Reactionary Republicanism

Reactionary Republicanism

How the Tea Party in the House Paved
the Way for Trump's Victory

BRYAN T. GERVAIS
and
IRWIN L. MORRIS

OXFORD
UNIVERSITY PRESS

OXFORD

UNIVERSITY PRESS

Oxford University Press is a department of the University of Oxford. It furthers
the University's objective of excellence in research, scholarship, and education
by publishing worldwide. Oxford is a registered trade mark of Oxford University
Press in the UK and certain other countries.

Published in the United States of America by Oxford University Press
198 Madison Avenue, New York, NY 10016, United States of America.

CIP data is on file at the Library of Congress
ISBN 978-0-19-087075-1 (pbk.)
ISBN 978-0-19-087074-4 (hbk.)

1 3 5 7 9 8 6 4 2

Paperback printed by WebCom, Inc., Canada
Hardback printed by Bridgeport National Bindery, Inc., United States of America

For Cameron, Maddie, and Chris (I.L.M.)

For Kathryn and Henry (B.T.G.)

CONTENTS

ACKNOWLEDGMENTS

We have been working on this project for what seems like a long time, at least half a dozen years. We just didn't realize it when we started. Our article "Reading the Tea Leaves" was not meant to be the beginning of a larger project, but after it was published and both of us had finalized other projects, we took another look at the Tea Party in the House. Never satisfied with standard measures of the movement's influence in the House, we were finally hooked by the realization that Tea Party organizations often made contributions to legislators who never joined the Tea Party Caucus. We owe this book to that early finding we did not expect and, frankly, did not understand (at least at the time).

Over the years, a lot of people have helped with this project. At Maryland, Irwin had a great group of students who worked on the project: Joe Wantz, Konrad Mugglestone, Gilbert Nunez, Raymond Williams, and Nick Miras, and a group of gifted undergraduates in the Center for American Politics and Citizenship's research program. We profited from comments received at the American Politics Workshop at the University of Maryland, and Frances Lee and David Karol provided very helpful comments on an early draft of the proposal that would become *Reactionary Republicanism*.

At the University of Texas, San Antonio, Bryan received able research assistance from several graduate students, including Dago Chavez, Edward Kelly, Matt Pina, and Sarah-Madeleine Torres, as well as a long list of very bright undergraduates participating in the UTSA Digital Politics Studio's research practicum program, whose hard work and ideas were indispensable to this project. Bryan's UTSA colleagues provided helpful feedback during sessions of the Department of Political Science and Geography's annual lecture series. Dan Engster, while serving as his department chair, provided Bryan with a vast amount of support and resources during the project, including a course release in the fall of 2016. Bryan is also grateful to Dan Gelo, Dean of the College of

Liberal and Fine Arts, for supporting the Digital Politics Fellowship during the fall of 2017.

Aspects of this project were presented at the 2014 and 2017 annual meetings of the American Political Science Association and the 2015 meeting of the Western Political Science Association. We are thankful to the discussants, chairs, and attendees of our panels for valuable feedback and suggestions, including (but not limited to) Larry Evans, Kim Fridkin, and Dan Shea. We are also grateful to our many colleagues who provided feedback and advice along the way, including Dan Biggers, Jim Curry, Mike Hanmer, Shanna Pearson-Merkowitz, Stella Rouse, and Ric Uslaner. Jeff Taylor played a crucial role in the project, helping to develop the measure of Tea Party salience. A grant from the Dirksen Congressional Center facilitated the collection of tweets during the 2016 campaign.

Working with the team at Oxford University Press has been a great experience. In particular, the early and consistent support of our editor, Dave McBride, played a crucial role in the development and completion of this project.

Finally, thanks to our families for putting up with us when we "had to work on the book." The book you hold in your hands is a testament to their love (and patience).

Reactionary Republicanism

Reactionary Republicanism

*How the Tea Party in the House Paved the Way
for Trump's Victory*

It is summer in Washington, and resentment is high. Anger and deep indignation are on display: at immigrants who take jobs from American workers, at minority students who take seats in college classrooms from white students, at the ill and infirm who don't deserve the medical care they receive.

Each of these groups is a target of the Trump administration's policy agenda. On the healthcare front, there is the effort to repeal and replace the Affordable Care Act (ACA, or "Obamacare"). On immigration, the president has just come out in support of a Senate proposal that will cut the number of legal immigrants in half. And on affirmative action, Attorney General Jeff Sessions has circulated a memo suggesting that the Justice Department plans to challenge long-accepted (and Supreme Court–approved) efforts to support campus diversity. Resentment in full flower.

President Trump's administration is singular in many respects. Trump was the first major party presidential candidate without the experience of elected office since Wendell Willkie in 1940; he is the first president without public service experience—as either an elected official or a high-ranking military officer—ever; he is the oldest elected president; and so on. It would be easy to attribute this resentful politics to him, and him alone. But that would be a flawed reading of the recent history of the Republican Party. This resentful politics has earlier—and deeper—roots. We trace it back to the Tea Party and, more specifically, the Tea Party in Congress (the House of Representatives).

We are not the first to characterize the Tea Party movement as resentful, but previous work in this vein has focused on the mass movement, not the manifestation of the movement in Congress. Through the course of our research, we have come to rethink much of what we took to be the conventional wisdom on the Tea Party movement in Congress. We found a larger, more institutionally significant group of legislators. We came to question the continued significance of "mainstream" Republicans. We found a group of legislators with conservative views on issues well beyond fiscal policy and a group of legislators who developed a distinctive "digital homestyle"—a systematically unhopeful, uncivil, and uncooperative Twitter persona. This persona resonated with a certain set of social media–savvy voters, and it subtly cultivated support—whether intentional or not—for the Trump candidacy. In this book, we follow the thread of "resentment" politics from Barack Obama's 2008 election and the full manifestation of the Tea Party to the Trump administration. This is the modern story of what has replaced "mainstream" Republicanism. This resentment fueled what we call *reactionary Republicanism*. But we are getting ahead of ourselves.

Background on the Tea Party

On December 16, 1773, over three hours aboard British vessels, a group of colonists tossed several dozen tons of tea into Boston Harbor. This singular act of defiance led to the closure of the port of Boston and, shortly thereafter, the British Parliament's enactment of the Intolerable Acts, a collection of acts that had the effect of reducing liberty and self-governance in the colony of Massachusetts—and interpreted by many colonists as a threat to liberty in the colonies more broadly (Middlekauf 2007). In response to the Intolerable Acts, the colonial governments gathered for the first Continental Congress in the late summer and fall of 1774. In April of the following year, the first shots of the American Revolution would be fired in Concord.

This eighteenth-century protest was the namesake of the twenty-first-century protest movement widely referred to as the Tea Party movement. The specific genesis of the modern movement is somewhat controversial. For example, the website TeaParty.org went live in 2004, and a number of local Tea Party organizations held events or protests during the later stages of George W. Bush's administration. In fact, one prominent Republican presidential hopeful held a Tea Party fundraising event in 2007 (Formisano 2012). But the most common reference point for the beginning of the modern Tea Party movement is CNBC correspondent Rick Santelli's early 2009 rant on the floor of the Chicago Mercantile Exchange opposing the Homeowners Affordability and Stability Plan. Santelli railed against the continuation of "bailout" politics begun during the George W. Bush administration and extended into the beginning of the Obama administration. Shortly thereafter, the "Taxed Enough Already" (TEA) Party became a massive national movement, the most significant conservative political movement—at least, to date—in the twenty-first century. As Paul Jossey (2016) has written:

The Tea Party movement began building in the George W. Bush years. Profligate spending and foreign adventurism with no discernable results nurtured disgust with Washington's habit of spending beyond its means and sending others to die in its wars. When President Obama made reorganizing the nation's health care system his foremost priority— and repeatedly misrepresented its effects in the process—anger at Washington exploded.

The significance of the Tea Party movement's impact stood in stark contrast to the organization of its leadership. The movement spawned any number of local organizations, and it included an array of national organizations. It also had deep-pocketed supporters, such as the Koch brothers and their political organization, and was promoted by experienced political elites, including former House majority leader Dick Armey (R-TX) (Skocpol and Williamson 2012). But the movement never had a single leader, nor was it ever effectively managed by a single organization. It was an odd mixture of grassroots activism and a number of tangentially related political organizations.

The lack of organization did not impede the movement's almost imme-diate efforts to hijack the national political debate and transform the electoral prospects of a host of Republican politicians. The Tea Party was the most in-teresting and visible political movement during the midterm elections of 2010, a year in which the Democrats lost more seats in the House than in any other midterm since the 1930s—including the watershed midterm elections in 1994. Though far from uniformly successful, Republican candidates aligned with the Tea Party—through endorsements or campaign contributions by Tea Party organizations—won numerous seats in Congress.

Officially founded during the 111th Congress (and the 2010 elections) by Congresswoman Michele Bachmann (R-MN), the Tea Party House Caucus at one point had, at least by some counts, sixty members. The Tea Party Caucus took positions on a number of policy issues facing Congress—consistently taking conserv-ative positions, often well to the right of the center of the Republican Conference, on fiscal and social policy issues. It was far more salient and successful than a Senate Tea Party Caucus constituted by then–South Carolina senator Jim DeMint.

Reconstituted in the 112th, 113th, and 114th Congresses, the House Tea Party Caucus grew less influential over the later part of this time period, during which it lost a significant number of members and took on a rather ep-isodic existence. It is rightfully considered dormant at the time of this writing. The Liberty Caucus (founded in 2012) and the Freedom Caucus (founded in 2015) shared both membership and a staunchly conservative ideological orien-tation with the Tea Party Caucus, but to this point, neither group has reached anything approximating the size of the Tea Party Caucus at its height.

The public goals and pronouncements of the Tea Party Caucus were not a straightforward reflection of the Tea Party movement in the electorate. Research on the mass Tea Party movement suggests that while it is clearly a "conservative" movement, it is a tapestry woven from several distinct brands of conservatism: fiscal or economic conservatism, social or religious conservatism, and racial/ethnic conservatism.

According to conventional wisdom, the sine qua non of Tea Party "orthodoxy" is fiscal conservatism. For a movement with a moniker derived from the phrase "Taxed Enough Already," this is no surprise. Tea Party members tend to support tax cuts and a variety of spending cuts (particularly cuts in domestic spending). Bailouts of large banks or troubled mortgage holders were unpopular. The expansion of the federal government's involvement in healthcare via the ACA ("Obamacare") was extremely unpopular among Tea Party stalwarts, and its repeal has long been a calling card. However, economizing on entitlement spending—particularly spending on Medicare and Social Security—has been far more controversial within the movement. While there has been some support, it is far from monolithic.

Limited government—even beyond that implied by fiscal conservatism— was also a key tenet of the Tea Party perspective. The limitations of particular interest—such as an emphasis on Second Amendment rights and the separation of church and state—resonated with conservative Christian groups, and the Tea Party naturally drew support from this demographic. In his book *Teavangelicals: The Inside Story of How the Evangelicals and the Tea Party Are Taking Back America*, David Brody (2012) highlights the broad consistency of the social policy objectives of Tea Party supporters and white Christian evangelicals— policy objectives that extend to opposition to same-sex marriage, abortion, and transgender rights. This social conservatism is not limited by gender. Women within the Tea Party ranks also take quite conservative positions on these social issues—and are often significantly more conservative than other Republican women (see Deckman 2016).

Finally, Tea Party conservatism includes a strain concentrating on issues with a significant racial/ethnic component. Tea Party conservatism opposes affirmative action and supports restrictions on immigration. The racially conservative segment of the Tea Party movement also seeks more severe penalties for illegal immigration and more support for immigration enforcement. Moreover, it opposes amnesty programs and DREAM programs that would provide educational resources for the children of undocumented immigrants. Data strongly suggest that those associated with the Tea Party movement are relatively negatively disposed toward African Americans and Latinos (Formisano 2012; Parker and Barreto 2013), and Tea Party supporters tend to be particularly racially resentful—in some cases, significantly more racially resentful than other Republicans.

This brand of conservatism was—on each ideological dimension—anathema to Barack Obama. In 2010, this ideological stew drove the extraordinarily successful Republican efforts to defeat Democrats in the House and the Senate. These Tea Party–led victories appeared to be a harbinger of success in the national elections in 2012, but that success failed to materialize. Was that the end of the Tea Party movement? Hardly.

On the surface, Mitt Romney did not appear to be an ideal Tea Party candidate. Campaigning since his failed bid to win the 2008 Republican nomination, Romney had difficulty attracting just the type of conservative Republicans who supported the Tea Party. He also faced opponents who could appeal to each dimension of Tea Party conservatism: Ron Paul (R-TX) for fiscal conservatives, Rick Santorum (R-PA) for social conservatives, and Newt Gingrich (R-GA) for racial/ethnic conservatives. But Romney made a concerted effort to attract Tea Party conservatives, promising the repeal of Obamacare, railing against illegal immigration, and proposing dramatic tax cuts. As one shrewd student of the Tea Party movement concluded:

> Romney has become the stealth tea party candidate, endorsing the essence of the movement while remaining unburdened by its public label. This makes him the ideal tea party candidate for the general-election battle against President Obama. (Skocpol 2012)

While he won the Republican nomination, Romney failed to defeat Obama, and the subsequent finger-pointing on the right of the Republican Party suggested Romney had failed to go far enough to fully energize the conservative base—to win the Tea Party voters. This failure would haunt Republican conservatives for four long years.

Following Romney's defeat of Tea Party candidates in 2012 and Obama's subsequent victory, the dwindling size of the Tea Party Caucus in the House was matched by the waning interest in the movement among the mass public. According to Gallup Poll data, the high-water mark for the mass movement came in early 2011, when 30 percent of Americans supported the Tea Party movement, 25 percent of Americans opposed the movement, and the remainder either had no opinion or neither supported nor opposed the movement.[1] By October 2015, support for the movement was just more than half of its peak level, opponents of the movement easily outnumbered supporters, and nearly 60 percent of survey respondents took no position on the movement. As an explicit mass movement, the Tea Party was dead.

But what happened to the objectives of the Tea Party, both in Congress and in the general population? Did the death of the Tea Party Caucus and the disintegration of the Tea Party movement among members of the mass public erase the reactionary conservatism that had briefly—but brilliantly—flowered within the Republican Party? We wondered. Shortly after the creation of the Tea Party movement and, more specifically, the Tea Party Caucus in the House of Representatives, we became interested in the economic, political, and social forces that drove the association of Republicans in the House with the Tea Party movement. As reported in a 2012 article, we found that district economics played a significant role in determining which House members joined the Caucus—the better-off the district (in terms of unemployment), the more likely a member was to attach her or his name to a movement ostensibly dedicated to gutting the social safety net. We concluded that "voters' 'anger,' which is widely presumed to drive the movement, is not so much a reaction to desperate economic circumstances but a reaction to government spending in response to the economic downturn."[2] This may be the right conclusion: constituents' anger over spending earmarked for others—not their own dire economic conditions—was driving representatives to hitch themselves to the Tea Party movement. But perhaps we did not do enough to characterize this anger as deep-seated feelings of resentment toward Washington, minority groups, and the former's perceived preference for the latter. Although this is a dynamic we did not focus on at the time, we have come to see, at the very least, attempts by House members associated with the Tea Party to foment enmity toward these targets among voters harboring preexisting, if latent, feelings of resentment.

What we saw among House members was apparently playing out in the general population as well. As Skocpol and Williamson (2012) describe in their indispensable study of Tea Party activists, many supporters of the movement were comparatively well-off during the Great Recession, yet were angry over the amount of taxpayer money going to "freeloading" social groups, which included the poor, "burdensome" immigrants, and "entitled" younger Americans. This was not anger over the state of their own finances, but resistance to the government helping others perceived as undeserving—a dynamic similar to what Kathy Cramer (2106a) describes in her (also indispensable) study of rural Wisconsinites and their support for the anti-government Scott Walker. America's fast-changing demographic makeup fuels this anger and engenders a dim view of the country's future. Pessimism about the future, a yearning for days past, and skepticism of demographic changes are hallmarks not just of hardcore Tea Party activists, but of supporters of the movement in general (Jones et al. 2015). Such supporters might be characterized as reactionary conservatives, as argued by Parker and Barreto (2013), who saw the 2008 election of Barack Obama, the nation's first nonwhite president, as the embodiment of the social and demographic changes they feared and resented.

The work that has morphed into this book began as an effort to more fully understand the distinctiveness of Tea Party legislators and the economic and political forces that drove their association with the Tea Party movement. Significantly, this interest in the institutional Tea Party movement—which has received far less attention than the Tea Party movement in the general population—preceded the Trump candidacy by several years. We certainly never expected to draw broad inferences between the manifestation of the Tea Party movement in the House and a presidential election.

By the same token, this project began well before the full flowering of Twitter. That the rise of the Tea Party was concurrent with the rise of a new means of communicating directly with constituents and activists has had profound consequences, as we argue throughout this book. Between Barack Obama's two presidential campaigns, in 2008 and 2012, political elites made substantial gains in the personalization of political communication via social media, particularly through the use of hashtags on the microblogging site Twitter (Bimber 2014; Bode et al. 2014). During this time, Twitter became one of the most active social network platforms among Americans and, significantly, a venue for activists associated with the Tea Party movement to connect and organize (this was also the case for the ephemeral, progressive Occupy Wall Street movement) (Agrawal et al. 2014; Duggan and Brenner 2013). Twitter thus provided political elites with a means not only to send messages directly to specific segments of the digital public (unfiltered by the news media), but to make common cause with energized, politically engaged groups of citizens. It is no surprise that the rate of Twitter adoption among members of Congress grew from about 1 in 3 in 2011 to nearly 100 percent by 2013.

Relatively early on in the project, we realized that the association between the Tea Party movement and members of Congress was a good deal more complicated than we had previously understood. Just as the mass Tea Party movement lacked formal leadership or coordinated focus, the manifestation of the Tea Party in Congress varied by member. Some members received campaign funds or other financial support from Tea Party organizations; others received endorsements from these organizations or the approbation of Tea Party activists. Some received all three. We characterize these members as ones receiving Tea Party *support*.

Some joined the Tea Party Caucus. Some tweeted support for the Tea Party and its policy objectives or attended Tea Party rallies to the point that journalists covering the campaigns in 2010 and 2012 identified them as Tea Party members. These were members who *attached* themselves to the Tea Party movement.

But far more frequently than we expected, financial support, organizational endorsements, activist approval, caucus memberships, tweets, and campaign events failed to overlap. While some members may have sought campaign funding and organizational endorsements, others sought neither (or needed neither) as long as they could attach their name to the Tea Party movement. Other members sought both attachment and support; other Republicans sought neither. Support did not imply attachment. Neither did attachment imply support. But members could also have both (or neither). Association—meaning attachment or support—with the Tea Party movement was obviously more complicated than we had appreciated.

The realization that the Tea Party movement in Congress was multidimensional —that association between House Republicans and Tea Party organizations could be a one-way street going in either direction, a two-way street, or a dead end—led us to consider the possibility that association with the Tea Party movement might have an equally complex strategic calculus.

The complexity of the Tea Party movement in the House obscured its size. A standard operationalization of Tea Party association in the House of Representatives has been membership in the Tea Party Caucus (e.g., Cline 2012; Mehta 2014; Pew Research Center 2011). If this is the only indicator of Tea Party association, then the movement was never close to a majority of the Republican Conference. In fact, even the most generous estimates of the size of the Tea Party Caucus never suggested it was even a third of the Republican Conference. But if the sole indicator of the Tea Party in the House is Tea Party Caucus membership, then many members who received significant campaign contributions from Tea Party organizations, and/or were endorsed by Tea Party organizations, and/or campaigned as Tea Party associates (at events, in public statements, and in tweets) would be excluded. The standard operationalization of the Tea Party movement in Congress fails to capture the full extent of that movement in the chamber. It fails to capture numerous members who received significant campaign contributions from the political action committees (PACs) of Tea Party organizations such as FreedomWorks, Tea Party Patriots, the Tea Party Express, Tea Party luminaries like former Alaska governor Sarah Palin, as well as smaller localized Tea Party groups. It ignores members who received endorsements from these same organizations.

Conversely, the presumption that Tea Party Caucus membership fully captured the Tea Party movement within Congress overstates the support Tea Party Caucus members received from Tea Party organizations. Just as some House Republicans who never joined the Tea Party Caucus received significant campaign funding and endorsements from the Tea Party organizations, some members of the Tea Party Caucus received little in the way of campaign contributions or endorsements from the most prominent Tea Party organizations.

Due in part to the lack of a clear, standard method for differentiating Tea Party members from "establishment" members, reporting on Congress since 2009 has typically included allusions to some amorphous Tea Party wing within the House, often imprecisely defined and lacking consistency. Sometimes discussions of the "Tea Party" legacy in Congress are simply references to the members elected during the "Tea Party wave" of 2010 (e.g., Davis 2016; Duran 2017; for a thoughtful review of this issue and the misappropriation of the "Tea Party" label in general, see Blake 2011). Other times, the label "Tea Party Caucus member" or "member of the Tea Party wing" is used as shorthand for more conservative, radical, or controversial members of the House (and lawmakers in general), regardless of whether they have formal membership in an official caucus or any other connection to the broader Tea Party movement (e.g., Balz 2014; Ho 2016; Pearlstein 2017).

In many instances, Tea Party members are differentiated from establishment types by their votes on specific bills or brinkmanship tactics—for example, "establishment" Republicans are those who were for raising the debt ceiling in 2011, while Tea Party Republicans withheld support until they could get what they wanted; "establishment" Republicans are those who voted against the 2013 government shutdown, while Tea Party members voted for it (e.g., Ball 2016; Bernstein 2010; Blodget 2013; Goldfarb 2013). However, premising that Tea Party members behave differently than establishment Republicans and then using differences in their behavior to sort Republicans into the two camps is a type of circular logic: if the goal is to determine whether the ideological positions and legislative behavior of the Tea Party faction are different from those of their mainstream counterparts, some metric other than ideology and legislative behavior must be used to determine who is in that faction.

Yet most often it has been membership in the official Tea Party Caucus or backing from some Tea Party organization that has been used to make the Tea Party–establishment distinction. We argue, first, that the size and scope of the Tea Party movement—even in the House—were not exclusively defined by the membership of the Tea Party Caucus, nor was the movement limited to House members who received campaign funds from Tea Party organizations, nor was it limited to the group of House members who received endorsements from Tea Party organizations. As we find, the overlap between these groups is relatively small. And even if we aggregated the memberships of these groups, we would still be ignoring a number of House members who attended Tea Party campaign rallies and events, explicitly espoused support for Tea Party policy objectives and/or the Tea Party movement more generally, and/or were widely considered by the media covering congressional campaigns to be associated with the Tea

Party. With a more complete picture of the Tea Party movement in Congress available to us, we realize that those members of Congress who were never associated with the Tea Party movement—no endorsements, no campaign contributions, no Tea Party Caucus, and so on—were a minority of the House Republican Conference.

Second, support for the Tea Party movement in Congress—and legislators associated with the Tea Party movement more specifically—was not driven primarily by economic deprivation. As we will see in Chapter 4, district-level economics played no significant role in the decisions of Tea Party organizations to support (or not) various House Republicans. Nor did constituents' economic circumstances drive House members' efforts to attach themselves to the Tea Party movement.

Third, the Tea Party movement in the House was not solely focused on small-government tax-and-spend issues. Our analysis indicates that Republicans who attached themselves to the Tea Party movement—but not those who received support from the movement—were significantly more conservative than their fellow Republicans. Our analysis suggests that the primary ideological distinction between those in the Tea Party movement and "mainstream" Republicans was based on issues of race and ethnicity.

Fourth, not only was the Tea Party movement in the House significantly larger than conventional wisdom suggests, those associated with the movement were more capable legislators than previously realized. This was not a movement of marginalized backbenchers. Members of Congress associated with the Tea Party movement tended to be the equal of their more mainstream Republican colleagues in terms of authoring bills, co-sponsorship activity, and producing legislation. In some contexts, we find that Tea Party Republicans were actually more legislatively effective than their fellow Republicans.

But legislators associated with the Tea Party movement, particularly those who made active efforts to attach themselves to the movement, were distinct from their more mainstream Republican colleagues in their political style, what we refer to as "digital homestyle." Taking our cue from Richard Fenno's seminal work of forty years ago, we focus on the way in which House members presented themselves to their constituents in a digital context. More specifically, focusing on their Twitter communications, we find that Tea Party Republicans were both (1) more emotionally negative and (2) more anti-deliberative than their more mainstream Republican counterparts. Tea Party Republicans were also less civil, and it is this incivility that provided the bridge to candidate Trump.

Trump's relationship with the vestiges of the Tea Party movement—both in the House and among the mass public—was never uncomplicated. Yet he was speaking to their people. If Romney was the stealth Tea Party candidate in 2012, Trump was that candidate in 2016. He was simply able to win.

Chapter Outline

Katherine Cramer (2016a) analyzes and elaborates on the deep-seated resentment of rural voters in Wisconsin—a core constituency of conservative Republican Scott Walker.[3] As Skocpol and Williamson (2012) effectively argue, Tea Party supporters are resentful if they are anything. In Chapter 2, we examine the shifting and varied targets of Tea Party resentment among the members of the movement. What may have begun as a response to frustration with big-bank bailouts quickly morphed into resentment toward those deemed unworthy of the support they were receiving from the government (and, implicitly or explicitly, taxpayers). During the early Obama administration, resentment toward the president and his policies—from responses to the bailout to criticism of the ACA—became resentment toward groups the president represented (or appeared to represent), including liberals, urban elites, minorities, and immigrants. Each type of conservative had a target of resentment. Fiscal conservatives resented liberal spendthrifts and bailout recipients. Social conservatives resented urban elites, gays, and the transgendered. And racial conservatives resented minorities and immigrants. We argue that this mass-level resentment within the movement helps us to understand the behavior of House Republicans and their reactionary politics.

In Chapter 3, we demonstrate that Tea Party Caucus membership is an extremely limiting operationalization of the Tea Party movement in the House. Some Republicans who never joined the Tea Party Caucus received electoral support from Tea Party organizations, were endorsed by Tea Party organizations, frequented Tea Party rallies, made public statements in support of the Tea Party, and were, at least in some cases, treated as Tea Party members by journalists covering their campaigns. The Tea Party in the House was broader and deeper than the Tea Party Caucus. Using a more comprehensive methodology for assessing a House member's association with the Tea Party movement, we are able to distinguish between Tea Party organizational efforts to *support* House members (primarily in their electoral efforts) and the efforts of House members to *attach* themselves to the Tea Party movement. Distinctive strategic dynamics drive these processes, and we are able to categorize House Republicans according to the extent to which they received support, sought attachment, both, or neither—referring to them as White Tea, Green Tea, Black Tea, and Coffee types. We also provide some preliminary evidence suggesting that the constituency bases for each of these Tea Party types were distinctive.

With a more complete understanding of the parameters of the Tea Party movement in Congress, in Chapter 4 we analyze the constituency forces that influenced the growth of the two key dimensions of Tea Party association in Congress. Here, we examine the impact of various district-level economic and demographic factors on the manifestation of Tea Party support and Tea Party attachment in the 112th Congress. Using data from the 2010 Cooperative Congressional Election Survey (CCES), we also examine the attitudinal foundations of Tea Party support and Tea Party attachment. Were Tea Party attachment and support driven by economic circumstances or fiscal conservatism among members' constituents, as the existing literature would suggest? Or were other factors—factors more directly associated with a broad-based politics of resentment—at work?

Assuming the equivalence of the Tea Party Caucus and the Tea Party movement in Congress obscures the institutional scope and diversity of the movement. It also masks the true policy orientations of key components of the Tea Party in the House. In Chapter 5, we investigate the ideological distinctiveness of the roll call voting of Tea Party members in the House. Here we are particularly interested in the extent to which Tea Party support and/or Tea Party attachment are associated with broad-based conservatism (as some research on the roll call voting patterns of Tea Party Caucus members would lead us to expect). In particular, we assess the hypothesis that Tea Party members are more fiscally conservative than their fellow partisans.

Conventional wisdom on the Tea Party movement in the House suggests that it was a collection of marginalized legislators intent on (and only capable of) obstructing the legislative process and the lawmaking efforts of others. In Chapter 6, we provide evidence that this perspective sells short the institutional capacity of the Tea Party movement. Our analysis suggests that House members associated with the Tea Party were significantly more institutionally active and institutionally effective than previous work admits.

While Tea Party Republicans and Republicans unassociated with the movement were equally adept at legislating—at least based on the standard of legislative effectiveness—the ways in which they related to their constituents tended to be distinct. In Chapter 7, we develop the concept of "digital homestyle." The conventional wisdom regarding the rhetoric of Tea Party elites is that it is angry and heated, often with the goal of inciting resentment toward Washington and out-groups. Leveraging a dataset consisting of every tweet issued by official congressional Twitter accounts during the 112th and 113th Congresses, we gauge whether the tweets of Tea Party Republicans are more likely to contain language meant to breed resentment, and detail various themes in this style of tweeting. We also consider whether Tea Party Republicans' reputation for being anti-compromise and anti-deliberative is reflected in the language they use on Twitter.

Tea Party rhetoric also has the reputation of being uncivil, something it has in common with the rhetoric of candidate and president Donald J. Trump. In Chapter 8, we explore the rhetoric of both, as well as the argument that Tea

Party rhetoric served as a bridge to Trumpian bombast. Utilizing a supervised learning program to code our dataset of congressional tweets for incivility, we test whether there are differences in the prevalence of incivility between Tea Party and non-Tea Party types. Although uncivil tweets were altogether rather infrequent, we find significant variation in the rate of incivility by Tea Party Attachment scores in the 113th Congress. Analyzing Trump's tweets in the same manner, we highlight similarities between the tweets of Tea Party Republicans and Trump in terms of affect, incivility, expressions, and targets.

Similarities in rhetoric raise the question as to what role the Tea Party in the House played in blazing the path to Trump's victory. In Chapter 9, we investigate the influence Tea Party representation has had on the biggest national stage—presidential elections. Specifically, we consider the endorsement behavior of members of Congress during the two elections that have passed since the Tea Party movement came to be (2012 and 2016) and whether our Tea Party Association measures predict endorsements for some presidential aspirants over others—namely, outsider, "establishment" candidates. Using data from the CCES, we also consider whether Tea Party representation influenced vote choice in the fight for the 2016 Republican nomination and the 2012 and 2016 general elections.

We examine the hypothesis that Tea Party House members paved the way for Trump's victory by normalizing political elites' use of uncivil, brash rhetoric on Twitter. As such, we analyze whether a representative's penchant for being uncivil on Twitter influenced the votes of social media users in the 2016 primaries and general election. Whereas uncivil rhetoric has likely always been a part of discourse of political elites, the style of uncivil rhetoric used and the frequency with which members of the mass public are exposed to it are unique to the Tea Party/social media era. It is no coincidence, we argue, that the election of a presidential candidate offering brash, populist, ethno-nationalist commentary on Twitter followed the rise of the Tea Party in the House.

In Chapter 10, we summarize our findings regarding which popular conceptions of the Tea Party in the House carry weight and which ones do not. We reflect on the choices made by leaders in the Republican Party, the path that these choices have put the party on, alternative paths some within the party have taken, and whether a "Tea Party on the left" might arise during the Trump era. And, rather soberly, we consider the prospects of political violence, amid increasingly hostile political discourse, in our time and the time to come.

2

Tea Party to Trump

Representing Resentful Republicans

With his "I'm mad as hell" rant against the Obama administration's mortgage refinancing program on the floor of the Chicago Mercantile Exchange, CNBC correspondent Rick Santelli gave birth to the Tea Party movement. The extent to which this apparently impromptu outbreak was actually unscripted is an open question (on this issue, see Formisano 2012), but in very short order, activists and moneyed interests formed Tea Party organizations, and Tea Party rallies popped up throughout the United States. Very deep pockets supported the Tea Party movement from the beginning. The Koch brothers were two of the wealthiest and most prominent early supporters (Mayer 2010), but the list of early supporters also includes other extremely wealthy individuals and foundations, from several of the Walmart Waltons, to Richard Mellon Scaife, to the Olin Foundation (Formisano 2012). These deep pockets facilitated the immediate growth of organizations like FreedomWorks and the Tea Party Express, and Tea Party demonstrations and rallies quickly illustrated the growing popularity of the nascent movement.

Populist movements have a long history in the United States. Even if we limit our time frame to the postcolonial era, populist protest is a frequently recurring theme throughout our nation's history. From the Whiskey Rebellion during Washington's administration to the Know Nothing Party in the 1850s, the People's Party of the 1890s, Thurmond's Dixiecrats in 1948, Wallace's American Independent Party two decades later, and Ross Perot's Reform Party in 1992, populist, anti-government protest has always played a role in American politics.

The "Tea" in Tea Party stands for "Taxed Enough Already," and early supporters of the movement traced its political lineage back to the anti-tax actions of the Sons of Liberty, who disposed of British Tea in the Boston Harbor in December 1773. According to movement supporters, the principles that drove the patriots to oppose British imperialism engendered the widespread opposition to economic policies promulgated first by the second Bush administration and then the Obama administration.

From its inception, the avowed guiding principle of this opposition movement was the value of limited government. As Foley (2012, 20–21) writes:

> The dominant theme of the Tea Party movement is its insistence on limited government. In the words of the movement's Contract from America, the movement seeks to "restore limited government consistent with the U.S. Constitution's meaning." The most prominent examples of this principle are the Tea Party's opposition to bailouts and health-care reform, although it is also evident in the movement's support of things like a rule requiring congressional bills to cite their constitutional power source and proposed constitutional amendments to require a balanced budget, to restore federalism, and to permit states to veto federal laws.

Postel (2012, 13) concurs by noting that "[t]he Tea Party's moral center is the market and the supposed freedom of the marketplace." Studies of the Tea Party movement uniformly describe it as a coalition without centralized leadership or formal structure. The absence of the conventional structure of a national political party precluded the development of an ideologically monolithic faction, but at least in its earliest manifestation, "the umbrella terms are *big government* and *spending*" (Formisano 2012, 13). As Postel (2012, 32) argues convincingly:

> [D]espite its heterogeneity, the Tea Party movement has maintained a degree of political coherence. It has done so by focusing on the corporate conservative agenda of fighting the "socialist" takeover: defeating health care reform, lowering taxes on the wealthy, lifting corporate regulations, and restricting union rights.

Although the genesis of the Tea Party occurred during the Obama administration, those in the conservative movement who would come together to form the Tea Party were also deeply disappointed with the Bush administration and its handling of the economic downturn referred to as the "Great Recession." Because of the timing of the genesis of the Tea Party movement—shortly after the beginning of the Obama administration—we may easily forget that early Tea Party members were disenchanted with the Republican Party more generally. Formisano (2012, 11) is correct in noting:

> Liberal critics of the Tea Party have underestimated the degree to which frustration with the Republican Party in the closing years of the Bush administration contributed to the rise of the Tea Party.

Even in the context of Tea Party supporters' aversion to the Bush administration and its Wall Street bailout, it is simply not possible to overstate the aversion of these same Tea Party supporters to President Obama and his administration. Maxwell and Parent (2012),[1] in their article entitled "The Obama Trigger: Presidential Approval and Tea Party Membership," provide compelling evidence that opposition to Obama was strongly associated with Tea Party membership. In fact, they argue that it was the key distinction between Tea Party members and nonmembers, more important even than attitudes on fiscal policy issues. They conclude that opposition to Obama was "an even more powerful driving force behind Tea Party identification than economic policy concerns" (Maxwell and Parent 2012, 1398). In their thoughtful and compelling book on the early Tea Party movement, Skocpol and Williamson (2012, 77) simply state that "[n]owhere are Tea Party fears more potently symbolized than in the presidency of Barack Hussein Obama." Shortly after his election, Obama came to be the symbol of this " 'socialist' take-over" for Tea Party supporters. As one pundit recalled:

> At a 2010 Tea Party meeting, former representative Tom Tancredo of Colorado drew cheers when he declared that in the 2008 election, "something really odd happened, mostly because I think that we do not have a civic literacy test before people can vote in the country. People who could not even spell the word 'vote,' or say it in English, put a *committed socialist* ideologue in the White House, name is Barack Hussein Obama." (Dionne 2016, 260)

But opposition to Obama extended beyond focused criticism of his political objectives and policy choices. For supporters of the Tea Party movement, Obama represented groups they opposed and resented. Ideologically based disagreements about various fiscal policy measures fail to explain the antipathy of Tea Party supporters to Obama. The visceral opposition to Obama, the main driver of the growth of Tea Party support, went well beyond a divergence with his policy positions. In talking with a host of self-avowed Tea Party supporters, Skocpol and Williamson (2012, 79) describe this pervasive dislike and distrust as follows:

> The son of an African father and a white American mother, Obama is perceived by many Tea Partiers as a foreigner, an invader pretending to be an American, a fifth columnist. Obama's past as a community organizer is taken as evidence that he works on behalf of the undeserving poor . . . His academic achievements and social ties put him in league with the country's intellectual elite, whose disdain feels very real to many Americans, and whose cosmopolitan leanings seem unpatriotic . . . Asked about the President, Tea Party members connect

Obama and his administration and political allies directly with those deemed undeserving—not just with African-Americans but also with illegal immigrants and criminals.

President Obama was simply "the Devil incarnate for Tea Partiers" (Skocpol and Williamson 2012, 28). Even accounting for the effect of respondents' positions on fiscal policy issues such as the stimulus package and the budget deficit, disapproval of Obama (among whites) was driven by racial stereotypes—an aspect of what the literature refers to as "old-fashioned racism" (see Tesler 2013, 2016b)—and "symbolic racism" (see Henry and Sears 2002; Kinder and Kam 2009; Kinder and Sears 1981; Tesler 2016b).

Parker and Barreto (2013) and Barreto et al. (2011) offer a related explanation for the rise of the Tea Party: Tea Partiers are reactionary conservatives who fear perceived social and demographic change in the United States—including the growth of minority and immigrant populations and the push for equal rights for ethnic/racial and sexual minorities. We realize that the term "conservative" is multifaceted (and contested). For us, conservatism embodies a respect for tradition and convention, an aversion to change, and a nostalgia for the past. Obama's presidency is viewed as the embodiment of the change that conservatives have such an aversion to (Parker and Barreto 2013, 186–187). The connection between sympathy for the Tea Party and viewing Obama as a subversive threat to the American way of life is so strong that Tea Party sympathy predicts negative opinions of Obama even after partisanship, political ideology, and a number of group-based discrimination measures (racial resentment, ethnocentrism, social dominance orientation, and authoritarianism) are controlled for (Parker and Barreto 2013, 212–217).

This group-focused opposition—a clear manifestation of "identity politics"—cannot be attributed to any systematized understanding of or perspective on the proper role of the government in the economic realm (whether in terms of tax policy, business regulation, or government spending). Decades of political behavior research teach us that Americans are not, in general, ideologically sophisticated (see, e.g., Campbell et al. 1960; Converse 1964; Zaller 1992). If this vast corpus of work is remotely accurate, then it seems that the ideological attractiveness of the conservative policy proposals of Tea Party leaders and umbrella organizations alone are insufficient to explain the dramatic rise in the popularity of the Tea Party movement. Decisions about the economic consequences of various policy responses to a dramatic downturn in home values are not dependent on the ethnic or cultural characteristics of the homeowners themselves. Many supporters of the Tea Party—even in its earliest days—would not have agreed.

Even the movement's most effective apologists admit that it is not ideologically monolithic; the Tea Party comprises groups and individuals with a diversity of opinions on a wide array of policy issues. As Foley (2012, 228) admits,

"The truth is that the Tea Party movement is a large umbrella, encompassing a diverse array of Americans from across the political spectrum." In short, "[t]he Tea Party can just as accurately be called the Tea Parties . . . because it exists on several levels and incorporates sometimes-competing factions as a loose confederation" (Formisano 2012, 7–8). But staunch supporters of the Tea Party argue that whatever racist misanthropes have been attracted to the movement, they are only the tiniest fraction of the support base. They criticize opponents of the movement for grossly overestimating the size of this segment, and some argue that opponents intentionally misrepresent its size in order to discredit the broader movement and its political ideals. Foley (2012, 228) writes, for example, that "progressives and liberals have invested so much time and energy into trying to discredit the Tea Party as a bunch of racist, homophobic, xenophobic, sexist zealots." And in light of the movement's diversity, its supporters highlight economic conservatism as the key distinguishing characteristic of the movement. In this vein, Foley (2012, 228) writes:

> Most [Tea Partiers] consider themselves conservative, but their conservatism is decidedly economic and libertarian in tone, emphasizing smaller government and greater individual liberty and responsibility. Social issues such as gay marriage and abortion, although they may be important to some individuals, are clearly not an agenda item of the Tea Party movement itself.

Other descriptions of the movement, even by those sympathetic to it, suggest that the ostensible focus on fiscal conservatism fails to capture the key policy orientations and objectives of significant components of the movement. For example, public opinion research on Tea Partiers indicates that social conservatives make up a significant component of the movement and that they are drawn to the movement because they view it as working for policy goals that are consistent with their culturally conservative objectives (e.g., Arceneaux and Nicholson 2012). The connection between social conservatives and the Tea Party movement manifests itself in a variety of ways. For example, belief in biblical literalism is positively associated with Tea Party membership (Maxwell 2016), and policy positions long associated with social conservatism—such as a pro-life orientation—are strongly associated with support for the Tea Party (Campbell and Putnam 2011; Clement and Green 2011). On this point, Campbell and Putnam (2011, A23) write:

> Next to being a Republican, the strongest predictor of being a Tea Party supporter today was a desire, back in 2006, to see religion play a prominent role in politics. And Tea Partiers continue to hold these

views: they seek "deeply religious" elected officials, approve of religious leaders' engaging in politics and want religion brought into political debates. The Tea Party's generals may say their overriding concern is a smaller government, but not their rank and file, who are more concerned about putting God in government.

As Dionne (2016, 259) writes, "Far from being an alternative to the religious right, the Tea Party was an overlapping form of political organization that gave voice to many of the same forms of social traditionalism that had animated followers of Jerry Falwell and Pat Robertson."[2]

Brown (2015) provides a more accurate—and less apologetic—description of the diversity within the movement, a diversity not always consistent with the ideologically succinct guiding principles promulgated by some Tea Party organizations. He also highlights the organizational significance of this political diversity:

> [C]ommon explanations of the beliefs of Tea Party supporters must be tempered by the empirical reality. Some in the Tea Party held deeply intolerant views toward other social groups, including African Americans, immigrants, and those in the lesbian, gay, bisexual and transgender (LGBT) community. Others in the Tea Party had little interest in changing social policy, instead—perhaps naively—they saw the Tea Party as a way to pursue solely economic aims connected to jobs and the size of government . . . While many supporters hewed in to the platform of the Republican Party, which aspects of that platform were most pressing *differed greatly.* (2015, 66, emphasis added)

So the empirical record of the Tea Party movement over time suggests that its supporters are distinct from other Americans—and often other Republicans—in one or more of three key areas: fiscal conservatism, social conservatism, and racial conservatism.[3] Let us be clear about what we mean by each of these terms.

Fiscal conservatives focus on the bread-and-butter issues associated with conventional descriptions of the Tea Party movement. They are concerned primarily about the growth of government, and they seek to curtail it. Fiscal conservatives seek significant spending cuts in an array of federal programs. For the most serious, reform of entitlement programs such as Medicaid, Medicare, and Social Security is a major policy goal. Fiscal conservatives also oppose new and expensive public programs such as the Affordable Care Act, support balanced-budget amendments, oppose extensions of the debt ceiling, and oppose government regulation—particularly when it pertains to commercial activities.

Social conservatives focus on policies related to cultural issues. These individuals tend to be pro-life, and they oppose any federal programs that they deem supportive of pro-choice rights. They oppose federal restrictions on state constraints on abortion rights, and they seek to overturn *Roe v. Wade*. Staunch social conservatives oppose gay marriage and generally oppose the extension of civil rights protections to those in the LGBTQ community. They support school choice, particularly plans that include funding for religious and parochial schools.

Social conservatives resent the cultural decline they see in modern America. They point back to what they consider a more wholesome time in their lives, a time they remember as one in which their own values were widely shared. Skocpol and Williamson (2012, 75) describe this behavior in the following manner:

> The nightmare of societal decline is usually painted in cultural hues, and the villains [those they resent] in the picture are freeloading social groups, liberal politicians, bossy professionals, big government, and the mainstream media.

Proponents of gay marriage and pro-choice activists could be added to the list.

Racial conservatives include those who manifest what scholars refer to as "old-fashioned racism" and/or "sophisticated racism." Old-fashioned racism is traditionally understood to be based on the presumption of the fundamental inferiority of individuals of a particular race. It includes, for example, the "desire for social distance between the races and beliefs in racial intellectual superiority" (Tesler 2013). Sophisticated racism, symbolic racism, or racial resentment is a subtler aversion to those of another race or ethnicity. Symbolic racism or racial resentment toward African Americans, for example, manifests in "attitudes that emphasize lack of black commitment to traditional American values" (Tesler 2013, 110). Parker and Barreto (2013, 89) describe this as "a new type of black antipathy . . . joining prejudice with the perception that blacks are in violation of the Protestant work ethic." The racially resentful tend to respond affirmatively to questions tapping into these attitudes. They agree or strongly agree that "Irish, Italian, Jewish, and many other minorities overcame prejudice and worked their way up. Black people should do the same without any special favors." Similarly, the racially resentful agree that "it's really a matter of some people not trying hard enough; if black people would only try harder they could be just as well off."

Racially resentful respondents also minimize the impact of a history of discrimination and racism on the current circumstances of African Americans. They strongly disagree with the statement "Over the past few years, black people have gotten less than they deserve." Similarly, they oppose the assertion "Generations of slavery and discrimination have created conditions that make it difficult for black people to work their way out of the lower class." Racial conservatives resent those of other races or ethnicities. This group tends also to resent illegal immigrants. Formisano (2012, 112) simply notes that "Tea Partiers are less favorably disposed to African Americans and Hispanics than most Americans." And Skocpol and Williamson (2012, 71) note that resentful "Tea Partiers regularly invoke illegal immigrants as prime examples of free-loaders who are draining public coffers."[4] The group-based animus of symbolic racism or racial resentment is less overt than that manifest in old-fashioned racism, but it is no less real. As López (2014, 152) writes, "Tea Party fury may not have come from old-style, hate-every-black-person racism, but it nevertheless stemmed from . . . racial hostilities." For our purposes, racial conservatism captures both manifestations of racial animus.

Significantly, *all* of these conservatives—fiscal conservatives, social conservatives, and racial conservatives—pine for an earlier era of American politics (though not necessarily the same era) that they consider to be more consistent with their view of the social and political world. Fiscal conservatives harken back to a time when government was smaller—to the Reagan administration or before. Social and racial conservatives often point to the halcyon days of the 1950s —a time before the women's and civil rights movements of the 1960s. Jones's thoughtful *The End of White Christian America* (2016) aptly captures the fears and apprehensions of social and racial conservatives. Gest (2016, 75) captures this nostalgia among working-class whites, a key Tea Party constituency, in the context of Youngstown, Ohio:

> There was a time—any local will tell you—when the city was the steel capital of the world, when the city's center was a bustling commercial hub, when you could step off the train on Monday and find a job on Tuesday. "This place was a boomtown," said John Avery, commencing the common narrative.

But today, "[t]here is a post-apocalyptic feel to Youngstown, Ohio" (Gest 2016, 74).

Survey data from the Public Religion Research Institute's 2015 American Values Survey reveal how widespread such sentiments are among those who identify with the Tea Party. Among Tea Party identifiers, 65 percent believe that America's greatest days are behind it, compared with 58 percent of other Republicans, 52 percent of independents, and 39 percent of Democrats who believe the same. Additionally, while this sentiment increased among all groups from 2012 to 2015, it increased the most among Tea Party identifiers. A significant majority of Tea Party and other Republicans (72 percent and 67 percent, respectively) also agreed that American culture and way of life have "mostly changed for the worse" since the 1950s and that immigrants burden the country rather than strengthen it (Jones et al. 2015).

"Take Our Country Back" (see Cassone and McCain 2012), a popular song that became an anthem of the Tea Party movement, captures this desire to return to an earlier, more socially and politically palatable era. Tea Partiers wish to be taken "back" to a time when their orientations and attitudes were the centerpiece of a dominant culture. But it also highlights the group-based animus of Tea Partiers who resent those they perceive to have taken their country—Wall Street bankers, gays, minorities, illegal aliens—and so they seek to take it back.

Qualitative research on the Tea Party movement—and on the growth of the broader conservative movement—reveals that resentment of various types played an important role in the growth of the mass movement. Regardless of the form of conservatism driving a Tea Party supporter, a target of resentment is always available. The fiscally conservative resent the Wall Street bankers and industrial titans saved by billions of dollars of federal aid. They also resent the federal bureaucracy, which they view as bloated and free-spending, the source of the regulatory red tape that inhibits economic growth. Social conservatives resent liberal elites, who they view as degrading their culture. And racial conservatives resent illegal immigrants, who they see as taking their jobs.

Cramer (2016a) makes a particularly compelling case for this perspective in her book, *The Politics of Resentment*. Rather than having a philosophical or ideological aversion to certain key policies, Tea Partiers oppose the benefits that these policies provide to those they consider undeserving. In some cases, the connection between the undeserving recipients and the policies themselves is so intimate—such as the connection between bank or commercial bailouts and the Wall Street interests that benefited from them or between members of the LGBTQ community and gay marriage—that opposition to one is tantamount to opposition to the other.

This "politics of resentment," however, is not uncomplicated. Resentment is not always targeted at others. Interviews and focus groups with self-identified Tea Party supporters indicate that they generally resent those they consider undeserving—and in this case the question is whether or not the individuals are deserving of the government benefits and support they received. For example, Cramer (2016a, 166) notes that during her fieldwork in Wisconsin, the idle rich, government employees, and the young were often highlighted on the list of the "lazy" and undeserving. But she also admits:

> The persistence of racial stereotypes that contain beliefs that some racial groups are lazier than others makes it likely that those arguments

activate racial resentment among many people . . . as we have seen in the mobilization of support for Tea Party candidates. (2016a, 166–167)

For these reasons, we think it appropriate to use the term "reactionary" to refer collectively to these different types of conservatism. Among Tea Party supporters in the general population, we see this reactionary orientation as flowing from both a sense of resentment and a desire to return to a more hospitable era. The movement is driven by a reaction to perceived undeserving others and the trajectory of history. Significantly, the "others" are not the same for all Tea Party supporters, nor do all supporters look back to the same idealized age.

So how does one represent constituents who are caught up in a movement like the Tea Party? Research on the Tea Party movement among members of the mass public dwarfs research on the Tea Party in Congress. We know a great deal about the demographics of Tea Party supporters. Various empirical analyses have uncovered their partisan attachments and ideological leanings, and scholars have offered insights into their policy orientations and political attitudes. This is not to say the literature is monolithic—which would be a surprise given the diversity of the population being studied—but we do understand the broad characteristics of the movement's participants.

Representing the Tea Party

The conventional wisdom regarding the Tea Party in Congress concentrates on the 2010 election and the dramatic influx of new Republican legislators under the banner of the Tea Party movement. The Tea Party Caucus in the House became the focal point for the movement in Congress. While certain Republican senators aligned themselves with the Tea Party movement, no similar formal organization existed in the Senate. The trajectory of the Tea Party Caucus is similar to that of a comet: a strikingly quick rise—actually beginning in the 111th Congress—and a similarly quick fall. The Tea Party Caucus stopped hosting public events during the summer before the 2012 elections, and the Tea Party Caucus website went dormant well before Election Day (Newhauser 2013). Though registered for the 113th Congress and reconstituted in the 114th Congress, the Caucus has yet to resume its previous level of activity or to return to anything like the height of its membership.

But the Tea Party in Congress represents much more than the history of the Tea Party Caucus, and the roll of Tea Party supporters among Republicans in Congress well exceeds that of the Tea Party Caucus—even at the height of its popularity. The manifestation of the Tea Party in Congress is complicated. Just as the Tea Party identifiers and sympathizers in the electorate are not monolithic, neither are Tea Party legislators cut from the same ideological cloth.

Given the wealth of recent research on the Tea Party movement among the electorate, we have a rather detailed (though certainly not complete) knowledge of Tea Party supporters. For the most part, these studies provide a broadly consistent outline of the movement, its character, and its components. The same cannot be said for our understanding of Tea Party legislators. Even for those aspects of the Tea Party in Congress that have received the most scholarly attention—the roll call voting behavior of Tea Party legislators and the role (and significance) of Tea Party organizations in the election of Tea Party legislators—conclusive results are rare. Scholars disagree about the ideological distinctiveness of the roll call voting of Tea Party legislators. Gallagher and Rock (2012) find no evidence of a distinctive ideological slant to the roll call voting of Tea Party legislators when compared with other House Republicans. Bailey et al. (2012) find evidence that the roll call votes of Tea Party legislators were distinctive on a small set of issues (dealing primarily with the debt ceiling and the funding of weapons systems). Gervais and Morris (2012) find that Tea Party legislators differ from other Republicans on tax policy, but they do not find any broader ideological differences. In contrast, Ragusa and Gaspar (2016) find evidence that Tea Party incumbents were generally more conservative than other Republicans in the 112th and 113th Congresses, and Bond (2013) makes a similar argument for freshmen in the 112th Congress. Obviously, the limited research on this group has yet to provide a consistent picture of the policy orientations, the institutional stature, the policy activity, or the public presentation of Tea Party legislators.

So how do Tea Party legislators represent the Tea Partiers in their districts? And what impact does the representation of Tea Party interests have on the subsequent manifestation of those interests? We must allow for the possibility that the legislative representation of the Tea Party movement reflects the diversity of the movement. While the movement began as a paean to fiscal conservatism, an increasingly large body of research clearly demonstrates its attractiveness to social conservatives and racial conservatives. The key is a shared opposition to the Obama administration and what it stands for; organizations, activists, and supporters may oppose Obama for very different reasons.

Just because Tea Party organizations lobby for greater fiscal conservatism in opposition to Obama administration fiscal policies, activists and supporters may oppose other Obama policies or resent groups that Obama represents or that he is presumed to favor (minorities, immigrants, urban elites, etc.). To the extent that Tea Party legislators are distinct, scholars have always assumed that the distinctiveness revolved around economic issues—"corporate welfare," tax policy, government spending, and business regulation (see Gervais and Morris 2012).

We consider the possibility that the distinctiveness of Tea Party legislators manifests in policies related to social issues and policies dealing with issues of race and ethnicity. In fact, we consider the possibility that the key distinction between the policy orientations of certain types of Tea Party legislators and other Republicans is based on issues related to race and/or social policy. If it's possible that Tea Party legislators are distinctive in their handling of issues related to race and ethnic politics, or on issues related to social policy, what is the source of this distinctiveness?

We can readily explain the presumed fiscal conservatism of Tea Party legislators. They seek the financial support or endorsement of Tea Party organizations. In some electoral contexts, this support might be crucial. But how do we explain the social and racial conservatism of Tea Party legislators? Those reactionary dimensions do not obviously flow from an effort to seek the support of Tea Party organizations. We see the racial and social conservatism of legislators as flowing from their representation of their constituencies—both primary and electoral—and their efforts to enlarge those constituencies through the mobilization of like-minded citizens. Members attach themselves to the Tea Party movement to reinforce and reinvigorate the support of their existing constituencies and to increase their support among new constituencies.

We posit the existence of a relationship between Tea Party legislators and their constituents. That relationship for Tea Party legislators who are focused solely on cultivating support from Tea Party organizations is relatively straightforward—and unidirectional. In contrast, Tea Party legislators who make an active effort to attach themselves to the movement cultivate a more complicated and more substantial relationship with their constituents.

Tea Party support depends on the strategic decisions of Tea Party organizations. Organizations associated with the movement have not given equal emphasis to the various types of Tea Party conservatism. Tea Party organizations have focused on fiscal conservatism, not to the complete exclusion of social and racial conservatism but generally so. As the literature on the Tea Party movement among the electorate indicates, however, the ideological attachment to small government and fiscal conservatism driving Tea Party organizations is not prevalent among citizens. Even the most expensive federal programs—such as Social Security, Medicare, and Medicaid—are rarely outright opposed by Tea Party supporters. Tea Party supporters tend to focus not on the programs but on the recipients. They oppose benefits—of any type—for recipients they deem unworthy or undeserving. That is not the same as opposing the program itself due to an ideological aversion to large government or expensive federal programs.

This disconnect between the political orientations of Tea Party organizations and the Tea Party movement among the electorate—again, not necessarily an ideological conflict but rather a significant difference in focus—mitigates against an energizing relationship between Tea Party support for a legislator and the growth and development of the movement in a legislator's district. This is particularly true for legislators who do not, once they have received support from Tea Party organizations, reinforce that association by making an effort to attach to the movement. Intuitively, we would think that organizational support and efforts to attach would be synonymous. It is just that, empirically, they are not (see Bailey et al. 2012; Ragusa and Gaspar 2016). We provide additional evidence for this and discuss it in greater detail in the next chapter.

Tea Party attachment, on the other hand, depends on the strategic decisions of Tea Party legislators. We see legislators' efforts to attach to the movement as efforts to cultivate support among movement activists and supporters. Efforts to attach to the movement also provide legitimation for the movement—as understood by the activists and supporters of the movement itself. So House members attaching themselves to the Tea Party movement—through Tea Party Caucus membership, attendance at Tea Party rallies, or marketing the Tea Party movement on Twitter—were not only trying to draw the support of Tea Party members; they were also cultivating the growth of the movement itself. We see this cultivation in constituency-level terms.

Again, this is a two-way relationship. Representatives make decisions about the level of their attachment to the Tea Party movement for strategic reasons. The nature of their constituencies plays a key role in determining members' incentives to attach to the Tea Party movement. In simplest terms, members who serve districts where the Tea Party is active are more likely, all else equal, to make an effort to attach to the Tea Party. By Tea Party activity, we mean active support for the Tea Party movement, as measured by the prevalence of voters who (1) indicate that they are members of the movement or (2) indicate that they support the movement. Active support for the movement among constituents is not the only key factor in members' decision-making calculus. As we have noted, the Tea Party movement is a loose collection of three types of conservatism: fiscal conservatism, social conservatism, and racial conservatism. As the relative prevalence of fiscal conservatives, social conservatives, and racial conservatives in a member's district increases, the more likely that member is to make an effort to attach to the Tea Party movement.

But attachment is not the only means of developing certain constituencies. In order to further understand the representational relationship between Tea Party legislators and their constituents, we take a closer look at one of the members' key mechanisms for advertising and position-taking: Twitter feeds—what we refer to as "digital homestyle." Representation is rarely a one-way street, and just as members' political affiliations, their policy orientations, and their institutional activities derive in large part from the preferences of their various constituencies—here we are thinking of personal primary, electoral, and geographic constituencies—members' actions and their communications to their constituencies, in turn, influence the political attitudes and actions of their constituents.

Tea Party members make direct efforts to cultivate constituencies that go beyond attachment to the Tea Party. Here, we also suggest that members' digital homestyles cultivate support by tapping into the cultural anxiety and racial resentment flowing from opposition to the Obama administration. This digital homestyle, which we examine in detail in Chapters 7 and 8, entails the frequent use of anti-deliberative and uncivil language by Tea Party legislators, as well as the invocation of emotional responses such as anger and sadness associated with the dystopian characterization of the present state of American politics. We argue that Tea Party legislators' digital homestyles provoke a sense of loss, one that breeds resentment and stokes, in particular, the existing social and racial conservatism within their districts.

In Chapter 4, we examine the proposition that efforts to attach to the Tea Party were driven, at least in part, by the economic, social, and racial conservatism of House members' districts. We are interested in the effects on members' primary, electoral, and geographic constituencies. Using data from Cooperative Congressional Election Surveys, we examine the connection between legislators and their various constituencies, focusing specifically on the distinctive constituency characteristics of Tea Party legislators. We are particularly interested in the relationship between attitudes associated with fiscal conservatism, social conservatism, and racial conservatism among constituents and the efforts of representatives to attach to the Tea Party.

We are also interested in the ways in which members associated with the Tea Party are distinct from other Republicans. Again, the literature on this set of issues is ambiguous, and if the representation of constituents' conservatism is simply association with a movement—absent distinctive policy orientations— then this association is of little value to members' constituents. That is, is the Tea Party label merely titular, something sought by members representing conservative constituencies? Or are there real differences in the positions that Tea Party and non-Tea Party Republicans take?

Similarly, we want to understand the institutional stature and capacity of legislators associated with the Tea Party movement. The "outsider" level implies limited institutional effectiveness, but is this characterization accurate, or is it a mere caricature? We seriously consider the possibility that Tea Party legislators are both more numerous than previously realized and more institutionally effective.

We examine the relative growth of the political attitudes associated with the Tea Party movement by legislative district. We hypothesize that representatives' efforts to attach themselves to the Tea Party would validate and legitimize the political orientations associated with the movement: fiscal conservatism, social conservatism, and racial conservatism. Our hypothesis implies that these three types of conservatism grow within congressional districts as a function of House members' attachment to the Tea Party movement.

Significantly, the growth of each type of conservatism in congressional districts is also a function of the extent to which a particular form of conservatism predated legislators' efforts to attach to the Tea Party movement. In simplest terms, we expect each type of conservatism to grow where it already existed. For example, if Tea Party supporters in a particular district are driven primarily by fiscal and social conservatism, then it is those dimensions of the Tea Party agenda that will be cultivated by members' efforts to attach to the Tea Party movement. Remember, the key is the manifestation of the movement as it exists in individual districts. Constituents see a member's efforts to attach to the movement as a validation of the constituents' own understanding of the movement (not necessarily the member's understanding of the movement).

We do not see members' attachment as introducing new types of conservatism to a constituency (be it primary, electoral, or geographic). Tea Party supporters activated by fiscal conservatism are unlikely to become racially conservative simply because their congressional representative has aligned her- or himself with the Tea Party movement. However, constituents who are already fiscally conservative (or socially conservative or racially conservative) may become more so, and their particular type of conservatism may have a greater impact on their decision to become politically active and the decisions they make about the types of policies and candidates they will support.

While the same dynamic may manifest with respect to members' digital homestyles, it is possible that members' advertising and position-taking through social media—Twitter specifically—could expand the dimensionality of the conservatism of their constituents. As members' advertising and position-taking identify new targets of resentment and/or prime emotional responses of fear or anger toward targets of resentment, it is possible that constituents' conservatism grows more complex (or more virulent). We evaluate this possibility in Chapter 9.

Stoking constituents' reactionary conservatism—rather than simply reflecting it—has implications not only for the future realization of the conservative goals of the Tea Party movement, but also for the success of candidates espousing those goals, whether or not they explicitly align with the Tea Party movement. The Tea Party movement has witnessed a dramatic decline in popular support. There are a variety of potential explanations for this decline, but one that has particular significance for us is the inability of the distinct strands of conservatism within the movement to effectively coalesce following Romney's nomination and Obama's subsequent re-election in 2012. In the aftermath of that election, and without the opportunity to unseat Obama, cooperation between the conservative groups became more difficult.

But the decline of the organizational Tea Party movement did not preclude the reactionary components of the movement—in whole or in part—from providing the political foundation for candidates espousing those ideals. We see the Trump candidacy and his electoral victories—first winning the Republican Party nomination for the presidency and then winning the presidency itself— as having been a direct result of the representation and effective cultivation of two dimensions of the Tea Party movement by House Republicans attached to the movement. The evidence suggests that his early supporters were drawn from the racial conservatives who favored the Tea Party. While competing with candidates with more overt connections to the Tea Party—such as Mario Rubio (R-FL) and Ted Cruz (R-TX)—made it somewhat more difficult to attract social conservatives, these conservatives began to align themselves with Trump as support for the other candidates declined . We argue that it was the resentment associated with this social and racial conservatism that boosted the Trump campaign to victory.

There are numerous parallels between the conservatives in the Tea Party movement and Trump supporters in the primary and general elections. Both groups were ardently anti-Obama. Both were racially resentful. Both favored immigration restrictions, Second Amendment rights, and budget cuts. Trump, like Tea Party legislators, consistently invoked a hopeless, doom-and-gloom attitude regarding the current political state of affairs. And—we argue—both activated largely latent white, working-class, non-college-educated whites.

In fact, President Trump's key insight about Tea Party supporters was their lack of strong ideological attachment to *fiscal* conservatism. This is also why a Tea Party darling like Ted Cruz failed to compete effectively for the Republican nomination. In Chapter 9, we consider the broader temporal and institutional implications of the Tea Party in Congress. We look at the presidential endorsement patterns of Republican House members—during both the campaign for the nomination and the general election campaign—to evaluate the distinctiveness of the decisions of Tea Party legislators. We also conduct district-level analyses of electoral support during the nominating campaign and the general election campaign to assess the following:

1. The impact of Tea Party *support* received by legislators on support for Trump in Republican primaries
2. The impact of legislators' efforts to *attach* to the Tea Party on support for Trump in the general election

3. The impact of legislators' *digital homestyle* on support for Trump in Republican primaries

4. The impact of legislators' *digital homestyle* on support for Trump in the general election

We contend that the representational strategy of members of Congress associated with the Tea Party movement enabled the election of Donald Trump. We discuss the significance of this finding in the conclusion.

Before analyzing the representational relationship between Tea Party supporters and Tea Party legislators, we need to understand just what a Tea Party legislator is—or more accurately, what Tea Party legislators are. We present theory and data on that issue in the next chapter.

3

The Tea Party in the House
of Representatives

Determining the partisan identification of members of Congress is easy. They nearly always begin their campaigns by registering to compete in the primary election of a specific party. They appear on a general election ballot as a member of a particular party. Their websites publicize their partisan attachments. They caucus with a particular party. And if they wish to change their partisan identification, it is a big deal. Changing one's partisan identification while one is a member of Congress is widely considered such an unusual and drastic event that when members do choose to align with a different party, they are expected to resign and run for the same seat (again) under their new party label.

But the Tea Party is not a conventional party, and it has proved very difficult to determine which members of Congress are members of the Tea Party and which are not. One reason for the dearth of research on the Tea Party in government is the difficulty of identifying which legislators are "true" Tea Party members. A survey of research on the Tea Party in Congress indicates that there is a surprising array of measurement strategies. Frankly, rarely are any two alike.

The earliest research on the Tea Party in the House uses the endorsements of Tea Party organizations to distinguish between members of the Tea Party and other Republicans.[1] Karpowitz et al. (2011) and Bullock and Hood (2012) use endorsement data from Tea Party organizations to distinguish between Tea Party members and other Republicans. But the application of Tea Party endorsements is not consistent. Karpowitz et al. (2011) use endorsements from FreedomWorks, Tea Party Express, Independence Caucus, Boston Tea Party, and an array of local Tea Party organizations to determine which candidates were associated with the Tea Party. Bullock and Hood (2012) use endorsement data from various Tea Party organizations as well, but they distinguish between the endorsements of Tea Party organizations and endorsements by former Alaska governor Sarah Palin, raising (but not resolving) the question of whether Palin's endorsements reflect the preferences of the broader movement. They do find that the relative success of the Tea Party candidates and the Palin candidates suggests distinct strategic objectives. Bailey, Mummolo, and Noel (2012) focus on FreedomWorks endorsements, but when they compare the effects of those endorsements with the effects of Tea Party Express endorsements and Sarah Palin's endorsements, they find no difference (in contrast to Bullock and Hood 2012).

Other researchers have focused exclusively on members' self-identification to determine association with the Tea Party movement. The most common and plausible means of identifying Tea Party legislators has been to consult the membership rolls of the Tea Party Caucus in the House of Representatives, formed by Michele Bachmann (R-MN) in 2010 (Gervais and Morris 2012). The one purely institutional manifestation of the Tea Party, the Caucus was also the only organizational entity associated with the Tea Party that recognized public and official claims by members of Congress to be associates of the popular movement. In contrast to organized parties, the Tea Party movement has no mechanism for recognizing formal membership. Similarly, the Caucus was established to further the interests of the Tea Party movement, and so legislators who join the Caucus might be expected to be those members of Congress most inclined to support the policy goals of the Tea Party (as diffuse as those might be). The measurement of self-identified association (or attachment) is based on membership in the Tea Party Caucus.

Ragusa and Gaspar (2016) use Tea Party Caucus membership to determine the "institutional" impact of the Tea Party movement on the voting behavior of members of Congress. They identify forty-six "permanent" members of the Tea Party Caucus, though it is not precisely clear what data they base this number on. They do, however, note that when they compared their list of Caucus members with that of Gallagher and Rock (2012), the match was perfect. They also use Tea Party organization endorsements as one measure of the "electoral" pressures members face to adjust their voting patterns in a conservative direction. They count endorsements from FreedomWorks and the Tea Party Express, but not Sarah Palin's endorsements or those from the Boston Tea Party, the Independence Caucus, or any of the local Tea Party organizations. Bailey, Mummolo, and Noel (2012) employ variables based on Tea Party Caucus membership in the 111th and 112th Congresses, but they do not specify how they identified the membership of the Caucus in either congress.

Clearly, Tea Party Caucus membership has been widely used to identify Tea Party members in scholarly research (Bailey et al. 2012; Gervais and Morris 2012; Ragusa and Gaspar 2016) and news media (Mehta 2014), but it is, unfortunately, a flawed measure. One issue is that while the Tea Party is in part a movement meant to purge the Republican ranks of those lacking ideological purity, it is doubtful that those in the Tea Party Caucus are "pure" conservatives in this sense (Weigel 2013). While Tea Party legislators have been labeled insurgents and have been associated with "brinkmanship" politics on controversial votes involving the debt ceiling and the 2013 government shutdown (Hook and O'Connor 2014), only a fraction of Tea Party Caucus members have been among those who have bucked leadership and not voted with the Republican "establishment" (Cilizza 2013a). This suggests that Tea Party Caucus membership has been used to strategically enhance conservative credentials, rather than simply serving as a reflection of a member's preexisting beliefs and legislative behavior.

While the House Tea Party Caucus is now dormant (see Newhauser 2013), several new groups—ostensibly affiliated with the Tea Party—have taken center stage in the House Republican Conference, orchestrating high-profile policy battles (e.g., the renewal of the Export-Import Bank's charter) and leadership shake-ups that have divided the Conference (Cadei 2015). The Liberty Caucus, instituted during the 113th Congress, has become the informal "home" for a younger, libertarian-minded cadre of House Republicans who consider themselves "true conservatives" and "real Tea Party Republicans" (Ferrechio 2014; Pareene 2014). The group, chaired by Justin Amash (R-MI), became a competitor of the "establishment" Republican Study Committee (Ferrechio 2014; Pareene 2014) and, according to some conservative-leaning media, the nexus of Tea Party–establishment conflict during the 113th Congress (Eddlem 2014). If the Tea Party existed in an institutional sense during the 113th Congress, it was as the Liberty Caucus. Yet the ranks of the Liberty Caucus are informal and nebulous, and its association with the Tea Party movement is more ambiguous than that with the Tea Party Caucus. Hence, like Tea Party Caucus membership, Liberty Caucus membership is an imperfect metric of "Tea Party-ness" on its own. In the 114th Congress, the Liberty Caucus was joined by the Freedom Caucus, which has since attracted many former members of the Tea Party Caucus. The Freedom Caucus (and, to a lesser extent, the Liberty Caucus) has been widely credited with forcing the resignation of Speaker John Boehner (R-OH) and Majority Leader Kevin McCarthy's (R-CA) decision to withdraw his name from the 2015 House speakership election (Matishak 2015; Walsh et al. 2015). Notably, Boehner's replacement, Paul Ryan (R-WI), would not accept the position without the blessing of affiliated members (or at least some measure of blessing) (*New York Times* Editorial Board 2015).

Another measurement strategy is to use an authoritative source for identifying Tea Party members. Carson and Pettigrew (2013) use the *New York Times* coding of Tea Party legislators for their analysis.[2] Unfortunately, the *Times* does not provide any explanation of its coding criteria or any description of its coding procedures. One can tell from the brief descriptions of the candidates identified as Tea Party members that some candidates were coded as Tea Party members because of the support or endorsements they had received from Tea Party organizations. For example, Todd Young (R-IN) was coded as a Tea Party member because "Mr. Young was endorsed by Freedom Works and the Independence Caucus" (*New York Times* 2010). Similarly, Bill Johnson (R-OH) "was supported by FreedomWorks and a $3,500 contribution from Sarah Palin's political action committee" (*New York Times* 2010).

Other members were associated with the Tea Party because of their own efforts rather than the support of Tea Party organizations. Marlin Stutzman (R-IN) was categorized as a Tea Party member because he "spoke at a Tea Party event in September that was headlined by Glenn Beck" (*New York Times* 2010). David McKinley (R-WV) was deemed a Tea Party member since he "said local Tea Party activists were going door to door on behalf of his campaign" (*New York Times* 2010).

In some cases, the justification for Tea Party member status includes no direct reference to any Tea Party organization or any Tea Party event. Trey Gowdy (R-SC) was seen as a Tea Party member because he "trounced a less conservative incumbent in the Republican primary in a district that has vocal Tea Party activists" (*New York Times* 2010), while Justin Amash was listed as a Tea Party member because he had

> acquired a reputation as a conservative maverick in the Michigan House, and dozens of Republicans have endorsed his Democratic opponent. In spite of attacks on him as being a libertarian ideologue, Mr. Amash beat two Republicans in the primary. (*New York Times* 2010)

In Amash's case, his reputation as a "maverick" and a "libertarian"—along with the fact that many Republicans endorsed his Democratic opponent—seems to have established his bona fides as a Tea Party member. Finally, in some cases, such as those of Jeff Landry (R-LA) and Vicky Hartzler (R-MO), there is no explanation at all.

This diversity of procedures for identifying Tea Party members among House Republicans would not concern us if the results of the analyses based on these varied coding procedures were consistent, but—not surprisingly—they are not. Bailey, Mummolo, and Noel (2012), for example, note that the correlation between the endorsements of various Tea Party groups is quite limited, as is the correlation between membership in the Tea Party Caucus and the lists of group endorsements. Ragusa and Gaspar (2016) find the same inconsistency with somewhat later data.

Consider the following examples. In 2010, Paul Gosar (R-AZ) won election to the House of Representatives from Arizona's First Congressional District. In 2012, he was re-elected to the House, this time from Arizona's Fourth Congressional

District. In 2010, Gosar received endorsements from a range of Tea Party organizations and individuals, including the Tea Party Express, FreedomWorks, and Sarah Palin. In 2012, he again received Sarah Palin's endorsement. Palin's political action committee, SarahPAC, contributed to Gosar's campaign in 2010 and 2012, and in 2012 the Tea Party–associated Club for Growth made independent expenditures in excess of $500,000 in support of Gosar's campaign. Media outlets also widely associated Gosar with the Tea Party movement (e.g., Santos 2012), but surprisingly, there is little evidence that Gosar was a member of the Tea Party Caucus in either the 111th or the 112th Congress.

Steve Southerland (R-FL) was also elected to the House of Representatives in 2010 and re-elected in 2012. Like Gosar, he received a considerable amount of support from Tea Party–related organizations and individuals. In 2010, Southerland was endorsed by FreedomWorks and Palin. His campaign also received direct contributions from FreedomWorks in 2010 and SarahPAC in 2012. Media outlets widely recognized Southerland as a Tea Party adherent. For example, the following is a brief section of an article on a Florida fundraising event held near Southerland's Second Congressional District shortly after the 2010 election:

> Al Kauses, chairman of the Panhandle Patriots Tea Party, whose members attended the event in matching blue T-shirts, said his organization comes to all meetings to try to hold elected officials accountable.
>
> "It was the Tea Party that got these people elected, most of them," he said. "If they hold to what they say they're going to do, they'll have the support of the people." (Reinlin 2011)

Like Gosar, Southerland appears never to have joined the Tea Party Caucus while it was still active.[3] At least, neither one is a member of the Tea Party Caucus according to Gallagher and Rock (2012) and Ragusa and Gaspar (2016). Members of Congress may also have a strong relationship with the Tea Party movement that does not involve explicit support from Tea Party organizations. Tom Price (R-GA), who was a member of the Tea Party Caucus, has consistently presented himself as associated with the Tea Party, and yet we find no evidence that Tea Party organizations have ever supported him.

These are not isolated issues. When Bailey, Mummolo, and Noel (2012) compare various measures of Tea Party association—Tea Party Caucus membership and Tea Party organizational support—they find relatively little overlap. Specifically, they write, "The correlation matrix across various affiliation types . . . makes it clear one cannot simply take one or another association and assume it completely embodies the nature of the Tea Party movement" (Bailey, Mummolo, and Noel 2012).

An additional problem with these coding schemes is the level of measurement. Existing coding schemes measure association at the nominal level: legislators are either members of the Tea Party or not. Endorsements from a set of Tea Party organizations and a single endorsement from one Tea Party organization are coded identically. A $1,000 contribution is the same as a $5,000 contribution. If the Tea Party were a traditional political party, this orientation to association would make sense. But as we noted at the beginning of the chapter, the Tea Party is not a traditional party. The Tea Party is a movement—a movement without a designated leader or any sort of coordinated structure. The policy goals of the various Tea Party organizations certainly overlap to an extent, but they were not and are not carbon copies. Again, association with a political movement is more complicated than identification with a political party.

When a political association is well organized and formally structured, there is a compelling logic to use explicit membership to determine the relative attachments of legislators to that association. But in the absence of formal structure and organization, the dichotomous quality of formal membership—whether in the party itself or a group associated with the party (e.g., the Tea Party Caucus)—fails to fully reflect the likely variance in the extent of association with the movement. This is a key issue with the Tea Party, such as it is, in Congress. We have no doubt that certain members of Congress are as closely aligned to the Tea Party movement as the rather amorphous character of that entity allows. Similarly, we expect that a number of legislators, even within the Republican Party, have no association with the movement at all. But we also expect that there are legislators whose association with the movement, while tangible, is more tenuous than that of the hard core.

Gervais and Taylor (2016) provide an interesting response to this problem. While they are focused on the public perception of a member of Congress's association with the Tea Party rather than actual association, their *Tea Party Salience* variable provides an interval-level measure of the relationship—or, technically, the public's perception of a relationship between the Tea Party and a member of Congress. Rather than being limited to the designation of a legislator as either a member of the Tea Party or not, this measure provides a means of capturing the extent of association between a legislator and the Tea Party. Gervais and Taylor assess the extent of a House member's association with the Tea Party movement by calculating the frequency with which print and television media described the member as a Tea Party candidate. Again, this is not a perfect measure of association. Neither candidates nor Tea Party organizations have control over the media, so any communication of a relationship between the member and the Tea Party organization will obviously be imperfect. Similarly, the frequency of news stories about a particularly candidate—whether or not the candidate is associated with the Tea Party—varies dramatically for reasons that have no impact on the extent of the underlying relationship between the candidate and the Tea Party. For example, in 2012, Paul Ryan had the highest Tea Party Salience score of any candidate. While Ryan did have ties to the Tea Party, the extreme value of his score was based on more than his association with the Tea Party; it was almost certainly a product of the fact that he was also the Republican nominee for the vice presidency.

Another key problem with existing measures of the association between a member of Congress and the Tea Party is that none capture the underlying dimensionality of this relationship. A member's association with the Tea Party is a two-way street; current measures of Tea Party association focus on only one lane of the road or the other. While Tea Party organizations may choose to associate with members of Congress, members of Congress may also choose to attach themselves with the Tea Party movement. Indicators derived from Tea Party organizations' endorsements or campaign contributions tap into what we refer to as *support* (Gervais and Morris 2014). Measures derived from membership in the Tea Party Caucus tap into what we refer to as *attachment* (Gervais and Morris 2014).

Strategic considerations drive both Tea Party support and Tea Party attachment, but the loci of the strategic decisions differ. Tea Party organizations make the decision to align with a legislator. Members of Congress make the decision to align with the Tea Party movement. As the decision-makers vary, so do the strategic considerations that drive the decision. A Tea Party organization might find a member an attractive standard-bearer to a far greater extent than the member views the Tea Party as a valuable ally. Similarly, a member who is rather less attractive to Tea Party organizations—for a variety of reasons—may be very interested in attaching her- or himself to the movement.

Tea Party organizations have policy goals. Efforts to achieve those goals through support for congressional candidates or members of Congress may take different forms. First, Tea Party organizations may focus their energies on helping candidates/members with compatible policy objectives win in particularly competitive electoral environments. Tea Party organizations may also support the efforts of acceptable candidates/members facing incumbents who are anathema to the Tea Party movement and who are in competitive electoral environments. Alternatively, Tea Party organizations may focus their support on the "true believers," the set of members whose policy preferences are the most closely aligned with the Tea Party organizations. Support in this case is intended to encourage the continuation of members' efforts to achieve policy goals consistent with those of the supporting organization. Finally, support may be directed to members with acceptable policy orientations who are particularly likely to win election or re-election. By supporting winners, the organization builds its own cache or brand so as to more effectively mobilize supporters and lobby members of the Congress in subsequent years.

Research on the two key types of Tea Party support—Tea Party organization endorsements and Tea Party campaign financing—suggests that there is some empirical support for each of these strategic rationales (see Bullock and Hood 2012). However, using endorsements alone to determine who is a "Tea Party" legislator is problematic. In the 2010 elections, FreedomWorks chose to endorse few incumbents and was strategic in choosing which candidates to back, favoring those in winnable races (Bailey et al. 2012; Karpowitz et al. 2011). The limited overlap between Tea Party group endorsements suggests that there is some difference of opinion among groups when it comes to who is deserving of Tea Party support (Bailey et al. 2012; *New York Times* 2010). Moreover, while a plethora of Tea Party groups were active during the 2012 elections, very few formally endorsed candidates (Beckel 2013).

Tea Party organizations also provided candidates with campaign contributions. When legislators are perceived to have conservative activists associated with these groups on their side, they are often described as "Tea Party–backed." However, as is the case with endorsements, Tea Party groups have been strategic about which candidates they wish to financially support and have generally made surprisingly few direct contributions to candidates (Gold 2014). Whether it is endorsements or contributions, we expect this support to be partially based on need, with candidates in "safe" seats less likely to draw valuable time and resources. Moreover, when support originates with one or more groups, thus suggesting approval of a candidate, it is unclear if other Tea Party groups or activists share these sentiments; with no single Tea Party "voice," it is possible for a candidate endorsed by a national Tea Party group to be disregarded by activists at home.

Legislators also make strategic decisions when determining the extent to which they will align with the Tea Party movement. Joining the Tea Party Caucus (or the Liberty Caucus or, now, the Freedom Caucus) communicates a member's attachment to the movement, but legislators can signal attachment through other means as well. Members of Congress may attend Tea Party rallies and then issue a traditional press release. This media activity would be likely to raise their score on Gervais and Taylor's (2016) Tea Party Salience index. The period since 2010 is notable for not just the rise of the Tea Party but also the rise of "digital homestyle," or how members of Congress present themselves to constituents and the broader public using social media. Before the 112th Congress began in January 2011, less than 30 percent of all legislators in the House and Senate had a verified Twitter account (Golbeck et al. 2010). By the time the 112th Congress was wrapping up in December 2012, the proportion of all members on Twitter was 95 percent (Hemphill et al. 2013). Thus, the 112th can be considered the first "tweeting" Congress. Both traditional and digital methods for connecting to constituents allow legislators to concoct a Tea Party image. Striving to identify with the Tea Party likely reflects some appreciation for and fidelity to the movement. However, as in the case of Tea Party Caucus membership, it is unclear how much of this is cover for less than impeccable ideological credentials and how much of it is represents a genuine commitment to the movement's principles and goals.

In some cases, the association between a legislator and the Tea Party movement is bidirectional. Some legislators attach to the movement, and organizations associated with the movement support the legislator. Conversely, some legislators who never received support from Tea Party organizations repudiate the movement themselves. But there may also be situations in which the association between a legislator and the Tea Party movement is a one-way street; for example, a legislator's efforts to attach to the movement may not be reciprocated with support, or a legislator may ignore the electoral support of Tea Party organizations.

We expect the character of this limited association to take one of two forms. The first form manifests in those cases in which a legislator's endeavors to be recognized as a Tea Party member have yet to be fully successful. Here we would expect to see claims of attachment to the movement that are not matched by comparable support from Tea Party organizations (maybe in the form of endorsements or campaign contributions).

But legislators' efforts to attach to the Tea Party movement are not necessarily attempts to win support from Tea Party organizations. As we discussed in the preceding chapter, Tea Party organizations are not synonymous with the Tea Party movement. Tea Party organizations tend to focus on policy objectives driven by fiscal conservatism. While there is some variation across Tea Party organizations—which should come as no surprise given the broader movement—fiscal conservatism is a central theme. Tea Party supporters among members of the mass public, however, tend to care far less about fiscal conservatism (apart from tax cuts) than Tea Party organizations or the movement's most ardent activists. The overhaul of entitlement programs, for example, is far more important to Tea Party organizations than it is to Tea Party voters. Conversely, Tea Party voters tend to be especially conservative on social issues, such as gay marriage and abortion—issues that are underemphasized (or ignored) by Tea Party organizations. Tea Party voters also tend to be more racially conservative, and these attitudes manifest on issues related to immigration, crime, and civil rights. In some cases, these issues are key for Tea Party organizations (such as immigration); in other cases, they are not (crime, civil rights). Legislators' efforts to attach to the Tea Party movement may be directed more at Tea Party supporters than at Tea Party organizations.

A second form of limited attachment manifests when members who are supported by Tea Party organizations manage their messages and public presentations in such a way as to limit the emphasis on Tea Party attachment (possibly in an effort to attract or retain more moderate components of an electoral constituency). That a member of Congress is attractive to Tea Party organizations—for reasons of ideological orientation or legislative effectiveness, for example—does not necessarily imply that the member is interested in aligning her- or himself with the movement. If a member's core constituency were somewhat less conservative on the fiscal issues so important to Tea Party organizations—or the social or racially tinged issues dear to Tea Party supporters in the general population—that member might shy away from attachment to the movement.

We reason that there are two largely distinct dimensions of Tea Party association: *Tea Party Support* and *Tea Party Attachment*. The discussion above provides various rationales for the limited overlap between the measures. At the very least, the discussion suggests that the influence of the Tea Party movement varied somewhat across legislators and the extent to which they displayed that influence also varied. It might also suggest that the Tea Party movement in Congress is either a small (and declining) splinter group or a broad but quite shallow collection of name-only Tea Party adherents. Another alternative is that the various manifestations of the movement in the House obscured the significance of the movement's impact on the behavior of a large number of legislators. In the next section, we describe the variables used to measure Tea Party support and Tea Party attachment.

Measuring Tea Party Association

The focus of our analysis is on the 112th and 113th Congresses. While this period was likely the high-water mark of the Tea Party in Congress, it was also clearly a time in which efforts to associate with the Tea Party movement were extensive and Tea Party organizations and activists widely advertised their support for members of Congress (and congressional candidates).

We have identified a set of indicators of Tea Party association that fall into each of these dimensions: support from Tea Party groups and activists (a *Support* dimension) and attempts by legislators to self-identify with the Tea Party movement (an *Attachment* dimension). We use three measures to tap legislators' attachment to the Tea Party:

1. Membership in the Tea Party Caucus or Liberty Caucus
2. Tea Party Self-identification with Social Media
3. Media Salience of Tea Party Connection

To gauge the organized Tea Party's support for legislators, we use the following indicators:

1. Tea Party Endorsements
2. Tea Party Campaign Contributions and Independent Expenditures
3. Tea Party Activism

Membership in the Tea Party Caucus was simply coded 1 if a legislator joined the Tea Party Caucus during the 112th Congress and 0 if she or he did not join the Caucus. Our list of Tea Party Caucus members in the 112th is based on the official membership list, which was made available on Michele Bachmann's website while the 112th Congress was in session. While the 112th was in session, sixty legislators, or about 25 percent of the House Republican Conference, joined the Tea Party Caucus.[4] Membership in the Liberty Caucus was simply coded 1 if a legislator joined the Liberty Caucus during the 113th Congress and 0 if she or he did not join. While attendance at Liberty Caucus meetings was by invitation only during the 113th Congress (see Ferrechio 2014; Pareene 2014), the Liberty Caucus does have an active (at least public) membership list (see Hohmann 2013); however, we were able to generate a list of its 113th membership from an official source that was formerly publicized.[5] This variable was coded 1 if a legislator was a member of the Liberty Caucus during the 113th Congress and 0 if she or he was not. Note that membership in the Tea Party Caucus did not affect coding for membership in the Liberty Caucus, nor did coding of membership in the Liberty Caucus affect coding of membership in the Tea Party Caucus.

While candidates can try to influence the coverage of their campaigns by traditional news outlets, social media has provided an avenue for campaigns to circumvent news media entirely and deliver unadulterated (and unvetted) messages directly to voters (Gainous and Wagner 2013). Thus, candidates who wish to connect themselves to the Tea Party movement have ample opportunity to do so with social media. As mentioned earlier, the 112th Congress was the first in which nearly all members of Congress had official congressional Twitter accounts (Hemphill et al. 2013). We made use of this wave by collecting every tweet generated by a Republican member's official account during both the 112th and 113th Congresses to assess Tea Party Self-identification with Social Media.[6] This database consists of hundreds of thousands of tweets and allows us to total the number of tweets, as well as calculate the percentage of a member's overall tweets that positively affiliate her- or himself with the Tea Party. Specifically, we searched each member's tweet collection for the terms "tea party" and "teaparty," the latter of which can identify use of the hashtag "#teaparty," as well as "#tpp," in reference to "tea party patriots" and "freedomworks." If a tweet was already identified as a Tea Party tweet, it was not counted again (i.e., if it included more than one of the search terms). All tweets were reviewed to ensure that references were positive and related to the Tea Party movement (e.g., "tpp" tweets were reviewed to ensure that they did not refer to Trans-Pacific Partnership). We created a Tea Party Tweet variable for both congresses, which we calculated by dividing the number of positive Tea Party tweets by the total number of tweets posted by a member's account within each congress.

Another avenue through which candidates can attach themselves to the Tea Party movement is the news media. Ubiquitous in many reports of Republican primary and general elections are the terms "Tea Party Republican" and "Tea Party candidate." Most voters' perceptions of who is and who is not a Tea Party legislator are based on how salient the Tea Party association is made in news media.[7] In regard to actual candidate control over this manner of association, news media connections are amalgamated: while much of the decision to connect a candidate to the Tea Party is ultimately at the discretion of journalists and media outlets, candidates can certainly influence the salience of the association. By appearing at Tea Party rallies, meeting with Tea Party organizations, and making Tea Party connections known to media outlets through the release of press releases, for example, candidates and their campaigns can increase the salience of their Tea Party association in news reports.

In the case of Media Salience of Tea Party Connection, we use a measure of how frequently candidates were positively connected to the Tea Party in print and in television transcripts of US news outlets during the 2010 election season (January 1, 2010, to November 1, 2010) and the 2012 election season (January 1, 2012, through November 5, 2012). The search was conducted using the LexisNexis news database, and results were reviewed to ensure that a candidate was truly attached to the Tea Party; other references were discounted (e.g., an article mentioning that an incumbent defeated a Tea Party challenger would not be counted as a positive association for the incumbent).

We follow the lead of previous works that have utilized Tea Party endorsements and focus on those issued by several national, high-profile Tea Party organizations and figures (Ansolabehere and Snyder 2011). We do this for several reasons. First, many Tea Party organizations decline to issue endorsements of candidates (Karpowitz et al. 2011). Second, even if collecting a comprehensive list of local and national Tea Party groups was feasible, the problem of retrieving complete and reliable endorsement lists from each would remain. Additionally, endorsements by some national Tea Party organizations were too few and indefinite to be leveraged. For example, the Independent Caucus "vetted" candidates through a questionnaire in 2010, but we hesitate to characterize these as endorsements in the same way we qualify FreedomWorks and Tea Party Express endorsements. Moreover, a large percentage of the "endorsed" candidates did not win the primary in 2010, never mind the general election. Likewise, the social media site Tea Party Nation called attention to specific candidates in on-line postings titled "Candidates you need to know about." However, in addition to there not being clear-cut endorsements, we identified only three "endorsed" candidates who went on to win in the 2010 general election.

Two national organizations that did make true endorsements in 2010 and 2012 were Tea Party Express and FreedomWorks. In addition, endorsements by former Alaska governor Sarah Palin have been treated as Tea Party endorsements (Bailey et al. 2012). We utilize the lists of endorsements made by Tea Party Express, FreedomWorks, and Sarah Palin to generate a Tea Party Endorsements variable on a scale of 0–3, with 3 indicating endorsements by all three, and 0 indicating endorsements by none of the three.

For the Tea Party Campaign Contributions and Independent Expenditures measure, we collected records of both direct and independent campaign contributions from Tea Party groups during the 2010 and 2012 election cycles and relied on the official returns that members of the House Republican Conference filed with the Federal Election Commission (FEC). We again collected data on the national Tea Party organizations Tea Party Express (whose fundraising arm is known as "Our Country Deserves Better PAC") and FreedomWorks, along with contributions from Palin's political action committee, SarahPAC. Additionally, we collected data on contributions by the fiscally conservative Club for Growth, which is often grouped with FreedomWorks and Our Country Deserves Better in accounts of outside "Tea Party" spending (Bump 2014; Weisman and Steinhauer 2014) and has evaluated legislators on Tea Party "purity" (Wasson 2012). While FreedomWorks and Club for Growth primarily made independent expenditures in support of candidates, Our Country Deserves Better was active in making direct and independent expenditures. SarahPAC, on the other hand, made direct contributions to candidate campaigns during the 2010 and 2012 election seasons.

We also collected direct contribution data on smaller, local Tea Party organizations by conducting a search for all groups reporting contributions to the FEC that had "Tea Party" in their name. For the 112th Congress, groups identified in this search included Independence Hall Tea Party PAC, the Llano Tea Party (of Texas), and Tea Party PAC USA. While other groups with "Tea Party" in their name were featured in the FEC database, they did not make any direct contributions during the 2010 election cycle and were thus excluded. For the 113th Congress, we collected expenditure data from the Tea Party Victory PAC.

As with many types of political activism, measuring Tea Party activism is difficult, but social media has made this much more feasible. Cho, Gimpel, and Shaw (2012), for example, used Meetup.org data to measure the geography of Tea Party activism during the fall of 2010. In order to measure support for a particular candidate, we turn to Twitter and the hashtag "#tcot," which stands for "top conservatives on Twitter," and is the most widely used hashtag among those associated with the movement (Bode et al. 2015). The hashtag, created by a self-described Tea Party activist, "provides a way for conservatives in particular and Republicans in general to locate and follow the tweets of their like-minded brethren," and, according to its founder, is "what really launched the Tea Party movement in February of 2009."[8] In short, it is a way that devout conservatives and Tea Party activists share information and mobilize support for ideas or candidates. Those who use the #tcot are essentially identifying themselves as Tea Party supporters (but see Bode et al. 2015 for a discussion of liberal users' "highjacking" of the hashtag). Using an online Twitter database, we conducted a search for the number of times #tcot and the candidate's name appeared together throughout the three weeks leading up to the November 2010 election (October 12, 2010, until November 2, 2010) and 2012 election (October 16, 2012, until November 6, 2012). Tweets that the search returned were reviewed to ensure that the messages were supportive and qualified as instances in which users were promoting a candidate via #tcot or in which the candidate's views or success were reported. Those that were not were discounted. In 2010, the Tea Party Activist variable ranged from 0 to 1,414, with an average of 18 supportive tweets per member. In 2012, the range dipped to 0 to 133, with an average of over 3 tweets per member.

Our Tea Party Attachment measure is a simple ordinal index ranging from 0 to 2. The prominence of membership in the Tea Party Caucus is reflected in our measure; members of the Tea Party Caucus are coded 2 in the 112th Congress. Legislators with values above zero on the standardized measures Tea Party Tweets and Tea Party Salience who were not members of the Tea Party Caucus were also coded 2. Legislators with values greater than zero on the standardized measure Tea Party Tweets *or* the standardized measure Tea Party Salience (but not both) who were not members of the Tea Party Caucus were coded 1. All other legislators in the 112th Congress were coded 0.

Because the connection of the Liberty Caucus to the Tea Party is more tenuous than the connection of the Tea Party Caucus to the Tea Party—and because the Liberty Caucus has played a less central role in the research on the Tea Party in Congress—it plays a less central role in the construction of our Tea Party Attachment measure in the 113th Congress than the Tea Party Caucus plays in our construction of Tea Party Attachment in the 112th Congress. In the 113th Congress, members who satisfied two of the following three criteria were coded 2:

1. Member of the Liberty Caucus
2. Scored above zero on the standardized Tea Party Tweets measure
3. Scored above zero on the standardized Tea Party Salience measure

Members who satisfied any one of the above criteria were coded 1" All other members were coded 0.

~~Our Tea Party Support Index is simply a sum of the standardized scores~~ of each of the component indicators: Tea Party Endorsements, Tea Party Contributions, and Tea Party Activism. Note that all of these are at least ordinal-level measures—unlike the caucus membership components of the Tea Party Attachment index. As in the case of our Tea Party Attachment measure, we do not view the components as tapping into a single underlying substantive dimension. They are distinct manifestations of support from a variety of participants in a broad and unstructured popular movement. We would expect to see some relationship between these components, but strong relationships would be surprising.[9]

While these measures are related, the relationships are not particularly strong. The strongest relationship, not surprisingly, was that between endorsements and campaign funding in 2012, with a correlation of nearly 0.50. (In 2010, the correlation between endorsements and campaign funding was only 0.26.) Overall, the Cronbach's alpha scale reliability coefficient is also relatively low (0.38 average for Tea Party Support across both election years and an average of 0.20 for the 112th and 113th Congresses for Tea Party Attachment). We also note that the Tea Party Attachment and Tea Party Support measures are largely unrelated. The correlation between them is less than 0.03 for the 112th Congress and less than 0.27 for the 113th Congress. Given the extant research, the distinctiveness of these measures is not surprising.

It is worth noting that the correlation is greater during the 113th Congress than during the 112th Congress, suggesting a coalescing of the movement and some greater level of coordination than existed in 2010. Along these lines, we note that the relationship between Tea Party Caucus membership in the 112th Congress is actually negatively associated (albeit weakly) with campaign support and endorsements in 2010. By the 113th Congress, the relationship between Liberty Caucus membership and campaign support and endorsements in 2012 is positive (though the relationship is still relatively weak, with correlations below 0.20).

But this subtle increase should not obscure the fact that a single latent dimension of Tea Party association simply does not exist. In the present context, the absence of a single unifying dimension for a diffuse mass political movement that lacks coordinated organization seems completely plausible. We see theoretical reasons for variance between a legislator's efforts to attach to the Tea Party movement and the extent to which the movement recognizes and reciprocates these efforts. Likewise, organizations within the movement—or prominent individuals associated with the movement—may in turn cultivate the support of legislators who do not fully reciprocate their efforts. This is preliminary evidence in support of this contention.

Tea Types and Their Exemplars

Tea Party support and Tea Party attachment will play a significant role in subsequent chapters. We will examine the relationship between Tea Party support and Tea Party attachment and legislators' ideology (as manifest in roll call voting). Are members of Congress associated with the Tea Party as conservative as popular media treatments suggest? Evidence of extreme conservatism among Tea Party legislators is mixed. Some research suggests that Tea Party legislators are significantly more conservative than other Republicans (Ragusa and Gaspar 2016). Other research indicates that Tea Party legislators are more conservative than fellow Republicans on only a few prominent issues directly associated with the Tea Party movement (Bailey et al. 2012; Gervais and Morris 2012). Still other research finds no evidence that Tea Party legislators are ideologically distinct from other Republicans (see Gallagher and Rock 2012).[10] We revisit this issue with our multidimensional Tea Party Association measure.

Subsequent chapters will also examine the extent to which Tea Party legislators differed from other Republicans on significant organizational dimensions. Previous research suggests that Tea Party legislators were backbenchers intent on being disruptive rather than producing public policy. We analyze the distinctiveness of Tea Party legislators in terms of leadership status, legislative productivity, and legislative effectiveness.

We also analyze the distinctiveness of Tea Party legislators' constituencies. Were Tea Party legislators serving different types of constituencies than other Republicans? If yes, in what ways were the constituencies different? Were Tea Party constituencies more or less racially and ethnically diverse? Poorer? Richer? More conservative? We address these questions in Chapter 4.

But before moving on to these other analyses, we examine the exemplars of the different types of Tea Party legislators implied by our measurement strategy. The types are as follows:

1. *Black Tea*: Legislators with this designation have *both* a high level of attachment to the Tea Party movement and a high level of support from the Tea Party movement.
2. *Green Tea*: These legislators score high on the Tea Party Attachment index, but they receive below-average levels of support from the organized Tea Party movement.
3. *White Tea*: Members of Congress in this category have below-average levels of attachment to the Tea Party but at the same time have above-average levels of support from Tea Party organizations.
4. *Coffee*: Legislators in this group have both below-average levels of attachment to the Tea Party and receive below-average levels of support from Tea Party organizations.

To illustrate how the indices divide up the Republican Conference, we will briefly discuss some exemplary cases of these types. First are the core Tea Party legislators: Black Tea Republicans. These legislators actively associate with the movement and are in turn embraced by the movement. Among the Black Tea legislators in the 112th or the 113th Congress are Sandy Adams (R-FL), Justin Amash, Michelle Bachmann, Jason Chaffetz (R-UT), Steve King (R-IA), Raul Labrador (R-ID), and Allen West (R-FL).

On the Tea Party Support dimension, each of these members of Congress received at least one endorsement from a Tea Party organization or Sarah Palin in 2010 or 2012, and a majority received multiple endorsements in at least one of these elections. FreedomWorks endorsed Adams, Amash, and West in 2010 and King in 2012. Amash also received the Tea Party Express endorsement in 2010, and Sarah Palin endorsed Adams, Bachman, and West in 2010. All received campaign funds from Tea Party organizations and SarahPAC in 2010 or 2012, and Bachmann—the titular leader of the Tea Party Caucus—received campaign funds from Tea Party organizations in 2010 and 2012. Amash and King received campaign support from FreedomWorks in 2012. Four of the Black Tea exemplars received funding from Our Country Deserves Better, and Bachmann received support from this group in 2010 and 2012. SarahPAC made contributions to Adams, Bachmann, and Labrador. All received multiple positive tweets from Tea Party activists in both 2010 and 2012 (if they campaigned in both years).

The Tea Party Attachment dimension was also high for each of these legislators. All were members of the Tea Party Caucus—with Bachmann and Labrador joining the Tea Party Caucus in the 111th Congress—or the Liberty Caucus. All had positive Tea Party Salience scores for either the 112th or 113th Congress, and all those who were members in both the 112th and 113th Congresses had high Tea Party Salience scores for both. Moreover, all had positive tweet rates for the Tea Party movement during either the 112th or 113th Congress, and most had positive tweet rates for both.

Green Tea Republicans —those attached to the movement who received little or no explicit support from the movement—were also prevalent during the 112th and 113th Congresses. Examples of Green Tea legislators include Todd Akin (R-MO), Randy Neugebauer (R-TX), Jeff Duncan (R-SC), Louie Gohmert (R-TX), and Tom Price. All of the Green Tea Republicans were members of the Tea Party Caucus in the 112th Congress, and all but Duncan were members of the Tea Party Caucus in the 111th Congress. Duncan was a member of the Liberty Caucus during the 113th Congress. Akin, Duncan, and Gohmert had positive Tea Party Salience scores in 2010 and 2012, and all five had positive Tea Party Salience scores in 2012. All had positive Tea Party Tweet rates in each of the congresses in which they served. On the Tea Party Attachment dimension, the Green Tea exemplars are indistinguishable from the Black Tea exemplars.

As for Tea Party support, Duncan was endorsed by FreedomWorks in 2010. None of the other members received endorsements from any of the main Tea Party organizations, and Duncan did not receive any other endorsements from these organizations in 2010 or 2012. Similarly, none of these candidates received any campaign funds from the major Tea Party organizations (including SarahPAC). Only Gohmert and Price received positive mentions from Tea Party activists, and Price received positive mentions only in 2010. Clearly, on the Tea Party Support dimension, the Green Tea exemplars are nothing like the Black Tea exemplars.

Among the White Tea Republicans, those who did not seek association with the movement but who were actively supported anyway, were Renee Ellmers (R-NC), Paul Gosar, Michael Grimm (R-NY), Reid Ribble (R-WI), and Daniel Webster (R-FL). All of the these exemplars were endorsed by major Tea Party organizations. In fact, FreedomWorks endorsed all five. Ellmers and Grimm also received endorsements from Sarah Palin, and the Tea Party Express endorsed Gosar. All of these endorsements were received during the 2010 election season. All of these members received campaign support from Tea Party organizations or SarahPAC in 2010, and SarahPAC made contributions to four of the five legislators. FreedomWorks contributed to Ribble's campaign in 2010 and 2012, and SarahPAC contributed to Ellmers and Gosar in both 2010 and 2012. All received positive comments from Tea Party activists in 2010, and except for Ribble, there were dozens of popular comments for each White Tea exemplar.

To the best of our knowledge, none of the White Tea exemplars were members of the Tea Party Caucus during either the 111th or 112th Congress. Only Ribble joined the Liberty Caucus. Tea Party Salience scores for the White Tea exemplars are all in the single digits. In comparison, the average Tea Party Salience score for the Black Tea exemplars was 147 in 2010 (and 165 in 2012). Three of the five White Tea exemplars made no positive Tea Party tweets during the 112th Congress, and the same is true for four of the five during the 113th Congress.

Finally, the 112th and 113th Congresses featured Coffee Republicans, or those who have little or no attachment to the movement and a comparable lack of support from the movement. Coffee Republicans included Spencer Bachus (R-AL), Shelley Moore Capito (R-WV),[11] Ileana Ros-Lehtinen (R-FL), John Shimkus (R-IL), and Mac Thornberry (R-TX).

Shelley Moore Capito received the Tea Party Express's endorsement in 2010, but not in 2012. None of the other Coffee Republicans received a Tea Party endorsement. None of the Coffee exemplars received campaign support from any of the major Tea Party organizations or SarahPAC. None of these Republicans received even positive mentions from Tea Party activists in 2012. None of the

Coffee exemplars were ever members of the Tea Party Caucus or the Liberty Caucus. Their average Tea Party Salience score in 2010 was 0.2, and for four of the five, we could not find any media reports connecting them in any way to the Tea Party in 2010. The same is true for all five in 2012 and 2014. Only Shimkus had a positive Tea Party Tweet rate in the 112th Congress, and none had a positive Tea Party Tweet rate during the 113th Congress. Clearly, these Republicans were not associated with the Tea Party movement. They made no effort to attach themselves to the movement, nor did they receive support from the movement.

In Chapter 4, we will examine the constituency, electoral, and institutional factors that led some members to make intense efforts to attach to the Tea Party movement and other members to ignore the movement. We also seek to understand which constituency, electoral, and institutional factors led Tea Party organizations and Tea Party activists to provide extensive support for some members and no support at all for others. But we can begin to uncover some of these dynamics by looking more closely at some of the key differences between the Black Tea, Green Tea, White Tea, and Coffee Republicans highlighted in this chapter.

First, from an ideological standpoint, Coffee Republicans are easily the least conservative type of Republican (see Figures 3.1 and 3.2). Using the first dimension of the DW-Nominate scores as an indicator of ideological orientation[12]— with higher scores indicating greater conservatism—we see that Coffee Republicans had the lowest scores in both the 112th and 113th Congresses and that their scores were well below the average in both congresses.[13] The Black Tea and Green Tea Republicans are by far the most conservative in both the 112th and 113th Congresses, with the Black Tea legislators leading in conservatism in the 112th and the Green Tea legislators leading in the 113th. This suggests that members' efforts to attach themselves to the Tea Party movement were more closely aligned with ideological conservatism—broadly measured—than

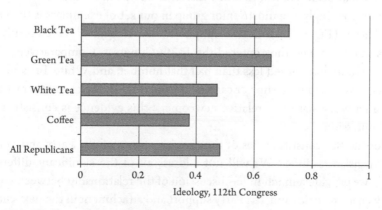

Figure 3.1 Ideology, 112th Congress.

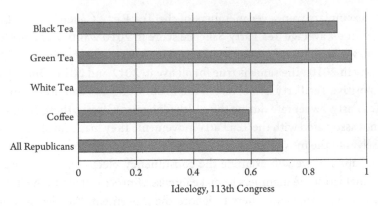

Figure 3.2 Ideology, 113th Congress.

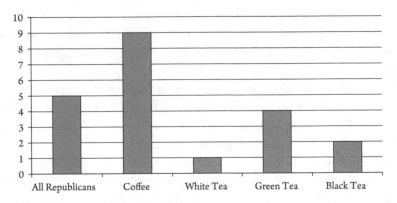

Figure 3.3 Terms in Office, 112th Congress.

support received from Tea Party organizations. Whether White Tea Republicans are less conservative than their fellow Tea Party legislators on fiscal issues alone remains to be seen. We will examine this issue further in Chapter 5.

Not surprisingly, the most senior group in our set of exemplars is the Coffee Republicans (Figure 3.3). Coffee legislators, on average, had served nearly nine terms in office when they entered the 112th Congress. Comparatively, Green Tea legislators had served less than half that number, and White Tea and Black Tea legislators had even shorter careers in Congress. To the extent that we think of Tea Party legislators as relative newcomers, this evidence is consistent with that impression.

How do the constituencies of these various types of Tea Party and non-Tea Party legislators differ? We will not address all of the significant differences here—we provide a much fuller discussion of the relationship between constituency characteristics and Tea Party support and attachment in the next chapter. But a brief overview of some of the key constituency distinctions will help clarify the intuition behind our argument regarding the differences between the types of Tea Party Republicans and the extent to which their constituents were likely to be supporters of Donald Trump.

At this point, we focus on district-level factors such as unemployment, percentage of immigrants, percentage of African Americans, and support for Obama in 2008 and 2012. First, the economic situations faced by constituents in these different types of districts vary considerably (Figures 3.4 and 3.5). Based on district-level unemployment rates leading into the 112th and 113th Congresses, Black Tea Republicans had the most economically vibrant constituencies. Conversely, White Tea Republicans tended to have the most economically troubled districts. Given our own previous research (Gervais and Morris 2012, 2014, 2015a), this is as expected. In the 112th Congress, those who were members of the Tea Party Caucus—remember that White Tea legislators scored high on the Tea Party Support measure but not on Tea Party Attachment, so they were not members of the Caucus—hailed from districts with below-average levels of

Figure 3.4 District Unemployment, 112th Congress.

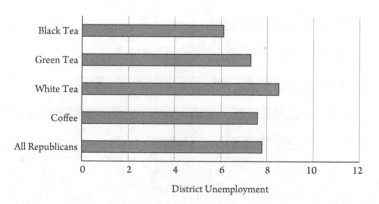

Figure 3.5 District Unemployment, 113th Congress.

unemployment. It is much easier to be fiscally conservative if the district you represent has relatively low unemployment; however, social and racial conservatism might easily be primed by economic discontent.

Variations in the racial/ethnic makeup of the various constituencies, as well as the immigrant composition of the electorate, are also important factors that differentiate the various types of Tea Party Republicans and non-Tea Party Republicans (Figures 3.6 and 3.7). Immigrants are significantly more common in Coffee Republican districts than they are in the districts of any other Tea Party Republicans. Immigrants are least common in Black Tea districts, somewhat more common in Green Tea districts, and even more common in White Tea districts.

The variation in the distribution of immigrants across the districts of different types of Tea Party legislators suggests that the electoral risks associated with the anti-immigrant orientation of the Tea Party also varied across districts. Where immigrants were relatively rare—in districts served by Black Tea Republicans

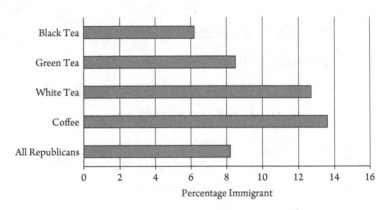

Figure 3.6 Percentage of Immigrants in District, 112th Congress.

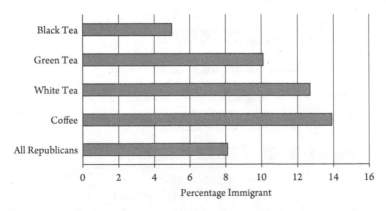

Figure 3.7 Percentage of Immigrants in District, 113th Congress.

and, to an admittedly lesser extent, Green Tea Republicans—attachment to the Tea Party posed relatively little electoral risk. In districts where immigrants were far more common—those served by Coffee or White Tea Republicans—attaching to a movement widely characterized as anti-immigrant could have posed serious electoral problems.

As in the case of immigrants, African Americans are rarest in Black Tea districts. They are most prevalent—and by a wide margin—in Green Tea districts (Figures 3.8 and 3.9). As African Americans are overwhelmingly Democratic, the presence of a large number of African Americans in the congressional districts of Green Tea Republicans suggests that these Republicans would need to win a particularly high percentage of white voters to remain in office. It is worth noting that four of the five Green Tea Republican exemplars are from southern states,[14] and there is a literature on the relationship between African American context and racial conservatism among southern whites going back to Key (1949).[15] This suggests that constituents in districts served by Green Tea

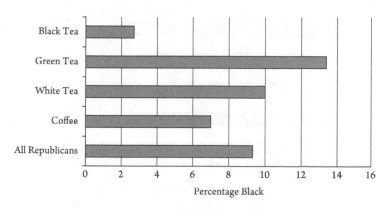

Figure 3.8 Percentage of Blacks in District, 112th Congress.

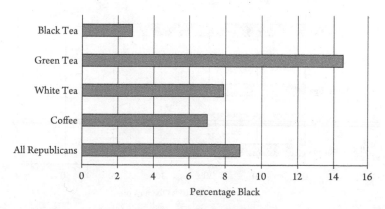

Figure 3.9 Percentage of Blacks in District, 113th Congress.

Republicans might tend to be more racially resentful than Republicans in other types of districts.

Support for Obama in 2008 and 2012 also varied by the type of Tea Party association manifested by Republican members of Congress (Figures 3.10 and 3.11). For our purposes, what stands out are (1) the very high level of support for Obama among the constituencies served by White Tea members and (2) the very low level of support for Obama among the constituencies served by Green Tea members. This is the first and only time we see the constituencies of the Coffee Republicans and the Black Tea Republicans falling in the interval *between* the constituencies of the Green Tea Republicans and the White Tea Republicans. This suggests that the Republicans most likely to face electoral pressure from the Left (from Democrats) were the White Tea Republicans. Strategically, White Tea Republicans have a strong incentive to accept campaign support from Tea Party organizations—they serve particularly competitive districts—but emphasizing and elaborating on an association with the Tea Party (i.e., Tea Party attachment)

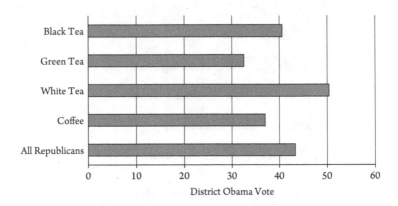

Figure 3.10 District Obama Vote, 2008.

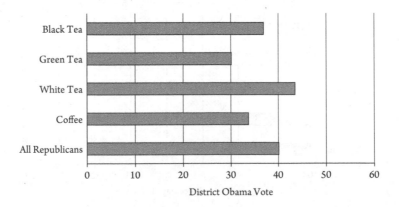

Figure 3.11 District Obama Vote, 2012.

would have been counterproductive in an environment in which the most serious threats would come from the Left.

On the other hand, the Green Tea Republicans were the most likely to face pressure from the Right (more conservative Republicans). Green Tea Republicans serve staunchly conservative districts in which the most likely challenge is from the Right. They have every incentive to align themselves with the Tea Party (Tea Party attachment) whether or not they receive a dime of support from Tea Party organizations.

Tea Party Types and House Republican Leadership

An important part of our argument and the general narrative about the Tea Party is its relationship with the leaders of the House Republican Conference. At various points in this book, we highlight, via anecdotes and data, the dynamics between the Tea Party movement and the five members who have held the top three positions in the Republican Conference since 2011 (through the time of this writing). These include John Boehner, who served as speaker of the House from January 2011 through September 2015; Eric Cantor (R-VA), who served as House majority leader from January 2011 through August 2014; Kevin McCarthy, who was promoted to majority Leader from majority whip after Cantor's resignation in August 2014; Paul Ryan, who became speaker of the House in September 2015 following Boehner's resignation; and Steve Scalise (R-LA), who succeeded McCarthy as majority whip in 2014.

The relationships between each of these members and the Tea Party are complicated. While each (with, so far, the exception of Scalise) would be treated as an adversary of the Tea Party, each could claim to have once had a connection to the insurgent forces that have served as a thorn in the side of House Republican leadership. As John Boehner once announced in an interview, "I was the Tea Party before there was a Tea Party."[16] Or, as now-Senator Richard Burr put it, "I think John was probably the first one that actually intended to drain the swamp. He was a radical. The closest example would be a Freedom Caucus guy today," (Alberta 2017).

In the early 1990s, at the outset of his congressional career, Boehner was part of a group of young members called the "Gang of Seven," who were aligned with Newt Gingrich (R-GA), the minority whip at the time (Mann and Ornstein 2012, 38). The "Gang" was known for confrontational, attention-grabbing stunts on the House floor, taking advantage of C-SPAN cameras to make the evening news (Mann and Ornstein 2012, 38; Hulse 2009). Following a series of scandals involving House Democrats, these Gingrich-aligned Republicans recognized a sense among voters that the political system was "broken." Accordingly, they presented themselves as anti-establishment outsiders and demonized Democratic president Bill Clinton and congressional Democrats with a number of uncivil terms in the run-up to the 1994 midterm election (e.g., "pathetic," "liar," "cheat," "traitor," "sick"). They would ultimately prevail in 1994, reclaiming majority status for Republicans in the House for the first time in forty years (Mann and Ornstein 2012, 39–40).

About a decade later, Boehner, now minority leader, seemed to still perceive himself as an insurgent and "rabble-rouser." Boehner, who had joined the House leadership following the Republicans' 1994 victory, was "semi-exiled" from the center of power in the late 1990s after Gingrich's downfall, and was welcomed back into leadership only in early 2006, after then–majority leader Tom Delay (R-TX) resigned amid the Jack Abramoff scandal (Hulse 2009). Boehner's succession of Delay was a surprise—he had been something of a dark horse candidate in a race that featured acting majority leader Roy Blunt (R-MO) and Arizona congressman John Shadegg (R-AZ) (Broder 2006; Murray 2006)—and many in the increasingly influential conservative blogosphere had preferred the "non-establishment" Shadegg over Boehner (Bolton 2006; Sullentrop 2006). (Shadegg, notably, would be a founding member of the Tea Party Caucus in the summer of 2010, before retiring at the end of the 111th Congress.) It did not help Boehner's cause that Republicans took a shellacking in the midterm election that November, allowing Democrats to regain control of the House for the first time since the 1994 "Republican Revolution" he helped orchestrate. To say the least, Boehner's hold on power was tenuous.

In the summer of 2009, Boehner, facing a Democratic majority in the House led by Speaker Nancy Pelosi (D-CA) and a new Democratic president, Barack Obama, dug into his old "bag of tricks" from his Gang of Seven days (Hulse 2009). It was during this same summer that the fledgling Tea Party movement emerged on the scene in full force, including the infamous healthcare reform town hall meetings, which featured Tea Party activists interrupting and heckling congressional Democrats (Bernstein 2010; Berry and Sobieraj 2014, 167–171). Concurrently, a new tool for direct communication with the public was starting to grow in popularity among members of Congress—Twitter. As we noted earlier, before the 112th Congress in January 2011, less than one in three congressional legislators had an official Twitter account, but by the time the 112th Congress came to a close, 95 percent of all members were on Twitter.

Boehner undoubtedly sensed the energy of the inchoate movement, understood it as the key to Republicans' retaking the House in 2010, and recognized the parallels with the 1994 midterms (e.g., the year before both the 1994 and 2010 midterm elections, a Democratic president promoted a controversial health reform bill). In fact, Boehner joined up with Kevin McCarthy in McCarthy's

California district for "one of the first major tea party protests," in April 2009 (Boyer 2010; Kane 2017). After returning to Washington, Boehner reputedly described the angry energy of the Tea Party protesters to the Republican Conference and announced: "I urge you to get in touch with these efforts and connect with them. The people participating in these protests will be the soldiers for our cause a year from now" (Boyer 2010).

Moreover, it is likely that Boehner, who, as a member of the Gang of Seven, took advantage of the advent of C-SPAN to communicate directly with the public, recognized the power of Twitter early on and that the contest for majority leader in 2006 led him to recognize the importance of currying favor with digital activists. Indeed, Boehner was among the earliest congressional adopters of Twitter, joining in the summer of 2007, slightly more than a year after the social media platform first launched and at a time when it was just starting to become popular.[17] For the remainder of his time in Congress, Boehner was among the most prolific congressional tweeters.

It was these factors that perhaps motivated him to reach into that old "bag of tricks," but to add a twenty-first-century digital twist. His very first tweet, in fact, was a cry back to the early 1990s, accusing the Democratic majority of corrupt behavior: "House investigating the outcome of a vote overturned and erased by the majority." He also returned to public relations stunts on the House floor, including one incident in July 2009, referred to as the "Boehner-buster," in which he stretched his prerogatives as a party leader to attack a climate change bill and effectively kill it. Indeed, in discussing the stunt with the *New York Times*, Boehner admitted that his intention was to draw attention:

> Republicans believe they can turn the energy fight [*sic*] to their favor. Mr. Boehner and his aides said his Boehner-buster brought thousands of favorable calls to his office, was a hit among Twitter followers and has been seen thousands of times on YouTube.
> "This is where the new media tools do help us," said Mr. Boehner. He said he received vocal encouragement for his push against the energy bill from spectators as he played in a Pro-Am golf tournament with Tiger Woods outside Washington on Wednesday. (Hulse 2009)

As the Tea Party movement thrived in the fall of 2010, and with the November elections around the corner, Boehner was happy to report, "There really is no difference between what Republicans believe in and what the Tea Party activists believe in" (Milbank 2010a).

As was the case in 1994, Republicans rode disenchantment with a Democratic president to victory in 2010, and in January 2011, at the start of the 112th Congress, Boehner was elected speaker of the House. His strategy appeared to work; as such, we can suppose he saw little reason not to continue courting the Tea Party and its energy in order to preserve and expand political power. Notably, Boehner qualified as a Black Tea Republican in the 112th. He attracted no endorsements or funds from Tea Party organizations, but received significant promotion from Tea Party activists online. In fact, only Allen West and Michelle Bachmann received more Tea Party promotion on Twitter in 2010 than Boehner.

This suggests that Boehner found success in currying favor with digital activists. Of course, the promotion of Boehner was also likely to have been driven by his position as minority leader during the 111th Congress. Elevating Boehner to House speaker symbolized not only majority status for Republicans in the 112th House, but the demotion of Nancy Pelosi—who served as a villain to the Right—and a major blow to Barack Obama and his agenda. Thus, forms of the refrain "Boehner for Speaker" were common rallying cries among Tea Party activists online before Election Day 2010, but this activity was more about victory for Republicans and defeating Democrats than it was about Boehner himself.

This might be interpreted as a limitation of our methodology—Boehner's connection to the Tea Party is enhanced simply because of his importance and profile. However, we believe it provides insight into Boehner, the Tea Party, and the changing dynamic between the two when considered alongside Boehner's attempts to attach himself to the movement and the support he received from the Tea Party in the 113th Congress.

In the 112th Congress, Boehner did not join the Tea Party Caucus, but his score on the Tea Party Tweet measure was greater than the median value for the Republican Conference, and his Tea Party Salience score was above average. That is, he made a modest effort to attach himself with the movement. In the 113th Congress, not only did Boehner lack an attachment to the Tea Party via caucus membership, he had the lowest possible scores for both the Tweet and Salience measures (0 for both on the unstandardized versions). That is, he made no effort to connect himself to the movement. At the same time, in addition to Boehner's failure to attract endorsements or funds from Tea Party organizations in 2012, his raw Tea Party Activism score fell from the third-highest within the Republican Conference in 2010 to not even cracking the top twenty in the 2012. Given the high profile of the speakership and the fact that few rank-and-file members enjoy national profiles, this is rather amazing. In short, Boehner went from qualifying as Black Tea in the 112th Congress to Coffee in the 113th.

It is likely that "Boehner for Speaker" carried less symbolic importance in 2012 than it did in 2010, and interest in House contests in general were eclipsed by the Romney–Ryan presidential ticket and the Republican bid to retake the Senate, which was still in Democratic hands. Nonetheless, we think this is evidence that the Boehner–Tea Party dynamic went from a cordial partnership in the 112th Congress to a lukewarm (at best) and perhaps hostile relationship in the 113th. This is best evinced by the refusal of nine Republican members to support Boehner for speaker at the start of the 113th Congress (Kasperowicz 2013)—all but one of whom were Black and Green Tea members of the 113th.[18] With the common goal of retaking the House, Boehner and the Tea Party embraced each other, but with this goal achieved, the relationship would significantly deteriorate before the 113th was over.

The relationship would only get worse. At the start of the 114th Congress in January 2015, most of these same members would again refuse to support Boehner in the vote for speaker, and the total number of defectors would grow to twenty-five—arguably the largest revolt against a speaker in a century (Blake 2015). A plurality of the defectors would join the Freedom and Liberty Caucuses, which would play an outsized role in forcing Boehner's resignation less than ten months later.[19]

The three other members who would serve as majority leader or speaker in the years after the Tea Party wave election of 2010 made up a group called the "Young Guns," who, as Mann and Ornstein (2012, 7) put it, endeavored to demonstrate their "commitment to new confrontational politics and in-your-face tactics designed to distinguish them from both their compromising predecessors and their accommodating senior colleagues." The members— Cantor, McCarthy, and Ryan—formed the group in the fall of 2010, releasing a coauthored manifesto in the run-up to the midterm elections entitled *Young Guns: A New Generation of Conservative Leaders* (Dionne 2016, 233; Lizza 2015; Mann and Ornstein 2012, 9; Milbank 2010a).

In the book, the three blasted uncontrolled spending, government take-over of healthcare, and political compromise. Much of this criticism was meant for Obama and congressional Democrats, but criticism was also leveled at the Republican establishment, who, they deemed, performed poorly—particularly with budgeting and spending—during the George W. Bush presidency (Dionne 2016, 233–234). (As Dionne [2016, 233] notes, the book conveniently fails to mention that Cantor and Ryan served for the entirety of the Bush presidency.) Presumably, the purpose of the manifesto was to separate the three from Republican leaders of the past (including Delay and even Boehner) and promote themselves as the next generation of Republican House leaders.

Like Boehner, the Young Guns also likely viewed the energy of the Tea Party movement as the key to retaking the House from the Democrats, blocking the Obama agenda and implementing their own agenda of greatly shrinking the size and scope of the federal government, and advancing their status within the House leadership structure. Essential to these goals would be to stock the House Republican Conference with staunch conservatives

who shared their anti-compromise zeal and would serve as loyal conservative allies (Steinhauer 2016). As Mann and Ornstein (2012: 9–10) write, the
Young Guns set out

> to recruit a new generation of highly ideological and uncompromising
> conservative candidates for the 2010 elections, provide them with
> money and technical support, and keep the focus on fiscal issues. The
> fiscal issues served two goals: they were meant to reinforce voters' un-
> happiness with Washington and the economy, and to accomplish a
> greater end, decreasing—by any means necessary—the size of govern-
> ment to pre-1960s Great Society levels.
>
> At the Young Guns' urging, many of those candidates began early in
> the 2010 campaign to talk about the debt ceiling as a core symbol of all
> that was wrong with Washington. They frequently mischaracterized a
> vote to lift the debt ceiling as a vote to add more debt. The Young Guns
> also appealed to the Tea Party movement that had emerged in 2009,
> fanning the seething populist anger that many activist conservatives felt.

In the short term, this strategy worked out. The Young Guns appeared to
succeed in portraying themselves as a part of the anti-establishment Tea Partiers
"rattling Washington," along with Sarah Palin and Senate candidates Rand
Paul and Christine O'Donnell (Millbank 2010a). And it brought victory: after
Republicans won a majority of seats in 2010, Obama faced a staunchly conservative Republican House that derailed his domestic agenda. Cantor rose to House
majority leader, and McCarthy became House majority whip, joining Speaker
Boehner to become the three highest-ranking Republicans in the majoritarian
House. Ryan would serve as chair of the powerful House Budget Committee
in the 112th and would become the Republican candidate for vice president
in 2012.

All of the Young Guns attached themselves to the Tea Party in the 112th
Congress, but their relationships with the movement were not identical. Cantor
qualified as a Green Tea, as determined entirely by his Tea Party Salience score,
the ninth-highest in the Republican Conference; he neither joined the Tea Party
Caucus nor attempted to connect to the Tea Party via Twitter. Additionally, like
Boehner, he attracted some digital activist support, and no endorsements or
funding from Tea Party organizations, but overall his Tea Party Support score
put him in the bottom half of the Conference. This might be interpreted as a
portent of the fate he would meet in the 113th Congress.

McCarthy qualified as a Green Tea member in the 112th as well. But his is
·an interesting case, which highlights some of the difficulties of measuring association with the Tea Party. While, like Cantor, his Tea Party Salience score

was on the higher end (fourteenth-highest in the Conference), it was still far below Cantor's. He posted a few positive Tea Party tweets in the course of the 112th, but his overall Tea Party Tweet rate ranked just eighty-third among all Republicans. He, too, did not join the Tea Party Caucus. Unlike Boehner and Cantor, he received little digital activist support, perhaps because he was a less prominent member at the time. However, while he would receive no funding support from Tea Party organizations, he did receive an endorsement from Tea Party Express. If, rather than defining Black Teas as those with Attachment and Support scores above average, we defined them as those with scores above the *median*, McCarthy would have been a Black Tea in the 112th. However, given that he had below-average scores on both dimensions, we think qualifying McCarthy as a core Tea Party member who actively associated with the movement and in turn was embraced by it would be a mistake. His low Tea Party Activist score and single endorsement do not signal a strong embrace by the movement. In fact, his endorsement from the Tea Party Express highlights the problems with relying on a single metric, as we argued earlier.

McCarthy, however, made efforts to connect to the Tea Party early (e.g., inviting Boehner to one of the first Tea Party rallies in the country in his hometown of Bakersfield, CA) and had an important connection to many of the freshman members of the Tea Party wave. He, of the three Young Guns, most obviously carried out the mission of filling the Conference with highly ideological and uncompromising conservative candidates, as he recruited a number of them to run in 2010 (Draper 2011). As majority whip in the 112th Congress, he championed and mentored many members associated with the Tea Party (Dickey 2015; Draper 2011); his office, which doubled as his Washington living quarters, served as something of a retreat (or rumpus room) for a number of Black, Green, and White Teas—complete with a basketball hoop on the back of a door (Draper 2011). In return, McCarthy was able to wield influence over the members and build support for policy proposals like the Ryan budget, in accordance with the Young Gun strategy (Draper 2011). Thus, during the 112th, McCarthy and segments of the Tea Party had use for each other, but it was not a serious romance.

Ryan also qualified as a Green Tea in the 112th Congress. Like the others we have highlighted in this section, he avoided joining Bachmann's Tea Party Caucus, and like Cantor and McCarthy, he had a fairly high Tea Party Salience score (eighteenth-highest in the Conference), but he made no attempt to connect with the Tea Party via Twitter. He also did not draw any funds or endorsements from Sarah Palin or Tea Party organizations. However, Ryan, like Cantor, appeared to have had a good rapport with Tea Party activists in 2010, receiving the ninth-highest Tea Party Activism score in Congress, though his overall Tea Party Support score was below average. This reflects the prevailing wisdom at the time, that the two possessed "both Tea Party credibility and governing experience [which would] determine much about the outcome of the conservative uprising of 2010" (Gerson 2010). But even then, there were doubts that Ryan could maintain this Tea Party credibility, as he needed to balance his new responsibilities as Budget Committee chair with the "pull of the Tea Party" (Milbank 2010c). Indeed, he seemed to denounce some of the inflexible talk laid out in the Young Gun manifesto when he declared in December 2010, "Compromise is not an ugly word" and promoted bipartisanship (Milbank 2010b).

Yet Ryan's association with the Tea Party would seemingly strengthen in the 113th Congress. He would again crack the top ten in Tea Party Activism scores,[20] and, as we noted earlier, he had the highest Tea Party Salience score among all members in 2012. No doubt this surge in salience was driven by Republican presidential nominee Mitt Romney's decision to name Ryan as his running mate. What is interesting is how becoming the party's nominee for vice president enhanced Ryan's Tea Party credibility in the minds of many. In a headline of the sort that would appear in countless publications after Romney announced his pick, the New York Times declared, "Ryan Brings the Tea Party to the Ticket." As the Times's Michael Shear (2012) elaborates, "Paul Ryan's ascendancy to the No. 2 spot on the Republican ticket is a signal event for a movement that counts him as one of their own. If Mitt Romney wins in November, a Tea Party favorite will be a heartbeat from the Oval Office . . . Mr. Ryan is now unquestionably the face of the Tea Party in Washington." The idea that the Tea Party movement counted Ryan as one of its own, never mind the face of the movement, might seem like a ridiculous claim by a mainstream news source misperceiving the movement, especially in light of Ryan's limited connection to the movement in the 112th Congress. Yet the Tea Party Express did embrace Ryan as one of its own in a press release titled "Congressman Paul Ryan: Strong Tea Party Choice for Vice President,"[21] citing Ryan's "Tea Party" economic policies and his popularity among Tea Party activists. Ryan otherwise did little to promote Tea Party ties during the 113th. For instance, he did not join Amash's Liberty Caucus and did not mention the Tea Party in any tweets from his official account. However, the Salience and Activist scores were enough to make Ryan a Black Tea in the 113th Congress.

Following Barack Obama's re-election in 2012, Ryan's status as Tea Party favorite would not last, and Ryan's case perhaps best represents the fluidity of association with the Tea Party and the importance of context. In the course of five years, Ryan would go from being perceived as a conservative legislator with some Tea Party credibility in the 112th, to the face of the Tea Party movement in Washington at the dawn of the 113th, to the Washington insider, whose powerful position would be under constant threat from Tea Party forces from within and outside the Republican Conference during the 114th Congress.

Ryan was not alone. In the long run, the anti-establishment Tea Party members the Young Guns helped recruit would turn on leadership, and the populist resentment they helped fan would backfire on them (Steinhauer 2016). In what has been referred to as the "Young Gun jinx," each would face setbacks in the years after 2011 emanating from these forces (Lizza 2015). Cantor, like Ryan, would qualify as Black Tea in the 113th, as he maintained support among Tea Party activists online during the 2012 election season (his score was in fact higher than Ryan's), and he had the sixth-highest Salience score in the Republican Conference, ahead of the likes of Steve King and Justin Amash. He also tweeted about meeting with local Tea Party groups on a pair of occasions, which represented the greatest effort any of the Young Guns made to connect to the movement online. At the start of the 113th Congress, he was portrayed as the leader of the Tea Party faction in the House. As the *New Yorker* magazine's Ryan Lizza (2013) asserts in a February 2013 profile of Cantor, "For the past two years, he has anchored the Tea Party, as the leader of House conservatives and the creator of a strategy to oppose and obstruct the Obama agenda." Lizza strongly suggests that Cantor might lead a Tea Party coup to unseat Boehner during the 114th.

Yet Cantor's connection to the Tea Party and the movement's activists would prove to be something of a facade, as he would be defeated by an anti-establishment challenger backed by Tea Party activists in his June 2014 primary race (Cohn 2014). When he resigned from Congress entirely in August, his defeat was described as the victory of a Tea Party outsider over a quintessential Washington insider (Mascaro et al. 2014). Cantor's story, like Ryan's, demonstrates the fluidity of association with the Tea Party and the importance of context. Their Tea Party stock would rise and fall at various points in the period after 2010, as it would for many other Republican members. Few have had consistently high Tea Party Association scores across both dimensions.

McCarthy, unlike his Young Gun brethren, remained a Green Tea Republican over the course of the 112th and 113th Congresses. However, his lack of support from the movement was more clear-cut in the 113th. He did not draw any endorsements from Tea Party organizations as he had in 2010. Though his profile was enhanced after he became whip, his Tea Party activist support—already miniscule in 2010—diminished further in 2012. Although he issued no Tea Party tweets and avoided joining the Liberty Caucus, his Tea Party Salience score did not change, indicative of moderate attachment to the Tea Party.

McCarthy, too, would face the Young Gun jinx. The man who was once credited with "wrangling" the Tea Party in Congress was defeated by it (Draper 2011) when his bid to succeed John Boehner as speaker in 2015 was blocked by the Liberty and Freedom Caucuses (Lizza 2015; Matishak 2015; Walsh et al. 2015). Among the members of those caucuses were Scott DesJarlais (R-TN),

Reid Ribble (R-WI), and Jason Chaffetz, each of whom McCarthy had mentored in some capacity in the early days of the 112th (Draper 2011). As if to add insult to injury, Chaffetz—whose insurgent style McCarthy once praised and encouraged—challenged McCarthy for the speakership, criticizing his leadership in the process (Dickey 2015; Howard 2015).

Ryan would instead succeed Boehner as House speaker, but his legislative agenda as speaker has thus far been derailed by an unbending Freedom Caucus and, since January 2017, the dysfunction of the Trump White House (Hesse 2017; Lizza 2015; Rubin 2017). There has been some discussion between Trump insiders and Freedom Caucus members about deposing Ryan altogether (Costa 2017). He has been targeted as an out-of-touch Washington insider by populist Trump supporters and has served as a scapegoat for difficulties Trump faced on the campaign trail and as president (Goldberg 2017; Mehta 2016) (and, according to one quick and messy method of measuring reactions to tweets, Ryan's tweets since becoming speaker have elicited far more negative reactions than those of any other prominent politician analyzed, including Trump).[22] Trump himself has threatened Ryan via the press (Steinhauer 2016) and has targeted Ryan on Twitter, most infamously with an October 2016 tweet that read, "Paul Ryan should spend more time on balancing the budget, jobs and illegal immigration and not waste his time on fighting Republican nominee." In the minds of many Republican voters, Paul Ryan has become what is wrong with Washington.

Of all the members of the House leadership we have highlighted thus far, Steve Scalise, who became majority whip following McCarthy's promotion to majority leader, might have the strongest claim to having been a Tea Party Republican in the 112th Congress, though upon closer inspection, this association was skin-deep. His connection to the movement is due entirely to his status in 2010 as a founding member of the Tea Party Caucus, of which he was a member in the 112th. However, he did little to promote his Tea Party ties, receiving the lowest possible score for Tea Party Salience (0 press mentions in the unstandardized version of the variable). He was also one of the very few Twitter holdouts in the House during the 112th, as he did not register an official account until early on in the 113th, making him one of the last incumbents to join the social media platform; obviously, then, he did not connect with Tea Party activists there. Not coincidentally, Scalise received no support from these digital activists, and he also failed to collect any endorsements or campaign funding from Palin or Tea Party organizations. Thus, although Scalise was a Green Tea during the 112th Congress, his association with the Tea Party was superficial, and his case highlights the problem with relying on Caucus membership alone to determine Tea Party status.

In the 113th Congress, with the Tea Party Caucus now defunct, Scalise would do little to maintain an attachment to the movement. Now a member of Twitter, he issued more than 2,200 tweets during the course of the congress, yet offered only one tweet connecting himself to the movement: a retweet of a post made by the official account of FreedomWorks. He again had the lowest possible Salience score and received no support from the Tea Party movement. In short, once the Tea Party Caucus ceased to be, Scalise went from Green Tea to Coffee.

This is but one facet of a story we wish to tell in the pages to come, that members of the House Republican leadership post-2010—and indeed the Republican Party writ large—endeavored to take advantage of an energized populist movement and simmering resentment among their base, sometimes through new digital communication tools, but were ultimately overcome by these forces. We argue that they enabled the rise of the Tea Party faction in the House in the 112th and 113th Congresses, whose political style would aggravate feelings of resentment, further damage the images of "establishment" (or experienced) politicians in the minds of Republican voters, and normalize certain types of legislative and extra-legislative behavior, including an uncivil style on Twitter. By the time the 114th Congress began in 2015 and would-be candidates began positioning themselves for the 2016 presidential election, conditions were ripe for an uncivil outsider, adroit with Twitter and willing to take advantage of (and further aggravate) high levels of resentment, to blaze a path to the Republican nomination, claim the White House, and effectively take over the Republican Party.

Rethinking the Tea Party in the House

We began this chapter by describing how researchers have gone about measuring various aspects of the Tea Party in the House of Representatives. While some work takes Tea Party Caucus or Liberty Caucus membership to be the sine qua non of association with the Tea Party, other work focuses on the endorsements of Tea Party organizations. Although both of these are indicators of the relationship between members of Congress and the Tea Party movement, they measure distinct aspects of this relationship. Caucus memberships are one manifestation of the attachment of legislators to the Tea Party; organizational endorsements are one manifestation of the Tea Party movement's support for House members. Distinct strategic dynamics drive Tea Party attachment and Tea Party support.[23]

In this chapter, we have laid out a methodology for independently measuring attachment and support. Caucus memberships are but one component of our measure of attachment, and support does not depend on organizational endorsements alone. In both cases, we extend the toolbox available to researchers intent on studying the institutional and electoral impact of the Tea Party in Congress.

Members' decision algorithms determine the extent to which they attach themselves to the Tea Party movement. Decisions made by Tea Party organizations to support (or not) a legislator are governed by the political costs and benefits they face. As we have seen in this chapter, House members and Tea Party organizations may make very different decisions about the extent to which they will associate with each other. In some cases (Black Tea legislators), both attachment and support manifest. In other cases (Coffee legislators), we see neither attachment nor support. Perhaps of most interest are those cases in which we see strong attachment but little or no support (Green Tea legislators) or considerable organizational support but little or no effort on the part of the member to attach to the movement (White Tea).

Realizing that the relationship between legislators and the Tea Party movement is multifaceted, composed of the distinct components of attachment and support, we see, first, that existing measures of the Tea Party in the House have grossly underestimated its prevalence. Measurement strategies focused solely on caucus memberships or organizational endorsements lead to significant underestimations of the role of the movement in congressional politics. A key implication of the application of a measurement strategy that captures the dimensionality of the Tea Party movement in Congress is that the number of legislators associated with the Tea Party movement—through attachment, support, or both—was far larger than previously realized.

A second important takeaway from this chapter is that the relationship between legislators and the Tea Party movement varied according to the strategic opportunities (and obstacles) flowing from the characteristics of their districts. Particularly in the case of members' efforts to attach themselves to the Tea Party movement, constituency characteristics appear to have played an important role. Black Tea, Green Tea, White Tea, and Coffee Republicans do not serve the same districts. As we consider the distinctiveness of the districts in the context of the most recent elections, we note that this variation is also related to the likelihood of constituents supporting Trump. In simplest terms, the constituency dynamics that drive Coffee Republicans are not conducive to the development of a vast cadre of Trump supporters. To a lesser extent, the same is true for White Tea Republicans. Even among the constituencies of Black Tea Republicans, the conditions are not perfect for the cultivation of Trump voters. It is in the constituencies of Green Tea Republicans where Trump should be particularly strong. In subsequent chapters, we will investigate that proposition.

4

The Representational Foundations of Tea Party Association in the House

Existing research on the Tea Party in Congress focuses relatively little on the constituency dynamics upon which Tea Party association is based. This is true whether we focus on Tea Party Caucus membership as the key determinant of Tea Party association or whether we focus on the support—financial support or endorsements—of Tea Party organizations.

Members of Congress serve in a representational context. They occupy a certain position in the institution from which they can serve their constituents. They face particular constellations of electoral pressures that also influence their capacity to represent. And they hail from distinctive geographic areas that are home to a wide array of constituents: constituents of different races and ethnicities, constituents who are immigrants, and constituents born in the United States. In some of these constituencies, unemployment rates are high; in others, few are unemployed. Poverty rates also vary dramatically. Constituencies also differ politically, and constituencies *served by Republicans* differ politically. Some are significantly more conservative than others. Some have a much higher percentage of Republicans than others. Religious attachments vary too, as do constituents' preferences on a wide array of policy issues.

So how do these differences help us understand the growth of the Tea Party movement in the House? Did Tea Party organizations target certain types of representatives for support, or did they target certain types of constituencies? Or both? And what factors fostered House Republicans' efforts to attach to the Tea Party movement? Did institutional factors drive these choices, or do constituency dynamics explain the wide variation in efforts to attach to the Tea Party brand?

At the end of Chapter 3, we presented data that suggested the variation in Tea Party support and Tea Party attachment has representational roots. Green Tea legislators tend not to serve the same types of districts as White Tea legislators. The same is true for Black Tea legislators and Coffee legislators. In this chapter, we dive deeper into the representational foundations of both Tea Party support and Tea Party attachment. We also investigate the representational foundations of Black Tea, Green Tea, White Tea, and Coffee identities.

In short, we find that the forces which lead to attachment to the Tea Party are dramatically different from the forces leading to support from the Tea Party. Given the distinctive strategic loci and logics of Tea Party attachment and Tea Party support—one driven by the strategic opportunities faced by members of Congress and the other driven by the strategic opportunities available to Tea Party organizations, this should not be a surprise. But given the way we have studied the Tea Party in Congress, it is a dramatic departure from what is reported in the existing literature—a departure that will provide a key to understanding the legislative behavior of Black Tea, Green Tea, White Tea, and Coffee Republicans in future chapters.

Representing the Tea Party Movement

Some of our own previous research on the Tea Party in the House focused specifically on the impact of economic and demographic contexts on the likelihood that a Republican would join the Tea Party Caucus. We found no evidence that constituency-level racial or ethnic dynamics drove decisions to participate in the Tea Party Caucus. Specifically, we found no significant relationship between the percentage of African Americans in a member's district and the likelihood that the member would join the Tea Party Caucus. The same was true for Hispanic context and Asian context.[1]

Where we did find contextual effects at the district level was on economic outcomes. Specifically, members serving constituencies with lower levels of unemployment were more likely to join the Tea Party Caucus. Our argument there was that constituents with higher levels of economic success were more concerned about the extent of their tax burden (think "Taxed Enough Already") and about what they considered wasteful federal spending on the undeserving—the benefits recipients they resented.

Other research on the Tea Party in Congress—specifically the Tea Party in the House—has focused either on (1) the ideological orientation or roll call voting behavior of Tea Party legislators (and the way in which it compares with the ideological orientation or roll call voting behavior of other Republicans/legislators) or on (2) the impact of Tea Party Caucus membership and/or support from Tea Party organizations (in the form of campaign funding or endorsements). What has not received significant attention—beyond our own limited work—is the representational distinctiveness of Republican House members associated with the Tea Party. We examine that here. More specifically, we look at the impact of the various factors related to a House member's representational capacity (i.e., institutional resources) and the member's representational focus (i.e., the characteristics of her or his constituency).

Evidence presented in the preceding chapter strongly suggested that the key dimensions of Tea Party association—Tea Party Attachment and Tea Party Support—were far from uniformly distributed across the House Republican Conference. Some Republicans received a great deal of support from Tea Party organizations; others literally received nothing. A host of legislators made extensive efforts to attach themselves to the Tea Party movement, from joining the Tea Party Caucus to frequently tweeting support for the movement. Others made no effort at all to attach themselves to the movement.

Evidence from the preceding chapter also suggested that the variation in Tea Party Support and the variation in Tea Party Attachment, while largely unrelated, were the result of systematic strategic decisions. In the case of Tea Party Support, the strategic decisions were made by Tea Party organizations. In the case of Tea Party Attachment, the strategic decisions were made by the House members themselves. Black Tea, Green Tea, White Tea, and Coffee Republicans seemed to enjoy different levels of seniority and to face electoral contexts of various degrees of security. They served constituencies of distinct racial and ethnic compositions, and their constituents were dealing with a wide variety of economic circumstances. In this chapter, we investigate the strategic dynamics associated with Tea Party Support and the (distinct) strategic dynamics associated with Tea Party Attachment in greater detail.

Understanding Variation in Tea Party Support

Research focused on explaining the variation in endorsements by Tea Party organizations or the distribution of campaign funds by Tea Party organizations is limited (but see Bullock and Hood 2012). There is more research on the impact of Tea Party organizations' endorsements, campaign financing, and independent expenditures (see, e.g., Bailey et al. 2012; Karpowitz et al. 2011; Ragusa and Gaspar 2016). Ironically, the findings regarding the impact of Tea Party organizational support on the electoral success of candidates or the subsequent ideological behavior of candidates is inconsistent. Bullock and Hood (2012) suggest that Palin's endorsements tended to go to candidates who were more likely to win elections than did the campaign contributions of formal Tea Party organizations. Karpowitz et al. (2011) find that FreedomWorks endorsements had a positive effect on Republican vote share; other Tea Party endorsements (e.g., by Tea Party Express, Sarah Palin, a local Tea Party organization, etc.) were unrelated to Republican vote share. Where Bailey et al. (2012) find limited evidence suggesting a relationship between Tea Party organizational campaign contributions and subsequent roll call voting behavior, Ragusa and Gaspar (2016) find no such evidence.

Rather than focusing on the instrumental effects of Tea Party support— greater electoral success and/or a change in roll call voting behavior—we examine the contextual effects that might have led to an endorsement or campaign contribution or independent expenditure in the first place. As we explained earlier, we theorize that variation in Tea Party support flows from a strategic logic focused on Tea Party organizations. As the level of Tea Party support is determined by the extent to which Tea Party organizations offer electoral support of various kinds—different types of campaign funding, endorsements—we argue that constituency factors play a role in the distribution of Tea Party support only to the extent that they play a role in the strategic context in which Tea Party organizations find themselves.

Theoretically, the members themselves have some limited ex post control over the level of support they accept from a Tea Party organization. For example, a member could always return a campaign contribution from a Tea Party organization if the member did not wish to be associated with the group. In practice, this sort of ex post rejection of support—particularly in the case of Tea Party organizations—is quite rare.[2] So what role might constituency dynamics play in the strategic calculus faced by Tea Party organizations? And what contribution might attitudinal variation make to the role of constituency dynamics in the strategic calculus faced by House Republicans making decisions about the extent to which they will attach themselves to the Tea Party movement?

Let us assume that Tea Party organizations are interested in supporting candidates who will support the Tea Party agenda. That implies that support would tend to go to legislators who served the most conservative districts. But organizational support is a limited resource. Obviously true in the case of financial support, it is also true for endorsements. Endorsements are valuable only if they are scarce; if all candidates—or even all Republican candidates—receive an endorsement, it is no longer a meaningful signal of support for a particular type of candidate.

The strategic use of limited resources such as support is not uncomplicated. While it would seem to make sense to support candidates who are likely to espouse the Tea Party movement's political goals, if they espouse those goals because of the character of their constituencies, then would an organization want to invest a scarce resource in them, given that they are already supportive of the movement's policy goals? Yes, it might—but only if these candidates were facing a competitive opponent.

Conversely, it might make sense for a Tea Party organization to support a candidate whose constituents are not particularly supportive of Tea Party movement ideals. Why would this be the case? The question is, what is the alternative? Assume that the potential support recipient's district is currently served by or, if the potential support recipient lost the election, would be served by—a legislator whose views are diametrically opposed to those of the Tea Party movement (whether or not that legislator is a Republican or a Democrat); then support from a Tea Party organization might play an instrumental role in the victory of a candidate who would be a clear improvement over the alternative.

What these scenarios suggest is that the strategic distribution of Tea Party support might not be limited to districts with Tea Party–oriented constituents. We may find a relationship between constituency characteristics and Tea Party support, but given the strategic dynamics, we do not expect to. These scenarios also suggest that Tea Party support is likely to be associated with electoral security. To the extent that this is the case, we should expect to see inverse relationships between margin of victory and Tea Party support and seniority and Tea Party support. Even limiting our analysis to the successful candidates— candidates who became members of Congress—we expect to find to find that Tea Party support flowed to (1) less senior legislators and (2) legislators facing more difficult electoral contests.

We posit that Tea Party organizations selected candidates for support based on the candidates' political resources and on the electoral contexts in which they were competing. But it is not possible for us to identify an ideal strategy because we cannot know the relative weights distinct Tea Party organizations assigned to certain objectives or values where trade-offs were unavoidable. For example, realizing that support—and even endorsements (if they are to be meaningful)— are a scarce resource, would a Tea Party organization prefer to support an institutionally powerful incumbent who is likely to win re-election regardless of the level of Tea Party support or would it prefer to support the challenger facing a stiff electoral test? Would an organization prefer to support a candidate replacing a retiring Republican from a conservative (and safely Republican) district or a challenger with a good chance to defeat an incumbent Democrat in a moderate swing district? Seniority and leadership positions on committees or within the party are significant institutional resources, but supporting a challenger—who would enjoy none of these resources—might be of greater value than supporting a safer, more institutionally advantaged incumbent. The thinking here is that legislators might be more responsive to early-career supporters than mid-career or late-career supporters.

The ideological complexity of the Tea Party movement also complicates the specification of uniform strategic expectations. Should Tea Party organizations focus their efforts (and their resources) on legislators serving constituencies that are likely to be fiscally conservative? Or legislators from constituencies likely to be socially conservative? Or racially conservative? And what if there are potential trade-offs here? It's also possible, as Bullock and Hood (2012) suggest, that different Tea Party organizations have distinct preferences regarding the relative trade-offs in these sorts of situations.

This strategic complexity prevents us from identifying an exhaustive list of ex ante expectations regarding the specific institutional, electoral, and constituency factors driving Tea Party support, but we can pose some preliminary hypotheses:

- *Tea Party Support is inversely related to district security.*
    Regardless of the ideological or institutional trade-offs, the distribution of scarce resources is likely to be driven—at least to some extent—by electoral security.
- *Tea Party Support is directly related to district opposition to Obama.*
    The overall ideological complexity of the Tea Party movement does not obscure its consistent opposition to President Obama and his policy agenda.

Understanding Tea Party Attachment

Tea Party attachment, on the other hand, results from legislators' reactions to the strategic contexts *they* face. As we discussed in Chapter 2, President Obama served as the focal point for the defining characteristic of the Tea Party movement in the electorate: the *politics of resentment*. Obama embodied the targets of resentment for conservatives enamored of the Tea Party movement. And while Obama might have represented groups that were targets of resentment for fiscal conservatives and social conservatives, he was clearly a target of resentment for racial/ethnic conservatives. We hypothesize that legislators attempting to attach themselves to the Tea Party movement did so to cultivate Tea Party–leaning conservative constituencies within their own districts. These efforts may have been intended to cultivate fiscal conservatives, or social conservatives, or racial/ethnic conservatives, or some mixture. We assess the empirical support for these targeting strategies in this chapter.

We conjecture that the constituency underpinnings of attachment to the Tea Party are more consistent than those for support from the Tea Party. Although institutional and electoral factors may play a role in the variation of Republican House members' efforts to attach themselves to the Tea Party movement, we expect the key factors to be associated with district-level conservatism. More specifically, we expect the primary engines of Tea Party attachment to be those factors associated with (1) opposition to Obama and (2) racial/ethnic conservatism.

The widespread growth of the Tea Party movement depended on a focal point of opposition: Obama. The resentfulness characteristic of supporters of the Tea Party movement required a target of blame. Initially, this target may have been Wall Street bankers, but it quickly became Obama and the groups he came to represent: minorities, immigrants, intellectuals, city dwellers, and the LGBTQ community. First, attachment to the Tea Party movement should have been more valuable for those candidates seeking to serve constituencies where Obama was relatively unpopular. We hypothesize:

- *Tea Party Attachment is inversely related to district support for Obama.*

Similarly, the benefits associated with Tea Party attachment were likely to be greater in those areas where groups linked to Obama (the targets of blame for reactionary, resentful Republicans) were relatively unpopular. In areas where immigrants are relatively unpopular, we would expect efforts to attach to the Tea Party movement to be more attractive. Republican candidates might also make strategic efforts to attach themselves to the Tea Party movement in those areas where racial/ethnic conservatism is high.

We have identified three types of conservatism—fiscal, social, and racial/ethnic—associated with the Tea Party movement. In the next chapter, we will investigate the extent to which the roll call voting patterns of Republican members of Congress on policy associated with each of these three types of conservatism are related to Tea Party support or Tea Party attachment. Here, we seek to determine whether it is possible to draw a direct connection between the various types of political conservatism found among House constituencies and our Tea Party Support or Tea Party Attachment measures.

To the extent that racial/ethnic conservatism plays a role in the Tea Party movement, we expect the relative size of the African American population and the relative size of the Hispanic population to be positively related to Tea Party association. More specifically, we expect the prevalence of African Americans and Hispanic to be a significant driver of attachment to the Tea Party.

At first glance, this may seem counterintuitive. Research suggests that supporters of the Tea Party movement are overwhelmingly white—partly a function of both the racial and ethnic composition of the Republican Party and the almost exclusive association of the Tea Party movement with the Republican Party. Given that, shouldn't we expect the relative size of the white population to directly affect Tea Party Attachment? We would if racial context had no impact on the political orientations of whites, but a growing body of research indicates that racial context—particularly the African American context and Hispanic context—has a strong conservative effect on white attitudes.

As far back as the 1940s, V. O. Key argued that white southerners living in areas with large numbers of African Americans would be more conservative than whites living in areas with few African Americans. The "Key hypothesis" would become one of the authoritative statements of the dynamics of group conflict theory. According to Key (1949), southern whites living in areas with large populations of African Americans—those living in the "Black belt"—saw these African Americans as a threat to their lives and livelihoods. As southern blacks were disenfranchised during this period, the perceived threat was one of an economic or physical nature. Writing about twenty-first-century southern politics, Hood, Kidd, and Morris (2012) argue that group conflict theory—and Key's own perspective on black context—played (and continues to play) a crucial role in the development of southern racial conservatism (as it manifests within the Republican Party). Although the perceived threat is now of a political nature, it still dominates the dynamics of race relations in the South. As the prevalence of mobilized African Americans grows, so does the Republican Party.

Recent work on the role of the Hispanic context on white political attitudes and orientations also suggests a group conflict dynamics. Just as Hood, Kidd, and Morris (2012) find that the mobilized black context fosters Republican growth in the South, Abrajano and Hajnal (2015) present evidence that the local Hispanic context fosters Republican growth. They also demonstrate that the local Hispanic context has a significant impact on white attitudes toward immigrants and immigration policy. As the relative size of the Hispanic context grows, white attitudes toward immigrants become more negative and white policy preferences become more conservative/anti-immigrant.

Minorities and immigrants are two of the target populations of Tea Party resentment. Candidates attempting to build support with constituencies where this targeted resentment is high would have a strategic incentive to attach themselves to the Tea Party movement. Constituencies where racial resentment is particularly high also offer candidates substantial incentives for attachment to the Tea Party movement. We argue that candidates identify with the Tea Party—and make efforts to attach themselves to the Tea Party movement—in order to build support among voters who share the racial/ethnic resentment common among supporters of the Tea Party movement. Note that these efforts are directed toward those who hold these racially conservative attitudes—whether or not they are active supporters of the Tea Party movement. We hypothesize:

- *As the relative size of the African American population increases, Tea Party Attachment scores will increase.*
- *As the relative size of the Hispanic population increases, Tea Party Attachment scores will increase.*
- *As racial resentment increases, Tea Party Attachment scores will increase.*

The relationship between constituents' economic conservatism or constituents' social conservatism and the strategic benefits of attachment to the Tea Party are more complicated. The explicit rationale for the formation of the Tea Party movement in the first place was economics. The devastation of the economic landscape in the aftermath of the Great Recession—and what was viewed by many as the government's failed (and unfair) response to the Great Recession—fomented the "Taxed Enough Already" Party movement. In another somewhat counterintuitive finding, the driving force behind the early Tea Party movement was not citizens who faced the direst economic circumstances, nor were the areas of greatest early strength the most economically destitute. As our own previous research shows, the constituencies of legislators associated with the Tea Party (as indicated by their membership in the Tea Party Caucus) were actually better off than the constituencies of other legislators in the Republican Conference. And this makes sense in the context of the concern for high taxes.

The commonly accepted narrative of the genesis and development of the Tea Party movement focuses on economic circumstances. The Great Recession brought about widespread economic misfortune, and the federal government's response to this misfortune was highly controversial, particularly within the Republican Party. According to conventional wisdom, the Tea Party was a response to this historic economic downturn and, maybe more specifically, the government's response to it. Resentful citizens—fueled by the deterioration of their own economic circumstances due to the Great Recession itself or the taxes associated with the federal government's response to the Great Recession—rallied to protest policies intended to mitigate the worst effects of the economic catastrophe. But the relationship between the movement and economics is complicated. Should we expect to find the strongest support for the movement in those areas most directly affected by the Great Recession itself? Or would it be more likely that the strength of the movement would be found in areas relatively untouched by the economic downturn, areas where the government's response to the downturn would be more likely to draw citizens' ire? Our previous research (Gervais and Morris 2012) suggests it is the latter, but the former is entirely plausible.

Attitudinal research on the Tea Party in the general population suggests that economic stress or economic deprivation may also influence association with the movement (Maxwell and Parent 2013; Tope et al. 2015). Maxwell and Parent (2013) find an inverse relationship between income and attitude toward the Tea Party movement among whites. Tope et al. (2015) uncover evidence that economic context—specifically the level of unemployment—is positively associated with the likelihood of identifying as a Tea Party member. Maxwell and Parent (2012) find an individual-level unemployment effect but no income effect. Hood, Kidd, and Morris (2015b) also find an income effect among southern primary voters. Given the inconsistency of these findings in the literature, we do not have a strong rationale for a directional hypothesis associating economic context and Tea Party support or economic context and Tea Party attachment.

If voters are driven to the Tea Party movement because of their own economic deprivation, then we would expect candidates' efforts to attach to the Tea Party (and thus build support among their constituents) to be inversely related to constituency-level measures of economic health. Conversely, if constituents are driven primarily by frustration with government efforts to bail out undeserving lenders and borrowers, the popularity of the Tea Party movement is likely to be greater in areas that enjoy relatively better economic circumstances. In this case, we would expect attachment to the Tea Party to be directly related to economic context. Economic context may drive Tea Party attachment, but we cannot ascertain, ex ante, the character of that relationship.

In the case of social conservatism, we have directional expectations—greater social conservatism among one's constituency would tend to enhance the strategic benefits associated with Tea Party attachment—but we also have reason to doubt the strength of the relationship (or the magnitude of the strategic benefits). Hood et al. (2015b) find a strong relationship between self-identification as a born-again Christian and support for the Tea Party movement among politically active southerners, but in their national sample, Maxwell and Parent (2013) find no relationship between self-identification as a Christian and support for the Tea Party movement. Other research (see, e.g., McNitt 2014) finds little evidence of a relationship between demographic factors or broad, district-level economic factors and Tea Party Caucus membership. It is also clear that Tea Party Caucus members are not limited to one (or even two) geographic areas.

Understanding the constituency-level attitudinal dynamics of Tea Party support and Tea Party attachment is also important for our broader argument regarding the impact of House Republicans' digital homestyle on their constituents' support for Trump. We must investigate the evidence of a causal relationship between constituents' attitudes and Tea Party support and Tea Party attachment. It may be that our causal interpretation of the relationship between constituents' attitudes and support for Trump (in a primary, the general election, or both) is more aptly attributed to the presence of underlying political attitudes (such as racial resentment—a constellation of attitudes that recent research has associated with support for Trump) prior to the election.

Analyzing Constituency Dynamics

Our primary independent variables are scales constructed from a variety of variables detailed in the preceding chapter. Tea Party Support is an index based on (1) the number of endorsements received from Tea Party organizations, (2) the amount of campaign contributions received from and the dollar value of independent expenditures made on behalf of the candidate by Tea Party organizations, and (3) Tea Party activist support for the candidate. Remember that Tea Party activist support is based on an analysis of the use of a key Tea Party hashtag when a candidate was being promoted on Twitter.

Tea Party Attachment is measured on an ordinal scale based on the following variables:

1. Membership in the Tea Party Caucus or Liberty Caucus.[3]
2. Tea Party Self-Identification with Social Media
3. Media Salience of Tea Party Connection

Tea Party Caucus membership is self-evident. Self-identification of members' attachment to the Tea Party movement is based on members' Tweets during the lead-up to an election—in the context of this chapter, the 2010 election. And our measure of media salience of the Tea Party connection is an update of the measure created by Gervais and Taylor (2016). Their measure captures the frequency of media articles and stories that positively associate a particular candidate with the Tea Party movement. Note that the media accounts differ significantly from Tea Party activists' tweets. While activist tweets are posted in an effort to build or cultivate Tea Party support for a candidate, media accounts are designed to reflect the existing attachment of the candidate to the Tea Party movement. Tea Party Attachment is a simple ordinal index ranging from 0 to 2. Tea Party Caucus members in the 112th Congress were coded 2. Legislators with positive values on the standardized measures of Tea Party Tweets *and* Tea Party Salience were also coded 2. Legislators with positive values on the standardized measures of Tea Party Tweets *or* Tea Party Salience—but not both—were coded 1. All other legislators were coded 0. Far more detail on both the Tea Party Support measure and the Tea Party Attachment measure can be found in the preceding chapter.

Our institutional and electoral variables are coded as follows:

1. Seniority—total number of terms served by a member through and including the 112th Congress. Note that the sample is limited to those members who won election or re-election in 2010.
2. District Security—a candidate's margin of victory in the 2010 congressional election. As margin of victory increased, district security is assumed to increase.[4]
3. Committee Leadership—coded 1 for individuals serving as ranking members of House committees during the 111th Congress. All others coded 0.

4. Party Leadership—coded 1 for individuals serving in the following posts: majority leader, majority whip, chief deputy whip, Republican Conference secretary, Republican Conference chair, Republican Conference vice chair, Campaign Committee chair, or Policy Committee chair in the 111th Congress. All others coded 0.

Our racial and ethnic context measures are the percentage of the relevant racial/ethnic group—African American, Hispanic, or Asian American—in a member's congressional district. These data are taken from US Census sources. Our district-level economic variables tap the unemployment rate and the percentage of constituents below the poverty level in each congressional district. These data are taken from the Census Bureau's American Community Survey.

We also included a number of attitudinal variables contained in the Cooperative Congressional Election Survey (CCES) from 2010 to more directly evaluate the extent to which constituency attitudes might have influenced Tea Party Support and Tea Party Attachment levels. These variables were based on survey responses to questions tapping overall conservatism, attitudes toward Obama, and racial resentment (two different questions). We also included a variable indicating whether or not a respondent considered her- or himself an evangelical Christian. Note that few of these variables ever reached a standard level of statistical significance, and with the exception of one measure of racial resentment (included in the final model for Tea Party Attachment) none were consistently significant over a variety of model specifications. We attribute the absence of robust attitudinal results—at least in part—to the relatively small average sample size per congressional district (less than seventy) and the variability of even these small samples. Finally, we also include the racial/ethnic identity and gender of the House member as control variables.

To assess the impact of these factors on Tea Party Support, we use ordinary least squares (OLS) regression with the House member as the unit of analysis, a standard tool for evaluating the independent impacts of each of a set of independent variables on an interval-level dependent variable. To evaluate the impact of these factors on Tea Party Attachment, we use ordered probit. We use ordered probit in this context—rather than OLS regression—because the dependent variable of interest is measured at the ordinal level rather than the interval level. The House member is again the unit of analysis. In both cases, reported significance levels are based on robust standard errors.

The results from a variety of model specifications indicate that two factors appear to dominate the strategic calculus of Tea Party organizations and Tea Party activists intent on providing support for House Republican candidates: Seniority (or lack thereof) and District Security (see Table 4.1).

Table 4.1 **Electoral Competition and Tea Party Support (112th Congress)**

Variable	Tea Party Support
Margin of Victory	**−0.02 (0.00)**
Terms in Office	**−0.14 (0.02)**
Constant	**1.44 (0.26)**
Districts (N)	241
R^2	0.23

Note: Coefficients are OLS regression. Robust standard errors are in parentheses. Boldface indicates significance at $p < .05$.

Tea Party Support is significantly and inversely related to legislators' seniority. All else equal, the most junior candidates received the highest levels of support. Remembering that this analysis is based on an analysis of *successful* House candidates—note that the only candidates in the dataset are those who won election to the 112th Congress—we conjecture that this result still probably underestimates the extent to which Tea Party organizations and activists supported the least senior House Republicans. Candidates receiving Tea Party support who were unsuccessful in their electoral bids were almost exclusively challengers (and thus without any seniority). Had these "losers" (and there were very few who reached the general election level) been included in the analysis, the magnitude of the Seniority variable would likely have been significantly larger.

Because of the construction of the Tea Party Support measure—incorporating endorsements as well as different types of financial support—illustrating the substantive significance of seniority (or competitiveness) is not trivial. One way to deal with this issue is to consider the relative position of candidates on a scale of support and then evaluate the predicted shift in their relative position resulting from a change in seniority (or competitiveness). If we assume that a House member is at the 50th percentile in Seniority and that the member's electoral margin is set to the mean for the sample of Republicans, what sort of effect would we expect to see if a member had been significantly more senior (say, by a standard deviation) or significantly less senior (again, by a standard deviation). Average Seniority for this sample is more than four and a half terms—more than nine years. The standard deviation for Seniority equates to approximately eight and a half years. Based on our model results, a shift from the average level of Seniority to a level of Seniority a standard deviation lower would result in a hypothetical candidate in the 74th percentile of Tea Party Support, a dramatic rise in relative position on the Tea Party Support measure. By the same token, a standard deviation increase in seniority would lead to a somewhat subtler change, a drop to the 43rd percentile in Tea Party Support. For strategic Tea Party organizations, one would expect the difference between a ten-year member and an eighteen-year member to pale in comparison to the difference between a new member or second-term member and a ten-year member, and the results support that expectation.

We also find that candidates in the most competitive races ceteris paribus received the highest levels of Tea Party support. Candidates in less competitive races received less Tea Party support. Whether or not this result would be enhanced by the inclusion of Republican "losers" who reached the general election level is unclear. As our focus is trying to understand the representational dynamics faced by successful candidates, this is not a significant issue. If we assume that a House member is at the 50th percentile for electoral security and that the member's Seniority is set to the mean for the sample of Republicans, what sort of effect would we expect to see if the race had been significantly more competitive (say by a standard deviation) or significantly less competitive (again, by a standard deviation)? Based on our model results, a one-standard-deviation decrease in competitiveness (i.e., larger electoral margin), we would expect our hypothetical candidate to drop to the 44th percentile in Tea Party Support. A one-standard-deviation increase in competitiveness, on the other hand, would push our hypothetical candidate up to the 73rd percentile. The asymmetric magnitude of the competitiveness effect makes sense in the context of the average level of campaign competitiveness. The average Republican in our sample had an electoral margin of more than 30 percent. At this point, we would expect any decrease in competitiveness to have little impact on support. The average candidate was clearly quite safe and would not need significant campaign support from Tea Party organizations. If Tea Party organizations are strategic about the distribution of their campaign resources, safe candidates would receive relatively little support in the first place. An increase in security should have little effect. On the other hand, a one-standard-deviation increase in competitiveness makes the race quite tight, and so a large swing in Tea Party Support is to be expected.

We find no evidence that Tea Party organizations and activists targeted candidates from congressional districts with particular racial/ethnic demographics or constituencies facing distinctive economic circumstances, whether good or bad. Nor do the data provide any support for our hypothesized relationship between opposition to Obama and Tea Party Support. The data also provide no support for the contention that Tea Party organizations targeted constituencies that were particularly conservative (in a broad sense). We do see some very limited evidence that racial resentment played a role in the distribution of Tea Party Support, but this result was not robust to model specification.

It is also worth noting that even this limited result suggested that racial resentment had a dampening effect on Tea Party Support. To the extent that we have evidence that racial conservatism played a role in the distribution of organizational support, higher levels of racial resentment resulted in lower levels of support. Clearly, we find no evidence that Tea Party organizations were targeting Republicans serving racially conservative constituencies. This could be because it was not a key issue for Tea Party organizations or because Tea Party organizations did not consider these areas particularly competitive. Beyond that, we would just be speculating. Finally, the variable tapping the prevalence of evangelical Christians is never statistically significant. If Tea Party organizations made efforts to support candidates in socially conservative areas, we see no evidence of that here.

There is some limited evidence that Tea Party organizations targeted the two African American Republicans in the 112th Congress—Tim Scott (R-SC) and Allen West (R-FL). The coefficient is large, but it falls just short of significance (at the .05 level). It is always risky to draw inferences from a couple of observations, but it is worth noting that Scott's association with the Tea Party movement followed him to the Senate, and research on the 2012 elections in South Carolina suggest that he received significant support from voters aligned with the Tea Party movement (Hood, Kidd, and Morris 2014). And West was a large enough outlier that a dummy variable for him was highly significant.

In short, the data indicate that Tea Party support was directed at relatively junior candidates in highly competitive races. Tea Party support was distributed in a manner intended to increase Republican victories; there is little evidence that the distribution strategy targeted candidates serving in any particular type of demographic or ideological constituency, and limited evidence suggests that support was actually less prevalent in (racially) conservative areas.

In contrast to the case for Tea Party Support, neither seniority nor electoral security influenced the level of Tea Party Attachment. Both junior members and senior members made efforts to attach themselves to the Tea Party movement. By the same token, both junior and senior members avoided association with the Tea Party movement (Table 4.2). Racial/ethnic context, on the other hand, played a key (and predictable) role in the decisions by Republican members of the House to attach themselves to the Tea Party movement.

As the relative size of the African American population increased, Tea Party Attachment increased (see Figure 4.1).[5] For each of the interval-level independent variables included in figures 4.1, 4.2, 4.3, and 4.4, "average" is the mean for the sample. "High" is a level consistent with a single standard deviation above the mean (for that variable), and "low" is a level consistent with a single standard deviation below the mean (again, for that variable). It

Table 4.2 **Determinants of Tea Party Attachment (112th Congress)**

Variable	Tea Party Attachment
Percent Black	**0.03 (0.01)**
Percent Hispanic	**0.015 (0.006)**
District Obama Vote	**−0.04 (0.01)**
Committee Leadership	**−0.78 (0.29)**
Racial Resentment B (% Who Somewhat Disagree)[a]	**0.04 (0.02)**
Cut 1 Constant	−0.19 (0.69)
Cut 2 Constant	0.23 (0.69)
Districts (N)	236
Pseudo R^2	0.078
Wald χ^2	38.55

Note: Coefficients are ordered probit regression. Robust standard errors are in parentheses. Boldface indicates significance at $p < .05$.

[a] Note that for this question on racial resentment, *disagreement* was the response considered more racially resentful.

is worth noting that the means and standard deviations for the various independent variables are based on our sample, which is limited to Republican House districts. "High Tea Party Attachment" indicates a representative with the highest score for Tea Party Attachment (2). "Some Tea Party Attachment" indicates a representative with a score of 1 on the Tea Party Attachment variable, and "No Tea Party Attachment" indicates a representative with a score of 0 on the Tea Party Attachment variable.

This is as we hypothesized. The effect is particularly striking for those in the High-Attachment category. A shift from one standard deviation below the mean in the African American context to one standard deviation above the mean would nearly double the likelihood that a House member would be in the High-Attachment category. African American context has been associated with white conservatism and identification with the Republican Party (see Hood, Kidd, and Morris 2012), and the racial and ethnic conservatism of the Tea Party movement would tend to be popular in areas with above average concentrations of African Americans. We expected Republicans candidates attempting to cultivate white support in areas with large African American populations (particularly in the

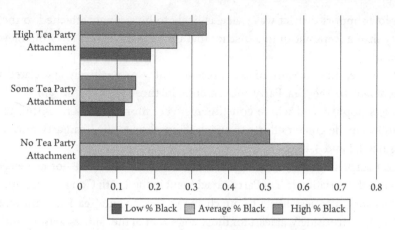

Figure 4.1 Likelihood of Tea Party Attachment and Percentage of Blacks in the Population.

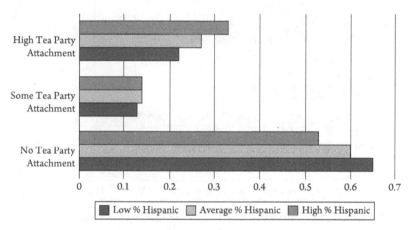

Figure 4.2 Likelihood of Tea Party Attachment and Percentage of Hispanics in the Population.

South, the focal region for the Republican Party) to attach themselves to the Tea Party, and our results suggest that is exactly what they did.

Likewise, as the relative size of the Hispanic population increased in their districts, Republicans made more concerted efforts to tie themselves to the Tea Party movement (Figure 4.2). While the effect of variation in Hispanic population has a less dramatic impact on Tea Party Attachment, it is still substantively (and statistically) significant.

District-level support for Obama was negatively associated with attachment to the Tea Party movement. Again, the shift in the probability of a House Republican seeking a high level of Tea Party attachment associated with a significant change in district-level support for Obama is quite dramatic. A Republican in a low-support district was twice as likely to be strongly attached to the Tea Party than a Republican in a district that gave Obama a relatively high level of support.

Likewise, one measure of racial resentment[6] was positively associated with attachment to the Tea Party movement.[7] In those districts in which Obama was less popular and where constituents were more racially resentful, House members made greater efforts to attach themselves to the Tea Party movement (Figures 4.3 and 4.4).

Not surprisingly, there is evidence of an institutional (but not an) electoral effect on the variation in Tea Party Attachment in the 112th Congress. Committee leaders were also less likely to attach themselves to the Tea Party movement. Somewhat surprisingly, at least for those cognizant of the "anti-establishment" reputation of the Tea Party, we find no evidence that party leaders were distinctive

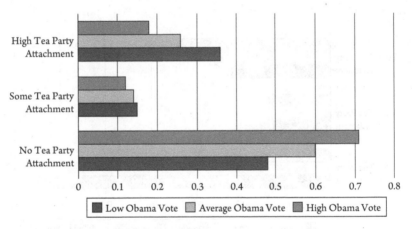

Figure 4.3 Likelihood of Tea Party Attachment and Support for Obama

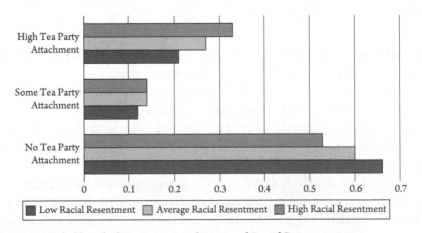

Figure 4.4 Likelihood of Tea Party Attachment and Racial Resentment

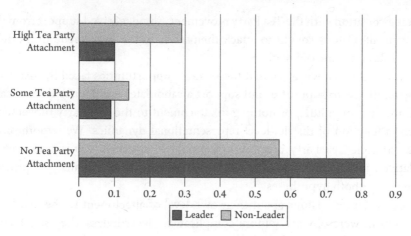

Figure 4.5 Likelihood of Committee Leadership and Tea Party Attachment

in their efforts to attach themselves to the Tea Party movement. They were neither more nor less likely to attach themselves to the Tea Party movement (Figure 4.5). This finding does, however, dovetail with our description (included in the preceding chapter) of several party leaders seeking to harness the energy of the Tea Party movement before and during the 112th Congress. Not every party leader made such an attempt, but efforts to attach to the Tea Party were not restricted to the rank-and-file, either.

The results suggest that Hispanic members of Congress might have been less likely to attach themselves to the Tea Party movement and that African American Republicans in Congress might have been slightly more likely to attach themselves to the Tea Party movement, but neither of these findings is statistically significant. As there was only a single Asian American Republican in our sample, we could not estimate a probability for Asian American members of Congress.

The same complications manifest in our efforts to analyze the relationship between constituency-level economic context and Tea Party Support. Tea Party organizations might well take economic context into account when offering support to candidates. However, we find no evidence that constituents' economic circumstances drove the distribution of Tea Party Support or that it influenced candidates' efforts to attach to the Tea Party movement.

Conclusions

Chapter 3 cited evidence suggesting that different types of Tea Party legislators served distinct constituencies and enjoyed different levels of institutional resources. Black Tea, Green Tea, White Tea, and Coffee legislators differed in their association with the Tea Party movement. Some received support from the movement. Others sought to attach themselves to the movement. Still others did both, and some did neither.

In this chapter, we argue that the strategic opportunities faced by Tea Party organizations (to support or not support a candidate) and House Republicans (to invest a lot, a little, or nothing in attachment to the Tea Party movement) were a function of district-level representational dynamics. We hypothesized that strategic Tea Party organizations would orient their scarce resources to relatively junior legislators in competitive districts, and our analyses provide support for both hypotheses.

Legislators' decisions about their own level of attachment to the Tea Party movement were obviously more complicated. Nevertheless, they still flowed from key constituency-level characteristics. And these constituency-level characteristics revolve around racial and ethnic context. Legislators' efforts to attach to the Tea Party movement are clearly and directly related to the relative size of the African American population in their district, the relative size of the Hispanic population in their district, and the opposition to Obama in their district. To a more limited extent, efforts to attach to the Tea Party movement are boosted by district-level racial resentment. Research suggests that Tea Party supporters tend to be more racially conservative. Our analysis suggests that legislators who made the most extensive efforts to attach to the Tea Party movement tended to serve the constituencies likely to be the most racially resentful.

In the next chapter, we investigate the legislative implications of Tea Party support and Tea Party attachment, specifically the ideological character of roll call voting in the 112th and 113th Congresses. Were those supported by Tea Party organizations more likely to support legislation associated with fiscal conservatism—the ostensible focus of nearly all Tea Party organizations—than other House Republicans? And were legislators who sought to curry favor with the most racially resentful constituents in their district through attachment to the Tea Party movement more likely to support a racially and ethnically conservative legislative agenda? We answer these questions next.

Tea Party-ness and Roll Call Voting in the House

In the preceding chapter, we provided some preliminary data suggesting that our Tea Party Attachment and Tea Party Support measures distinguished between legislators from different types of districts and legislators with different types of voting records. Those findings were based on only a small sample of exemplary cases of each of the types of House Republicans. In this chapter, we extend one aspect of that analysis—the examination of legislators' roll call voting behavior—to the full sample of House Republicans. More specifically, we assess the extent to which Tea Party Attachment and Tea Party Support are independently associated with distinctive roll call voting behavior.

We focus initially on the overall ideological tenor of a legislator's roll call voting behavior. We then examine the relationship between roll call voting behavior and particular issues scholars have associated with the Tea Party in Congress and the Tea Party movement more generally.

Roll Calls and the Tea Party in the House: Background and Theory

Research on the Tea Party in the electorate is extensive. Journalists and scholars have investigated the demographic profile of Tea Party supporters. They have analyzed their positions on a variety of policy issues, and they have evaluated their impact on multiple elections. Research on the impact of Tea Party supporters on House elections includes that of Carson and Pettigrew (2013), Karpowitz et al. (2011), and McNitt (2014). Analyses of the demographic characteristics and ideological leanings of supporters are even more extensive (see, e.g., Barreto et al. 2011; Campbell and Putnam 2011; Clement and Green 2011; Hood et al.

2015a, b; Maxwell and Parent 2012, 2013; Parker 2010; Parker and Barreto 2013; Skocpol and Williamson 2012; Tope et al. 2015; Williamson et al. 2011).

The extensive body of research on the Tea Party movement at the mass level has not been matched by research on the Tea Party in Congress (either the House or Senate). Research on the ideological distinctiveness of Tea Party legislators—versus analyses of the campaign contribution or endorsement strategies of Tea Party organizations or research on the impact of Tea Party association on members' electoral fortunes—is particularly limited. The few analyses of the ideological distinctiveness of Tea Party legislators offer inconsistent findings.

In one of the earliest—if not the earliest—studies of the Tea Party in Congress, Gallagher and Rock (2012) examine various dimensions in which we might expect Tea Party members to distinguish themselves, from roll call voting to bill sponsorship to personal demographics to media activity. Gallagher and Rock (2012) find that Tea Party members—and they operationalize Tea Party membership solely on the basis of Tea Party Caucus membership—are more likely to seek media attention than more mainstream (or in our terms, Coffee) Republicans. On bill sponsorship leading to new law, Gallagher and Rock (2012, 111) find that Tea Party legislators are less active than other Republicans, but on roll call voting, Tea Party members are "indistinguishable from other Republicans." They conclude that "if being a Tea Partier is a meaningful distinction, it doesn't seem to reveal itself in how congressmen vote" (Gallagher and Rock 2012, 112).

Bailey et al.'s (2012) analysis reflects the broad contours of Gallagher and Rock's research. While Bailey et al. (2012) find some evidence that Tea Party Caucus membership is associated with DW-Nominate scores (a standard, though hardly uncontroversial measure of legislator ideology), this relationship disappears when they control for previous DW-Nominate scores. This control is problematic because it significantly curtails their sample—nearly cuts it in half—but this still suggests that the relationship between Tea Party Caucus membership (and, in this case, the number of Tea Party activists in a district, Tea Party endorsements, and district-level Tea Party favorability) and legislators' ideology is weak or nonexistent.[1] On more specialized legislation—such as debt-ceiling roll calls or votes on the funding of a particular jet fighter engine—Bailey et al. (2012) find evidence that some measures of Tea Party influence (whether from activists in members' districts or, more rarely, Tea Party organization endorsements) did influence members' votes. Evidence that Tea Party Caucus membership influenced roll call voting, even on these specialized votes, is limited.

Some of our own previous work in this area (Gervais and Morris 2012) is consistent with the presence of a focused roll call voting effect. Looking at roll call voting on tax policy in the 112th Congress, we find that members of the Tea

Party Caucus took more conservative positions on various tax policy votes than other members of the House Republican Conference (an effect robust to the inclusion of standard control variables). We did not find evidence of a roll call voting effect that extended beyond this specific set of issues, nor did we investigate the impact of various constituency or organizational Tea Party variables on roll call votes cast on these tax policy issues.

More recent research suggests the presence of a more substantial ideological distinction between Tea Party legislators and other members of the Republican Conference. Bond (2013) presents evidence indicating that Tea Party freshmen—those elected in 2010—were far less supportive of President Obama's legislative initiatives than other conservative Republicans. Although not the same as a measure of ideology, President Obama's agenda during the 112th Congress was multifaceted and ranged well beyond the more limited set of issues that were the primary focus of the positive results referenced earlier. Another distinctive aspect of this analysis is the exclusive focus on freshmen associated with the Tea Party; this is a far smaller group than that produced by other conventional measures of Tea Party membership (such as Tea Party Caucus membership). Bond (2013) does not provide any evidence that this aversion to Obama's agenda was shared among incumbent Tea Party members.

More recently, Ragusa and Gaspar (2016) produced the most compelling evidence for the general ideological distinctiveness of Tea Party members in the House. Their analysis of DW-Nominate scores indicates that Tea Party Caucus members grew significantly more conservative during the 112th Congress than did Democrats or other Republicans. Their evidence also indicates that this increase in conservatism lasted well into the 113th Congress. While Democrats or non-Tea Party Republicans who became more conservative during the 112th Congress bounced back (had a liberal reversion) during the 113th Congress, the same was not true for Tea Party Republicans. Ragusa and Gaspar (2016) found that the relative size of district-level activism influenced ideological voting in a manner consistent with Tea Party Caucus membership (though, as they note, for different reasons). Organizational variables—such as Tea Party organization endorsements—failed to produce a comparable effect.

A particularly interesting aspect of Ragusa and Gaspar's analysis is their focus on change in ideology rather than ideology itself. To measure this change, they had to limit their sample to those members of the House who served in both the 111th and 112th Congresses, so, somewhat ironically, the sample of Tea Party Republicans has no overlap with the sample of Tea Party Republicans in Bond's (2013) study (in one case, incumbency is required; in the other, it is prohibited). Focusing on ideological change also places a rather significant constraint on the sample size. Their measure of Tea Party Caucus membership limits the

Tea Party membership in the House to less than 20 percent of the full Republican Conference. The case they make for the ideological distinctiveness of Tea Party members in the House is compelling, but it is also a case based on a particularly restrictive understanding of Tea Party association. The question remains, if our understanding of the pervasiveness of Tea Party attachment and/or Tea Party support is more inclusive, do we see, or should we expect to see, ideological differentiation among legislators associated with the Tea Party?

Our analysis differs from existing work in several respects. First, we argue that there are various ways to associate with the Tea Party movement. As we explained in Chapter 3, legislators may *attach* themselves to the movement, or they may receive *support* from the movement, or both. Second, our measures of attachment and support both extend well beyond what has been presented in the existing literature. We are not the first to notice that legislators who received campaign contributions from Tea Party organizations aren't necessarily the same ones who joined the Tea Party Caucus (e.g., Bailey et al. 2012). Nor were we the first to point out that there was considerable variation in the funding and endorsement patterns for legislators among Tea Party organizations (Bailey et al. 2012; Bullock and Hood 2012; Karpowitz et al. 2011). But the array of measures we use to capture attachment and support extend well beyond existing work. Third, we make a novel contribution to the literature by highlighting the distinctive strategic dynamics that drive Tea Party attachment and Tea Party support and explaining how these dynamics should be associated with identifiable patterns of behavior among legislators.

But the unique aspects of our analysis to this point then raise important questions related to our characterization of the legislators ranging across the dimensions of our Tea Party Attachment and Tea Party Support measures. We argue for new concepts and broader, more extensive methodologies of measurement. For what purpose? Are the legislators who range across these dimensions different in the ways we would expect? Our preliminary analysis at the end of Chapter 3 suggests that the answer is yes, but in this chapter we intend to make a more compelling case based on a more rigorous analysis of the full sample of House Republicans in the 112th and 113th Congresses—not just an analysis of exemplary cases of various types of Tea and Coffee Republicans. To this effort we now turn.

Tea Party Attachment, Tea Party Support, and Ideological Conservatism

Specific strategic dynamics drive Tea Party attachment and Tea Party support. Legislators' political calculations—particularly as they relate to electoral risks and opportunities—influence the decisions they make regarding the extent to which they *attach* themselves to the Tea Party movement through membership in the Tea Party Caucus, membership in the Liberty Caucus, social media promotion of the Tea Party movement, or participation in the types of campaign events and political rallies that foster media attention. Conversely, it is the strategic opportunities available to Tea Party organizations that influence decisions about the level and character of the organizational backing legislators receive. Should an organization endorse a candidate? Should an organization make a campaign contribution to a particular candidate or offer independent support to that candidate? And if there is a decision to provide financial support, what level of support should be provided? The answer to each of these questions depends on the strategic objectives and obstacles faced by the organization. Does a particular organization seek to support members with a long record of support for Tea Party policy initiatives? Or does the organization seek to support the freshmen with the potential to replace Democrats or less supportive Republicans? Or is the organization intent on supporting only those candidates most likely to win? The literature provides some support for each of these objectives (see Bullock and Hood 2012). Members of Congress almost certainly provide information for each organization's decision-making process, but the members don't make the decisions. In short, members *attach*; organizations *support*.

The focal points of the decision-making processes regarding Tea Party attachment and Tea Party support are different, and because their distinct decision-making processes are driven by specific political dynamics, we should not expect the same relationship between a legislator's ideology and Tea Party support as between Tea Party attachment and a legislator's ideology. We view Tea Party attachment as the result of members' efforts to associate themselves with the Tea Party movement and the political orientations of its supporters. As we discussed in Chapter 2, we heavily discount the possibility that Tea Party attachment is cheap talk. We see little reason for a "relatively" liberal member of the Republican Conference to invest in an association with the Tea Party. In a general election, association with the Tea Party would clearly alienate more moderate constituents—constituents the member has likely depended on for electoral support in the past. And in a primary contest where partisans tend to be more knowledgeable and politically engaged, claims to an association with the Tea Party for a liberal Republican would not be credible. From the standpoint of organizational support, the dynamics are similar. The more moderate organizations that had supported the candidate in the past would be alienated by efforts to attach to the Tea Party movement. Tea Party organizations, conversely, would be unlikely to base an offer of support on attachment efforts divorced from actual policy orientations.

If legislators' efforts to attach to the movement are not cheap talk, we expect attachment efforts to be strongly associated with ideological conservatism. We view attachment to the Tea Party as an amalgam of advertising and position-taking (Mayhew 1974). It is an "effort to disseminate one's name among constituents in such a fashion as to create a favorable image" (Mayhew 1974, 49), but Tea Party attachment clearly has the sort of political content commonly seen in position-taking—more elaborate than a simple roll call vote, but still, we argue, indicative of a particular (conservative) political orientation. Thus, we expect efforts to attach to the Tea Party to be coincident with ideological conservatism, and this ideological conservatism should be multidimensional.

As we discussed in Chapter 2, the fiscal conservatism so consistently associated with the Tea Party movement—and Tea Party organizations in particular—is less common among Tea Party supporters in the general public. These Tea Party supporters tend to hold views that reflect racial conservatism and social conservatism more consistently than fiscal conservatism (see Skocpol and Williamson 2012, 45–85; also see Barreto et al. 2011).[2] The primary audience for legislators' efforts to attach to the Tea Party movement are their constituents.[3] We argue that efforts to attach to the Tea Party are directed primarily at constituents (rather than Tea Party organizations). Legislators attempting to attach to the Tea Party hope to cultivate support among constituents associated with the Tea Party (or constituents positively disposed to the Tea Party), and these constituents are more likely to hold conservative views on racial and social issues than on fiscal issues. Conservative views on fiscal issues, while potentially crucial for organizations, tend not to be of particular significance for Tea Party adherents in the general public. We don't presume an inverse relationship between Tea Party attachment and fiscal conservatism, but that ideological dimension is unlikely to be the primary driver of a member's efforts to communicate an association with the Tea Party movement.

Tea Party organizations, on the other hand, are likely to pay more attention to legislators' support for the tenets of fiscal conservatism than Tea Party adherents among the electorate. For that reason, we might expect a member's adherence to fiscal conservatism to play a more important role in the acquisition of support from Tea Party organizations than other dimensions of conservatism. Given Tea Party organizations' focus on fiscal conservatism—not exclusively, but more consistently than that of Tea Party supporters in the general population—we may well find that the association between Tea Party support and the general ideological orientation of a legislator is either quite weak or nonexistent.

As we have noted, the literature provides inconsistent answers to the question of the ideological distinctiveness of Tea Party legislators, due largely to the variation in the strategies used to measure the movement in Congress. These strategies consistently underestimate the significance and the scope of the movement in Congress. We offer a novel solution to this problem by reconceptualizing Tea Party association and creating measurement strategies for both of the key conceptual components of association—attachment and support. We present the empirical implications of these theoretical innovations below.

Tea Party Attachment, Tea Party Support, and Roll Call Voting

We seek to understand the relationship between a legislator's ideology and our dimensions of Tea Party association: Tea Party Attachment and Tea Party Support. To gauge the level of conservatism of each Republican member of the 112th and 113th Congresses, we use scores from the first dimension of the DW-Nominate scale developed by Poole and Rosenthal (1997). We realize that this is an imperfect measure. Most significantly, as the scores are based solely on roll calls, there are no substantive standards for descriptors such as "liberal" and "conservative." Knowing that a legislator's score indicates greater conservatism relative to her or his colleagues does not necessarily imply that the legislator is conservative. However, these scores—especially the variant we have selected, DW-Nominate—are the standard measure of ideology in the literature (limited though it may be) on the manifestation of the Tea Party movement in Congress (Bailey et al. 2012; Gallagher and Rock 2012; Ragusa and Gaspar 2016). As we intend to contribute to this particular literature, we do not see an alternative to the use of these scores, nor would one be appropriate. Our key independent variables—Tea Party Attachment and Tea Party Support—were described in detail in Chapter 3. We begin by focusing on the relationship between overall ideology and efforts to attach to the Tea Party movement.

Looking first at the average DW-Nominate scores for varying levels of attachment, we find clear evidence tying Tea Party Attachment to greater conservatism in both the 112th and the 113th Congresses. Figures 5.1 and 5.2 depict the average DW-Nominate score for each category of Tea Party Attachment (with 0 indicating the least attachment and 2 indicating the most attachment). For both the 112th and 113th Congresses, legislators scoring a 1 on the Attachment scale had significantly more conservative voting records than their Republican colleagues scoring a 0 on the Attachment scale, and legislators scoring a 2 on the Attachment scale had even more conservative voting records than those who scored a 1 on the Attachment scale.

We base these inferences on simple descriptive statistics, so we must consider the possibility that these results are an artifact of related differences between the legislators who attached to the Tea Party movement and those who

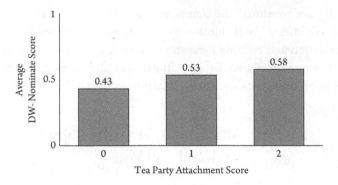

Figure 5.1 Tea Party Attachment and Ideology, 112th Congress

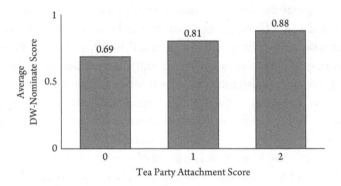

Figure 5.2 Tea Party Attachment and Ideology, 113th Congress

did not. For example, it may be that seniority is driving ideology and that Tea Party legislators are simply more junior than other Republicans. Or Tea Party legislators may enjoy greater electoral security, and so they are able to take more conservative positions than their fellow Republicans. Or those making an effort to attach to the Tea Party may play less significant roles in conference or committee leadership, and so, again, they may be freer to take more extreme conservative stances than the "establishment" Republicans who are more likely to be in leadership roles. We incorporate a measure of seniority, a dummy variable for party leadership status,[4] and a dummy variable for committee leadership status.[5]

Constituency-level factors may also influence roll call voting behavior. For example, legislators' voting patterns may simply be a response to the underlying ideological orientation of their districts. If their efforts to attach to the Tea Party are driven solely by the same force, then what appears to be a relationship between attachment and roll call voting should disappear when constituency ideology is controlled for. We use Obama's percentage of the two-party vote to gauge constituency ideology and partisanship. For the 112th Congress analysis, we use the Obama vote percentage from the 2008 election. For the 113th Congress analysis, we use the Obama vote percentage from the 2012 election. Another constituency-level factor that could explain the apparent relationship between Tea Party attachment and roll call voting is the variation in the presence of a particularly relevant political group: Tea Party activists. We use Burghart and Zeskind's (2010) calculations for the district-level presence of Tea Party activism in the 112th Congress. For the 113th Congress, we use Burghart and Zeskind's (2015) data but we produce our own calculations.[6]

In multivariate models—one for the 112th Congress and one for the 113th Congress—we assess these alternative explanations for the variance in roll call voting behavior manifest in the descriptive analyses.[7] The results for both the 112th and 113th Congresses strongly support the contention that it was the more conservative members of the Republican Conference who made the most concerted efforts to attach themselves to the Tea Party movement (Figures 5.3 and 5.4).

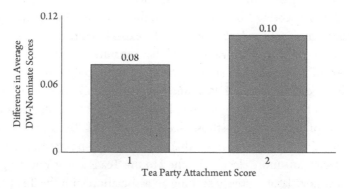

Figure 5.3 Estimated Impact of Tea Party Attachment on Ideology, 112th Congress

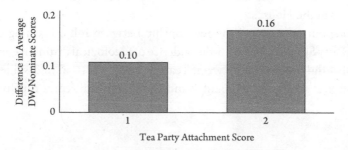

Figure 5.4 Estimated Impact of Tea Party Attachment on Ideology, 113th Congress

Even after controlling for additional factors, Tea Party Attachment is still significantly associated with greater roll call voting conservatism. The estimated increase in conservatism associated with a shift from 0 to 1 on the Tea Party Attachment scale is just less than half of the standard deviation of DW-Nominate scores for the Republican Conference in the 112th Congress. The estimated increase in conservatism associated with a shift from 0 to 2 on the Tea Party Attachment scale is considerably more than half of the standard deviation of the DW-Nominate scores for the Conference in the 112th Congress. The results also indicate that the estimated difference between legislators scoring 1 on the index and those scoring 2 is substantively and statistically significant (and, obviously, in the expected direction).

Analysis of data from the 113th Congress tells the same story, though the magnitude of the estimated differences—those present after other variables are accounted for—is greater than in the 112th Congress. The estimated increase in conservatism associated with a shift from 0 to 1 on the Tea Party Attachment scale is well more than half of the standard deviation of DW-Nominate scores for the Conference in the 113th Congress. And the estimated increase in conservatism associated with a shift from 0 to 2 on the Tea Party Attachment scale is nearly a full standard deviation of the DW-Nominate scores for the Conference in the 113th Congress. The results also indicate that the estimated difference between legislators scoring 1 on the index and those scoring 2 is substantively and statistically significant (and, obviously, in the expected direction).

One of the more striking aspects of these results is that they occurred in the context of a caucus-wide shift to the right by Republicans. Consider that the gap between the average DW-Nominate score for Democrats in the 112th Congress and the 113th Congress was less than 0.01.[8] Even the least conservative group of Republicans—those scoring 0 on the Tea Party Attachment scale—shifted to the right by more than a quarter of a point. The conservative shifts for legislators more closely attached to the Tea Party were even greater in magnitude.[9] Legislators actively seeking an association with the Tea Party were significantly more conservative than other Republican Conference members at a time when these other members were themselves moving farther away from Democrats in the House.

Turning our attention to the relationship between roll call voting behavior and Tea Party Support, we find little evidence of ideological distinctiveness. First, we see that the correlation between Tea Party Support—an interval-level variable, unlike Tea Party Attachment—and DW-Nominate scores is paltry. In the

112th Congress, the correlation is less than 0.10, and in the 113th Congress, the correlation is less than 0.12. In the 112th Congress, the average DW-Nominate score for a Republican was nearly identical (within 0.03) to the average DW-Nominate score for a Republican with a Tea Party Support score a standard deviation above the average. The 113th Congress exhibits a similar pattern. The average DW-Nominate score for a Republican with a Tea Party Support score a standard deviation above the average is within 0.04 of the average score for all Republicans.

Multivariate analyses offer no additional support for the ideological distinctiveness of Republicans who enjoyed significant Tea Party support. We included Tea Party Support as a variable in the models estimated to assess the impact of Tea Party attachment on roll call voting behavior, and in neither the model for the 112th Congress nor the model for the 113th Congress did either Support variable come close to reaching a standard level of significance. Evidently, either Tea Party organizations did not try to target distinctively conservative Republicans or they failed to effectively target distinctively conservative Republicans.

One plausible explanation for the lack of evidence of a relationship between Tea Party Support and roll call voting behavior is that our measure of roll call voting—DW-Nominate scores—is too general. One could argue that Tea Party organizations were focused on fiscal conservatism and that a measure of roll call voting that covers a much wider array of issues—technically, for DW-Nominate scores, all issues—is insufficiently focused and that analyses based on this general indicator are biased against manifesting a relationship focused on only a single policy dimension within the broad set encompassed by the indicator.

To examine this possibility, we evaluate the relationship between Tea Party Support and a more focused measure of fiscal policy conservatism, the vote scores calculated by the National Federation of Independent Business (NFIB).[10] The roll calls selected for inclusion in the NFIB vote scores reflect the types of tax and regulatory issues that have been highlighted by Tea Party organizations since the beginning of the movement. In the 112th Congress, the roll calls included the following:

- H.R. 2, Repeal of the Patient Protection and Affordable Care Act of 2010.
- H.R. 4, Small Business Paperwork Mandate Elimination Act—repeals certain tax-reporting requirements for small businesses.

- H.R. 910, Energy Tax Prevention Act—prohibits the Environmental Protection Agency (EPA) regulation of stationary sources of greenhouse gases.
- H.R. 2587, Protecting Jobs from Government Interference Act—prohibits the National Labor Relations Board (NLRB) from preventing the transfer of jobs to right-to-work states.
- H. J. Res. 2, Balanced Budget Amendment.
- H.R. 527, Regulatory Flexibility Improvements Act—requires agencies to conduct additional analyses of the economic impact of new rules and regulations on small businesses.
- H.R. 436, Health Care Cost Reduction Act—repeals excise tax on medical devices.
- H.R. 8, Job Protection and Recession Prevention Act—extends Bush era tax rates for individual income, capital gains, dividends, and estate taxes.

The list of roll calls in the 113th Congress consisted of a similar set of bills focused on limiting government (or, more specifically, limiting the federal government). They included the following:

- H.R. 2668, Fairness for American Families Act—delays the Affordable Care Act (ACA) individual mandate.
- H.R. 2231, Offshore Energy and Jobs Act—expands domestic energy production by lifting the moratorium on offshore drilling.
- H.R. 1120, Preventing Greater Uncertainty in Labor-Management Relations Act—prohibits NLRB decision-making prior to resolution of the constitutionality of the current board.
- H.R. 4457, America's Small Business Tax Relief Act of 2014—makes permanent the temporary maximum small-business expensing level.
- H.R. 2575, Save American Workers Act of 2014—prohibits the use of the thirty-hour work week standard established by the ACA for purposes of the employer mandate.
- H.R. 2804, All Economic Regulations Are Transparent Act—requires extensive analysis of the economic impact on small businesses of all new rules and regulations.

While the bills, amendments, and resolutions incorporated in the NFIB vote scores deal with a variety of issues, they all relate to the fiscal and regulatory focus of even the earliest manifestations of the Tea Party movement and the related organizations. Whether in the realm of fiscal issues—such as a balanced budget amendment or a variety of tax relief bills—or regulatory issues, the efforts of both congresses to increase the fact-finding and analysis required for new rules or regulations, and to limit the actions of regulatory boards or agencies such as the NLRB and the EPA, are meant to limit the size and reach of the federal government.

Legislators enjoying Tea Party support may not be more conservative than their fellow Republicans on the full range of issues addressed by Congress. But if they are noticeably more conservative on any particular set of issues, it should be these. Surprisingly, we found little evidence that legislators associated with the Tea Party—both those who made efforts to attach themselves to the Tea Party movement and those who received support from Tea Party organizations—cast more fiscally conservative roll call votes than fellow Conference members who were Coffee Republicans.

We do find slight evidence of a relationship between Tea Party Attachment and fiscal conservatism and Tea Party Support and fiscal conservatism. Legislators scoring 1 or 2 on the Tea Party Attachment scale have slightly higher NFIB fiscal conservatism scores than legislators who scored 0 on the Tea Party Attachment scale, but the average substantive differences are tiny—never more than 1.5 points on the 100-point scale. And while Tea Party Support is positively correlated with fiscal conservatism in both the 112th and 113th Congresses, the magnitudes of the relationships are very small (less than 0.01 in the 112th Congress and less than 0.07 in the 113th Congress). In multivariate models that included the same controls as our models of DW-Nominate scores, neither the Tea Party Attachment variable nor the Tea Party Support variable was ever statistically significant.

We posit that the primary reason for the absence of a significant relationship between Tea Party Attachment and fiscal conservatism and Tea Party Support and fiscal conservatism is the generally high level of fiscal conservatism throughout the Republican Conference. In both the 112th and 113th Congresses, Republicans were, as a group, quite conservative on fiscal issues. The average Republican scored more than 98 on the 0–100 NFIB scale (with higher scores indicating greater fiscal conservatism) in both the 112th and 113th Congresses, and with standard deviations below 5 in both cases, we can see a high level of fiscal conservatism throughout the Republican Conference.

If the variation in roll call voting is not due to distinctions in fiscal policy preferences, then on what issues might Tea Party Republicans be different from their fellow Conference members? We suggest that important differences may exist on issues relating to civil rights—particularly as they pertain to minorities and immigrants—and social policy issues.

Our measure of social policy is a collection of roll call votes derived from those used to create vote scores for the Heritage Action Scorecard and the FRC Action Scorecard. Heritage Action is the legislative affiliate of the conservative standard bearer, the Heritage Foundation. FRC Action is the legislative affiliate of the conservative Family Research Council. Examples of votes included in these scorecards for the 112th Congress are as follows:

- H.R. 2, Repeal of the Job-Killing Health Care Law Act (the ACA allows for taxpayer-funded abortions).
- H. Amdt. 95 to H.R. 1, Defunding of Planned Parenthood.
- H.R. 3, No Taxpayer Funding for Abortion Act.
- H. Amdt. 1084 to Commerce, Justice and Science Appropriations Act of 2013 (H.R. 5326)—would have prevented the use of Department of Justice funding to prohibit state legalization of medicinal marijuana.
- H.R. 1076, Ban on funding for National Public Radio.

Examples of votes included in these scorecards for the 113th Congress are as follows:

- H. Amdt. 2 to Continuing Resolution of 2015 (H.J. Res. 59)—would have delayed implementation of the ACA and provided for conscientious objections to the Department of Health and Human Services employer-mandated coverage for contraception.
- H.R. 1797, Pain-Capable Unborn Child Protection Act.
- H. Amdt. to H.R. 4486, Military Construction and Veterans Affairs Appropriations Act—would have allowed medical providers to recommend medicinal marijuana.
- H. Amdt. 101, Creation of additional work requirements for Supplemental Nutritional Assistance Program (SNAP) recipients and reduction in program spending by $31 billion.
- H. Amdt. 375 to H.R. 2397, Department of Defense Appropriations Act—would have required that chaplains have the endorsement of a qualified religious organization.
- H. Amdt. 748 to H.R. 4660, Commerce, Justice, Science and Related Agencies Appropriations Act—would restrict Department of Justice enforcement of the Controlled Substances Act in cases where states legalized the use of marijuana for medicinal purposes.

We use the roll call vote scores calculated by the Leadership Conference on Civil and Human Rights to measure voting patterns on civil rights issues. The Leadership Conference uses a relatively expansive understanding of "civil rights" to select votes for its perennial roll call vote scorecard. Votes selected from the 112th Congress included the following:

- Duncan Amendment to H.R.1, which would have cut field funding for the Legal Services Corporation.
- Webster Amendment to H.R. 5326, which would have eliminated funding for the American Community Survey.
- H.R. 1315, Consumer Financial Protection Bureau Restructuring, which was designed to weaken the Consumer Financial Protection Bureau (CFBP).
- H.R. 6079, Repeal of the Patient Protection and Affordable Care Act.
- Black Amendment to the Commerce, Justice and Science Appropriations bill for 2013, which was intended to prohibit the Department of Justice from challenging controversial state immigration laws.
- King Amendment to H.R. 2112, which would have prohibited the expenditure of federal funds for the Department of Justice settlement agreement with African American farmers in the *In re Black Farmers Discrimination Litigation.*
- King Amendment to Department of Homeland Security Appropriations Act (H.R. 5855), which would have prohibited funding for the enforcement of Executive Order 13166 directing federal agencies to provide foreign language support for those with marginal English capability.
- H. Amdt. 1075 prohibiting expenditure of Department of Justice funds from challenging any state voter identification law.

In the 113th Congress, the set of roll call votes included the following:

- H. Admt. 96 to H.R. 2216, which would have eliminated prevailing wage requirements.
- Ellison Amendment to H.R. 4660, which would have prohibited the use of federal funds to contract with commercials interests that had violated the Fair Labor Standards Act.
- Gosar Amendment to Transportation–Housing and Urban Development (HUD) appropriations bill, which prohibited HUD use of federal funds to implement "Affirmatively Furthering Fair Housing" regulation.
- H.R. 3193, Consumer Financial Protection Bureau Overhaul.
- King Amendment to H.R. 4660, prohibiting federal funds for "sanctuary cities."
- H.R. 5272, Defunding of "Deferred Action for Childhood Arrivals."
- H.R. 2217, Eliminating "Bed Mandate" for Immigration Detention and Eliminating Prosecutorial Discretion in Immigration Enforcement.
- H.R. 4935, Child Tax Credit Expansion.

Some of these roll call votes directly concern race and ethnicity. Others concern issues that have a greater impact on minority communities than on white communities. Any legislation relating to services or benefits for the poor or working class, for example, would have a disproportionate effect on minority communities because of the relatively high prevalence of minorities among the poor and working class.[11] Legislation relating to consumer protection, the child tax credit, prevailing wage requirements, legal services for the indigent, and protection of fair labor standards would clearly fit within this category.

The Republican Conference showed somewhat more variability on issues related to social conservatism and racial conservatism—core issues for supporters of the Tea Party movement in the general population. On our index of issues tapping social conservatism, the average Republican score, while still quite high, was not as high as the average score for fiscal conservatism. In the 112th Congress, the average score on the Social Conservatism index was 97, and in the 113th Congress, the average score was 84. The standard deviations for both indices were also higher than those for the Fiscal Conservatism indices, nearly 7 in the 112th Congress and nearly 18 in the 113th Congress.

Still, in the 112th Congress, the differences between the levels of social conservatism for members with varying associations with the Tea Party are quite small. Average scores on the Social Conservatism index are above 96 for all groups, with the average score for members receiving a 1 on the Tea Party Attachment index about one point higher than members receiving a 0 on the Tea Party Attachment index. Members receiving a 2 on the Tea Party Attachment index score just less than a point higher than members receiving a 1 on the Tea Party Attachment index. In a multivariate model for the Social Conservatism index in the 112th Congress, neither of the Tea Party Attachment variables are significant. We also find relatively little evidence that support from the Tea Party is associated with social conservatism. In the 112th Congress, the Tea Party Support index is actually negatively correlated (albeit very weakly) with scores on the Social Conservatism scale. In the 113th Congress, the correlation is less than 0.05. In neither congress is the Tea Party Support variable significant in the multivariate model.

However, in the 113th Congress, we do find a more robust relationship between attachment to the Tea Party and social conservatism. Averages for our Social Policy Roll Call index vary significantly across the levels of Tea Party Attachment in the 113th Congress (Figure 5.5).

The descriptive results suggest that legislators who made an effort to attach themselves to the Tea Party movement were more conservative on social policy issues than other Republicans. Significantly, more extensive efforts to attach to

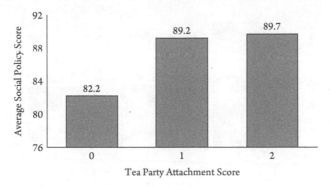

Figure 5.5 Tea Party Attachment and Social Policy, 113th Congress

the movement do not appear to be associated with greater social conservatism. These results find some support in the multivariate analysis. Those scoring a 1 on the Tea Party Attachment scale are clearly more socially conservative than those scoring 0; however, the dummy variable for those scoring a 2 on the Tea Party Attachment scale is not significant. Note that the descriptive difference between 1s and 2s is quite small. The small number of 2s also mitigates against a significant result. Still, we have more evidence of significant differences on social policy issues than we do on fiscal policy.

With civil rights issues—those most closely associated with the treatment of minority communities—there is even greater evidence of a distinction between legislators associated with the Tea Party movement and other Republicans. In terms of roll call voting on civil rights, we see that the average Republican was farther away from the endpoint—in this case, 0 on a 0–100 scale—than she or he was on our measure of fiscal conservatism in both the 112th and 113th Congresses. We also note that the standard deviation of scores on the Civil Rights scale was significantly higher than the standard deviation of the Fiscal Conservatism scale in both the 112th and 113th Congresses. We do not mean to suggest that there was wide variance within the Republican Conference on issues related to minority populations, but there was clearly far more variation than that which manifest on fiscal policy issues (Figure 5.6).

As attachment to the Tea Party increased, so did anti–civil rights roll call voting. Members who made little or no effort to attach themselves to the Tea Party had scores on the Civil Rights index that were more than twice as high as the scores of legislators who made greater efforts to attach themselves to the Tea Party. In fairness, even the Republicans in the lowest attachment category were still quite conservative—less than 10 on a scale from 0 to 100 (with higher scores indicating greater support for civil rights). But those members who made some significant effort to attach themselves to the Tea Party had scores below 5,

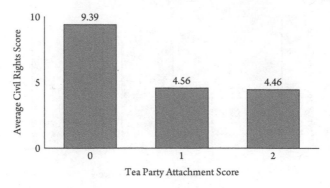

Figure 5.6 Tea Party Attachment and Civil Rights, 112th Congress

and the members who made the greatest effort to attach themselves to the Tea Party had even lower scores (though only slightly).

The multivariate analyses bear out the relationships we see in the descriptive results. Both of the Tea Party Attachment dummy variables—one for moderate attachment and one for extensive attachment—are substantively and statistically significant. The coefficients for dummy variables exceeded 3—actually –3— and given that the Republican average for the Civil Rights index in the 112th Congress was less than 7.5, this is a substantial effect. Also, both variables were significant at the .01 level. Though we saw little evidence of a Tea Party support effect in the descriptive data, the Tea Party Support variable is significant and signed appropriately in the multivariate analysis. This provides at least some limited evidence of a connection between Tea Party support and roll call voting on civil rights issues.

In the 113th Congress, we see a somewhat more complex relationship between Tea Party attachment and civil rights voting. While those in the "no effort to attach" category were more supportive of civil rights than those in the "moderate effort to attach" category, the Republicans in the "most effort to attach" category actually had roll call voting records that were most supportive of civil rights. Noting that the category capturing those who made the most extensive attachment efforts in the 113th Congress is quite small (fifteen members), it would be easy to overstate the significance of this result.[12] And while the multivariate results strongly support the distinctiveness of the "moderate attachment" and the "no attachment" Republicans, the distinctiveness of the small number of legislators who made the most concerted efforts to attach to the Tea Party movement is open to question. We also find no support in the multivariate analysis for the presence of a relationship between Tea Party support and civil rights voting.

Roll Call Voting and the Tea Party in the House

The limited research on the Tea Party in Congress presents conflicting findings regarding the relationship between legislators' association with the Tea Party and roll call voting patterns. Gallagher and Rock (2012) find no relationship with Tea Party Caucus membership—their measure of association—while Ragusa and Gaspar (2016) find evidence that incumbents who joined the Tea Party Caucus became significantly more conservative during the 112th Congress and that they maintained this conservatism during the 113th Congress. Bond (2013) finds a comparable general effect—opposition to the full range of the Obama agenda—but the analysis focuses solely on freshmen Republicans associated with the Tea Party movement. Our earlier work (Gervais and Morris 2012) indicates that Tea Party association influenced only a narrow set of roll calls, a finding similar to that of Bailey et al. (2012).

The existing literature suffers from a number of shortcomings. The analyses focus on different groups of Tea Party Republicans (sometimes freshmen, sometimes incumbents, sometimes both). The time frames of the analyses are sometimes limited. Bailey et al. (2012) base their analysis on well less than a year of roll call votes. And we (Gervais and Morris 2012) focused solely on the impact of Tea Party association on tax policy.

Without ignoring these issues, we argue that a more serious problem obscures our understanding of the breadth and depth of the differences between the policy preferences of Tea Party legislators and those of fellow members of the Republican Conference: a failure to adequately conceptualize the dimensionality of Tea Party association. We view Tea Party association as composed of Tea Party attachment (driven by members' political objectives) and Tea Party support (driven by Tea Party organizations' political objectives). This conceptualization of Tea Party association also leads us to rethink the measurement of Tea Party "members" in the first place. The strategic dynamics that produce different levels of Tea Party support are not the same as those that produce different levels of Tea Party attachment, and so Tea Party Caucus membership does not denote or connote the same relationship as does an endorsement by a Tea Party organization.[13] Nor do existing measures of Tea Party association fully capture either the dimension of Tea Party attachment or the dimension of Tea Party support. Members' efforts to attach themselves to the Tea Party movement go well beyond Tea Party Caucus membership (see Gervais and Taylor 2016), and Tea Party organizations can provide support beyond simple endorsements.

In Chapters 3 and 4, we demonstrated that Republican House members in the 112th and 113th Congresses varied on both dimensions of Tea Party association. While some made extensive efforts to attach themselves to the movement, others made no efforts at all. While some received various types of support from Tea Party organizations, others received nothing at all. Significantly, the presence of attachment did not ensure support, or vice versa. Certain members did have quite high scores on both Tea Party Attachment and Tea Party Support—those we refer to as the Black Tea Republicans—and others made no efforts to attach to the Tea Party movement, nor did they receive any support from it (the Coffee Republicans). But perhaps most interestingly, a number of legislators made extensive efforts to attach themselves to the Tea Party movement yet received little or no support from Tea Party organizations (Green Tea Republicans). And even extensive organizational support from the Tea Party was no guarantee that a legislator would reciprocate with an effort of attachment; in fact, some legislators never did (White Tea Republicans). Using a small set of examples, we illustrated the distinctive strategic dynamics producing the different types of "tea" and "coffee."

In this chapter, we generalize a key finding of the limited analysis in the preceding chapter: legislators who make an effort to attach themselves to the Tea Party movement have significantly more conservative roll call voting records than fellow Republicans who are not attached to the Tea Party. And those legislators who make the most extensive efforts at attachment—Tea Party Caucus membership, pro-Tea Party tweets, frequent attendance at Tea Party events likely to be covered or noticed by journalists—have the most conservative voting records of all. The results suggested by our brief examination of a handful of legislators are borne out by multivariate analyses of the Republican Conference in the 112th and 113th Congresses.

We also present evidence indicating that the ideological distinctiveness of Republicans intent on attaching themselves to the Tea Party movement is not a function of attitudes toward fiscal policy. The Tea Party is ostensibly a fiscally conservative, small-government movement, but we find little evidence that members' views on fiscal issues motivate them to attach to the Tea Party. Our data indicate that Republicans are quite fiscally conservative whether or not they align themselves with the Tea Party. Some very limited evidence suggests that Tea Party attachment is associated with social conservatism. To the extent that we can identify the policy areas where Tea Party attachment has a significant and noticeable effect, it would seem to be those dealing with civil rights and an array of minority communities. Legislators keen to align themselves with the Tea Party have voting records that stand out on issues related to fair housing, consumer protection, immigration policy, voter ID laws, healthcare, and programs providing support for the poor and working class. Each of these policies has a disproportionate effect on minority communities, and it is in these policy areas where the brand of conservatism espoused by Tea Party adherents in the general population is most clearly apparent.

We acknowledge the difficulties associated with the use of roll call vote scorecards created by organizations to highlight particular policy agendas. Members cast hundreds of votes in a congress, and focusing on a small set always has the potential to lead to a mischaracterization of legislators' policy preferences. But we do see clear patterns on important votes in key policy areas. And those patterns strongly suggest that the members making an effort to imbue themselves with the Tea Party brand are ideologically different from other Republicans on issues that disproportionately affect minority communities, particularly racial and ethnic minorities.

Counterintuitively, given the organizational history of the movement, fiscal policy does not divide Republicans along Tea Party lines. This appears to be true whether we are thinking in terms of members receiving Tea Party support or members attaching themselves to the Tea Party movement. It is worth remembering here that Tea Party support is rarely related to differences in members' policy preferences.

Finally, we want to highlight the fact that one of our control variables—a district-level measure of Tea Party membership—played a far more important role in determining roll call voting patterns in the 113th Congress than in the 112th Congress. At the same time that support for the Tea Party in the general electorate appeared to be declining, the significance of Tea Party activists increased, regardless of the level of Tea Party support received by a member or the member's efforts to attach to the Tea Party. We argue that the impact of the Tea Party movement in the House is longer-lasting and more pervasive than previously realized. These results are fully consistent with that argument.

In the next chapter, we examine the institutional distinctiveness of legislators associated with the Tea Party movement. Conventional wisdom suggests that the movement attracted backbench outsiders and freshman troublemakers, neither of whom were intent on actually making policy. Using bill sponsorship patterns and a new measure of legislative effectiveness, we evaluate the conventional wisdom. Did the Tea Party attract only legislators with marginal institutional capacity? That's the question for the next chapter.

Appendix

Tables 5A.1 and 5A.2 provide the full set of multivariate results for the roll call voting for the 112th and 113th Congress.

Table 5A.1 **Roll Call Voting in the 112th Congress**

Variable	DW-Nominate, First Dimension	Racial Policy Roll Call Score	Social Policy Roll Call Score	Fiscal Policy Roll Call Score
Tea Party Attachment = 1	**0.077** **(0.031)**	**−3.703** **(1.189)**	0.320 (1.380)	0.478 (0.648)
Tea Party Attachment = 2	**0.103** **(0.023)**	**−3.158** **(0.906)**	1.237 (0.787)	0.186 (0.555)
Tea Party Support Score	0.005 (0.006)	**−0.614** **(0.253)**	1.445 (0.212)	0.133 (0.105)
Obama 2008 Vote Share	**−0.006** **(0.001)**	**0.363** **(0.090)**	**−0.202** **(0.071)**	**−0.097** **(0.038)**
Margin of Victory for 112th Congress	−0.000 (0.000)	0.0134 (0.027)	−0.001 (0.017)	0.006 (0.012)
Years in Office	**−0.004** **(0.001)**	0.054 (0.062)	−0.065 (0.058)	−0.076 (0.052)
Tea Party 2010 Members	**0.000** **(0.000)**	−0.002 (0.003)	−0.002 (0.002)	**0.003** **(0.002)**
Leadership Party Status	−0.037 (0.070)	**−6.486** **(1.254)**	**3.019** **(0.883)**	0.710 (1.024)
Committee Chair Status	0.011 (0.028)	**−3.286** **(1.554)**	**2.762** **(0.948)**	−0.671 (1.114)
Hispanic Representative	0.001 (0.028)	**11.090** **(4.766)**	0.045 (1.611)	−0.188 (0.995)
Asian Representative	**−0.034** **(0.0172)**	(0.013) (1.069)	**2.947** **(1.053)**	**1.856** **(0.543)**
Gender	−0.029 (0.027)	1.429 (2.325)	−2.252 (2.101)	−0.315 (0.718)
Constant	**0.648** **(0.087)**	−6.870 (4.583)	**107.096** **(3.686)**	**101.395** **2.166**
Observations	241	240	240	240
R^2	0.307	0.260	0.082	0.105

Note: Coefficients are the results of OLS regression. Robust standard errors are in parentheses. Boldface indicates significance at $p < .05$ (one-tailed test).

Table 5A.2 **Roll Call Voting in the 113th Congress**

Variable	DW-Nominate, First Dimension	Racial Policy Roll Call Score	Social Policy Roll Call Score	Fiscal Policy Roll Call Score
Tea Party Attachment = 1	**0.099** **(0.021)**	−2.134 **(0.923)**	**5.360** **(2.133)**	0.632 (0.601)
Tea Party Attachment = 2	**0.162** **(0.076)**	5.149 (2.715)	1.662 (4.005)	−0.216 (0.910)
Tea Party Support Score	0.001 (0.007)	−0.079 (0.201)	0.087 (0.455)	0.155 0.099
Obama 2012 Vote Share	**−0.003** **(0.002)**	**0.410** **(0.087)**	**−0.887** **(0.188)**	**−0.135** **(0.054)**
Margin of Victory for 113th Congress	−0.034 (0.038)	1.620 (2.112)	−1.697 (5.457)	0.547 (1.000)
Years in Office	−0.003 (0.002)	**0.0135** **(0.081)**	−0.181 (0.154)	−0.049 (0.063)
Tea Party 2012 Members	**0.001** **(0.000)**	**−0.004** **(0.002)**	**0.006** **(0.003)**	**0.002** **(0.001)**
Leadership Party Status	0.068 (0.055)	**−4.859** **(1.148)**	−9.059 (11.415)	**1.351** **(0.493)**
Committee Chair Status	0.037 (0.037)	**−3.151** **(1.170)**	0.909 (3.006)	**2.045** **(0.716)**
Hispanic Representative	−0.002 (0.040)	5.007 (4.008)	2.130 (2.683)	**2.756** **(1.063)**
Asian Representative	Omitted	Omitted	Omitted	Omitted
Gender	−0.0570 (0.035)	−1.035 (1.280)	3.779 (2.865)	**1.219** **(0.425)**
Constant	**0.737** **(0.085)**	**−8.047** **(4.200)**	113.130 9.699	101.413 2.596
Observations	230	229	229	229
R^2	(0.226)	(0.256)	(0.224)	(0.125)

Note: Coefficients are the results of OLS regression. Robust standard errors are in parentheses. Boldface indicates significance at $p < .05$ (one-tailed test).

6

Tea Party-ness, Bill Sponsorship, and Legislative Effectiveness

The Tea Party can perhaps point to no greater single electoral victory than the defeat of House Majority Leader Eric Cantor (R-VA) in 2014. Cantor at the time was the second most powerful Republican in the House of Representatives and Speaker Boehner's (R-OH) presumed successor. Yet in what was billed as one of the "most stunning electoral upsets" in recent history, Cantor lost the Republican primary for the Seventh District of Virginia in June 2014 to David Brat (R-VA)—a little-known economics professor who was backed by local Tea Party activists (Cohn 2014). Barred from running as an independent under Virginia's "sore loser" law (Mascaro et al. 2014), Cantor resigned, with Brat finishing out Cantor's term in the 113th Congress (Weiner 2014).

Tea Party activists celebrated Brat's win as a victory for the Tea Party movement (Mascaro et al. 2014). But Tea Partiers were not alone in orchestrating the defeat of Cantor: as a local Democratic Party consultant named Brian Umana (2014) explained in a *Washington Post* op-ed, it was an alliance of activists on the right and left that helped the Tea Party underdog emerge triumphant. The motivation for liberal activists was simple: they viewed replacing the conservative majority leader with a Tea Party newcomer as an excellent trade-off; Brat's views might be more extreme than Cantor's, but he wouldn't be nearly as influential, or so the thinking went. After the election, however, Umana (2014) expressed some reservations about the outcome:

> Was my deal with the tea party an even trade? On one hand, Cantor used his power in the federal government to weaken our country and to make our politics more acrimonious, and I think one more tea party backbencher in the House, provided that House does not include Eric Cantor, is a good deal for Democrats. On the other hand, I had not realized that the tea party in Virginia could field a candidate as skilled as Dave Brat appears he may be.

This quote highlights a common assumption about Tea Party legislators—that they are neither effective in enacting policy nor eager to do so. This assumption, we think, is born of additional assumptions about the profile of the average Tea Party member. First, in contrast with established, long-tenured incumbents, Tea Party legislators are presumed to be political neophytes, generally lacking the seniority, stature, professional relationships, and overall experience to usher bills through the legislative process. An assertion made by a number of political observers is that the Tea Party movement, in its esteem for outsiders, has elevated individuals into political positions for which they are neither experientially nor temperamentally prepared (Tomasky 2014). This reputation is likely partially a result of some high-profile losses by "fringe" Tea Party candidates in Senate races deemed "very winnable" for Republicans (Spivak 2012). Observers assume that the ineptitude of Christine O'Donnell, Todd Akin (R-MO), Sharron Angle, and other failed Tea Party candidates is a trait shared by those Tea Party candidates who win their seats, too.

This view of Tea Partiers dovetails with the perspective that despite all the attention the Tea Party faction receives, it has yet to truly make its mark on policy in Congress. As one former senior congressional adviser explained, the tactics and tone of Tea Party members may influence the "terms of national debate ... [but the Tea Party] has yet to produce one real policy gain. Think about that. On what major federal issue has the tea party left a permanent, meaningful stamp since John Boehner claimed the speaker's gavel with its help?" (Clancy 2014). Adherents of this view can perhaps point to no greater example of this than former Tea Party Caucus chair Michele Bachmann (R-MN), whose reputation for being "more of a bomb thrower than a legislator" was undergirded by an almost nonexistent legislative record coupled with a national profile (Bresnahan and Sherman 2011; Linkins 2013). Tea Partiers may know how to get themselves in the news, so the thinking goes, but they do not understand or are unwilling to put in the work of ushering bills through the legislative process.

Second, observers on the left and right have suggested that Tea Partiers are not just backbenchers, but "intransigent backbenchers" (Douthat 2015), more concerned with obstruction and brinksmanship than with enacting policy. These observers are referring not only to Tea Partiers' conflicts with Democrats, but also to their conflicts with the Republican Party leadership—perhaps best exemplified by the 2013 government shutdown (e.g., Carney 2013). Such media coverage suggests that Tea Party members are less motivated than the average legislator to pass legislation and are more motivated to impede lawmaking. For example, when (in a reversal of Cantor's 2014 loss) incumbent Tea Partier Tim Huelskamp (R-KS) lost his primary race to the "establishment-backed" Roger Marshall in August 2016, observers suggested that voters were frustrated by the lack of legislating by Huelskamp and other Tea Party members. Reflecting on

Huelskamp's loss and the failure of Tea Party challengers to defeat any "establish-ment" Republicans in other primary races in 2016, the political director of the Chamber of Commerce told *Politico*:

> The lesson is that local beats national, and good candidates who focus on governing win elections. Instead of getting in the boat and rowing, and pushing back against President Obama, Senate Minority Leader Harry Reid and House Minority Leader Nancy Pelosi, some candidates chose to . . . only say "no" to everything and marginalize themselves. Voters want candidates who represent their districts and who are proposing real solutions. (Bade and Schneider 2016)

We doubt that Tea Party legislators are truly the obstructionist backbenchers with little interest in legislating they are often portrayed to be. For one, as we and others have noted previously, many long-tenured incumbents have adopted the Tea Party mantle. The Tea Party Caucus was launched in the summer of 2010 during the 111th Congress, and although the November 2010 election would usher in a new crop of Tea Party–aligned legislators, the first fifty-two Tea Party members were incumbents (Gervais and Morris 2012). While membership in the Tea Party Caucus, endorsements from Tea Party organizations, and pressure from activists might influence legislators, it does not stand to reason that this would make them less effective—rather, the type of legislation they sponsor might change. This appears to be the case with legislative behavior more broadly. As Ragusa and Gaspar (2016) show, those who joined the Tea Party Caucus or whose district was home to a number of Tea Party activists became more con-servative in the 112th Congress compared with the 111th (although, notably, endorsements from organizations did not contribute to this). Likewise, our results in the preceding chapter demonstrated that attachment to the Tea Party is associated with more conservative roll call voting.

Moreover, contrary to claims that the Tea Party has had no meaningful policy impact beyond stifling the creation of opponents' legislation, others suggest that the Tea Party's agenda has been adopted by Republicans in Congress (Capehart 2014). As Herman Cain, a 2012 candidate for the Republican nomination for president and a Tea Party darling, keenly put it, "I never expected tea party–backed candidates . . . to take Congress by storm . . . [b]ut I think the key thing is it's causing many of the incumbents to move more to the right relative to what the tea party message is" (Capehart 2014). Lest we think this is the biased opinion of a Tea Party supporter, journalists and scholars have suggested that a focus in the news media on who is winning and losing primaries is an insuffi-cient way to gauge the Tea Party's influence in Congress, belying their impact on the Republican Conference's rightward shifts (Skocpol 2014; Waldman 2014).

Skocpol (2014) argues that looking beyond primary wins and losses reveals that "Tea Party pincers [have kept] a stranglehold on GOP leaders and legislative agendas," and Tea Partiers have succeeded in pushing congressional Republicans farther right on policy issues. While part of this agenda-setting influence can be attributed to obstruction tactics by Tea Party legislators and by party leaders and other members crafting legislation amenable to the Tea Party factions, we expect that members associated with the Tea Party have contributed through active sponsorship of legislation.

Finally, as we have argued, some facets of the Tea Party movement—namely, the national organizations—are likely to support legislators with compatible policy objectives. But another factor in an organization's strategic calculus may be which members can successfully implement their agenda: if Tea Party organizations' resources are finite (which they are) and influencing policy is among their goals (a safe assumption), then it would make sense to direct resources to members with similar policy goals and to those they believe can help make these goals a reality. Helping to elect or re-elect a legislator who cannot legislate is a waste of time and resources.

In this chapter, we test these competing claims regarding the legislative performance of Tea Party members, examining whether our Tea Party Association measures predict both (1) less sponsorship activity and (2) less legislative effectiveness. That is, we investigate whether, during the 112th and 113th Congresses, Black, Green, and White Tea Republicans were any less likely to sponsor bills than Coffee Republicans and, ultimately, if they were just as effective at lawmaking.

For us, this is a key issue. We argue that Tea Party legislators—especially those who made a concerted effort to attach themselves to the movement—cultivated a representational relationship with their constituents in which their own status as Tea Partiers and their support for one or more of the reactionary dimensions of the Tea Party movement were crucial elements. Meaningful representation presumes some level of institutional effectiveness. If Tea Partiers are simply marginal backbenchers, their standing with—and influence on—constituents would be negligible. If the Tea Party "emperors" have no institutional "clothes," then it would be quite difficult for them to build the representational relationships that we presume exist.

Tea Party Association and Bill Sponsorship

We first consider the sponsorship behavior of Republican Conference members in the 112th and 113th Congresses. For data on bill sponsorship, we turn to Adler and Wilkerson's Congressional Bills Project, a dataset that includes every bill introduced in Congress since 1947, along with its sponsor and final status

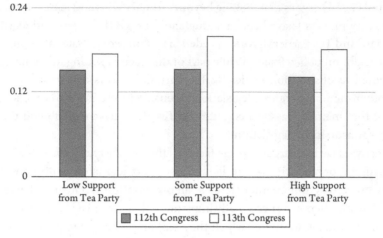

Figure 6.1 Percentage of Bills Sponsored That Passed the House by Tea Party Support.
Note: Differences in the percentage of sponsored bills passed at different levels of Tea Party Support were not significant in the 112th Congress ($F = 0.07, p > .05$) or the 113th Congress ($F = 0.35, p > .05$).

(i.e., did not pass the House, passed the House but did not become law, or became law). Using these data, we can determine whether those associated with the Tea Party were any less active than other Republicans in sponsoring legislation and can take a cursory look at how successful they were in ushering their bills through the legislative process.

We first look at an essential element of lawmaking for House members—ushering bills out of the House. Is the percentage of bills sponsored that passed the House lower among those with higher scores on our Tea Party measures? Figure 6.1 displays the average percentage of sponsored bills that made it out of the House by Tea Party Support.[1] Here, we break down Tea Party Support into three groups—those with the lowest scores on the standardized Support measure, those with medium scores on the Support measure, and those with high scores on the Support measure both the 112th and 113th Congresses.[2] As can be seen, within each Congress, there is little difference in success rates among members with different levels of support from the Tea Party. Those who received a medium level of support from the Tea Party in the 113th had slightly higher (20 percent)—but not statistically significant—rates of success than those with low (17.4 percent) and high support (18.1 percent), but otherwise success is evenly distributed. Somewhat notably, success rates were better overall in the 113th Congress (17.9 percent) than in the 112th (14.8 percent).

What about those who endeavored to link themselves with the Tea Party movement? Figure 6.2 displays the average percentage of bills that passed the House by Tea Party Attachment. In the 112th Congress, the average percentage of bills making it out of the House is somewhat lower among those with high

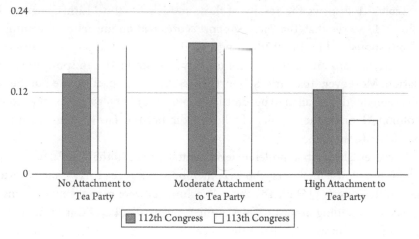

Figure 6.2 Percentage of Bills Sponsored That Passed the House by Tea Party Attachment.

Note: In the 112th Congress, there were no significant differences in the percentage of sponsored bills passed at different levels of Tea Party Attachment ($F = 1.48, p > .05$). In the 113th Congress, differences between the three groups are significant ($F = 2.54, p < .05$).

attachment (12.5 percent) than it is for those with some (19.4 percent) and no attachment (14.8 percent), but the differences between the groups are not significant. However, in the 113th Congress, members with high attachment saw only 8.0 percent of their bills pass the House—a full ten percentage points lower than the averages for those with some (18.5 percent) and no attachment (19.0 percent).

The percentage of bills passing the House can be misleading, however. It would not be correct to conclude that a member who sponsored only two bills with both passing the House is a more influential legislator than a member who sponsored thirty bills, with a third passing the House. Moreover, we cannot rule out other factors that might influence bill sponsorship activity (e.g., ideology, seniority) by looking at the means alone. We thus estimate a series of negative binomial regression models, in which the number of bills that a member sponsored, the number of the member's bills that passed the House, and the number of the member's bills that did not pass the House are regressed on Tea Party Support and Tea Party Association. In addition, we also consider whether the Tea Party Association variables predict the number of sponsored bills that did and did not become law. As we have done in previous chapters, we break Tea Party Attachment into two dichotomous variables. We also control for a number of individual factors, including the member's ideology (first-dimension DW-Nominate scores), the member's gender, the year the member took office, whether the member held a party leadership position, and whether the member held a committee leadership post.

Table 6.1 displays the results of these models for the 112th Congress. In column 1, we see that Tea Party Support scores had no impact on the number of bills sponsored in the 112th Congress. That is, those supported by external Tea Party groups and activists were not any less productive in sponsoring legislation. Moreover, Tea Party Support scores had no impact on the number of bills sponsored that failed to become law (column 2) or failed to pass the House (column 3), or on the number of bills that did become law (column 4) or pass the House (column 5).

However, although a moderate level of attachment to the Tea Party was not significant, House members who were members of the Tea Party Caucus during the 112th Congress (High Tea Party Attachment) were more likely to sponsor legislation. Holding other variables at their means, Tea Party Caucus members sponsored 3.1 more bills than other members of the Republican conference.[3] It is important to note that although those who attached themselves to the Tea Party may have sponsored more bills, this did not necessarily translate into legislative success. As shown in column 2 of Table 6.1, High Tea Party Attachment had a positive effect on the number of sponsored bills that did not become law—members with high attachment to the Tea Party producing about 3.0 more failed bills than those with weaker or no ties.

The area where Caucus membership (High Tea Party Attachment) had the most impact in the 112th Congress was on the number of bills sponsored that did not pass the House (column 3). That is, members who made efforts to connect themselves to the movement produced a larger body of sponsored bills that did not make it out of the House. Controlling for a number of individual factors, a member with the strongest attachment (a Caucus member) saw about 16.9 bills fail to pass a House vote, while all other members averaged 13.6.

Interestingly, as shown in columns 4 and 5, neither Tea Party Attachment variable affected the number of successful bills in terms of becoming law and passing the House. That is, those with the strongest attachment to the Tea Party produced laws at a rate comparable to other members of the Republican Conference. They simply produced more failed bills. We would be wrong, then, to categorize them as less eager or effective legislators—less efficient perhaps but, if anything, more eager than other legislators to produce legislation. Keeping in mind that non-Tea Party Caucus members with some attachment (as indicated by Tea Party Tweets and Tea Party Salience scores) and those receiving support from the Tea Party performed no differently than those with no attachment, controlling for other factors, it is fairly clear that members associated with the Tea Party in the 112th Congress were not a do-nothing group of backbenchers who merely obstructed the passage of bills they did not support.

That members of the Tea Party Caucus introduced more failed bills, on average, than other members is an interesting finding. We see two plausible explanations.

Table 6.1 **Tea Party Association and Bill Sponsorship in the 112th Congress**

Variable	Total Bills Sponsored (1)	Total Bills Sponsored: Did Not Become Law (2)	Total Bills Sponsored: Did Not Pass House (3)	Total Bills Sponsored: Became Law (4)	Total Bills Sponsored· Passed House (5)
Tea Party Support	−0.01 (0.022)	−0.01 (0.02)	−0.01 (0.02)	−0.08 (0.09)	−0.04 (0.05)
High Tea Party Attachment	**0.17** **(0.10)**	**0.17** **(0.10)**	**0.21** **(0.11)**	0.20 (0.31)	−0.10 (0.22)
Moderate Tea Party Attachment	0.10 (0.12)	0.10 (0.12)	0.08 (0.13)	−0.03 (0.41)	0.06 (0.28)
DW-Nominate	−0.10 (0.24)	−0.08 (0.25)	−0.19 (0.27)	−1.17 (0.88)	0.36 (0.60)
Gender	0.01 (0.13)	0.02 (0.13)	0.02 (0.14)	−0.49 (0.47)	−0.04 (0.30)
Year Took Office	**−0.01** **(0.01)**	**−0.01** **(0.01)**	**−0.01** **(0.01)**	−0.02 (0.01)	−0.01 (0.01)
Party Leadership	−0.06 (0.22)	−0.07 (0.22)·	−0.37 (0.25)	0.18 (0.69)	**1.01** **(0.47)**
Committee Leadership	**0.36** **(0.15)**	**0.32** **(0.15)**	0.24 (0.16)	**1.08** **(0.38)**	**0.97** **(0.32)**
Constant	**27.44** **(10.99)**	**26.30** **(11.23)**	**26.94** **(12.08)**	44.41 (32.36)	22.94 (24.85)
Log Likelihood	−867.23	−862.47	−45.90	−243.16	−485.90
Observations	240	240	240	240	240
Pseudo R^2	0.01	0.01	0.01	0.05	0.03

Note: Coefficients are results of negative binomial regression. Standard errors are in parentheses. Boldface indicates significance at $p < .05$ (one-tailed test).

First, Caucus members, energized by the Tea Party movement, were merely more exuberant than other members, sponsoring bills that had little chance of success. Second, while the Republican Party may have embraced those with Tea Party ties to achieve electoral success and reclaim the House of Representatives in the 2010 elections, Tea Party members (including incumbents) were initially marginalized, needing to sponsor more bills to produce similar levels of successful legislation. These explanations are not mutually exclusive, and we see both as playing a role in this institutional dynamic.

It was a different story in the 113th House. With the Tea Party Caucus ceasing to operate, opportunities to align with the Tea Party in an institutional sense diminished, consisting mainly of alignment with the Amash-led libertarian Liberty Caucus. Indeed, as shown in Table 6.2, neither high nor moderate attachment to the Tea Party had any significant impact on any of the five count variables. That is, the significant differences displayed in Figure 6.2 disappear when other factors are controlled for.

The change between the 112th and 113th Congresses may be due in part to the changing nature of attachment to the Tea Party, but we see this change as indicative of the Tea Party forging more influence in Congress. If those who chose to associate with the Tea Party were regarded as insurgent outsiders prior to or during the 113th, efforts to institutionally marginalize them were clearly ineffective. That those linked to the Tea Party produced roughly the same number of successful bills as other members could be evidence of the Tea Party's becoming embedded within the Republican establishment—and Tea Party policy positions became more mainstream.

As evidence of this latter explanation, in the 113th Congress Tea Party Support scores had a positive relationship with the number of sponsored bills that became law. In other words, other factors being controlled for, the more support a member received from Tea Party groups and activists, the larger the member's tally of bills signed into law. Those backed by the movement did not sponsor more bills or have more unsuccessful bills. Interestingly, Tea Party–supported legislators also did not see more bills pass the House, but when their bills did make it out of the House, they were more successful than bills sponsored by those with less or no support from the movement.

In addition to suggesting the "mainstreaming" of Tea Party legislators, this finding aligns with a point that we and others have made: Tea Party organizations are strategic. With finite resources to divvy out, the most rational behavior is to support legislators who they believe can successfully shepherd their policies into law—and the percentage of bills passing the House that were ultimately enacted is higher among those aided by the Tea Party movement. House Republicans below the 50th percentile in Tea Party Support saw 24.7 percent of their bills that passed the House signed into law, on average. This rate of success does not improve much through the 95th percentile (around 25.2 percent). However, among the legislators in the top 5 percent of Tea Party Support,[4] the rate swells to 45.5 percent! Note that we are not talking about a huge collection of bills (ten becoming law of twenty-one that passed the House), and three of these legislators did not see any bills pass the House at all. Yet, astonishingly, only two members among this group were not freshman legislators[5]—and even these two members were relatively new to Congress (Jason Chaffetz (R-UT), came to office in 2009, and Paul Gosar (R-AZ) was among those in the first Tea Party wave of 2011).

Table 6.2 **Tea Party Association and Bill Sponsorship in the 113th Congress**

Variable	Total Bills Sponsored (1)	Total Bills Sponsored: Did Not Become Law (2)	Total Bills Sponsored: Did Not Pass House (3)	Total Bills Sponsored: Became Law (4)	Total Bills Sponsored: Passed House (5)
Tea Party Support	0.03 (0.02)	0.03 (0.02)	0.03 (0.02)	**0.11** **(0.04)**	0.02 (0.04)
High Tea Party Attachment	−0.13 (0.18)	−0.12 (0.18)	−0.06 (0.19)	−0.47 (0.51)	−0.57 (0.36)
Moderate Tea Party Attachment	−0.04 (0.10)	−0.05 (0.10)	−0.01 (0.11)	0.13 (0.23)	−0.15 (0.18)
DW-Nominate	0.09 (0.24)	0.12 (0.24)	0.07 (0.26)	−0.58 (0.60)	0.13 (0.43)
Gender	0.12 (0.15)	0.13 (0.15)	0.05 (0.16)	0.09 (0.35)	0.24 (0.26)
Year Took Office	**−0.02** **(0.01)**	**−0.01** **(0.01)**	**−0.01** **(0.01)**	**−0.03** **(0.01)**	**−0.02** **(0.01)**
Party Leadership	−0.29 (0.25)	−0.31 (0.25)	**−0.75** **(0.27)**	0.19 (0.53)	**0.76** **(0.39)**
Committee Leadership	−0.04 (0.15)	−0.11 0.03	**−0.43** **(0.16)**	**0.92** **(0.25)**	**0.92** **(0.23)**
Constant	**32.09** **(10.65)**	**30.66** **(10.82)**	**26.25** **(11.02)**	**66.37** **(21.23)**	**46.20** **(18.45)**
Log Likelihood	−804.00	−796.05	−763.75	−241.75	−481.64
Observations	230	230	230	230	230
Pseudo R^2	0.01	0.01	0.01	0.07	0.05

Note: Coefficients are results of negative binomial regression. Standard errors are in parentheses. Boldface indicates significance at $p < .05$ (one-tailed test).

To further parse the legislative success of those backed by the Tea Party, we took a closer look at the ten bills sponsored by those in the top 5 percent of Tea Party Support that became law. Three of the bills were ceremonial, involving the naming of federal buildings (two post offices and a veterans affairs center), and two focused on transportation (regulating Transportation Security Administration (TSA) technology acquisition programs and limiting fees charged to passengers of air carriers). The remaining five all concerned the federal regulation of public lands, an issue that has been portrayed as a shibboleth of

Tea Party Republicans from western states (Cottle 2016; Marcotte 2016; Tobias 2016a,b).[6] Indeed, we find that Tea Party Support predicts sponsorship of unsuccessful public lands legislation in the 112th Congress (see Table 6A.1 in the appendix).[7] That Tea Party Support predicts successful sponsorship of bills in the 113th Congress—some of which deal with public lands—is suggestive of a Tea Party policy agenda gaining traction over time. However, we will be careful not to make too much of this: only one of the bills involved devolution of federal lands to state control, and all received bipartisan support. In general, then, none of the bills are particularly significant (at least from an ideological standpoint)—and so perhaps it is no surprise that they became laws. Regardless, in the context of a congress where few laws passed (see DeSilver 2014), the success of Tea Party–backed members ushering their bills into law indicates that they were not a marginalized fringe group in the 113th Congress, nor do they appear to have been a group uninterested in legislating.

Legislative Effectiveness

We have thus far, with the exception of the ten bills sponsored by members with the highest Tea Part Attachment scores, treated all bills the same. However, they clearly are not the same—successfully ushering a bill naming a post office into law, for example, is a much less significant legislative accomplishment than one changing the tax code. We thus turn to a more rigorous measure of legislative effectiveness—the LES-to-Benchmark ratio developed by Volden and Wiseman (2014)—and calculate a legislator's effectiveness by comparing the legislator with other members of similar status within her or his party.

One part of this measure is the Legislative Effectiveness Score (LES), a multistage approach to measuring members' legislative effectiveness. The LES approach incorporates not only the number of bills each member sponsors, but how many make it to each step in the legislative process (action in committee, passed out of committee, action on the House floor, passed out of the House, passed into law). Bills are weighted by their significance, with commemorative bills counting the least and substantively significant bills counting the most. The second part of the LES-to-Benchmark ratio are Benchmark scores, which are predicted values for each member's LES based on the member's seniority in Congress, whether she or he was a member of the majority party, and whether she or he was chair of a committee/subcommittee. To formulate the LES-to-Benchmark ratio, we follow the lead of Volden and Wiseman and simply divide the true LES by the Benchmark score. Thus, a higher score indicates above-average legislative effectiveness for a member's profile.[8] The range of scores in the 112th Congress was 0 to 8.75, and the range in the 113th was 0 to 6.03.

Table 6.3 displays the results of two models, one for the 112th Congress and one for the 113th Congress, with the LES-to-Benchmark ratios regressed onto the Tea Party Association variables (Tea Party Attachment is divided into two dichotomous variables). The normal set of control variables are included as well.

The results for the 112th Congress are shown in column 1. Tea Party Support is not significant, indicating that those backed by the Tea Party movement were just as effective legislators as those of similar standing in the chamber. While

Table 6.3 **Tea Party Association and Legislative Effectiveness Scores Relative to Benchmark Scores**

Variable	112th Congress (1)	113th Congress (2)
Tea Party Support	0.03	0.02
	(0.03)	(0.03)
High Tea Party Attachment	0.19	−0.13
	(0.15)	(0.20)
Moderate Tea Party Attachment	**0.36**	0.12
	(0.21)	(0.18)
DW-Nominate	**−0.87**	−0.37
	(0.44)	(0.34)
Gender	−0.06	0.06
	(0.18)	(0.19)
Year Took Office	−0.00	−0.01
	(0.01)	(0.01)
Party Leadership	0.46	−0.03
	(0.96)	(0.36)
Committee Leadership	0.11	0.12
	(0.22)	(0.31)
Constant	2.05	19.92
	(15.11)	(15.29)
Observations	242	230
R^2	0.04	0.02

Note: Coefficients are results of OLS regression. Robust standard errors are in parentheses. Boldface indicates significance at $p < .05$ (one-tailed test).

High Tea Party Attachment (those who joined the Tea Party Caucus) was also insignificant, Moderate Tea Party Attachment had a positive effect on LES-to-Benchmark ratios. That is, those who made some effort to align themselves with the Tea Party movement without joining Bachmann's Tea Party Caucus were more effective than similar legislators who did not do so. In the model for the 113th Congress (column 2), no variable was significant—including the measures of Tea Party Association.

Tea Partiers as Legislators

The results of the LES-to-Benchmark analysis reveal that members associated with the Tea Party were not any less effective at legislating than Coffee (or "establishment") Republicans. Indeed, in the 112th Congress, those who attached themselves to the Tea Party via means other than becoming members of the official Tea Party Caucus were more effective legislators than members with similar profiles. Considered along with findings that, in the 112th, Tea Party Caucus members actively sponsored (all types) of legislation and that, in the 113th, greater support from the Tea Party movement was associated with a larger number of bills successfully ushered into law, it is very difficult to conclude that Tea Party legislators are less effective in enacting policy or less eager to do so.

We can point to some evidence of Tea Partiers lacking efficiency—those with high Tea Party Attachment in both the 112th and 113th Congresses struggled more with bills getting enacted into law (although factors other than Tea Party Attachment may account for this in the 113th, as seen in Table 6.2). Perhaps this is evidence of some resistance to the Tea Party policy goals. However, when considering the substantive importance of the legislation and how members with similar profiles performed, we find that Tea Party members performed comparably. As Brian Umana, the Democratic consultant who helped defeat Eric Cantor learned, Tea Party–aligned legislators may be more skilled than many presume. Rather than merely obstructing from the backbench or finding themselves marginalized by a skeptical Republican Conference and leadership, Black, Green, and White Tea Republicans appear to want to enact policy and in turn enjoy some institutional cachet. There is simply no evidence that Tea Party legislators were less institutionally active or less effective than their more mainstream Republican colleagues.

That is not to say that some Tea Party legislators have not embraced brinkmanship tactics or that the policies enacted by Tea Party legislators are no different from the bills sponsored by Coffee members. And other legislative behavior of Tea Party members does differ from that of Republicans not associated with the movement: as we showed in the preceding chapter, Tea Party Attachment predicts more conservative voting patterns. Moreover, it says nothing about the extra-legislative behavior of Tea Party members, including the nature of their rhetoric and their supposed expressed disdain for compromise and bipartisanship. In the next chapter, we take a close a look at the rhetoric of Tea Party members, focusing on their digital discourse.

Appendix

Table 6A.1 **Tea Party Support and Sponsorship of Public Lands Legislation That Did Not Become Law in the 112th Congress**

Variable	Total Public Lands Bills Sponsored: Did Not Become Law
Tea Party Support	**0.14**
	(0.08)
High Tea Party Attachment	0.27
	(0.28)
Moderate Tea Party Attachment	0.43
	(0.33)
DW-Nominate	−0.60
	(0.75)
Gender	−0.17
	(0.38)
Year Took Office	**−0.04**
	(0.02)
Party Leadership	**−1.96**
	(1.13)
Committee Leadership	0.50
	(0.39)
Constant	**77.19**
	(30.76)
Observations	239
Pseudo R^2	0.04

Note: Coefficients are results of negative binomial regression. Standard errors are in parentheses. Boldface indicates significance at $p < .05$ (one-tailed test).

7

Tea Party-ness and
Public Presentation

Aversion-Inducing and Anti-Deliberative Rhetoric

We have thus far considered how the constituencies and legislative behavior of members associated with the Tea Party movement differ from those of mainstream, Coffee Republicans. In this chapter and the next, we examine Tea Party members' extra-legislative behavior—namely, how they present themselves on Twitter to the public. Myriad essays have described the angry, outrageous, anti-deliberative behavior of those associated with the Tea Party—including that of legislators. As a writer for the liberal outlet the *Daily Kos* put it:

> Some of the things that Tea Party politicians and candidates say is pretty outrageous. Recently candidates or commentators aligned with the Tea Party have called for succession (sic), mutiny, and armed revolt. They routinely call Obama a Muslim, and a Senate Candidate in Wyoming called Hillary Clinton the "anti-Christ." They have convinced themselves that liberals are destroying the nation, and they must do something to stop it. They're angry at the state of affairs, and desperate to do something. So how angry is the Tea Party? (Coblenz 2014)

Likewise, David Brooks (2016), the conservative *New York Times* columnist, has argued that the Tea Party exemplifies people who

> delegitimize compromise and deal-making. They're willing to trample the customs and rules that give legitimacy to legislative decision-making if it helps them gain power. Ultimately, they don't recognize other people. They suffer from a form of political narcissism, in which they don't accept the legitimacy of other interests and opinions. They

don't recognize restraints. They want total victories for themselves and their doctrine.

These quotes reflect the conventional wisdom about the Tea Party in government. Journalists and pundits have made a wide range of claims about the dispositions and behavior of Tea Party legislators and how they differ in tone and tactic from those of "establishment" Republicans (e.g., Blodget 2013; Cilizza 2013; Egan 2012; Gans 2013). Often, they are described as employing overheated "red meat" populist rhetoric, with the aim of confronting President Obama, Democrats, and the Republican establishment. A significant amount of attention has been given to their putative commitment not to compromise and their broader anti-deliberative approach to politics (e.g., Frum 2010; Gans 2013; Klein 2013; Malone 2011).

The ascendency of Donald Trump prompted renewed efforts among observers to trace the GOP embrace of (or capitulation to) Trump's well-documented brashness (see Barbaro 2015; Lee and Quealy 2016) to the rise of Sarah Palin and the Tea Party (Gonyea 2016). As former Obama chief of staff William Daley (2015) penned in the *Washington Post*, "Palin became a Fox News fixture, reinforcing the newly formed tea party's 'never compromise' demands. Bombast, not reason, reigned. Now the 'settle for flash' aura of Palin's candidacy looks like a warning that the party was prizing glib, red-meat rhetoric over reasoned solutions."

The assertion that Tea Party rhetoric is angry, heated, and anti deliberative has not just been leveled by those outside conservative circles, as the above quote from the David Brooks article suggests. Supporters of the Republican "establishment" have criticized the "extreme rhetoric" of the Tea Party and its rejection of bipartisanship while lamenting the absence of William F. Buckley, the conservative icon and founder of the *National Review*—the traditional conservative flagship news source (Welch 2012). Other self-identified conservatives not aligned with the Tea Party have bemoaned the movement's promotion of candidates who object to compromise and its rejection of candidates who express an openness to negotiation over policy (Friedersdorf 2011).

But are these claims about Tea Party rhetoric just media narrative, or are the behavior and rhetoric of Tea Party–aligned legislators truly more heated, confrontational, uncivil, and anti-deliberative? In this chapter, we begin our analysis by focusing on the affective undercurrent of legislators' social media rhetoric and the extent to which their behavior is anti-deliberative. We continue this analysis in Chapter 8, examining whether Tea Party rhetoric is more uncivil than that of establishment Republicans and examining its similarities to the rhetoric of Donald Trump.

Affect in Tea Party Rhetoric

From the outset, the Tea Party movement has been linked with anger. The movement has been characterized as "boiling mad,"[1] while "seething anger" is said to serve as "an indigenous aspect of the Tea Party movement" (Bernstein 2010). Some empirical evidence backs up these claims: at least through the end of 2012, more than half of Tea Party supporters said they were angry, compared with less than one in five in the general public saying the same (Montopoli 2012).

Although descriptions of the Tea Party as angry are widespread, research on the movement suggests there are alternative emotions to consider. One is anxiety. In fact, scholars have argued that extensive out-group anxiety is what differentiates Tea Party sympathizers from mainstream conservatives (Barreto et al. 2011). In their observations of Tea Party activist meetings, Skocpol and Williamson (2012) describe witnessing an anxiety based not on racism but on fear over societal decline—with immigrant and young people at the vanguard—and, at least at the meetings they attended, fear was more common than anger.

We might expect that Tea Party elites channel the anger or anxiety supposedly underlying the broader movement and that the rhetoric of these elites, as fixtures of the movement, incorporates the same emotions. Anecdotal descriptions of the Tea Party faction in Congress suggest that the group is driven by the same organic emotion as the broader movement. For example, as Donald Trump's competitiveness became a reality in the fall of 2015, the Freedom Caucus flexed its muscles by removing Boehner (R-OH) and blocking McCarthy (R-CA), leading some to conclude that the uprisings were one in the same: that both lawmakers and activists aligned with the Tea Party were fueled by frustration with the Republican establishment (Hook and O'Connor 2015).

An alternative view is that Tea Party leaders themselves are not angry or anxious but that their rhetoric fuels these existing emotions in the public. As we discussed in Chapter 2, pessimism about the future, a sense of loss, a sense that the federal government looks out for Americans other than themselves, a deep concern about cultural change and immigration, and a nostalgia for the past are feelings that Republicans, especially Americans identifying with the Tea Party, are likely to hold (Jones et al. 2015). Data from the 2015 Public Religion Institute survey reveal that the sentiment that America's "greatest days are behind us" is higher among Tea Party identifiers than among other Republicans, Democrats, and independents. Moreover, while this sentiment increased among all groups from 2012 to 2015, it increased the most among Tea Party identifiers. With the 2016 presidential primary season around the corner, pessimism and resentment were especially strong among those who identified with the Tea Party (Jones et al. 2015).

The subsequent upheaval of American politics that Donald Trump's ascendancy represents did not come out of nowhere. In all likelihood, any monocausal explanation will be insufficient. Rather, a confluence of factors made Trump's rise possible. Data collected by the collaborative Democracy Fund Voter Study Group reveal that those who voted for Trump in the general election were not a single homogeneous bloc, but a coalition of voters. However, perhaps the group most critical to Trump's victory were so-called American preservationists, who, Elkins (2017) argues, "comprise the core Trump constituency that propelled him to victory in the early Republican primaries." Characteristics of American preservationists include a low level of formal education, a desire to be around people similar to themselves, and a belief that the system is "rigged." In addition, compared with other groups in the Trump coalition,

> [t]hey are far more likely to have a strong sense of their own racial identity . . . They take the most restrictionist approach to immigration— staunchly opposing not just illegal but legal immigration as well, and intensely supporting a temporary Muslim travel ban. They feel the greatest amount of angst over race relations: they believe that anti-white discrimination is as pervasive as other forms of discrimination, and they have cooler feelings (as measured on a feeling thermometer scale) toward minorities. They agree in overwhelming numbers that real Americans need to have been born in America or have lived here most of their lives and be Christian. (Elkins 2017)

This account suggests that a key to Trump's early success was appealing to a group of white Americans who were resentful of out-groups and believed they were losing out to minorities. The sociologist Arlie Russell Hochschild (2016) suggests that the groundwork for such resentment was laid well before 2015. She argues that the social movements of the 1960s and 1970s left white Americans with the sense that they were " 'waiting in line' and laid down a simmering fire of resentment which was to flame up years later as the Tea Party" (2016, 212). All that Tea Party candidates needed to do to take advantage of this latent antipathy was douse the simmering fire with a little gas. The right rhetoric on the campaign trail could mobilize individuals mourning a loss of a way of life and predisposed to be resentful.

Another hypothesis concerning the affective undercurrent of Tea Party members' rhetoric, then, is that it is designed to foment or aggravate broader cultural and economic resentment. The language used would not come across as angry but would instead describe a world in decline, a sad state of affairs in which hardworking whites were losing out. Such discourse would intimate that their culture was being subverted, that resources were being directed to other groups, and that elites and institutions had failed them. Ultimately, the rhetoric would incorporate a language of loss, suffering, injustice, and blame—language we associate with sadness.

Sad rhetoric used to drum up support for populist movements has been observed outside of the American national scene. In fostering a politics of resentment, in generating feelings that the system is unfair and emphasizing loss, British political parties fueled reactionary populism among the white working class prior to the 2010 parliamentary elections (Hoggett et al. 2013).

Stateside, this has been observed at the subnational level and in the rhetoric of prominent politicians aligned with the Tea Party. In an extensive qualitative analysis, Cramer (2016a, 24) documents how Republicans in Wisconsin, particularly Governor Scott Walker, tapped "into resentment to win elections and further their policy goals" by using this type of rhetoric. Walker, who "campaigned on a Tea Party platform" and won the Wisconsin governorship in the movement's wave election of 2010, successfully tapped into the rural consciousness of many Wisconsinites, and their view that the state spent an extravagant number of tax dollars on lazy, out-of-touch urbanites and public employees, while few public expenditures were directed toward hardworking (and deserving) rural folks (Cramer 2016a, 184–203).

Similar descriptions characterize the rhetoric of other American politicians linked to the Tea Party. Engels (2015, 110, 116) identifies the Tea Party as a movement that "seeks to capitalize on widespread feelings of powerlessness, frustration, and victimhood" suggests that the rhetoric of Tea Party politicians encourages white Americans to blame and resent liberals and minority groups for the failure of neoliberal economic policies. In particular, Engels (2015, 125) focuses on the rhetoric of the most "vocal representative of such victimage," Sarah Palin, which, he argues, "amplifies, rather than alleviates, the feelings of injustice and loss."

Likewise, Ted Cruz's (R-TX) rhetoric is said to incorporate a "sadness [that] reflects his belief that the United States is drifting aimlessly . . . Whether the topic is 'the Washington cartel' or illegal immigration, Cruz conveys a feeling that the status quo is painfully unacceptable. His look of sorrow effectively reinforces his call for change. It also suggests that he empathetically feels the voters' pain" (Hill 2015).

It is possible that Walker, Palin, Cruz, and others genuinely feel a sense of sadness about the state of the country. Yet we might expect to detect "sad" language in the rhetoric of Tea Party members because it plays into the narrative that members of the white working class have faced loss, injustice, devastation, suffering, and abandonment at the hands of an establishment, or "Washington cartel," that places the interests of other groups first. This rhetoric plays on an indigenous pessimism—it confirms and reminds listeners that establishment policies have failed them, that they are losing out, and that things will continue to get worse.

Affect in the Rhetoric of the Tea Party Legislators

We test the claim that House members attached to the Tea Party were especially likely to use resentful rhetoric in order to appeal to simmering resentment among some white voters. In addition, we begin to make the case that one factor that paved the way for Trump was the rhetoric espoused by Tea Party members in the years before 2015. To do so, we again turn to the official tweet dataset. As before, we treat the tweets as if they were posted directly by a member, even though a staffer or third-party organization might be running the account, because the messages have the tacit approval of the legislator. That is, the tweets are effectively the voice of the member, even when she or he is not the individual typing the tweet.

There are several reasons to focus on members' rhetoric in tweets. First, the number of Americans following elected officials on Twitter is growing, and thus legislators' tweets have the potential to directly affect public opinion (e.g., Anderson 2015; Gainous and Wagner 2013). Yet members of the public do not need to be followers of legislators or even Twitter users to be influenced by their posts, as traditional news media increasingly report on what elites tweet (Lefky 2015). The attention Donald Trump's tweets have received—both before and after he became president—is the most obvious case (Grynbaum and Ember 2016). But Trump's tweets are not the only ones that receive coverage. For example, the *Washington Post* reported on Republicans' social media reaction to Obama's January 2016 gun control announcement and featured the verbatim tweets of Trent Franks (R-AZ), Louie Gohmert (R-TX), Charles Boustany (R-LA), and Kevin McCarthy, among others (Van Dongen 2016).

In addition, a raft of recent studies has found that what political elites (especially members of Congress) tweet about can influence the issues that traditional news media cover[2] and that members are likely to be strategic about which issues to prioritize on Twitter in order to influence journalists (Conway et al. 2015; Neuman et al. 2014; Shapiro and Hemphill 2016). As such, when legislators' tweets focus on the tribulations and dangers of Obamacare, a stagnant economy, the decline of manufacturing jobs, or illegal immigration, these issues are more likely to be covered in mainstream news sources. In short, what members say in their tweets can directly and indirectly influence public opinion, and we speculate that emotional tweets are especially likely to be noticed, retweeted, and interpreted as newsworthy. Finally, to the extent that the issues legislators tweet about are similar to the issues they emphasize in other media, such as television ads (and there is some evidence they are—see Kang et al. 2018), then their rhetoric in tweets should serve as a proxy for their public communication more generally.

To measure affect in legislators' tweets, we turn to Linguistic Inquiry and Word Count (LIWC), a text-analysis program developed by psychologists at the University of Texas at Austin (Tausczik and Pennebaker 2010), capable of measuring affective, linguistic, and cognitive components in texts.[3] LIWC has been previously utilized to analyze political-themed tweets (Tumasjan et al. 2010),[4] including the overall levels of positive and negative affect in the posts, as well as discrete emotions like anger, anxiety, and sadness. To calculate anger scores, LIWC searches for a set of 230 words or word stems, a set of 116 words/stems to calculate anxiety scores, and 136 words/stems to calculate sadness scores.[5]

An average of just less than 4 percent of the words used by Republicans in the 112th Congress were considered affective, with about 3 percent associated with positive emotions and 1 percent associated with negative emotions. The numbers were nearly identical in the 113th Congress: slightly more than 4 percent of the words members used, on average, were affective, the majority of which (more than 3 percent) were again words associated with positive emotions. Republican members of Congress, then (at least in the 112th and 113th Congresses), were much more likely to tweet positive words than negative words. Still, about 1 of every 100 words a member tweeted was negative. What percentage of words were associated with each of the discrete emotions of anger, anxiety, and sadness? Table 7.1 displays the average percentages of angry, anxious, and sad words used by Republicans in the 112th and 113th Congresses.

In the 112th Congress, about 0.27 percent of words used by Republicans were categorized as angry, 0.11 percent were categorized as anxious, and 0.26 were sad. In the 113th, the rates were nearly identical—0.28 percent were angry words, 0.12 percent were anxious words, and 0.24 were sad words. Given that the average total words for each legislator in the 112th Congress was about 17,650, this means that, on average, each member tweeted an angry word about forty-eight times, an anxious word just under twenty times, and a sad word about

Table 7.1 **Percentage of Angry, Anxious, and Sad Words Used by Republicans in the 112th and 113th Congresses**

	Avg. Percentage of Angry Words	Avg. Percentage of Anxious Words	Avg. Percentage of Sad Words
112th Congress	0.27	0.11	0.26
113th Congress	0.28	0.12	0.24

Note: Values are the percentage of words that qualify as angry, anxious, or sad according to the Linguistic Inquiry Word Count 2015 Internal Dictionary.

forty-six times. In the 113th Congress, the average total word count for each legislator over the two-year period was just under 25,000. On average, then, each member tweeted an angry word about seventy times, an anxious word about thirty times, and a sad word about sixty times.

If the claim that Tea Party elites are more likely to adopt resentful rhetoric is true, then these rates should be higher among those associated with the Tea Party. To test this, we generate models that regress the percentage of total words that are categorized as angry, anxious, or sad onto the Tea Party Support and Tea Party Attachment measures, controlling for the same factors we have in previous models.[6] The results for the 112th and 113th Congresses can be seen in Tables 7.2 and 7.3, respectively.

As we have previously discussed, members who draw support from the Tea Party movement are not necessarily members with the strongest conservative credentials, specifically on the dimensions of conservatism most closely associated with resentment: social and racial conservatism. Where support goes is largely the result of tactical decision-making on behalf of Tea Party groups and activists— their money and energy go to where they are likely to get the most bang for their buck. Moreover, legislators who score high on this scale and low on the Tea Party Association scale are not necessarily seeking to publicly connect themselves to the movement, and thus would not try to adopt or mimic the movement's rhetoric. Accordingly, as shown in Table 7.2, Tea Party Support was not connected to the use of any of the discrete emotions in legislators' tweets in the 112th Congress.[7]

Yet the same cannot be said for Tea Party Attachment. Although, as shown in Table 7.2, attachment did not have a significant relationship with affect in the 112th, we again we see evidence of changes between the 112th and 113th Congresses. Results for the 113th, displayed in Table 7.3, indicate that Tea Party Support again has no relationship with the proclivity to use emotional words. However, the Tea Party Attachment measure was positively related to a pair of discrete emotions: anger and sadness.[8]

As shown Table 7.3, those high in Tea Party Attachment used a greater number of angry words. Controlling for other factors, the percentage of angry words among those in the highest category of Tea Party Attachment was 0.08 points higher than those with no attachment, holding all else constant, or roughly twenty more angry words. This finding appears to fit with the conventional wisdom regarding the Tea Party fueling an angry, populist revolt, although the differences in the proclivity of angry rhetoric are small. However, this relationship appears to be driven by the rhetoric of those with the strongest attachment, not those who merely tangentially linked themselves to the movement. Looking at the raw mean percentages, the fifteen members who had the highest Tea Party Attachment scores in the 113th Congress averaged 0.41 angry words, while those in the two lower categories (some and no attachment) both averaged 0.27.

Table 7.2 **Affect in the Twitter Rhetoric of 112th House Republicans**

Variable	Anger	Anxiety	Sadness
Tea Party Support	0.01	0.01	0.00
	(0.01)	(0.00)	(0.01)
Tea Party Attachment	−0.00	−0.01	0.00
	(0.02)	(0.01)	(0.01)
DW-Nominate	0.14	0.01	**0.12**
	(0.10)	(0.05)	**(0.05)**
Gender	0.04	−0.02	−0.02
	(0.04)	(0.02)	(0.02)
Year Took Office	**−0.01**	**−0.00**	−0.00
	(0.01)	**(0.00)**	(0.00)
Party Leadership	**−0.11**	−0.02	0.03
	(0.06)	(0.03)	(0.04)
Committee Leadership	−0.11	0.02	**0.04**
	(0.08)	(0.05)	**(0.03)**
Total Tweets (112th Congress)	**0.00**	**0.00**	0.00
	(0.00)	**(0.00)**	(0.00)
Constant	**19.50**	**7.65**	1.51
	(9.68)	**(4.29)**	(2.96)
Observations	207	207	207
R^2	0.11	0.10	0.07

Note: Standard errors are in parentheses. Boldface indicates significance at $p < .05$ (one-tailed test).

The most interesting results, we think, involve the use of sad words. Tea Party Attachment had a positive effect on the percentage of sad words members incorporated into their tweets in the 113th Congress, as shown in Table 7.3. This effect occurred even when ideology was controlled for (conservatism also had a positive effect) and suggests that reports of Tea Party elites using simmering resentment for political gain have some merit.

Looking at the members with the highest percentages of sad words further reveals the connection between members attached to the Tea Party. Joe Wilson (R-SC), a Black Tea Republican in the 113th Congress, had the highest percentage, with 0.52 percent. Green Tea members Tim Huelskamp (R-KS) (0.49 percent), Trent Franks (0.45 percent), Sam Johnson (R-TX) (0.44 percent), Marlin Stutzman (R-IN) (0.43 percent), and Morgan Griffith (R-VA) (0.42 percent) had the third-, fourth-, sixth-, eighth-, and ninth-highest rates,

Table 7.3 **Affect in the Twitter Rhetoric of 113th House Republicans**

Variable	Anger	Anxiety	Sadness
Tea Party Support	0.00	0.00	−0.00
	(0.01)	(0.00)	(0.00)
Tea Party Attachment	**0.04**	−0.00	**0.02**
	(0.02)	(0.01)	**(0.01)**
DW-Nominate	0.04	**0.07**	**0.08**
	(0.08)	**(0.03)**	**(0.04)**
Gender	0.01	−0.01	−0.02
	(0.03)	(0.01)	(0.01)
Year Took Office	**−0.00**	**−0.00**	−0.00
	(0.00)	**(0.00)**	(0.00)
Party Leadership	**−0.07**	**−0.03**	0.02
	(0.03)	**(0.02)**	(0.03)
Committee Leadership	−0.02	−0.04	0.00
	(0.04)	(0.03)	(0.02)
Total Tweets (113th Congress)	0.00	**0.00**	0.00
	(0.00)	**(0.00)**	(0.00)
Constant	**8.96**	**5.49**	2.57
	(4.04)	**(1.95)**	(1.53)
Observations	214	214	214
R^2	0.07	0.08	0.08

Note: Coefficients are the results of OLS regression. Robust standard errors are in parentheses. Boldface indicates significance at $p < .05$ (one-tailed test).

respectively. The other members who made the "top ten" in the 113th (Rob Aderholt, R-AL; John Fleming, R-LA; Pete Olson, R-TX; and Kenny Marchant, R-TX) were all Coffee members in the 113th, but each was also a Green Tea member during the 112th. Other 113th Black and Green Tea Republicans were not far outside the top ten, including Green Tea Jim Bridenstine (R-OK), whose rate of 0.40 percent was good for thirteenth-highest, Green Tea Scott Garrett (R-NJ), with a rate of 0.36 percent, and Black Tea Michele Bachmann and Green Tea Dave Camp (R-MI), both with 0.35 percent.

To further investigate this, we took a closer look at the sad language those with high Tea Party Attachment scores used in the 113th Congress by pulling out some common examples that we found in members' tweets.[9] The words identified as sad are italicized. When it came to sadness, there was significant discussion of *lost* and *inferior* healthcare coverage, doctors, benefits, life savings, and jobs; of *low* employment rates and workforce participation; of *discouraged* workers; of *broke* and *broken* programs (e.g., Medicare, Social Security); of millions and billions of taxpayer dollars *lost* to waste; of the *devastating* effects of *failed* and *failing* leaders and leadership (e.g., Obama and Nancy Pelosi,), *failing* and *failed* policies (e.g., Obamacare, "Obamanomics," the stimulus program, housing policies, education policies, energy policies, tax policies, national security policies, securing the border, the combat readiness of the military, the handling of terrorism and ISIS), and *failing* and *failed* institutions (e.g., the Veterans Administration); of programs that haven't failed yet but are *doomed* to *fail* and other *failures* to come; of programs that have caused Americans and American industry to *suffer* and *hurt* job creation; of *overwhelming* regulations; of *empty* words, rhetoric, and promises; of *inadequate* performances in office; of *lowering* bars of achievement for students; of students forced into *low*-performing schools; of Obama not lifting a finger to address *tragedies* and *failing* to act; of Obama and others allowing soldiers, veterans, and diplomats to *suffer tragic* deaths; of Americans *losing* hope and hope changing to *despair* under Obama; of Americans showing *remorse* over electing Obama; of *missing* the days of Reagan; of *hurting* job markets, patients, pensioners, children, seniors, American families, and Americans; of Americans *losing* faith in their government and in America; of *lost* liberty.

The common refrain of all this sad rhetoric is that Americans have experienced a loss of material resources and standards at the hands of a failing (and sometimes uncaring, if not outright abusive) federal government. Why is it that members of Congress with high Tea Party Attachment scores are so angry and so sad? First, this is likely a type of digital homestyle, in which members attempt to cultivate trust and support with the public (Fenno 1978). By channeling these attitudes and emotions, legislators are not only attempting to connect with their constituents who share them, but also are attempting to build broader supportive constituencies (Gainous and Wagner 2014), something White Tea Republicans (those with only Tea Party support) are not looking to do. Second, and less cynically, perhaps members legitimately possess these feelings. They feel the country is in decline and that government institutions continue to fail—and sometimes abuse—the American people. Thus, the angry and sad sentiments they express and their public identification with the Tea Party movement are both the fruit of genuine feelings about the state of country.

There is, finally, the possibility that members are attempting not only to tap into but to aggravate latent feelings of resentment and loss. Members describing the declining performance of a declining nation—and one with unfair or immoral social policies—do so not merely to connect with constituents and the broader public or because they are genuine feelings, but because they recognize they can arouse these emotions among groups of voters and that this is a politically expedient strategy. In support of this final explanation, there is evidence that Tea Party elites have attempted to take advantage of underlying racial resentment. Banks (2014, 140–148) found that angry campaign rhetoric by 2010 Tea Party candidates (as identified in the 2010 *New York Times* list) increased the weight of racial considerations in the voting behavior of whites and ultimately increased support for Republican candidates among whites harboring some racial prejudice.

We argue that sad rhetoric has a similar effect in breeding resentment and that anger and despair are associated with the view that the country is in decline and that unfair burdens are being placed on certain groups, much in line with the arguments of Cramer (2016a) and Hochschild (2016). And while we do not find a connection between either measure of Tea Party Association and affect in the 112th Congress (although we do not examine tweets issued by campaign Twitter accounts), we do see evidence of affective rhetoric in the tweets of members who made some efforts to attach themselves to the Tea Party in the 113th—the same individuals who tended to have conservative racial policy roll call scores (except those in the highest category; see Chapter 5). In short, members cultivating Tea Party constituencies attempt to capitalize on feelings of resentment toward perceived undeserving others—and this is reflected in their rhetoric and roll call votes.

This is our take, of course, and we have no doubt that others, including the members who leverage this style of rhetoric, see it differently. In personal correspondence with us, Tim Huelskamp (2017), now out of office and serving as president of a conservative think tank, took issue with our argument that legislators' rhetoric aggravated feelings of resentment. He instead suggested that Tea Party Republicans like himself were merely channeling the frustrations of the public. As he put it, we (the authors) "missed not only the point of the Tea Party movement or 'Drain the Swamp': the American people are fed up with Washington. These [sic] wasn't driven by Tea Party congresswoman [sic] or congressman [sic]—it is what the electorate thought and still thinks." Yet Huelskamp also allowed that the Tea Party in the House might have contributed to the political earthquake that was to come, telling us that "the concern, the doubt, and distrust of big government and the Washington Establishment in particular [are] what motivated America to elect Donald Trump. If I played any such role in that race, I'm happy to take credit."

Rhetoric Regarding Compromise, Bipartisanship, and Negotiation

Rhetoric is not the only feature commonly thought to distinguish Tea Party members from other Republicans—they are perhaps more notorious (or renowned) for intransigence. The 112th Congress featured two monumental budgetary impasses: the showdown over raising the debt ceiling in 2011 and, in the waning days of the 112th, the so-called fiscal cliff crisis. During both crises, Tea Party members were reportedly unwilling to compromise, or did so reluctantly at the last minute (Acosta 2012; Farenthold et al. 2013). Yet the Tea Party faction's reputation as an anti-compromise, obstructionist, and oppositionist bloc is not limited to these two crises—it is often suggested that this type of behavior is endemic to association with the Tea Party. As the *Economist* (2011) put it:

> [T]he tea-party movement is animated by an oppositional spirit of partisanship rather more than policy concerns. They aren't just calling for a restoration of conservative principles; they're out to get the people who are perceived as giving comfort to the enemy, in this case, the Democrats.

It would be inaccurate to place blame for dysfunction in Congress solely at the feet of Tea Party–aligned legislators. At the very least, even the harshest critics of Tea Party members must admit that hyperpartisanship and gridlock in Washington predate the movement's formal launch in early 2009 (Mann and Ornstein 2012), and prominent members commonly portrayed as establishment types—including former speaker John Boehner—have rejected the word.[10] Yet proponents of the Tea Party likewise must admit (or perhaps might happily tout the fact) that "compromise" has been a dirty word within the movement. Empirical assessments provide some support for this. Grossman and Hopkins (2015) argue that Republican primary voters' preference for politicians who stick to principle rather than compromise has enabled the election of Tea Party–backed candidates, and Tea Party organizations have applied significant pressure on incumbents not to stray from conservative principles. Skocpol and Williamson (2012, 173) could find no examples of the word "compromise" in Tea Party organization promotional materials, nor did they witness any Tea Party activists positively refer to the concept.

Comity in Congress has been on the decline for some time (Uslaner 1993), and rhetorical rejections of bipartisanship and compromise had been in vogue among Gingrich-aligned congressional Republicans even before the Republican Revolution of 1994 (Mann and Ornstein 2012, 39). Yet the Tea Party era is thought to be different, in that the commitment not to compromise appears to be not just a rhetorical device to gain and hold onto power,[11] but a core tenet of the Republican Conference, perhaps because members fear earning the wrath of the Tea Party movement. *Washington Post* columnist Dana Milbank (2010b), reflecting on the differences between the Gingrich era and the Tea Party era in the days before the 2010 wave election, argues:

[T]here is no Bob Dole in the Republican leadership today; there isn't even a Newt Gingrich. There is nobody with the clout to tell Tea Party–inspired backbenchers when it's time to put down the grenades and negotiate. Rather, there are weak leaders who, frightened by the Tea Party radicals, have become unquestioning followers of a radical approach.

Indeed, observers have suggested that a reputation for not compromising and rejecting bipartisanship is perceived to be an asset, if not a necessity, among Tea Party supporters (Friedersdorf 2011). Likewise, a reputation for working with Democrats or partnering with the Obama White House could provoke protestations from Tea Party activists. For example, when Republicans—including many purported Tea Party legislators—voted yes on the compromise deal to end the 2011 debt ceiling crises, Tea Party activists were incensed and threatened to unseat the members who voted for it (Blackmon and Levitz 2011). It was the same story following the passage of the 2013 fiscal cliff deal (Freedlander 2013).

A reliable conservative record did not absolve Republicans from the sin of compromise. Veteran Indiana senator Dick Lugar was neither the most conservative nor most liberal Republican senator during the 112th Congress but, on occasion, crossed the aisle to make deals with Democrats and was known to have a good working relationship with Obama (earning the label "Obama's favorite Republican") (Prokop 2012). This reputation appeared to be enough for him to lose his 2012 primary race to a Tea Party–backed state treasurer who openly expressed disdain for any compromise and bipartisanship (and ultimately lost the election due in part, ostensibly, to outrageous commentary) (Dionne 2016, 360–361).[12] Even the mere suggestion of crossing the aisle might earn Tea Party disdain: Kansas senator Jerry Moran's suggestion in early 2016 that he was open to giving Obama's doomed Supreme Court nominee, Merrick Garland, a hearing prompted Tea Party Patriots to threaten Moran with a primary challenge for his "outrageous behavior." Moran, who was endorsed by Tea Party Express in 2010, quickly changed tunes (Rauch 2016).[13]

If this is true, then an anti-deliberative stance is something those high in Tea Party Attachment (namely, Black and Green Tea Republicans) would wish to promote, as it enables legislators to avoid earning the disfavor of the Tea Party's activist base and maintains the Tea Party bona fides that they have fashioned. Thus, we could expect such legislators (1) to discuss compromise, bipartisanship, and negotiation less frequently than those with low Tea Party Association and (2) when they do mention them, to be more likely to discuss them in negative terms. Negative references to compromise may be mere lip service to principled stances, and analyzing how members talk about compromise cannot tell us if those high in Tea Party Association are more anti-deliberative in practice. As the saying goes, talk is cheap. Yet we think such rhetoric reinforces partisan identity and undermines openness to compromise among members of the public. Certainly, elite rhetoric can inflame mass partisanship and negative attitudes toward the out-group (e.g., Hetherington 2001; Iyengar et al. 2012), and because there is an inherent interactivity between public and elite opinion, a base resistant to compromise will reinforce these sentiments among elected representatives (Jacobson 2000; Layman et al. 2006; Saunders and Abramowitz 2004; Stasavage 2007). Thus, anti-deliberative rhetoric has consequences. For those curious about measuring anti-deliberative behavior via cross-cutting political talk (Mutz 2006), we consider and discuss this method in the appendix to this chapter.

To assess whether members with high Tea Party Association scores were less likely than those with low scores to reference pro-deliberative terms, and more likely to reference them in negative terms, we searched for the terms "compromise" and "bipartisanship,"[14] along with the stem " negotiat*" in the database of congressional tweets.[15] In the 112th Congress dataset, this search returned a collection of 271 tweets. In the 113th Congress, the search returned a larger collection of 742 tweets. Each of the tweets were then independently reviewed and coded by a group of three research assistants and put in one of five categories: "supports compromise/bipartisanship"; "principled rejection"; "not enough from other side"; "neutral"; and "irrelevant."[16]

A tweet was categorized as "supports compromise/bipartisanship" if the member did any or all of the following in the tweet: spoke positively about compromise/bipartisanship in general or specific terms; spoke positively about the need for compromise/bipartisanship in general or specific terms; or praised others for their willingness to engage in compromise/bipartisanship. Although the standards for a "supportive" tweet may seem generous, they do not result in a significant number of tweets categorized as such.

Many tweets fell into the two negative categories. A tweet was categorized as "principled rejection" if the member blatantly rejected compromise and bipartisanship as concepts in the tweet. An invented example (and the one the coders used as a guide, is "I am unwilling to compromise on the issue of Obamacare—repeal is the only option"). A tweet was categorized as "not enough from other side" if the member did any or all of the following: argued that proposal/bill did not include enough concessions on issues important to the Republican Party (e.g., "There are not nearly enough spending cuts in this bill for me to support it"); argued that the "other side" hadn't done enough or was unwilling to compromise (e.g., "The Democrats have given up essentially nothing"); or the member was dismissive of or belittled the compromise proposal issued by "other side" (e.g., "This 'compromise' offer is pretty pathetic").

A tweet was categorized as "neutral" if the member mentioned compromise/bipartisanship, but it was unclear what her or his position was (e.g., "I will be talking about the budget compromise at noon"). In many instances, it would not be a stretch to assume positive connotations—however, in an effort to err on the conservative side, such tweets were coded as neither positive nor negative.

Finally, a tweet was categorized as "irrelevant" if it featured one of the search terms but the word was not used in the context of bipartisan compromise/co-operation (e.g., "We cannot compromise safety"). Among the 112th tweets, a total of thirty-two were coded as irrelevant, while eighty-three were coded as such among the 113th tweets; these tweets were subsequently removed from the dataset, ensuring the analyses to follow were focused on deliberative talk in the context of partisan politics.

We first turn attention to whether those high in Tea Party Attachment are less likely to reference pro-deliberative terms. If much of the conventional wisdom about Tea Party legislators is true, we should see Tea Party members using the terms less frequently. To do so, we estimate a pair of negative binomial regression models for each of the two congresses, estimating whether Tea Party Attachment affects the number of times deliberative terms were used, controlling for the usual set of factors. The first column of Table 7.4 displays the results for the 112th Congress. As we expected, and in alignment with the conventional wisdom, those high in Tea Party Association were less likely to reference compromise, bipartisanship, and negotiation in the context of American partisan politics. Although these words were not utilized widely during the 112th, among those looking to promote Tea Party connections, these words were even more sparse. We might say that among a multitude of Republicans hesitant to reference deliberative terms, Black and Green Tea members managed to speak about them even less.

When Black and Green Tea members did mention deliberative terms, did they have a negative connotation? Figure 7.1 breaks down the average number of references that fell into the positive/neutral categories and negative categories ("principled rejection" or "not enough from other side") at each level of Tea Party Attachment.[17] While the numbers are small, in general we see a pattern in which stronger Tea Party Attachment correlates with less positive and more negative references to compromise, bipartisanship, and negotiation. Of the 1.3 tweets averaged by those with no attachment to the Tea Party (Coffee or White Tea Republicans), 1.0 were positive or neutral, and only about 0.3 discussed deliberative terms in a negative fashion. Among those with moderate Attachment scores, who averaged 1.0 tweets referencing deliberative terms in total, the breakdown skewed more negative throughout the 112th Congress: they averaged 0.6 positive or neutral references and about 0.4 negative references. Those with high Attachment scores—Black and Green Tea Republicans—who averaged only 0.7 references to deliberative terms in total, had the smallest average of positive or neutral references, at 0.3, and averaged the same amount

Table 7.4 **References to Compromise, Bipartisanship, and Negotiation in the Tweets of Congressional Republicans**

Variable	*Number of References to Deliberative Terms*	
	112th Congress	*113th Congress*
Tea Party Support	0.05	0.07
	(0.07)	(0.04)
Tea Party Attachment	**–0.30**	0.12
	(0.14)	(0.17)
DW-Nominate	0.19	**1.66**
	(0.68)	**(0.59)**
Gender	0.10	0.22
	(0.35)	(0.37)
Year Took Office	0.01	**–0.02**
	(0.02)	**(0.01)**
Party Leadership	–0.67	–0.22
	(0.78)	(0.57)
Committee Leadership	0.12	–0.21
	(0.42)	(0.37)
Constant	–25.83	**41.57**
	(32.77)	**(25.17)**
Log Likelihood	–313.23	–475.04
Observations	223	225
Pseudo R^2	0.01	0.02

Note: Coefficients are the results of negative binomial regression. Standard errors are in parentheses. Boldface indicate significance at $p < .05$ (one-tailed test).

of negative references (0.4) as those with some attachment. Thus, in the 112th Congress, not only were those with high Tea Party Attachment scores less likely to mention deliberative terms, but when they did mention them, a larger share of the terms had a negative connotation than did references tweeted by those with low Attachment scores.

If the raw counts are any indication, deliberative terms were more widely used in the 113th Congress than in the 112th (658 vs. 239 times). As shown in the second column of Table 7.4, this proves to be true: Tea Party Attachment ceases to have a significant impact on mentions of deliberative terms[18] in the 113th Congress—but note that the direction of the coefficient has flipped—and Tea Party Support also continues to be insignificant. The phenomena witnessed

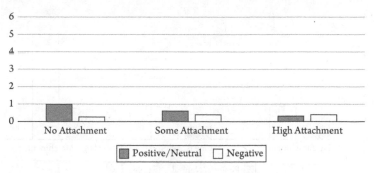

Figure 7.1 Average Number of Positive/Neutral and Negative References to Deliberative Terms by Tea Party Attachment, 112th Congress

during the early years of the Tea Party movement—avoidance of the term "compromise" by those affiliated with the Tea Party—appears to have dissipated. Indeed, looking at simple averages, the small group of legislators with the highest Tea Party Attachment scores averaged 7.0 (SD = 10.7) references to deliberative terms, far outpacing those with some (2.3, SD = 2.4) and no attachment (2.7, SD = 8.1). But were Black and Green Tea members talking about the deliberative terms in a positive way?

As Figure 7.2 reveals, negative references to compromise, bipartisanship, and negotiation were far more prevalent during the 113th Congress. Those with no attachment averaged about 1.1 positive references—nearly identical to the group's average in the 112th—but the average number of negative references increased to nearly 1.6 (SD = 7.3). Likewise, the average number of positive references among those with some attachment, at 0.6 positive references, was also unchanged from the group's average in the 112th. However, the average number of negative mentions more than quadrupled to about 1.6 (SD = 1.9).

It is among those with high attachment that we see the most dramatic changes from the 112th to the 113th Congress. The average number of positive references to deliberative concepts increased to about 2.3 among Black and Green Tea members; however, the number of positive references was dwarfed by the nearly 7 negative references (SD = 9.6) that those with high attachment averaged, which is about seven times the average from the 112th. In the 113th, four of the six members with the most negative references to compromise had high Tea Party Attachment scores.[19] Thus, while Black and Green Tea Republicans talked a lot about compromise, bipartisanship, and negotiation with the Obama White House and Democrats on social media during the 113th, the vast majority of these references were either a principled rejection of the concepts or suggestions that the "other side" needed to give more.

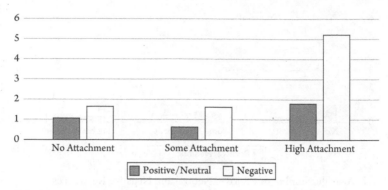

Figure 7.2 Average Number of Positive/Neutral and Negative References to Deliberative Terms by Tea Party Attachment, 113th Congress

Emotional and Anti-Deliberative Public Presentations

Throughout this chapter we have found evidence that the extra-legislative behavior of Tea Party members—specifically, those who attempt to attach themselves to the movement—does differ from that of mainstream Republicans and those who do not foster public connections to the movement. This was especially true in the 113th Congress. On Twitter, the rhetoric of Black and Green Tea Republicans incorporated more angry and sad language than the rhetoric of those with no attachment to the movement, consistent with claims that Tea Party members have attempted to aggravate latent resentment toward outgroups and the federal government.

Moreover, those who attached themselves to the Tea Party also became more anti-deliberative in the 113th Congress. In the 112th, high Tea Party Attachment scores were associated with avoiding the mention of compromise, bipartisanship, and negotiation, especially positive allusions to these deliberative terms. In the 113th, deliberative terms became a hot topic of conversation among conservatives—but, unlike the situation in the 112th, a majority of these terms now carried a negative connotation. Those with high Tea Party Attachment scores were especially likely to post tweets that negatively discussed deliberative terms.

In sum, we find support for the conventional wisdom regarding the affective and anti-deliberative tone of Tea Party members' public presentations. From a political psychology perspective, that members who avoid or criticize deliberative processes and choose not to engage with the out-party also employ rhetoric meant to incite resentment makes some sense. Affective Intelligence Theory (AIT) links aversive emotions, including anger and resentment, to anti-deliberative attitudes and more partisan behavior (MacKuen et al. 2006,

2010). According to AIT, however, the role of aversion is a mediating one—it is a link in the causal chain between some stimulus (usually an elite message) and more anti-deliberative attitudes. From what we can gather from anecdotal evidence, the causal arrow is flipped—more deliberative or bipartisan behavior by legislators incites anger in Tea Party activists. As one official associated with the Tea Party movement said following the 2013 fiscal cliff deal: "If you think 2010 was the Tea Party Congress, just wait until 2014. You will see people even more angry and up in arms. I don't think we have seen nothing [sic] yet" (Freedlander 2013).

But this makes some sense, too: if Tea Party activists, as well as the much larger group of Americans who identify with the movement, are enthused by candidates who reject compromise on principle, then for Republicans wishing to attach themselves to the movement, a way to earn the enthusiasm of voters is to practice anti-deliberative behavior (Grossman and Hopkins 2015; also see Schouten 2013). As work in AIT and related theories have shown, enthusiasm, along with anger and resentment, are mobilizing forces (Brader 2006; Groenendyk and Banks 2014; Valentino et al. 2011; Weber 2013). For members hoping to take advantage of Tea Party energy, there is perhaps no better recipe than a public presentation of aversion-inducing rhetoric and anti-deliberative behavior. The reasons that those who attached themselves to the Tea Party followed this recipe differed between the 112th and 113th Congresses, something we take up in Chapter 9. Also in the next chapter, we examine the extent to which Tea Party legislators took the next step to incivility.

Appendix

Cross-Party Communication on Twitter

While measuring deliberative behavior is a notably difficult task for social scientists and has been an area of dispute between political theorists and empirical political scientists, Mutz (2006) offers a simple yet sufficient method for doing so: measuring the extent to which one engages with cross-cutting political talk. It would be difficult, if not impossible, to measure cross-cutting *face-to-face* talk among legislators, but we might consider the extent to which they engage with each other via Twitter. Twitter enables users to "@-mention" other users, for the purposes of contacting, reaching out to, or acknowledging them; in turn, users can "@-reply" (i.e., reply) to users who @-mention them, enabling dialogue (Tromble 2016). Thus, we can look at how often Republicans "@-mention" Democrats using their official Twitter handles, a requisite for digital dialogue.

This type of analysis is not ideal, for a couple of reasons. First, merely referencing a colleague from across the aisle is far different from having a cross-cutting conversation about politics and policies. Such tweets might be devoid of substantive content altogether. Second, outreach to the other side is likely to be limited among legislators—Democrats and Republicans-—as the Twitter community is characterized by relatively high levels of political homophily (Barberá 2014; Colleoni et al. 2014). And when they do interact, they may not do so in a deliberative fashion. Bode et al. (2015) found that Tea Party–aligned Twitter users were more likely to "highjack" the hashtags of progressive groups—not for the sake of deliberation but to agitate and proselytize. Moreover, members of Congress do engage in partisan "blame and shame" in their tweets (Hemphill et al. 2013).

However, while engagement with the other side for negative purposes such as these is a concern, we expect that the number of such tweets that include Democrats' official Twitter handles will be limited, for a pair of reasons. First, norms might limit the extent to which members call out their Democratic colleagues in such a confrontational and public fashion. While comity in Congress has declined and the prevalence of public attacks on congressional colleagues has been increasing for some time (Uslaner 1993), there are still few instances in which the integrity of a member is impugned on the House floor (Jamieson 2011)—at least through the 111th Congress. House rules (or the interpretation of such) may also minimize direct, personal critiques, as they restrict the use of official Twitter accounts to "official business" and prohibit their use for campaign and political usage.[20]

Our review of Republican tweets generally supports this. On average, 1 percent of Republicans' tweets in the 112th Congress and 2 percent of their tweets in the 113th included congressional Democrats' Twitter handles. However, while the tweets were not devoid of direct criticisms (many were those of Republicans eager to direct criticisms to @NancyPelosi and @SenatorReid, the official Twitter accounts of House Democratic leader Nancy Pelosi and Senate Democratic leader Harry Reid), many other tweets were cordial and professional. Often, members took to Twitter to acknowledge partnerships and thank congressional Democrats for work on a bill important to them. For example, Ed Royce (R-CA) touted his co-sponsoring of Democrat Jim McGovern's (D-MA) bill,[21] and Jim Gerlach (R-PA) thanked Democrat Jason Altmire (D-PA) for his help in securing the Medal of Honor for a veteran of the Vietnam War.[22] Others, though, while cordial and personal, were not very substantive, such as Darrell Issa's (R-CA) tweets welcoming longtime Democrat and Dean of the House John Dingell (D-MI) to the social media platform[23] and wishing Democratic Whip Steny Hoyer (D-MD) a happy birthday.[24]

Certainly, pleasantries like these fall short of deliberation, but they may be indicative of some level of bipartisan comradery and collegiality, elements essential to more substantive cooperation—commitments to which Tea Party legislators reputedly lack (e.g., Gans 2013). Indeed, lest we dismiss birthday messages as trivial, even they appear to have a partisan dimension: Tea Party Caucus chair Michelle Bachmann, for example, wished thirty-seven legislators a happy birthday during the 112th Congress—all of them Republicans (Bachmann's birthday wishes were only more bipartisan in the 113th).[25] Beyond factoids like this, is there evidence that those with a high level of attachment to the Tea Party are less likely to engage in digital dialogue with Democrats? In Table 7.A1, we regress the percentage of a members' tweets that include a congressional

Table 7.A1 **Percentage of Republicans' Tweets That Include Congressional Democrats' Twitter Handles**

Variable	112th Congress	113th Congress
Tea Party Support	−0.00	−0.00
	(0.000)	(0.001)
Tea Party Attachment	−0.00	**−0.01**
	(0.001)	**(0.002)**
DW-Nominate	**−0.01**	−0.01
	(0.005)	(0.012)
Gender	**−0.00**	0.00
	(0.002)	(0.003)
Year Took Office	0.00	0.00
	(0.000)	(0.000)
Party Leadership	0.00	−0.00
	(0.005)	(0.004)
Committee Leadership	0.00	−0.00
	(0.006)	(0.005)
Total Tweets	**0.00**	0.00
	(0.000)	(0.000)
Constant	−0.23	−0.05
	(0.339)	(0.478)
Observations	207	215
R^2	0.06	0.03

Note: Coefficients are the results of OLS regression. Robust standard errors are in parentheses. Boldface indicates significance at $p < .05$ (one-tailed test).

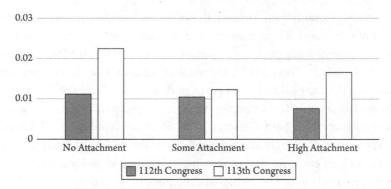

Figure 7.A1 Percentage of Tweets Directed toward Congressional Democrats by Tea Party Attachment, 112th and 113th Congresses

Democrat's Twitter handle onto the Tea Party Association measures, as well as the standard set of control variables.

The first column displays the results for the 112th Congress. While conservatism had a significant negative effect on the percentage of tweets mentioning Democrats, neither Tea Party measure was significant. In the 113th, displayed in the second column, it was the opposite: conservatism ceased to be significant, but Tea Party Attachment was, reducing the percentage of tweets by one percentage point (again, only 2 percent of Republicans' tweets referenced Democrats in the 113th, on average). That is, those who chose to align themselves with the Tea Party publicly were less likely to engage with Democrats on Twitter.

Interestingly, it was not those with the highest level of attachment to the Tea Party who were driving this result, but those with some attachment. As displayed in Figure 7.A1, whereas those with no attachment and high attachment to the Tea Party both doubled their rates between the 112th and 113th Congresses, those in the middle averaged about the same percentage of tweets mentioning Democrats in both congresses.

Civility and Tea Party Rhetoric

The Bridge to Trumpian Bombast?

"Maybe our memories are too short, but the level of anger, disrespect, and incivility seems to be at an all-time high right now." This is what *NBC News* journalist Chuck Todd had to say about the 2010 midterm elections.[1] If Todd had a crystal ball, he might have seen that the acrimonious 2010 cycle would seem quaint, if not halcyon, after the 2016 presidential election, in which incivility was said to have reached "epidemic proportions."[2]

The acrimony would begin well before the first debate of the primaries in the summer of 2015. In July, Senator Ted Cruz (R-TX) took to the floor of the Senate to accuse Majority Leader Mitch McConnell (R-KY) of lying to Cruz and other Republican senators about a vote on the much-maligned Import-Export Bank. As reported by *Politico*, "The bank has become a flashpoint in the battle between the GOP's business and tea party wings" (Raju 2015). Cruz, the Tea Party's stalwart in the Senate,[3] not only bucked his own party's leadership, but impugned his party's leader on the floor, breaching the decorum of a historically deliberative upper chamber (Raju 2015). Congressional watchers, as well as fellow Republican senators, described Cruz's behavior as unusual and inappropriate, suggesting that it was in part (or completely) motivated by his presidential ambitions (Barrett 2015; Bump 2015).

Cruz would not be the only 2016 presidential aspirant to draw headlines for uncivil rhetoric and behavior. Neurosurgeon-cum-Republican candidate Ben Carson made regular use of Nazi analogies in his critiques of the Obama administration (Wehner 2015); Senator Marco Rubio (R-FL) experimented with decidedly lowbrow remarks during the primaries (Sargent 2016); and eventual Democratic nominee Hillary Clinton's Twitter snark elicited debates about presidential tone (Azari 2016).

However, it was the eventual Republican nominee and general election winner, Donald Trump, whose rhetoric and behavior drew the most attention (and condemnation). About a month before Cruz's attack on McConnell,

Trump threw his hat in the ring, descending an escalator of Trump Tower with wife Melania in hand, to make his announcement. At a time when few believed Trump's bid was anything more than a publicity stunt, perhaps the most notable aspect of Trump's announcement was his line regarding undocumented immigrants from Mexico: "They're bringing drugs. They're bringing crime. They're rapists. And some, I assume, are good people" (Ross 2016).

Trump would offer up plenty more lines of questionable civility. Throughout the campaign, political scientists and presidential historians testified that Trump violated norms of campaign discourse that were rarely, if ever, violated by previous candidates (Jackson 2016). While his antics before and during debates spurred myriad analyses (e.g., Healy and Martin 2016; Tumulty and Rucker 2015), it was his commentary on Twitter that was both novel and perhaps the most incendiary (Barbaro 2015; Jackson 2016). Notably, Trump's tweets were (and continue to be) headline news, increasing the exposure of his tweets to an audience well beyond his Twitter followers and users of the platform (Grynbaum 2016).

In January 2016, the *New York Times* began a running list of people and things Trump has insulted on Twitter.[4] Many of the targets include Democrats (especially Clinton), liberals, the media, and anyone airing public criticism of Trump. But also among Trump's targets have been other Republicans, including Rubio, Cruz, Carson, John Kasich, Jeb Bush, and Paul Ryan (R-WI). If Trump's attacks on fellow Republicans crossed a line for some conservatives, his were not the first to do so (e.g., Cruz's impugnment of McConnell). Writers for *National Review* have reflected on "intra-conservative incivility" aimed at them by Tea Party–aligned politicians for supposedly falling in line with the Republican establishment (French 2013).

In this chapter, we test the widely shared assumption that Tea Party legislators are more uncivil than their "establishment" colleagues. Specifically, we assess the level of incivility in the tweets of members of the 112th and 113th Congresses and determine whether our measures of Tea Party association predict higher levels of incivility. We then compare Tea Party tweet rhetoric with that of Trump and see if House Tea Partiers' rhetoric served as a bridge from an era of partisan acrimony to the current era of Trumpian bluster.

The Tea Party and Incivility

Many observers have highlighted the connection between anger, "outrage" incivility, and the Tea Party movement (e.g., Coblenz 2014). Among scholars, Tea Party rhetoric has been described as "the very antithesis to civil discourse," stemming from perceived inherently violent undertones (Harcourt 2012;

Skocpol and Williamson 2012, 32–33). Parker and Barreto (2013) find that outrageous, hyperbolic, and conspiratorial rhetoric is significantly more common among Tea Party supporters than it is in mainstream conservative outlets (e.g., *National Review Online*); and they find that the same is true for personal attacks on Barack Obama (2013, 46–48), which they in part attribute to anger over the election of the first African American president (2013, 53–54, 238–239). Perhaps there is no better indicator of the Tea Party's reputation for incivility than the fact that the mantle of "Tea Party imitators" has been applied to other groups that have adopted uncivil tactics (Ward 2015).

Reports of uncivil behavior have dogged the movement since its inception. High-profile incidents include the now infamous summer of 2009 town hall meetings on healthcare reform, featuring crowds of Tea Party activists who interrupted and heckled congressional Democrats (Berry and Sobieraj 2014, 167–171; Bernstein 2010). In the early days of the movement, Tea Party protesters were also accused of extremely reprehensible behavior, such as spitting on Democratic lawmakers and addressing them with racial slurs (Kane 2010).

These accusations apply not only to Tea Party activists, but to elites as well. Among the anecdotal evidence cited is an ad produced by Sarah Palin's political action committee that featured crosshairs over congressional districts that the PAC hoped to turn red (Harcourt 2012). The 2011 attack in Tucson, Arizona, that left six people dead and critically injured thirteen others, including Congresswoman Gabrielle Giffords (D-AZ), whose district was included in the ad, brought national attention to Tea Party tactics and rhetoric and renewed calls for civil discourse (e.g., Cooper and Zeleny 2011). There is no evidence that the shooter was motivated by the ad, and Palin would later unsuccessfully attempt to sue the *New York Times* for libel for suggesting that this was the case (and, unfortunately, a similar event would occur in 2017, resulting in the wounding of Majority Whip Steve Scalise (R-LA), with many Republicans now lamenting the dearth of civil discourse) (Borchers 2017; Weigel 2017). But this was not the first or last time Palin was connected to incivility. As Herbst (2010, 53–57) notes, Palin's strategic use of incivility was a constant on the 2008 campaign trail, which served to electrify and bond supporters.

Perhaps there is no more infamous example of incivility in the contemporary era than that which occurred during the earliest days of the Tea Party movement, when future Tea Party Caucus member Joe Wilson (R-SC) exclaimed, "You lie!" while President Obama was addressing a joint session of Congress in 2009 (Hulse 2009)—an incident that bought Wilson fame and swelled his campaign coffers (Berry and Sobieraj 2014, 191–192; Herbst 2010, 171n).

Anecdotes abound of the uncivil, controversial, and outrageous commentary of other former and current House members ubiquitously linked to the Tea Party—including, but not limited to, Todd Akin (R-MO) (Eligon and Schwirtz

2012), Michele Bachmann (R-MN) (Bouie 2013), Louie Gohmert (R-TX) (Barrouquere 2017; Livingston 2016), Steve King (R-IA) (Bump 2016), and Allen West (R-FL) (Alvarez 2012). King's comments in particular have drawn scorn due to their apparent racism; these include a 2017 tweet in which he stated that "culture and demographics are our destiny. We can't restore our civilization with somebody else's babies" (Graham 2017).

Of course, Tea Partiers do not have a monopoly on incivility and have themselves been the target of uncivil attacks. For example, former vice president Joe Biden purportedly referred to them as "terrorists" (Allen and Breshanan 2011), and Arizona senator John McCain referred to Tea Party lawmakers as "hobbits" and "wacko birds" (Cohn 2011; Weiner 2013). Moreover, our assertion is not that the discourse of Democrats or liberals is devoid of uncivil and outrageous claims.[5] Indeed, one of the noteworthy trends of the Trump era has been Democrats' embrace of conspiracy theories (Nyhan 2017). Rather, our purpose here is to determine if a distinguishing feature of Tea Party and non-Tea Party Republican legislators is the frequency with which incivility is utilized, specifically in digital communications, and the extent to which uncivil rhetoric has become institutionalized in the House.

Identifying Political Incivility Online

Testing the claim that Tea Party members are more outrageous and uncivil than their Coffee colleagues, particularly in their social media commentary, requires defining what we mean by outrage and incivility. The increasing diversity of media outlets during the past two decades, coupled with the advent of an interactive web, has prompted an apparent rise in political incivility—along with a robust scholarly literature defining and operationalizing political incivility. Additionally, scholars have noted the connection between conservative sensationalist media and the Tea Party. This includes not only Rick Santelli's CNBC rant in 2009 but also the role of Fox News in incubating the young movement and inculcating its viewers with the values of the Tea Party (Berry and Sobieraj 2014, 156; Weaver and Scacco 2013; Skocpol and Williamson 2012, 130–138).

Berry and Sobieraj (2014, 161–162) find that while many Tea Party identifiers have relied on Fox News, the relationship between the network and the movement is more nuanced, with some identifiers preferring more extreme voices on talk radio. Instead, they argue that Fox News is part of a broader "outrage industry" that includes conservative talk radio and digital content, and that the "outrage" rhetoric of the conservative media establishment helped to give rise to and sustain the Tea Party movement. A central feature of the relationship between the Tea Party movement and the "outrage industry" during the 112th and 113th Congresses was reciprocity: the movement grew due to coverage of its events and message, outrage media served as a "communications hub" for the decentralized movement, and the views and efforts of movement activists were validated by outrage industry outlets (Berry and Sobieraj 2014; 181–182). Likewise, the Tea Party provided the outlets with great material; mobilized, fixated niche audiences; and validation for the ominous warnings of many "outrage" personalities about the threat the Obama administration posed (Berry and Sobieraj 2014, 181–182).

Notably, Berry and Sobieraj (2014) identify "outrage" incivility as a variety of rhetoric within the broader category of political incivility. For example, they argue that while all outrage is uncivil, not all incivility is outrageous. The distinguishing feature of outrage is that it is purposeful, that it is used to provoke emotion, and that malfeasant inaccuracy is used to diminish targets (Berry and Sobieraj 2014, 6–7). Mutz and Reeves (2005) operationalize political incivility as exchanges that include "gratuitous asides that suggested a lack of respect and/or frustration with the opposition"—many of which would be likely to qualify as outrage incivility according Berry and Sobieraj's (2014, 245–248) codebook.[6]

Whether the distinguishing features Berry and Sobieraj attribute to outrage incivility are absent from political incivility more generally is a debate for another time and place. However, for our purposes, we argue that the two are sufficiently closely related that we do not make a distinction but rather treat political incivility and outrage incivility as one and the same. We accept that political incivility is purposeful and often meant to provoke emotion. So how does it differ conceptually from the angry and sad populist rhetoric—which we argued is intended to provoke resentment—discussed in the preceding chapter? There is certainly overlap among the phrases identified as both angry/sad language and political incivility. For example, the stems "kill*" and "destroy*" are included as angry words in the LIWC dictionary, while "fail*" is included as a sad word, and our coders identified gratuitous adjectives such as "job-killing," "job-destroying," and "failed" as examples of invective and hyperbole in certain contexts. The use of "lie," "liar," and other forms of "lie" can also make a tweet both angry and uncivil. However, plenty of words and stems listed as "angry" and "sad" are not alone sufficient to make a tweet uncivil—for example, "grim," "critical," and "lost." Moreover, there are plenty of uncivil remarks that include none of the words listed as "sad" and "angry." Conceptually speaking, unlike most political incivility, angry/sad rhetoric meant to breed resentment does not always have a target; one can paint a picture of a declining country or people without explicitly pointing a finger at a begetter of these effects. Likewise, a message might be uncivil because of how it is delivered, but the substance of the message is devoid of any type of emotional language. In short, while both types of rhetoric are likely employed with the intent to incite anger or resentment in others, they are not one and the same.

Gervais (2014, 2015, 2017a), reviewing the research on political incivility identifies four main types that can be found in digital political communication: *invectives and ridicule; hyperbole and distortion; digital stridency;* and *conspiracy theories.* The first type, invectives and ridicule, which includes ad hominem attacks, character assassination, mockery, name-calling, and other insults, is a common (and commonly identified) form of political incivility (Anderson et al. 2014; Berry and Sobieraj 2014; Brooks and Geer 2007; Coe et al. 2014; Fridkin and Kenney 2008; Massaro and Stryker 2012; Mutz 2015; Thorson et al. 2010). However, hyperbole and distortion, which can be defined as attempts to paint targets and their actions as corrupt, immoral, or radical, is prevalent as well (Berry and Sobieraj 2014; Gervais 2014, 2015, 2017a; Massaro and Stryker 2012).

Particularly relevant to digital communication is what Gervais (2017a) refers to as digital stridency, which includes vocalistic "surrogates" for shouting, sarcasm, and other types of incivility displayed in audiovisual communication (Sobieraj and Berry 2011). Examples of digital stridency include strategically capitalized words, multiple punctuation marks, ellipses, and quotation marks (Kalman and Gergle 2014). Strategic typing in all caps, the text equivalent of shouting, is a notable feature of many of Trump's tweets (Guarino 2017).

Conspiracy theories, the fourth type of incivility, include accusations of very sinister motives and actions that are prima facie baseless (Gervais 2014). Sobieraj and Berry (2011, 28) do not initially consider conspiracy theories to be a type of outrage incivility but note, after realizing its prevalence, that it should be treated as such in the future, which they do in their subsequent volume (Berry and Sobieraj 2014, 10, 13).[7]

Much of the focus on elite political incivility in the political communication and psychology literatures has been on audiovisual incivility—namely, uncivil political discourse on television. This is for good reason—as Mutz (2015) finds, uncivil political television can be "in-your-face" in two senses: norms of political discourse are violated, but the filming of political debaters up close also violates spatial norms. The combination of these elements makes for an arousing experience for viewers, which heightens attention but also diminishes political trust and the perceived legitimacy of the other side.

Mutz (2015, 153–177) casts doubt on the ability of text-based digital discourse to induce affective reactions to the extent that audiovisual incivility can, or at all. Recent research by Gervais (2017a, 2017b), however, suggests that when elites are uncivil online, they can induce affective reactions. Even tweets issued by elites, restricted to 140 (or 280) characters or fewer, can elicit affective reactions (namely anger) when they incorporate incivility, as well as anti-deliberative attitudes. This is particularly true when they utilize digital stridency and when the message is oppositional—that is, it attacks the partisan in-group (Gervais 2017b).

Thus, if political elites incorporate incivility in their digital communications, there may be serious consequences for openness to compromise and bipartisanship among members of the public.[8] Given the Tea Party's connection with outrageous incivility and the widespread reporting of Tea Party legislators' outrageous comments, we expect our Tea Party Association measures to predict the presence of incivility in members' tweets. Because we are using members' official Twitter accounts, outrageous incivility may be somewhat rare (as only a nonrandom selection of legislators have personal and campaigns accounts, using such for our analysis of rhetoric in tweets may result in biased inferences). The content of social media posts issued by members' accounts is comparable to the content featured in other types of media utilized by members (e.g., newsletters, press releases, and websites) and, thus, are generally self-promotional and positive (Golbeck et al. 2010; Hemphill et al. 2013a; Lassen and Brown 2010; Lawless 2012). That is, members normally talk about their policy positions and their activities, especially intra-district events.

However, while official congressional Twitter feeds may generally resemble high-tech newsletters, there is variation in use among members. Partisan stripes account for some differences in Twitter behavior—including the topics representatives tweet about (Gainous and Wagner 2014; Hemphill et al. 2013a; Lawless 2012) and the hashtags members leverage to frame debates (Hemphill et al. 2013b). Moreover, we can expect intra-party and intra-ideological groups to emphasize different identities and promote different movements, policies, and ideas (Bode et al. 2014; Gervais and Wilson 2017). In an analysis of the hashtag use of congressional and gubernatorial candidates and their followers during the 2010 midterm elections, Bode et al. (2014) found evidence of various "clusters" of Twitter users within larger liberal and conservative groups. The largest cluster within the conservative digital community was one associated with ostensible Tea Party politicians (the most frequently used hashtags in this grouping were "#tcot" and "#teaparty") (Bode et al. 2014). This suggests that Tea Party members—both elites and digital activists—have a distinct identity online. We expect, therefore, to see differences in tone and tactic between Republicans associated with the Tea Party and those not.

Coding of Members' Tweets for Incivility

Our complete dataset of tweets issued from official Republican member accounts consisted of slightly more than 168,000 tweets in the 112th Congress and about 255,000 tweets in the 113th Congress. Hand coding the entire dataset of 423,000 tweets would not have been feasible. However, advances in machine and supervised learning programs have enabled the coding of databases of this size and have been used by political scientists in recent years to code comparably large datasets of political content (Collingwood and Wilkerson 2011; Grimmer and Stewart 2013). The key advantage of supervised learning programs is that, rather than looking for patterns in the data, they follow the lead of human coders who have coded a sample of the dataset; this hand-coded sample is used to "train" an algorithm for the purposes of coding the remainder of the dataset (Collingwood and Wilkerson 2011). In fact, we are not the first to use a supervised learning program to measure political incivility or related concepts in tweets and other social media posts. Theocharis et al. (2016) used a supervised learning program to code tweets aimed at European candidates for incivility, although their definition of "incivility" differs significantly from ours, focusing on moral issues and democracy (i.e., tweets that impolitely reference human rights, social harmony, law and order, etc.). Similarly, the Pew Research Center (2017) utilized machine learning methods to code thousands of Facebook postings by members of Congress for "indignant disagreement" with the other side.

We first selected a random sample of each member's tweets from each congress—about 7 percent of the member's total[9]—to hand-code. For example, if a member served in both the 112th and 113th Congresses, about 7 percent of her or his tweets from the 112th and about 7 percent from the 113th were selected. This sample collection alone amounted to more than 28,000 tweets. We chose a sample set this large for the sake of inter-unit and intra-unit representativeness. We are open to the possibility that different members incorporate different rhetorical styles in their tweets, and so every member has to be included. Moreover, we want to be sure the sample set for each member is representative; many members issued only several hundred tweets (the median for the 112th Congress was 622 and that for the 113th it was 908.5), and so selecting 1 percent of their tweets would mean coding only two or three tweets, which we deemed insufficient.

Details on the coding process can be found in the appendix. In short, the process involved a multitude of coders and two rounds of coding before a master training set was finalized. In the end, about 1.4 percent of the sample tweets in the 112th Congress and 1.5 percent of the tweets in the 113th were deemed uncivil. The vast majority of the uncivil tweets were criticisms of Barack Obama and hyperbolic assessments of the ills of Obamacare and the harm Obama's policies were having on the economy.

A tweet from the 112th Congress that was representative of those labeled "uncivil" by coders included this October 2011 tweet by Mary Bono Mack (R-CA): "Simply put, this administration's failed 'pay now, suffer later' fiscal policies are driving our economy into the ground." This June 2012 tweet from Blake Farenthold (R-TX) was also representative of tweets marked as uncivil in the 112th: "@BarackObama: #IndividualMandate is 'absolutely not a tax increase.' Obama lied to us all to push this through. #FullRepeal of #Obamacare." In the 113th Congress, representative tweets included a post by Tom Graves (R-GA) that read, "I spoke to @seanhannity about #SOTU and how the president seemed to laugh off the #Obamacare disaster," and one by Mike Kelly (R-PA) that read, "Obama admin's defense cuts are a dangerous disgrace to the world's most important military power & must be opposed."

To complete the automated coding, we utilized a maximum entropy (ME) exponential model.[10] The ME model, in essence, models all the known attributes of the data and ignores the unknown (Collingwood and Wilkerson 2011). The larger the training sample, the more accurate the algorithm. However, even for larger sample sizes, accuracy rates of 75 to 85 percent are to be expected (Collingwood and Wilkerson 2011).

In the appendix, we present twenty randomly selected tweets that were marked "uncivil" by the program (see Table 8A.1). In most cases, we think the label is justifiable. Hyperbolic remarks and gratuitous, besmirching adjectives, including "train wreck," "nightmarish," "failed," and "devastating," are used to attack Obama administration policies and their impact (especially Obamacare). Obama himself is referred to as "despicable" and a "failure," and he is often accused of breaking his promises. Digital stridency is also evident, taking the form of strategically capitalized words (e.g., "ADMITTED"). In a few cases, the tweets seem mismarked. For instance, Adam Nunnelee's (R-MS) tweet, "Disaster aid, like all spending, isn't free, we either pay for it now or pay later with interest; I think we should have paid for it now," does not seem very uncivil. It is likely that the program picked up on the terms "disaster" and "spending." In general, the accuracy appears to be in line other studies using this approach.

Incivility Use and Tea Party Association

The average number of tweets labeled "uncivil" per member during the two-year period was 17.1. As members averaged a total of 800 tweets during the 112th Congress, the average uncivil tweet rate was about 1.5 percent—nearly identical to the rate in the hand-coded sample (1.4 percent). In the 113th Congress, the average number of uncivil tweets was 18.3; given that members averaged 1,141 tweets during the two-year period, the total average uncivil rate was 1.6 percent—again, nearly identical to the rate in the hand-coded sample. In short, there was a slight uptick in the average number of uncivil tweets by members in the 113th from the 112th, but the ratio of uncivil to civil tweets was nearly the same—in both congresses, less than 2 in 100 tweets included uncivil elements.[11] All the same, this is the equivalent of about 3.5 uncivil tweets per day (collectively) from Republican members during the 112th, and more than 5.5 uncivil tweets per day during the 113th.

Although uncivil tweets issued by official accounts were rare relative to the total number of tweets posted, there was significant variation among members when it came to incivility. The member with the highest incivility rate during the 112th Congress was Dana Rohrabacher (R-CA), who fell close to the border between Green Tea and Coffee in the 112th, with a rate of about 33 percent. A rate this high—about 1 in 3 tweets—was an extreme outlier. We mentioned in an endnote in the preceding chapter that Rohrabacher's Twitter behavior is rather unique among members of Congress, in that he personally engages with the public on the platform (constituents and otherwise), something that is rare among legislators (Glassman et al. 2009; Gulati and Williams 2015, 46–47). Engagement on social media platforms increases the chances of uncivil interactions, but Rohrabacher's responses to Twitter users who "@-tweeted" him were often especially dismissive and combative (or at least they struck us as such).[12] Rounding out the top ten in the 112th Congress were Coffee member Sam Graves (R-MO), with 11.3 percent; White Tea Ken Calvert (R-CA), with 6.6 percent; Green Tea Steve King, with 6.3 percent; White Tea Bill Johnson (OH-6), with 4.9 percent; Coffee Kevin Brady (R-TX), with 4.3 percent; Green Tea Rich Nugent (R-FL) and White Tea Justin Amash (R-MI), with 4.1 percent; Coffee Sam Johnson (R-TX), with 3.8 percent; and, notably, then–Speaker of the House John Boehner (R-OH), who qualified as a Black Tea member in the 112th, with 3.7 percent.

It is noteworthy that Boehner was the only Black Tea Republican to crack the top ten, although the White Tea Amash fell just outside the threshold, and both he and the Green Tea Steve King qualify as Black Tea in the 113th. Another member with a reputation for outrageous commentary, Allen West, was not far outside the top ten, ranking thirteenth. Among West's uncivil tweets was one posted on July 2011 that included the line, "Anyone with an Obama 2012 bumper sticker, I recognize them as a threat to the gene pool," which would draw significant attention.[13]

Boehner's inclusion in the top ten might surprise some—but a review of his tweets marked "uncivil" makes it quite clear that he made ample use of hyperbolic distortion, invectives, and mockery, with the intention of insulting President Barack Obama and other Democrats. Adjectives such as "job-killing," "job-destroying," and "failed" were liberally used to describe Obama, his administration, and his policies, and he appeared to mock the Obama "stimulus" package (the American Recovery and Reinvestment Act of 2009) through the use of quotation marks on a number of occasions. While it is known that Boehner and House Republican leaders made the calculation to tolerate strongly worded anti-Obama rhetoric, borrowed from the "fringe," during the 112th Congress

(Dionne 2016, 300–303), Boehner's own use of this type of rhetoric has been chalked up to his offering "lip service" to Tea Party talking points (Cassidy 2015). What this finding highlights is the extent to which John Boehner himself was on the offensive during the 112th—he was not offering up an uncivil line from time to time for political cover, but was among the leaders of the pack when it came to uncivil discourse via Twitter, something we discuss further later in the chapter.

This likely hints at a general mindset within the House Republican Conference held by both Tea Party and Coffee Republicans. To demonstrate the extent to which the Republican Conference leveraged incivility during the 112th Congress, we report the raw rates of incivility in tweets among those associated and not associated with the Tea Party movement. In addition to showing the average incivility at all three levels of Tea Party Attachment, we break down Tea Party Support into three groups for both congresses—those with the lowest scores on the standardized Support measures, those with moderate scores on the Support measures, and those with high Support scores.

As displayed in Figure 8.1, there was little difference in the rate of incivility use across all levels of both Tea Party Association dimensions in the 112th Congress. Indeed, the range across levels and dimensions is 1.3 to 1.7 percent, not too distinct from the rate of 1.5 percent for the entire 112th Conference. To further assess whether either dimension of Tea Party Association predicts incivility use, we turn to regression analysis, in which incivility rates are regressed on Tea Party Support and Tea Party Association. We also control for a number of individual-level factors, including the member's ideology (first-dimension DW-Nominate scores), the member's gender, the year the member took office,

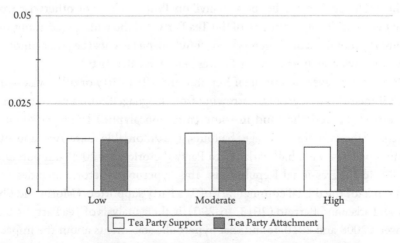

Figure 8.1 Average Incivility Rates by Tea Party Support and Tea Party Attachment, 112th Congress.

whether the member held a party leadership position, whether she or he held a committee leadership post, and the total number of tweets the member issued during the 112th Congress.

Table 8.1 includes the results of the analysis. As we have done previously, we consider the effects of attachment to the Tea Party as a single, three-category variable and as two dichotomous variables (Moderate Tea Party Attachment and High Tea Party Attachment) in two separate models. Consistent with the averages in Figure 8.1, neither Tea Party Support nor Tea Party Attachment is significant, nor does it matter whether Tea Party Attachment is included as a single variable (Table 8.1, column 1) or broken down into two variables (column 2).

DW-Nominate is significant in both models, however, indicating that more conservative members had a higher rate of incivility use. The year the member took office is also significant, indicating that longer-serving members also had a slightly higher rate of uncivil rhetoric on Twitter. The significance of total tweets in both models suggests that the more members tweeted, the higher was the percentage of uncivil tweets, but as with the tenure variable, the coefficient is miniscule.

It would seem that despite all of the attention given to the Tea Party's penchant for outrageous commentary, members affiliated with the movement were not any more likely to post uncivil tweets than Coffee members after the 2010 Tea Party wave. Conservatism and tenure of office drove some members to use more uncivil rhetoric on Twitter, but association with the Tea Party did not predict more incendiary rhetoric. One conclusion (which we elaborate on later) might be that Republicans, regardless of their association with the movement, adopted some of the uncivil rhetoric of the movement in the early days of the movement. Demonstrating that the Tea Party movement spurred congressional Republicans in the 112th Congress to be more uncivil on Twitter than they otherwise would have been is difficult, as the rise of the Tea Party and the widespread adoption of Twitter by members of Congress were simultaneous events (i.e., we cannot look at how uncivil members were on Twitter before the Tea Party).

We can, however, determine if Republicans—Tea Party or otherwise—used uncivil rhetoric strategically, borrowing from language themes prevalent in the movement. Hyperbolic (and in some cases apocalyptic) language about the effects of the stimulus package, bailouts, the Affordable Care Act, and other Obama policies was a hallmark of Tea Party rhetoric after 2009 and potentially a boon to congressional Republicans. This hyperbolic rhetoric includes (or is particular to) the digital commentary of Tea Party supporters (Morin and Flynn 2014). Parker and Barreto (2013, 46, 290), in their analysis of Tea Party websites between 2008 and 2010, found that hyperbolic statements about the impact of Obama policies on the economy were prevalent, including language emphasizing "destruction" and suggestions that the policies were "ruining America" (language

Table 8.1 **Tea Party Association and Incivility Rates in Tweets during the 112th Congress**

Variable	Incivility Rate, 112th (1)	Incivility Rate, 112th (2)
Tea Party Support	0.00	0.00
	(0.00)	(0.00)
Tea Party Attachment	−0.00	—
	(0.00)	—
Moderate Tea Party Attachment	—	−0.00
	—	(0.01)
High Tea Party Attachment	—	−0.00
	—	(0.00)
DW-Nominate	**0.03**	**0.03**
	(0.01)	**(0.01)**
Gender	−0.01	−0.01
	(0.01)	(0.01)
Year Took Office	**−0.00**	**−0.00**
	(0.00)	**(0.00)**
Party Leadership	−0.01	−0.01
	(0.01)	(0.01)
Committee Leadership	−0.01	−0.01
	(0.01)	(0.01)
Total Tweets	**0.00**	**0.00**
	(0.00)	**(0.00)**
Constant	**1.76**	**1.75**
	(0.55)	**(0.55)**
Observations	205	205
R^2	0.17	0.17

Note: Coefficients are results of OLS regression. Standard errors are in parentheses. Boldface indicates significance at $p < .05$ (one-tailed test).

that was far less prominent in the mainstream *National Review Online*). Tea Party rhetoric would provide an opportunity for Republicans, before and after the 2010 elections, to reshape the topics of debate from "change we can believe in" and Wall Street reform to Obamacare, government tyranny, ballooning deficits, and the effects of Obama's policies on the economy (Dionne 2016, 324; Skocpol and Williamson 2013, 160).

If the key to Republican success—before and after 2010—was to highlight the inadequacy of Obama administration policies and to secure, appease, and mobilize Tea Party supporters, then we would expect to see echoes of Tea Party hyperbole regarding the impact of Obama policies in House Republicans' rhetoric (e.g., "Tell them what they want to hear"). It is not surprising, then, that the House Republican Conference collectively issued well over 2,000 tweets describing Obama's "failed," "job-crushing," "job-killing," and "job-destroying" policies and presidency during the 112th Congress.[14] Often, these phrases were superfluous, meant to exaggerate their negative impact on policies and paint a picture of an economy being devastated. For example, Boehner tweeted in March 2011, "ObamaCare worsens our job-crushing debt crisis," and Green Tea Blake Farenthold tweeted in July 2012, "@BarackObama has made #recovery harder by allowing 106 new major job killing #regulations costing us over $46 billion." Removing "job-crushing" or "job killing" does not make these tweets any less critical of the healthcare law or Obama, nor does it alter their core claims (see Mutz and Reeves 2005). Moreover, there are other ways to make the point that Obama's policies have a negative economic impact; for example, "ObamaCare worsens our debt crisis and slows job growth." Yet phrases like "slow job growth" and even "hurt economic growth," are less dramatic, less severe, and arguably, in the minds of Republicans, less effective at mobilizing support.

Indeed, many of these tweets were written in a manner to suggest that Obama (and Democrats) were not just harming the economy, but doing so maliciously. For example, Tim Walberg (R-MI) tweeted in October 2011, "Do you think the Obama Administration has a job killing regulatory agenda?" and Ken Calvert tweeted in February 2012, "Obama wants to have it both ways on Keystone: wants 2 hide anti-jobs agenda while appeasing extreme enviros in party." Many of these tweets were designed seemingly to elicit outrage. Take this June 14, 2011, tweet from then–Republican whip (and Green Tea member) Kevin McCarthy(R-CA): "Unemployment at 9.1% while Obama laughs off failed economic policies that cost taxpayers trillions."[15] This post, the language of which was ostensibly borrowed from the Heritage Foundation,[16] was retweeted by ten other official congressional Republican Twitter accounts. A day later, McCarthy issued another tweet with language similar to this (e.g., "Can no longer tolerate broken promises & the WH laughing at its failed polices . . ."). Tweets of this type have a lot packed into them. They simultaneously make the argument that (1) Obama's policies are not fixing the economy (but are breaking promises to the American people), while also insinuating that (2) he is hurting hardworking, taxpaying Americans, and (3) is laughing about it. The first point alone might tap into frustration with the bailout and anger over economic conditions, but the last two points are meant to aggravate these sentiments and incite populist resentment toward the Obama administration and liberal elites more gener-ally by deriding who and what the government was spending money on and their attempts to regulate behavior, common concerns of Tea Party supporters (Barstow 2010; Cramer 2016; Skocpol and Williamson 2012, 79–80).

One of the most prevalent themes in the anti-Obama rhetoric of the mass-level Tea Party was the claim that he was a dangerous, socialist radical (Parker and Barreto 2013; Skocpol and Williamson 2012). Whether an accurate de-scription or not, "socialist" is generally regarded as a loaded term with a negative connotation in American politics (Senator Bernie Sanders's (I-VT) embrace of the term "democratic socialist" is noteworthy because it defies convention; it is the exception that proves the rule).[17] As argued by Berry and Sobieraj (2014, 50–53), the term is often used to vilify Democrats by associating them with left-wing extremism. Likewise, Herbst (2010, 55–56) notes that applying the "so-cialist" label to Democrats is an example of the strategic uses of incivility.

While legislators' tweets contained a number of allusions to socialist "creep" in the United States,[18] direct references to Obama as a socialist or to his policies as socialist or "socialized" was rare in tweets of the 112th Congress: we could identify only ten instances (see Table 8A.2). However, all but one of the tweets was made by either a Black Tea (Michele Bachmann and Allen West) or Green Tea member (Rob Aderholt (R-AL), Justin Amash, Paul Broun (R-GA), Trent Franks (R-AZ), Tim Huelskamp (R-KS), and Dennis Ross (R-FL)). The ex-ception was Rohrabacher, whose relationship with the Tea Party we discussed earlier. Tea Party rhetoric is also notable for the promotion of conspiracy theories regarding Obama's place of birth and his birth certificate. We could identify only two tweets referencing Obama's birth certificate in the 112th: both were made by Green Tea members from Texas, John Carter and Louie Gohmert, and both chastised Obama for his slow release of his long-form birth certificate (the tweets were issued after the White House announced he would do so), rather than promoting the conspiracy. In short, the "birther" conspiracy was not promoted by Republican members via their official Twitter accounts.

While incivility rates were more or less even across different levels of Tea Party Association in the 112th, this was not the case in the 113th Congress. As we have already noted, the amount of incivility in the 113th Congress ticked up slightly, compared with the 112th Congress—yet the change appears to have been driven solely by those who attached themselves to the Tea Party. Figure 8.2 displays the average incivility rate at different levels of both Tea Party Association dimensions during the 113th Congress. While those with low Attachment scores (i.e., those who made no effort to attach themselves to the Tea Party) had an in-civility rate of just 1.3 percent, those with moderate and high scores had an av-erage rate of 2.4 percent. This difference is the equivalent of about 12.5 additional uncivil tweets during the 113th Congress. On the other hand, we see that there

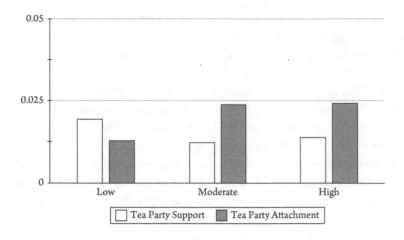

Figure 8.2 Average Incivility Rates by Tea Party Support and Tea Party Attachment, 113th Congress

is little connection between Tea Party Support—backing from the Tea Party movement—and the presence of incivility in tweets. In fact, the causal arrow appears to go in the opposite direction: the highest rates of incivility are among those with the lowest Tea Party Support scores (note that this group would include Green Teas).

Given some of our earlier findings, this is no surprise. Members who draw support from the Tea Party movement are not necessarily those with the strongest conservative credentials, particularly on the dimensions of social and racial conservatism. Where support goes is largely the result of tactical decision-making on behalf of Tea Party groups and activists—their money and energy go to where they are likely to get the most bang for their buck. It makes sense then that Tea Party Support has little connection to the more outrageous rhetoric of the Tea Party, as the legislators who score high on this scale are not seeking to publicly connect themselves to the movement and thus would not adopt or mimic its rhetoric. Nonetheless, those who had below-average Tea Party Support scores and who made no efforts to attach themselves to the movement—Coffee Republicans— had a below-average incivility rate in the 113th Congress of less than 1.3 percent (SD = 1.1). Non-Coffee members averaged almost a percentage point higher, with a rate of 2.2 percent, but there was also greater variation among these members (SD = 4.2). Contrast this with data for the 112th: Coffee Republicans had an average incivility level slightly above the average of 1.5 percent (SD = 3.8), whereas the Tea Partiers had an average slightly below 1.5 percent. The differences were not enormous but highlight the fact that things had changed in the 113th Congress.

As with the 112th Congress, we used regression analysis to control for potential confounding factors. The results of the model are shown in column 1 of

Table 8.2 **Tea Party Association and Incivility Rates in Tweets during the 113th Congress**

Variable	Incivility Rate, 113th (1)	Incivility Rate, 113th (2)
Tea Party Support	−0.00	−0.00
	(0.00)	(0.00)
Tea Party Attachment	**0.01**	—
	(0.00)	—
Moderate Tea Party Attachment	—	**0.01**
	—	**(0.01)**
High Tea Party Attachment	—	0.01
	—	(0.01)
DW-Nominate	0.02	0.01
	(0.01)	(0.01)
Gender	0.00	0.00
	(0.01)	(0.01)
Year Took Office	−0.00	−0.00
	(0.00)	(0.00)
Party Leadership	−0.00	−0.00
	(0.01)	(0.01)
Committee Leadership	−0.00	−0.00
	(0.07)	(0.01)
Total Tweets	0.00	0.00
	(0.00)	(0.00)
Constant	0.49	0.50
	(0.45)	(0.50)
Observations	220	220
R^2	0.05	0.05

Note: Coefficients are results of OLS regression. Standard errors are in parentheses. Boldface indicates significance at $p < .05$ (one-tailed test).

Table 8.2. Consistent with the raw averages in Figure 8.2, Tea Party Support is not significant in the model. However, Tea Party Attachment has a positive effect on incivility rates, increasing the rate by one percentage point with each move up the three-category variable, holding all else constant. Unlike what we found for the 112th, no other variable (including DW-Nominate scores, total number of tweets posted, and tenure of office) was significant in the model.

Is the effect of Tea Party Attachment on incivility rates linear, or do high levels of attachment not necessarily mean higher rates than moderate levels of attachment? This is a question worthy of investigation, as we have seen this previously with the 113th Congress. In part, this is because we use Liberty Caucus membership to construct our 113th Tea Party Attachment variable: only a small, niche group of fourteen members was included on Amash's official list, compared with the sixty official members of the Tea Party Caucus in the 112th. Thus, many who had high scores on the Attachment dimension in the 112th were "demoted" in the 113th due to the lack of a broad, popular Tea Party–oriented caucus in the 113th (again, we do not equate the two caucuses). As displayed in column 2 of Table 8.2, we see this dynamic play out again: holding all else constant, high-level Tea Party Attachment is not significant. However, the moderate-level Tea Party Attachment coefficient is significant and in the expected direction: those who made some efforts to attach themselves to the Tea Party had an incivility rate one percentage point higher than other Republican members, holding all else constant.

The significance of Tea Party Attachment, along with the insignificance of Tea Party Support, is a result similar to our findings on other tweeting behavior in the 113th Congress. In the preceding chapter, we reported that Tea Party Attachment in the 113th predicted higher levels of angry and sad rhetoric, which we interpreted as efforts to aggravate latent resentment. We also determined that Tea Party Attachment predicted more negative allusions to compromise, bipartisanship, and negotiation—behavior we consider indicative of anti-deliberative attitudes. Evidence that those who align themselves with the Tea Party use rhetoric tonally and attitudinally distinct from those who do not is in line with the conventional wisdom about the Tea Party elites we reviewed earlier. However, as we have seen in this chapter, Tea Party Attachment did not predict anger or sadness in the 112th Congress. In short, there seems to be a pattern in which the digital rhetoric of those attached to the Tea Party did not differ much from that of non-Tea Party Republicans in the 112th, but differences emerged for the 113th.

One explanation for this is the demise of the Tea Party Caucus, which in the 112th had served as a prime vehicle for Republicans with less than orthodox conservative records to boost conservative bona fides and take advantage of the energy of the movement. In addition, the Caucus's end in the 113th Congress was simultaneous with—or more likely endogenous to—the Tea Party brand's loss of some cachet: according to Gallup, by the fall of 2013, the number of Americans claiming to be supporters of the Tea Party movement had declined ten points from its high-water mark of 32 percent in November 2010 (Norman 2015). By the end of the 113th Congress, fewer than one in five would claim to be a supporter. Significantly, much of this drop in support was due to Republicans' and conservatives' increasing indifference to the movement: a growing share claimed to neither support nor oppose it. Thus, there was less incentive (and indeed more risk) for non-"true believers" to connect themselves to the movement.

To the extent that these members were not "true believers," we might expect that the degree to which their rhetoric—in terms of incivility and affective tones—mirrored that of the Tea Party would be tempered. That is, they posted tweets similar to McCarthy's tweets, and they did so infrequently. Once they no longer could or cared to attach themselves to the movement, only the "true believers" were left, and their rhetoric fits the mold of Tea Party members. These members, who truly perceived themselves to be part of the Tea Party, made substantial efforts to attach themselves to the movement. And as this happened in the 113th Congress, we can see how their rhetoric differs from that of other Republicans—it is more frequently uncivil, it more frequently strives to breed resentment, and it is anti-deliberative. To test this we looked at the nineteen legislators who went from Tea Party Caucus members in the 112th to scoring 0 on the Tea Party Attachment index in the 113th and who tweeted in both congresses.[19] As can be seen in Figure 8.3, the averages provide some support for this explanation: in the 112th, this group averaged an incivility rate of 1.4 percent (just below the average rate of 1.5 percent for the entire conference), and in the 113th, it averaged 1.5 percent (again, just below the conference average of 1.6 percent). When we look at the twenty-four who were members of the Tea Party Caucus in the 112th and remained attached to the Tea Party in the 113th, we see a surge in incivility use: this group had an incivility rate of 1.7 percent (SD = 1.3) in the 112th, which increased to 4.0 percent (SD = 7.1) in the 113th. Note the high standard deviation—this average for the group was propped up by the inclusion of the tweeters with the two highest incivility rates in the 113th—but even excluding these two extreme outliers, the group average was 2.3 percent (SD = 1.5).

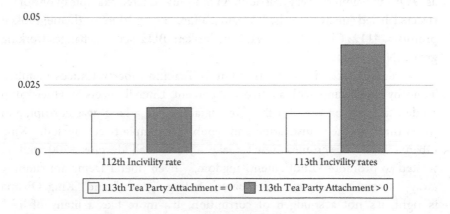

Figure 8.3 Incivility Rates Among Tea Party Caucus Members Who Served in 112th and 113th Congresses

Thus, another part of the answer seems to be that members who attached themselves to the movement became more emboldened and used more incivility in the 113th Congress than in the 112th. Of the sixty-nine members who score a 1 or 2 on the Tea Party Attachment index in the 113th, fifty-two also served in the 112th (and tweeted in both congresses).[20] We compared their 113th incivility rates with the 112th incivility rates. The results are clear-cut: whereas this group averaged an incivility rate of 1.6 percent (SD = 1.2) during the 112th—very close to the average of 1.5 percent for the entire conference—they averaged 2.6 percent (SD = 5.1) during the 113th, an entire percentage point more and well above the 1.6 percent all Republicans averaged during the 113th. Moreover, this difference is not driven by some members attaching themselves to the Tea Party in the 113th after scoring 0 on the index in the 112th. In fact, when these members are excluded, the difference between the congresses becomes larger: the average among the thirty-eight members who consistently had some attachment to the Tea Party in both congresses was just under 1.6 (SD = 1.2) percent in the 112th, but swelled to 3.0 (SD = 6.0) in the 113th. Note again the high standard deviation in the 113th. When the two outliers already mentioned are excluded, the 112th rate falls to 1.5 (SD = 1.2) and 113th rate falls to 2.0 (SD = 1.3)—not as impressive a difference, but still indicative of the fact that those who attached themselves to the Tea Party were more uncivil in the 113th Congress than in the 112th.

So who were these outliers? The lineup of members with the highest incivility rates during the 113th Congress changed from the lineup in the 112th. The top spot was now claimed by Green Tea member Trent Franks, who traded the Tea Party Caucus for the Liberty Caucus (and also made the top ten in the 112th). Franks averaged an absurd rate of 36.2 percent and, like Rohrabacher in the 112th, was an extreme outlier. One reason the rate was this high was that for several days in July 2014, Franks's account decided to tweet out what was referred to as "#ObamaFailures" every half hour. A randomly selected example of one of his tweets labeled "uncivil" reads, "#ObamaFailures every 30 mins Theme: broken promises. #112: Claim: "Fine. Nat'l site broken. BUT state exchanges working great!" Nope. #tcot."

Coming in second was another Green Tea and Liberty Caucus member, Timothy Huelskamp, with a rate of 7.2 percent. Uncivil tweets by Huelskamp tended to focus on the idea that Obama acted like a king, was corrupt, and was a threat to the Constitution and republic. Example tweets include "King Obama says his #cronies didn't make a #HardSell despite $700 million wasted to promote #EntitlementKingdom," "Even liberal Dems are running away—screaming—from King Obama's failing agenda," and "King Obama is right, it's not a smidgen of corruption. It's more like a litany of lies." Huelskamp also repeatedly spoke of the devastation Obama's policies were supposedly wreaking on the economy, using terms like "ObamaScare" (his phrase for Obamacare) and the "#Obummer economy." Huelskamp would also link Obama to socialism on several occasions; for example, referencing a Fox News poll indicating low support for government efforts to reduce income inequality, he tweeted, "Voters choose founders & free enterprise over Obama & his socialism."

Following Huelskamp was another Green Tea Republican, the freshman member Jim Bridenstine (R-OK) with 6.8 percent. Bridenstine, who, like Franks and Huelskamp, would (informally) join the Freedom Caucus in the 114th Congress, also posted that Obama posed a danger to the republic ("Obama's attempt to rule by decree is unconstitutional, and dangerous to our republic. #Obamacare") and repeatedly described an irresponsible, unresponsive, and out-of-control Obama-run federal government using the hashtag "#ObamaGovtGoneWild." Bridenstine, too, would link Obama policies with socialism, arguing, "The purpose of Obamacare is to further the goal of implementing socialized medicine. #DefundObamacare." Overall, tweets connecting Obama to socialism ticked up only slightly in the 113th—but, again, nearly all were issued by Black and Green Tea members.

Rounding out the top ten were Roger Williams (R-TX) with 5.5 percent, Pete Olson (R-TX) with 5.4 percent, Renee Ellmers (R-NC) with 5.2 percent, Doc Hastings (R-WA) with 5.1 percent, and Mike Kelly (R-PA), Dana Rohrabacher, and Diane Black (R-TN), all with 5.0 percent. Of this group, Ellmers and Black qualified as Green Tea Republicans, and Kelly qualified as a White Tea Republican. Collectively, the top ten issued almost 1,000 tweets marked uncivil throughout the 113th. Members with reputations for uncivil behavior and making controversial remarks were not too far down in the rankings. Steve King's rate of 4.0 percent was good enough for fifteenth-highest in the conference, while Joe Wilson ranked twentieth, with a rate of 3.3 percent. Bachmann's rate of 2.3 percent was comparatively pedestrian but still above average, placing her in the top forty.

Notably absent from the top ten in the 113th Congress was John Boehner. Having made the top ten in the 112th Congress, with a rate of 3.7 percent, he fell to thirty-fifth in the Republican conference in the 113th, with a "mere" 2.4 percent. We do not and cannot know what was going on in the Speaker's head, but we do not think this reflects a change of heart regarding tactics. Indeed, Boehner claimed to have left office in September 2015 "with no regrets or burdens" (Sheshgreen 2015). A lifelong Catholic, he has been described as being "at peace" in the days and hours leading up to his resignation, following his meeting with Pope Francis during the pontiff's visit to Congress (Costa 2015). And he actually posted more uncivil tweets in the 113th Congress than the 112th, as he made more than double the amount of tweets overall in the latter congress. In general, his incivility rates were above average, and it is a fair assumption that many members followed his lead as Speaker when it came to digital discourse (e.g., we found more than 4,600 retweets of Boehner by the official accounts of other Republicans during both congresses). Hence, celebrating Boehner's "commitment to civility, cross-party dialogue and compromise," as the University of Notre Dame did in 2016, might strike some as curious (Capehart 2016).[21] What Boehner's fall in the rankings indicates is less a change of heart regarding rhetoric—his 113th rate would have put him in the top twenty uncivil tweeters in the 112th—than an acceleration of the uncivil rhetoric of others in the Republican Conference. And the data indicate that it was primarily those who attached themselves to the Tea Party who were moving up the rankings.

Accepting the Mantle of Anger: The Rhetoric of Donald Trump

Tellingly, the few media presentations that have received credit for "predicting" the rise of Donald Trump in some form or fashion in the years before 2015 have been satirical. They include a fake news video (and by "fake news," we really mean fake news) produced by *The Onion* soon after Obama's 2012 re-election, entitled "After Obama Victory, Shrieking White-Hot Sphere of Pure Rage Early GOP Front-Runner for 2016."[22] A "reporter" for the piece announces that "this screaming orb just might be the only one who really taps into the deep-seated seething fear felt by so many Republicans right now," while a disappointed "voter" notes, "Mitt Romney just didn't get me fired up enough to vote, but that sphere of anger really speaks to me."

We refuse to call Donald Trump a "shrieking white-hot sphere of pure rage," because that would not be politically correct,[23] Instead, we will call his ascendancy the manifestation of resentment provoked in part by members of the Republican Party. Trump's rhetoric—accentuating the decline of the white working class and forgoing any and all pretenses of civilized discourse—is a more extreme (and perhaps more potent) version of the rhetoric espoused by Black and Green Tea Republicans. Despite the lack of premonitions regarding his rise, *The Onion* notwithstanding, the Trump phenomenon did not come out of nowhere—and neither did his rhetoric.

In this section, we will analyze the rhetoric of Trump, focusing not only on his incivility but also on the affective tone of his tweets. We expect to see not only high levels of incivility, but also the presence of angry and sad rhetoric. Commonly, Trump's rhetoric is described as angry, with intent to breed resentment—much in line with our Tea Party rhetoric findings described in Chapter 7.

Ethnic Nationalism, Populism, and Resentment

Commentators have asserted that Trump's rhetoric reflects ethnic nation-alism, which views trade and international relations as a zero-sum game (Brooks 2016; *Economist* 2016). While he claims to support some free trade (e.g., Schwartz 2016), his view that the United States is "losing" by engaging in many free-trade deals and accepting immigrants is well documented. In line with ethnic nationalist rhetoric, Trump's rhetoric is thought to express aggression toward out-groups and nostalgia for past greatness ("Make America Great Again") and focuses on race and ethnicity (*Economist* 2016; Rothwell and Diego-Rosell 2016).

This last point is reflected in the number of preliminary analyses linking Trump supporters to ethnocentric views. Analyses based on the 2016 American National Election Studies data found that Trump supporters are more likely to have cold feelings toward many groups, but warmer feelings toward whites, than are supporters of other Republican presidential aspirants (Ingraham 2016; Kalkan 2016; McDaniel and McElwee 2016). Moreover, white identity appears to matter more to Trump supporters, with stronger attachment to white identity predicting cooler feelings toward Hispanics and Muslims (McDaniel and McElwee 2016). Similarly, racial isolation and a lack of exposure to Latin American immigrants have been connected to Trump support (Rothwell and Diego-Rosell 2016). Ethnocentric attitudes may be latent, but they can be acti-vated and aggravated by elite manipulation.

If this sounds familiar to you—not unlike the argument Cramer (2016a) made regarding Walker and the Tea Party's attempts to breed resentment in rural Wisconsinites—then you are not the only one. Cramer (2016b), writing in the *Washington Post*, argued:

> What happened in Wisconsin is now happening nationwide. Trump is capitalizing on that same resentment, and blaming others for voters' sense of being dismissed, disrespected, and left behind. This is how Donald Trump will win the Rust Belt, and probably the Republican nomination. *He is turning up the flame under resentment that has been simmering for years.* The strategy will likely work, despite the Republican Party's attempts to put out the fire. [emphasis added]

Indeed, as we found with Tea Party rhetoric in the preceding chapter, Trump's rhetoric is said to remind (or suggest to) his base that they have suffered so-cial and material losses, along with a loss of freedom and status. Thomas Edsall (2016a), writing in the *New York Times*, notes that Trump's success reflects a "triumph of resentment." The push for tolerance, diversity, inclusiveness, and multiculturalism by progressives, Edsall suggests, has given rise to psychological reactance among many older white males, leading them to take steps to restore freedom and autonomy. Trump, the "PC-puncher," not only endorses these sentiments, but encourages and aggravates them.

A related argument that has received significant attention (and has been thoroughly explicated by Amanda Taub in a 2016 piece for *Vox*) is that Trump's rhetoric—particularly the "law and order" and punitive elements, Manichaean reasoning, and claims that he alone can fix problems that weaker politicians have failed to solve—is consistent with authoritarianism and that support for Trump is a symptom of the rise of authoritarianism within the Republican base (Taub 2016). As Hetherington and Weiler (2009) argue, since the Republican Party reinvented itself as a party of "law and order" and traditional values in the 1960s, authoritarians have gradually gravitated toward the party. The social change the country has undergone in recent years—increasing diversity and greater acceptance of members of the LGBTQ community—is experienced by people with authoritarian personalities as personally threatening, spurring them to rally behind someone who, in the words of social psychologist Jonathan Haidt, promises to "lock down the borders, kick out those who are different, and punish those who are morally deviant" (Taub 2016).

Whether Trump's ascendancy can be best explained by his embrace of ethnic nationalism, ethnocentrism, authoritarianism, some combination of each, all three, or something entirely different, we leave to others, but we argue that the common thread that runs through each of these theories is the aggravation of feelings of resentment among the white working class.[24] Moreover, we assert that there are extensive similarities between the rhetoric of Tea Party Republicans and Trump. The answer to the question of "Why Trump, why now?" is that Tea Party rhetoric primed white working-class Republicans to find Trumpian rhetoric acceptable and attractive.

The claim that Republican rhetoric in the Tea Party era helps explain the rise of Trump has many adherents. Robert Kagan (2016), writing in the *Washington Post*, argues that the Republican Party's rhetoric and tactics in recent years, led to the "creation" of Trump, describing him as

> its Frankenstein's monster, brought to life by the party, fed by the party and now made strong enough to destroy its maker . . . We are supposed to believe that Trump's legion of "angry" people are angry about wage stagnation. No, they are angry about all the things Republicans have told them to be angry about these past 7½ years, and it has been Trump's good fortune to be the guy to sweep them up and become their standard-bearer. He is the Napoleon who has harvested the fruit of the revolution.

Kagan is far from the only person to describe Trump as the Republicans' Frankenstein monster; many observers have noted a similarity between the rhetoric of Trump and that of the Tea Party, arguing that they both have drawn upon and aggravated latent ethno-nationalist sentiment, promoted conspiracy theories, and adopted breaches of decorum as a core tactic (Chait 2016; Steinhauer 2016).[25] Trump's policy stances differed little from those of two of his rivals for the 2016 Republican nomination, Cruz and Rubio, both of whom had Tea Party ties. But while there was little difference in policy positions, Trump delivered a different type of "salesmanship . . . [which included] more entertaining oratory and online insults; better campaign swag; and more overt appeals to racism and xenophobia. (He makes dog whistles audible to humans.) Trump may be less civil than the others, but in the age of reality TV, incivility sells" (Rampell 2016).

Thus, what made Trump different from the others was not the originality of his messages, but the intensity and conspicuousness of his points. Yet if the rhetorical styles that had been previously reserved for political commentators on talk radio, cable news, and internet forums not gained a foothold in government with the rise of the Tea Party in the House, then Trump's rhetoric would seem all the more abrasive and unacceptable. Not only did Tea Party rhetoric render uncivil and resentful talk from the mouths (or keypads) of the people's representatives a normality, increased reliance on the resentful appeals and uncivil brazenness of Black and Green Tea members of the 113th Congress enhanced the appeal of Trump.

We have focused primarily on the style of rhetoric, but there are similarities between Trump and the Tea Party when it comes to subjects. Political scientist Rachel Blum has found that many of the topics found on Tea Party websites, as well as the framing of those topics, are remarkably similar to the rhetoric of Trump; among these topics are the media, American exceptionalism, law and order, foreign countries, and immigration (Blum 2017). We believe that Trumpian bombast is a natural outgrowth of Tea Party rhetoric, though perhaps a more extreme version. The appeal, acceptance, and embrace of Trump's commentary would not have been possible if the Tea Party had not normalized this style of political talk before Trump's foray into politics.

Of course, Trump was fanning the flames himself during this period. For example, he began to question Obama's country of birth, and thus his eligibility for the presidency, in early 2011, questions that have been widely considered part and parcel of racist conspiracy theories (Parker and Eder 2016; Sargent 2016). And it could be that members of Congress borrowed rhetoric from Trump. Thus, it is possible, or even likely, that Trump helped to create the conditions that enabled his own rise. But imagine if Republican members of Congress had resisted this style of rhetoric. Imagine if they had offered plenty of critiques of Obama, but resoundingly and publicly rejected conspiracy theories about Obama's country of birth and religion. Imagine if their tweets had promoted their policy ideas and picked apart the policies of Democrats, but were delivered in a decorous, civil manner. If Trump and other firebrands were kept on the fringes, their tactics rejected and their language censured, would feelings of resentment had hit the fever pitch that they did during the Obama years?

Trump may have had a healthy Twitter following during this time and a friendly conservative media establishment that could expand his reach. These were necessary conditions, but not sufficient. If congressional Republicans had taken a different tack in 2010, approaching anti-Obama furor far more tepidly and rebuking those inside and outside of government who offered the most incendiary claims, this would have tempered resentment, and the appetite for Trumpian bombast would have been less voracious come 2015. To believe otherwise is to deny congressional Republicans any agency—it is to say that they were merely swept along on this wave and that there was nothing they could have done or said that would have changed the course of events that brought us to the Trump presidency. Depending on your perspective, this line of thought absolves them of any guilt or denies them any credit. Perhaps all can agree that it is unlikely that Tea Party rhetoric had no role in fostering resentment during the 112th and 113th Congresses.

Instead, we think that Tea Party members of the House helped create the conditions for Trump's victories—conditions that were necessary but, on their own, not sufficient. Trump needed to have credence among a segment of the Republican electorate, and so his tweeting behavior in the years leading up to 2015 was essential. It is likely that the conservative media establishment helped blaze the path to Trump's rise as well. But they had willing partners in the Tea Party faction of the House GOP who were more eager than other Republicans to leverage incendiary rhetoric and continuously reminded voters that elected officials did not have to sound like statesmen. Once Pandora's box was opened, expectations were set, and rhetoric could not be toned down, only ratcheted up.

Affect in Trump's Tweet Rhetoric and Its Antecedents

In Chapter 7, we demonstrated that House members attached to the Tea Party in the 113th Congress were more likely than others to embrace aversion-inducing rhetoric, including allusions to what Americans had lost and how the federal government had failed them. Tweets incorporating angry words were strongly tied to our Tea Party Attachment measure. Donald Trump himself would likely admit that he discusses these themes and has embraced "anger." As he stated in a Republican presidential primary debate in January 2016: "I will gladly accept the mantle of anger . . . Our military is a disaster. Our healthcare is a horror show . . . Illegal immigration is beyond belief. Our country is being run by incompetent people. And yes, I am angry . . . because our country is a mess" (McManus 2016).

We consider this claim further by examining the affect underlying Trump's tweets, again with the aid of LIWC. The data include about 4,300 tweets from Trump's personal Twitter account (@realdonaldtrump) made from February 2016 through May 2017 and tweets from the official presidential account (@ POTUS) made from January 2017 through May 2017. Comparing analyses of Trump's tweets with analyses of Congress members' tweets has limitations: tweets from both of Trump's accounts are not subject to the same rules as tweets from members' official accounts, and the "official" account often retweets posts from the "unofficial" account, or both accounts issue the same tweet. Moreover, most of the tweets we will analyze were made when Trump did not hold elected office (although he was the de facto or official Republican nominee for president for much of this period). With these caveats in mind, measuring affect in Trump's tweets can provide insight into how much his rhetoric resembled that of members attached to the Tea Party.

As shown in Table 8.3, there are some differences in the frequency of angry, anxious, and sad words in Trump's personal and official accounts. Angry and anxious words appeared only slightly less frequently in the tweets of the official account: 0.51 percent of all words tweeted by the personal account were angry, versus 0.42 percent of words tweeted by the official account, and 0.21 percent of words tweeted by the unofficial account were anxious, compared with 0.14 percent of the words from the official account. When it came to sad words, there were much larger differences: 0.43 percent of the words tweeted by the unofficial account were sad, whereas just 0.15 percent of words from the official account were sad. Part of this discrepancy has to do with the fact that Trump

Table 8.3 **Percentage of Angry, Anxious, and Sad Words in the Tweets of Trump**

Twitter Handle	Anger	Anxiety	Sadness
Unofficial: @RealDonaldTrump (4,292 tweets)	0.51	0.21	0.43
Official: @POTUS (616 tweets)	0.42	0.14	0.15

Note: Values are the percentage of words that qualify as angry, anxious, or sad, according to the Linguistic Inquiry Word Count 2015 Internal Dictionary.

often alluded to "failing" institutions (e.g., "the failing New York Times") throughout the campaign season and often ended his tweets deriding others with his trademark exclamation "Sad!," which is meant as an insult. When the stems "fail*" and "sad*" are excluded, the percentage of words qualifying as "sad" falls to 0.26, and the official account percentage falls to 0.11.[26] Even then, some of Trump's "sad" rhetoric referred to "low" ratings and to "losers" and people who "lost" badly to him.

Nonetheless, there was also rhetoric painting a picture of a country in decline, disappointed by failed leadership. While Trump was singled out before and after the campaign for having a doom-and-gloom message, he was not the first to make the case for a nation in a downward spiral. Indeed, there are some remarkable similarities between the sad rhetoric of Trump and the sad rhetoric of some of the Black and Green Tea members of the 113th Congress we highlighted in Chapter 7.

One predictably common theme is the perils of Obamacare. For example, while Michele Bachmann tweeted in September 2014, "Obamacare is doomed for [sic] failure," and Jim Bridenstine tweeted in August 2013, "Obamacare is a disaster. It is damaging our economy and hurting American families. #DefundObamacare," Trump issued a tweet with similar language in October 2016: "Obamacare is a disaster. Rates going through the sky—ready to explode. I will fix it. Hillary can't! #ObamacareFailed."

Beyond anti-Obamacare rhetoric, there were other thematic similarities, including poor leadership and increasing despair under Obama, in the tweets of Tea Partiers and Trump. Bridenstine wrapped up a tweetstorm about Obama's approval ratings in July 2014 with a post (retweeted by Black Tea Thomas Massie), "#42Reasons Obama's approval rating is 42%—Final Reason—FAILED LEADERSHIP. #tcot." Likewise, Trump posted a link in August 2016 with the text, "STATEMENT IN RESPONSE TO PRESIDENT OBAMA'S FAILED LEADERSHIP." Tim Huelskamp tweeted in October 2014: "#Obummer: Americans continue to view the country on the wrong track. 6 years of #hope has changed into despair." Trump echoed in July 2016, "Our country does not feel 'great already' to the millions of wonderful people living in poverty, violence and despair."

One of Trump's notable themes during the 2016 campaign was that the recovery from the Great Recession was the slowest since the Great Depression seven decades prior.[27] For example, Trump tweeted in July 2016, "We are suffering through the worst long-term unemployment in the last 70 years. I want change—Crooked Hillary Clinton does not," and in August 2016, "Obama's disastrous judgment gave us ISIS, rise of Iran, and the worst economic numbers since the Great Depression!" This theme is also present in the tweets of Tea Partiers in the 113th: Huelskamp tweeted in April 2014, "The #ObummerEconomy #FastFoodRecovery is the worst since the Great

Depression," while Bachmann posted in July 2013, "Pres. Obama repeated his usual jobs speech, but numbers dont [*sic*] lie: worst economic recovery since Great Depression. #SpeechesDontHire," and Trent Franks posted in July 2014, "#ObamaFailures every half-hour until list is complete. #146 Unemployment rates almost unheard of since Great Depression. #tcot."

Trump and Tea Party House members also both tweeted that other aspects of the American economy were at their lowest point in decades. While Green Tea Renee Ellmers tweeted in January 2014, "The Labor Force Participation Rate is at it's [*sic*] lowest since April 1978 w/ a shocking 91.27 MILLION Americans NOT in the labor force today," Trump tweeted in July 2016, "American home-ownership rate in Q2 2016 was 62.9%—lowest rate in 51yrs. WE will bring back the 'American Dream!'" And when John Boehner tweeted in January 2014, "Lower incomes, more Americans living in poverty the #newnormal under President Obama," Donald Trump followed up with the August 2016 post "A vote for Hillary Clinton is a vote for another generation of poverty, high crime, & lost opportunities. #ImWithYou." Boehner may have been a Coffee member in the 113th, but his rhetoric belied this.

Polls throughout 2016 indicated that Americans were pessimistic about the economy and that American leadership was unwilling or unable to look out for the average American, despite the fact that macroeconomic meas-ures indicated a robust economy (see Long 2016 and White 2016). Although members of the white working class were, on average, better off economically than members of the nonwhite working class, it was the latter group that was far more optimistic about America's economic future and more likely to be-lieve the American Dream was "alive and well" (Casselman 2016). However, Trump's apparent "doom-and-gloom" rhetoric in 2016 was not the origin of these dichotomies. In the years before 2016, political elites in the House recounted the ways Americans had been failed. In the 113th Congress, this type of language increased among Black and Green Teas—those hoping to attach themselves to the populist movement fueled by resentment. They offered not optimism, but confirmation that "average Americans" were not getting what they deserve, and then some. "Average Americans" were informed that liberals in government thought they were stupid and that "federal job-killing over regulations" were costing them tens of thousands of dollars per year (as Huelskamp claimed in a pair of 2014 tweets).[28] Americans were also told that amnesty for illegal immigrants would cause labor rates to further de-cline and cost taxpayers trillions of dollars (Bridenstine claimed this in a pair of 2014 tweets).[29]

Other themes in Trump's rhetoric had antecedents in themes House members attached to the Tea Party in the 113th Congress touched on, themes that non-Tea Party legislators largely avoided. Before Trump announced in

2015 that he would build a border wall and that Mexico would pay for it, Green Tea member Todd Rokita (R-IN) tweeted out an idea in September 2013 that illegal immigrants should be used to build it.[30] Before Trump warned of the lawlessness and criminality that Obama's immigration policies had spawned, declared he would bring back law and order, and recruited his supporters to "keep an eye out" for fraudulent voters, Black Tea member Steve King took to Twitter during the 113th to warn Americans of the dangers of "Obama's lawless [amnesty] order" and recruited his fellow Iowans to "keep an eye out" for a "busload of UAC [Unaccompanied Alien Child] #illegals" coming their way.[31] Before Trump tweeted about the "WEAK leadership of Obama" and that Obama "Only makes bad deals!" Green Tea member John Carter asked Americans in a September 2014 tweet if they agreed that "Obama's weak leadership led us to our current position internationally." In addition, before Trump tweeted in March 2016, "Obama, and all others, have been so weak, and so politically correct, that terror groups are forming and getting stronger! Shame," Carter was sharing his thoughts on Twitter in 2013 that the 2009 Fort Hood shooting was "the cost of being politically correct."[32] Before Trump announced in December 2015 that he was "calling for a complete shutdown of Muslims entering the United States,"[33] Green Tea member Louie Gohmert promoted a story on Twitter that the Department of Homeland Security would be giving "deference to Muslim extremists,"[34] and fellow Green Tea member Walter Jones (R-NC) shared that he was against National Endowment for the Humanities (NEH) funding going to a program that would promote "Muslim cultures" at a community college.[35]

Before Trump tweeted throughout 2016 that the "dishonest media" had it out for him and was underestimating his strength among the grassroots, Huelskamp tweeted out an article in June 2014 emphasizing the strength of the Tea Party grassroots with the message, "Guess what liberal media . . . Tea Party is alive and well!" Before Trump tweeted in February 2017, "The FAKE NEWS media (failing @nytimes, @NBCNews, @ABC, @CBS, @CNN) is not my enemy, it is the enemy of the American People!" Lamar Smith (R-TX), a Green Tea member in the 112th Congress, tweeted in March 2014, "Liberal media bias is a threat to our #democracy." And before Trump tweeted in October 2016, "We must bring the truth directly to hard-working Americans who want to take our country back," Green Tea member Jeff Duncan (R-SC) promoted the idea on Twitter in 2013 that the country needed to be moved "back towards the Constitution" and reclaimed.[36]

Trump announced in his 2017 inauguration speech, "From this day forward, it's going to be only America First. America First,"(Bennett 2017). The slogan "America First" has a long and controversial history, with connections to anti-Semitism, isolationism, sympathy for fascism, and ethnic nationalism (Bennett 2017; Calamur 2017). Trump has stated that his use of the phrase is meant to convey that he wants America to stop being "disrespected, mocked, and ripped off" by other countries and that he plans to withdraw from or renegotiate free-trade pacts (Bennett 2017). One of Trump's core arguments before and after the 2016 campaign was that "weak leaders" had allowed Mexico and other countries to take advantage of the United States; as he tweeted soon after taking office in January 2017, "Mexico has taken advantage of the U.S. for long enough. Massive trade deficits & little help on the very weak border must change, NOW!"

Several Coffee members used variants of the phrase "America first" in tweets during the 113th Congress, but with far different connotations than Trump's. For example, Scott Rigell (R-VA) tweeted about his "America First" plan (as in country before party) that would restore cuts resulting from the 2013 budget sequestration.[37] A pair of other Coffee members—Larry Buchshon (R-IN) and Randy Hultgren (R-IL)—tweeted about plans to keep "America first" in research, science, and innovation. Only one member of the 113th—Black Tea member Randy Weber (R-TX)—used the phrase in a sense similar to Trump's, including a tweet from July 2014 referencing Mexico, "It's Time To Put America First! Tell Obama to use existing authority & resources to secure border. Take $ from foreign aid & send them back!," and a tweet from November 2014, "Minimalize Obama's lies, keep our eyes on the prize: 'The beautiful for spacious skies.' America matters Mr. President. Put America first!"

In sum, we find that legislators attached to the Tea Party were making Trumpian points before Trump announced his candidacy in 2015—and making the case for a candidate like Trump. Slamming the Obama administration in a September 2014 tweet, Black Tea member Steve Southerland (R-FL) asked, "Will Americans get the leadership they deserve?" For Americans listening and waiting for an answer, Trump's February 2016 tweet (in response to an announcement that Carrier was laying off 1,400 workers in Indiana) might have seemed like salvation: "I am the only one who can fix this. Very sad. Will not happen under my watch! #MakeAmericaGreatAgain." Trump's claim that America needed to be restored to greatness would have seemed a no-brainer, as the case that the country was supposedly in free fall had already been made. Notably, even Trump's infamous slogan was not original to him: while Ronald Reagan first used "make America great again" in 1980 (and Bill Clinton, ironically, did so in his first campaign for president) (Margolin 2016), versions of the slogan were used on Twitter by several Black and Green Tea Republicans during the 112th Congress, and as early as 2011.[38]

Frequency of Incivility in Trump's Tweets

Trump's tweet rhetoric, as we noted at the beginning of this chapter, has a reputation for incivility. As we have shown, those who attached themselves to the Tea Party in the 113th Congress, on average, were more uncivil than Coffee and White Tea Republicans. Using the same training set and method that we used to code the congressional tweets,[39] we gauge what percentage of Trump's tweets qualify as uncivil.

Overall, close to 12.5 percent of Trump's unofficial (i.e., personal account) tweets were labeled uncivil, and only around 2 percent of his official account tweets were uncivil. This variance is consistent with reports that the official @ POTUS account "presents an official, subdued version of the administration, while the other provides access to the president's stream of consciousness" (Hemmer 2017). Yet given Trump's reputation as a tweeter, some may be surprised that the percentage of uncivil tweets from his personal, unofficial account is not higher. We offer several thoughts. First, reviewing the tweets the program did not label "uncivil," we presume that the program may have missed some tweets that would likely qualify as uncivil—so Trump's rate might be slightly underestimated. Second, perhaps an underreported aspect of Trump's Twitter behavior is the extent to which he positively reflects on himself and his campaign—not unlike Congress members' promotion of themselves and their activities within their districts. He often exaggerated the historic implications of his campaign (e.g., "I have been drawing very big and enthusiastic crowds, but the media refuses to show or discuss them. Something very big is happening!"). A significant number of tweets were dedicated to encouraging his supporters, ginning up enthusiasm, selling his candidacy, and thanking supporters and news media for good news (e.g., "Thank you for your support! TOGETHER we will MAKE AMERICA GREAT AGAIN!" and "Thank you to @foxandfriends for the great review of the speech on immigration last night. Thank you also to the great people of Arizona!"). He also often retweeted supporters, thanking them for their kind words. In total, nearly 14 percent of all of his tweets contained the words "thank you." Trump's tweet rhetoric, consisting of gratitude to and encouragement for his supporters, alongside biting disparagement of opponents, is not unlike Palin's rhetorical balancing act during the 2008 presidential campaign (Herbst 2010, 48–49).

That said, Trump's average is plenty high, and although it is bested by the official accounts of two members of Congress—Rohrabacher in the 112th and Franks in the 113th—it is likely that few congressional tweets pack in as much incivility as Trump's. Trump's adeptness at incivility allows him to make multiple (often disparaging) points in very few words, such as this February 2016 tweet: "Little Marco Rubio treated America's ICE officers 'like absolute trash' in order to pass Obama's amnesty." Rubio is given a belittling sobriquet, is accused of offensive behavior toward law enforcement, is tied to Obama, and both Rubio and Obama are tied to amnesty, a policy unpopular with conservatives   in just sixteen words. Trump's frequent use of disparaging, belittling adjectives for his opponents is often coupled with hyperbole and digitally strident elements (e.g., "#CrookedHillary has FAILED all over the world! #BigLeagueTruth" and "Little Marco Rubio gave amnesty to criminal aliens guilty of 'sex offenses.' DISGRACE!"). Trump's tweets also referred to conspiracy theories, such as his infamous March 2017 tweet, "Terrible! Just found out that Obama had my 'wires tapped' in Trump Tower just before the victory. Nothing found. This is McCarthyism!" They also contained threats, such as a tweet directed toward Republican primary opponent Ted Cruz, "Lyin' Ted Cruz just used a picture of Melania from a G.Q. shoot in his ad. Be careful, Lyin' Ted, or I will spill the beans on your wife!," and a May 12, 2017 tweet directed toward former FBI director James Comey, whom Trump had fired the day before, "James Comey better hope that there are no 'tapes' of our conversations before he starts leaking to the press!" (Shear and Apuzzo 2017).

Trump's surprising 2016 victories and penchant for controversial tweets has inspired countless analyses of how he utilizes the platform.[40] However, we assert that it is not the novelty of Trump's uncivil tweeting style that we should focus on, but the frequency and extremity of his tweets. Elite discourse on Twitter was not devoid of incivility before Trump came along; as we have shown, Trump's tweets are stylistically and thematically similar to those of legislators attached to the Tea Party—especially the tweets of Black and Green Tea Republicans in the 113th Congress. There are exceptions, of course. That is not to say that these members inspired Trump to tweet the way he does, but rather that they created an appetite (or perhaps a compulsion) for Trump's Twitter style. Their rhetoric was the bridge that took us from a political culture largely devoid of uncivil social media use two election cycles prior to one in which the ultimate winner relied on incivility throughout the campaign. The Twitter style of Black and Green Tea members not only helped normalize uncivil political messages on Twitter but, as we showed in the preceding chapter, helped to stir up resentment within the populace that would lead a segment of the Republican base to accept only messages delivered in "politically incorrect" terms. They paved the way for Trump.

Institutionalized Incivility and Resentment: The Tea Party's Legacy

Incivility has always been a part of American political discourse, and those in search of a golden era of civility are likely to come up short. Yet a common contention of political observers of late is that the United States has entered a "golden era of incivility."[41] Political scientists and historians rightly point to other eras when American politics was consumed by outrageous rhetoric or worse, or argue that temporal changes in context and norms make comparing eras a difficult if not impossible task (e.g., Herbst 2010; Sapiro 1999). Nonetheless, the frequency of elite political incivility for public consumption, we argue, is most likely unique to our time. We believe this for several reasons.

The first is simply logistics. The advent of cable television weakened the president's "monopolistic access to the public," a mainstay of the broadcast era, as members of Congress now had means to communicate directly with the public (Kernell 2006, 215–216). The rise of social media has dramatically enhanced members' ability to do this, as platforms enable them to send messages to the public instantaneously and as frequently as they wish. And while it is not always the member tweeting from her or his account, and while public relations strategy factors into the equation, the same factors that embolden members of the mass public to be more uncivil in their digital communications than they are in face-to-face discourse embolden members and their staffs as well. Perhaps if our twenty-first-century telecommunications had been available in earlier periods in American history, members of Congress would also have made use of incivility—and this would have occurred in some periods more than others. The point is that only today's legislators have these capabilities at their fingertips—which gives them a means and perhaps encourages them to broadcast red meat rhetoric to the electorate. Newt Gingrich (R-GA) may have once inferred that Democrats were "the enemy of normal Americans," in the weeks prior to the 1994 midterm elections (Devroy and Babcock 1994), but these words could not go viral as Trump's infamous tweet describing the media in the same manner did (see Johnson and Gold 2017).

That the 112th Congress also served as the first true "tweeting" congress is not trivial; the congress that would see a majority of its members adopt a new medium for public presentation could set the norms and mores for such. Uncivil discourse was normalized within the institution and encouraged by House leadership immediately before and during the 112th. Put another way, incivility became institutionalized, due to *motive* (the goal of retaking the House and, subsequently, appeasing and appealing to a bitter base) and *means* (the ability to quickly broadcast uncivil remarks via social media). For the House, already a partisan chamber in a polarized era, this meant that incivility became a permanent part of its culture. If the social media revolution had come when politics was less polarized and volatile, one wonders, would the culture of congressional tweeting have a different, more deliberative tone?

Certainly, incivility is commonplace in campaign discourse, and political incivility had been used strategically prior to 2010. It has even been a prominent part of campaign strategy in recent history. The 1994 Republican Revolution was likely a precursor of the Tea Party wave of 2010 (certainly Boehner serves as a direct connection between both),[42] and Sarah Palin's strategic use of incivility on the 2008 campaign trail perhaps set the tone for the subsequent Tea Party era (and Palin's vice presidential candidacy is probably the true starting point of the movement) in that her demonization of Obama and Democrats electrified segments of the Republican base (Herbst 2010).

What was different about the era after 2010 is that House members were motivated *and* able to keep the campaign atmosphere going during the 112th Congress. In previous eras, members and parties would not continuously air uncivil and negative ads once Election Day had passed, because, among other things, doing so would be very expensive. Rank-and-file members could try their best to make the evening news by conducting stunts in front of C-SPAN cameras, but this took effort, and public exposure was far from guaranteed. However, tweeting out uncivil messages is quick, easy, and free.

Moreover, conditions were right for certain purveyors of political incivility (which, colloquially, might be termed "anti-politically correct" talk) to reap rewards. The Republican Party was in a particularly good position to do so in 2010; Republicans were the out-party heading into the first midterm election in the presidency of the country's first African American president, whom sizable segments of their base believed to be a socialist, a Muslim, foreign-born, or all three. Demonization of Obama—before and after the midterms—could mobilize these voters, and thus uncivil tweeting was not limited to an insurgent group of backbenchers during the 112th Congress. Boehner, the head of the Republican Conference, was a leader of the pack when it came to uncivil tweets. McCarthy and Paul Ryan (R-WI) also had above-average incivility rates (both more than 2 percent). The finding that members of the House leadership were among the most uncivil aligns with previous findings that they attempted to demonize Obama during this period—especially when it came to Obamacare.[43] Winning control of the House in 2010 would prove that, instead of a liability, apoplectic anti-Obamacare rhetoric brought rewards. It would not end in the 112th or in the 113th. And, as we mentioned earlier, Boehner's use of incivility did not let up in the 113th, despite his coming under siege from members associated with the Tea Party. House Republican leaders ostensibly have continued to utilize incivility more than the rank-and-file on average, although their levels of incivility are dwarfed by those of Black and Green Tea members.[44]

Palin's story exemplifies another, more personal type of reward that incivility offered Republicans, as she became wealthy and a star in conservative media after her ticket lost the 2008 election. The conservative outrage industry is a media phenomenon unique to our time; partisan media has been the norm, not the exception, in American history, but today's telecommunications have multiplied the volume of outrage and the venues hosting it (Sobieraj and Berry 2013, 12). There are also unique benefits available to political elites who earn the industry's approbation.

Palin's formula of making outrageous claims to gain riches, fame, and support among conservatives is a strategy House Republicans aligned with the Tea Party have followed. Joe Wilson's "You lie!" moment in January 2009, which made him a star and enriched his campaign, best encapsulates this.[45] Michele Bachmann, despite a lackluster legislative record, also gained fame (Bresnahan and Sherman 2011; Linkins 2013) and was briefly touted as a strong contender for the 2012 nomination by conservative media outlets (e.g., Fox News 2011). In a 2012 interview with National Public Radio (NPR), former longtime House member Lee Hamilton notes, "When you do show disrespect, when you yell out at the State of the Union or you shake your finger at the president, you get a lot of support. You raise a lot of money and get a lot of plaudits and emails for standing up" (Greenblatt 2012). Echoing Hamilton in the same NPR piece, political scientist George Edwards notes that the current political climate incentivizes attacks on politicians from the other party, while discouraging collaboration and compromise.

In addition, if a career in Congress does not work despite (or perhaps because of) outrageous comments, a career in the conservative outrage industry awaits. Allen West became "a darling of Fox and other conservative outrage outlets" after making the "McCarthyish" claim that as many as eighty Democratic members of the House of Representatives were Communists (Berry and Sobieraj 2014, 179). Out of office, West (like Palin) would become employed by Fox News (Weiner 2013), as would former Black Tea member Jason Chaffetz (R-UT) (Gold 2017), himself no stranger to controversial comments.[46] There are opportunities outside of Fox News, too: former Green Tea member Joe Walsh (R-IL) has found a second career as a conservative talk radio and Twitter provocateur,[47] and, following his 2016 defeat, fellow former Green Tea Republican Tim Huelskamp was named president of a conservative think tank known for its attacks on climate science.[48] It is not that outlandish to suggest that the career calculations that some members make, then, have shifted, and the failure to get re-elected is not as devastating to careers as it once was (Fenno 1978; Mayhew 1974).

The flip side of rewards for incivility is punishment for not engaging in it. During the 112th Congress, Republicans notably pivoted to the right to avoid antagonizing the Tea Party movement and forces intimately connected to it. Rhetoric insufficiently acidic might be enough to draw the damning label of "RINO" (Republican in Name Only) from influential voices in the conservative outrage industry (Sobieraj and Berry 2013, 223), and anything less than a "principled" reputation might instigate national, well-financed Tea Party organizations to sponsor primary challenges (Grossman and Hopkins 2015). An efficient way to avoid being branded with the scarlet "R" and ward off challenges from the movement was to adopt its rhetorical style. Even in the absence of any real legislative productivity (as was the case in the 112th and 113th Congresses) symbolic and rhetorical attacks on Obamacare could assuage activists aligned with the Tea Party movement (Grossman and Hopkins 2015). Members who did not actively attach themselves to the movement or receive support from it might still benefit from leveraging Tea Party rhetoric. It was an ideal middle ground for some: a member could avoid the risk that comes with being labeled a Tea Party Republican. At the same time, by offering enough tough talk about Obama and Democrats, they could appease and perhaps mobilize Tea Party supporters in their districts and keep would-be primary opponents at bay. This is why incivility was utilized equally across the Tea Party Association index in the 112th.

This remained true in the 113th Congress. However, the institutionalization of incivility in the 112th gave legislators willing to use it more frequently the green light, with the pull of rewards and specter of punishment providing plenty of incentive. The effects of these forces would be compounded by the strengthening of Tea Party power in the 113th, emboldening those who attached themselves to the movement. For one, House Tea Partiers would gain an important ally in the Senate in Ted Cruz, whose obstructionist tactics and uncivil behavior in the 113th would bring the freshman senator infamy. Despite having few allies in the Senate, Cruz gained notoriety (and a strong position for the Republican presidential nomination in 2016) for his anti-compromise positions and incendiary commentary (see Schreckinger 2015), suggesting once again that incivility brings rewards.

Notably, Cruz quickly developed significant clout among the Tea Party faction in the House, and his presidential candidacy would be buoyed by support from a number of the Black and Green Tea Republicans, including Steve King, Jim Bridenstine, Mark Meadows (R-NC), Jeff Duncan, Tim Huelskamp, Louie Gohmert, and Randy Weber—something we explore further in the next chapter (Jalonick 2016; Palmer and French 2015). On numerous occasions in the 113th Congress, Cruz would inspire (or direct) them to challenge Boehner and House leaders (Skocpol 2014), as well as introduce his bills (Jalonick 2016). In many ways, he replaced Bachmann (who would serve as a Cruz ally) as the true leader of the Tea Party "caucus," leading critics to suggest that the freshman senator had become the House speaker "in all but name" (Costa 2014). Rallied by Cruz, the Tea Party faction in the House would force Boehner and the House leadership to cave in to their demands throughout the congress (Kane and O'Keefe 2014; Palmer and French 2015)—leading Boehner to later refer to Cruz as "Lucifer in the flesh," (Alberta 2017).

While Boehner had to deal with Cruz's rising influence, the Liberty Caucus, led by Justin Amash, would be launched in the 113th Congress and serve as both a precursor and contemporary of the more notorious Freedom Caucus. As we noted in Chapter 3, a group of nine members, consisting of Black and Green Tea Republicans, save one, refused to support Boehner in the speaker vote at the start of the congress (Kasperowicz 2013). Even had he wanted to rein in incivility, Speaker Boehner was losing control of his caucus in the 113th and was forced to resign before the end of the first session of the 114th. Despite leading the charge with anti-Obama rhetoric, despite pioneering outreach to activists on social media, despite adapting his old bag of confrontational tricks to the twenty-first century, the old ringleader of the Gang of Seven, the man who described himself as the "Tea Party before the Tea Party," could not keep up with the rapid pace at which his conference was embracing ever more outrageous rhetoric. In the end, he was not confrontational enough. As congressional scholar Sarah Binder (2015) wrote in the *New York Times* after Boehner's resignation:

> Fresh from deposing a compromising leader they viewed as too accommodating to Democrats, the far right of the G.O.P. seems emboldened to pursue a no-holds-barred strategy to secure its political and policy aims— a strategy that might pay off back home but at considerable cost to their party's national reputation and to Congress's capacity to solve problems.

This refers to legislative behavior, but we think it applies to rhetoric as well. It might be poetic justice that, upon resigning, Boehner was treated to uncivil farewells from a variety of political foes, Tea Party and otherwise (Rubin 2015). As if to add insult to injury, a Tea Party–backed candidate would claim Boehner's vacated House seat in a 2016 special election (Phillips 2016). Following the election, won by Warren Davidson (R-OH), Justin Amash— consistently one of the most prolific congressional tweeters—took to Twitter to crow, "A @freedomcaucus congressman will now hold Eric Cantor's former seat AND John Boehner's former seat. Congratulations, @Vote_Davidson!" The men who helped cultivate a culture of incivility on congressional Twitter were now targeted by it.

In addition to enabling the institutionalization of incivility, the Republican leadership's tolerance and embrace of this type of language has had other consequences. First, compromise with the other side (and thus governing) has become nearly impossible—not because the other side is too offended to work with you (although this, too, is a risk; see Gutmann and Thompson 2012, 123; Jamieson 2011; Uslaner 1993), but because any agreement will be perceived as a deal with the devil among the parishioners you have been preaching to. As Dionne (2016, 328), who blames Boehner for the 2011 debt ceiling crisis, put it, "[I]f Barack Obama was as corrupt and dangerous as so many in the party's base devoutly believed, how could the Republicans engage him in a normal give-and-take?" Less compromise generates more government dysfunction, which only strengthens the anti-government message of the Tea Party.

In addition, for elites, it means you cannot let up on the incivility. When elected officials echo the talking points of the outrage industry, their arguments are granted a legitimacy they heretofore lacked, and they become a new powerful voice in the conservative echo chamber (Jamieson and Cappella 2009). Yet the potency of uncivil attacks reduces legislators' latitude and impunity: you cannot convincingly demonize an opponent for years, then tone down the rhetoric and not expect a backlash. Increasing resentment among the electorate (as we saw in the preceding chapter, Black and Green Tea Republicans played a role in fostering resentment in the 113th Congress) means that more incivility is required. And so the demand for political incivility—characterized as not being "politically correct" talk—among a segment of the electorate would only grow. To connect with an angry, populist Republican electorate, fed up with Washington's elite, and not be a target, meant being on the offense. It meant more railing against Washington, demonizing opponents, and tolerating (if not promoting) conspiracy theories. When incivility becomes institutionalized, it is no longer just a useful tactic; it becomes required.

The House leadership's habit of encouraging hostility toward Obama in the electorate dates back to the fall of 2010, when the Young Guns released their manifesto celebrating "angry citizens" fed up with the Obama administration, and Boehner, in his bid for speaker, contrived to encourage resentment. Consider this excerpt from a September 2010 *Washington Post* article on the relationship between Boehner and Cantor:

> [T]he rise of the "tea party" and the growing opposition to Obama merged their approaches in many ways. Republican activists at tea party rallies have shown little desire to hear GOP ideas beyond opposition to Obama, and many of these activists say they don't want to follow the edicts of party leaders, but rather want Republicans in Congress to listen more to the public.
>
> So instead of touting their own policy ideas, Republicans, led by Cantor and Boehner, this spring launched a program called "America Speaking Out" that created a Web site and town halls to solicit ideas from the public. And they kept their focus on attacking Obama. (Bacon 2010)

A (still live, as of May 2017) announcement of the "American Speaking Out" program posted on Boehner's official webpage, which decries Obama's "stunning failure of leadership" and "Washington Democrats' out-of-control spending spree and its devastating impact on small businesses and our economy as a whole," provides insight into Boehner's strategy to aggravate resentment as well as connect with and encourage digital activists:

> Too many in Washington forget that we work for the people, not the other way around. Taxpayers are just fed up, and they want us to stop spending their hard-earned money.
>
> That's why, through the America Speaking Out project, Republicans are providing Americans with a megaphone to make their voices heard and help build a better, more responsive government. If you have an idea to cut wasteful Washington spending, log on to AmericaSpeakingOut. com right now and start a discussion about it.

Boehner also refused to fully quash conspiracy theories about Obama's country of birth and religion upon becoming Speaker in February 2011, arguing that it was not his job to do so and that Americans had a right to believe whatever they wished (Dionne 2016, 302–303). But tolerating such talk, perhaps in the hope that it would fade away, led to its expansion among segments of the Republican Party; "birtherism" grew into a conflagration. Not a month after Boehner punted on the chance to discourage "birther" talk, Donald Trump publicly expressed doubt about Obama's birth certificate for the first time (Parker and Eder 2016).

This would all catch up with the leadership of the Republican Party. Fanning the flames would bring rewards, including electoral victories in 2010 and 2014, but it would also enable the rise of a hardline faction in the 113th Congress that was even more willing to put aside old discursive norms and ramp up uncivil rhetoric. Succeeding Boehner as speaker, Paul Ryan would be continually tested, hamstrung, and punished by a powerful Freedom Caucus in the 114th (See Bade 2016; Cottle 2016; and *New York Times* Editorial Board 2015).

On another front, the "angry citizens" professional politicians had encouraged would begin to direct their ire at them. Having disparaged the incumbent administration and government more generally, Tea Party rhetoric would affirm for a suspicious white working class that they were getting a raw deal. The rhetoric would help create the conditions for widespread resentment and a fervor for "anti-politically correct" discourse. As the end of 2015 rolled around and 2016 presidential primaries were set to begin, it became clear that the fire Republicans helped build had consumed their party.

Appendix

Details on the Coding of Training Set Tweets for Incivility

Two rounds of coding took place. During the first round, two dozen under-graduate coders (UCs) were tasked with determining if each of the training set tweets was "civil" or "uncivil." The UCs completed the coding as part of a one-credit lab. To determine whether a tweet was uncivil, the UCs were instructed to follow a rubric, which can be seen in Table 8A.3. If they thought the tweet was civil (i.e., lacked uncivil elements, per the rubric), they were to score the tweet 0. If they thought the tweet qualified as uncivil, they were to score the tweet 1. Before coding the sample dataset, the UCs received training and feedback on their coding on several practice sets. The tweets the UCs coded were de-identified—that is, House members' names were not attached to the tweets (although given members' propensity to refer to themselves and include identifying information in the text of the tweets, it remained possible to deter-mine the tweeter's identity).

Each tweet was individually coded by three different coders, but each coder's set of tweets differed, ensuring he or she had to use individual judgment. Thus, while "coder 1," "coder 2," and "coder 3" appeared in our spreadsheet, each "coder" was actually eight different people. This is an unorthodox method for coding, but we adopted it for two reasons: (1) more coders meant a larger di-versity of perspectives, thus reducing the chance that the collection of tweets labeled "uncivil" was a biased set; (2) it allowed us to use a larger sample as the training set, ensuring a representative set of tweets for each member.

During this first round of coding, intercoder reliability, in terms of percent agreement was good: for 83 percent of the 112th tweets and 84 percent of the 113th tweets, all three coders agreed. However, a test of Krippendorf's alpha, a more rigorous test of intercoder reliability, produced an alpha of only 0.28 for the 112th and 0.24 for the 113th, scores below the acceptable limit. This is likely for two reasons. The first has to do with the fact that the measure assumes the "coders" are constant, and not, as in our case, composites of multiple coders. In short, the more rigorous approach makes high intercoder reliability harder to achieve. It would be quite the feat if we received acceptable alphas using this approach, but alas we did not.

The second reason has to do with the nature of the data, the level of vari-ability in the coding, and how the measure calculates reliability. In about 84 percent of cases, all three "coders" gave the tweet a 0. This is consistent with previous content analyses of members' tweets: they are self-promotional, and

Table 8A.1 **Random Selection of 113th Congress Tweets Marked as Uncivil by Algorithm**

Member of Congress	Tweet
Bachmann, Michelle (R-MN)	Seniors were promised Medicare would be safe. Obamacare = losing access to doctors, health benefits. http://t.co/Y4RWOOI8Wp #BrokenPromises Mar 23, 2014
Brady, Kevin (R-TX)	SPREAD THE WORD—OCare created the hardship you can claim in order to be exempted from OCare—Sebelius vs. Accuracy http://t.co/chXDUqYAQ7 Mar 13, 2014
Latham, Tom (R-IA)	Want a better idea of how nightmarish the #trainwreck of implementing #Obamacare is? All of this has to be done fast: http://t.co/SfknnWqM6Q Jun 26, 2013
Franks, Trent (R-AZ)	Tweeting #ObamaFailures every half-hour: #64 Civilian trial for Ghailani led to acquittal of terrorist who ADMITTED to his activities. #tcot Jul 18, 2014
Weber, Randy (R-TX)	RT @RepKevinBrady: Another day, another White House delay. #BrokenPromises http://t.co/NLKyFkZDmJ Mar 26, 2014
DesJarlais, Scott (R-TN)	President Obama talks like he only wants tax the wealthy but #Obamacare will be a tax on everyone #TN04 #healthcare Mar 14, 2013
Denham, Jeff (R-CA)	There are #jobs waiting to be created while the Administration delays yet again on #KeystoneXL http://t.co/yDnC5Wu2lp Apr 21, 2014
Latham, Tom (R-IA)	NY times raises new concerns with how #Obamacare is unfair to rural America. Points out the law lacks #FairnessForAll http://t.co/69pZviMNqV Oct 24, 2013
Ellmers, Renee (R-NC)	VIDEO: Obama SOTU: Same Speech, Same Result http://t.co/PU9QPH2JYG More #BrokenPromises Jan 27, 2014
Cantor, Eric (R-VA)	How much more proof do we need of Obamacare's devastating effects before Dems finally admit the law they enacted isn't working for America? Feb 04, 2014
Huelskamp, Timothy (R-KS)	#Despicable, the death of an American journalist won't stop King Obama from fundraising or golf. http://t.co/LXUG3Bs6r9 Aug 21, 2014

Table 8A.1. **Continued**

Member of Congress	Tweet
Price, Tom (R-GA)	POTUS says #Obamacare is "doing what it's designed to do." What? Raise costs? Limit access to care? Kill jobs? Jul 19, 2013
Cantor, Eric (R-VA)	At this point, one has to ask: What else is the Administration hiding about ObamaCare? Dec 03, 2013
Nunnelee, Alan (R-MS)	Disaster aid, like all spending, isn't free, we either pay for it now or pay later with interest; I think we should have paid for it now. Jan 16, 2013
Johnson, Sam (R-TX)	Rather than lecturing on his failed econ policies, @BarackObama's time would be better spent witnessing the crisis on Texas' southern border Jul 08, 2014
Weber, Randy (R-TX)	RT @PeteKTheBlaze: 'Most transparent administration' ever says it will veto EPA transparency bills: http://t.co/yOqTssuY8v Nov 18, 2014
Lummis, Cynthia (R-WY)	I voted no on the funding bill because I think it should've blocked Obama's #amnesty for millions of illegal immigrants #IllegalImmigration Dec 12, 2014
Franks, Trent (R-AZ)	#ObamaFailures every half hour until list complete. #139 Unnecessarily halting White House tours to punish Americans for political point. Jul 23, 2014
Palazzo, Steven (R-MS)	We're serious about balancing the budget. POTUS is serious about his bracket http://t.co/oTIixu64OY #marchmadness #BalancedBudgetMar 20, 2013
Rokita, Todd (R-IN).txt	How many more jobs will the #ObamaCare #TrainWreck cost America? Video: http://t.co/jGV4pM79M8 May 16, 2013

Table 8A.2 **References to Obama and Socialism in 112th Congress Tweets**

Member of Congress	Tweet	Type of Member	Date
Justin Amash (R-MI)	Pres. Obama's rhetoric is becoming less and less distinguishable from that of Hugo Chavez and other socialist... fb.me/1cHOhksi2	Green Tea	Aug. 16, 2011
Robert Aderholt (R-AL)	The SCOTUS decision on #obamacare today is a devastating step toward socialized medicine in the US. http://t.co/v1U51jqi	Green Tea	June 28, 2012
Michele Bachmann (R-MN)	#Obamacare will do to America what socialized medicine did to Ontario: government picks winners and losers http://t.co/mygnniiN#tcot	Black Tea	Oct. 23, 2012
Paul Broun (R-GA)	Mr. President, you don't believe in the Constitution. You believe in socialism.	Green Tea	Jan. 26, 2011
Trent Franks (R-AZ)	Instead of apologizing for all the socialist policies his own Admin has proposed, Mr. Biden seeks to spin the truth for political gain.	Green Tea	Mar. 20, 2011
Timothy Huelskamp (R-KS)	RT @ RepublicanStudy: It must be crystal clear in '12 who backs govt mandates and venture socialism vs. liberty and free enterprise. http . . .	Black Tea	Jan. 17, 2012

Table 8A.2 **Continued**

Member of Congress	Tweet	Type of Member	Date
Dana Rohrabacher (R-CA)	@Timmmaaay Sanders is a good friend of mine but that doesn't make him any less a socialist, at least he's more honest about it than Obama @TahoeTrekker saying POTUS is socialist disrespect? labeling Reagan capitalist? neither purists both impacted by those ideologies	Green Tea	Dec. 3, 2012; Feb. 5, 2012
Dennis Ross (R-FL)	Charlie Crist socialized property insurance in Florida. Seems a perfect fit w/the Pres. who socialized medicine in America. #ConsumersLose	Green Tea	Aug. 28, 2012
Allen West (R-FL)	Watching Pres in London—it's humorous to me that he who promotes socialist economic policy is quoting Adam Smith & free market principles	Black Tea	May 25, 2011

thus positive. What this means is that only a small segment (less than 17 percent in the 112th and 15 percent in the 113th) of the tweets received at least a single 1. Among the tweets that did not receive all nulls, there was plenty of disagreement, however: in only 3 percent of these cases in the 112th and 5 percent in the 113th did a tweet receive three 1s. Thus, we had low diversity of coded values overall, coupled with significant disagreement among tweets that did not received all 0s. When overall variability is low, Krippendorf's alpha expects an especially low level of disagreement (the formula for the alpha is 1 – (observed disagreement – expected disagreement)).

Table 8A.3 **Incivility Rubric Utilized by Human Coders**

Criteria of Incivility	*Example Claim*	*Type*	*Example Statement*
Criterion 1: "Namecalling, Mockery, Sarcasm, and Character Assassination"	The candidate may not have been completely sincere	Civil Negative	"The candidate has not been completely forthright with the American people about his voting record."
Additional superfluous adverbs and adjectives that add no new information but are purposefully insulting, belittling, and condescending		Uncivil Negative	"The <u>unethical</u> and <u>deceitful</u> candidate has not been completely forthright with the American people about his voting record." "The candidate has not been forthright about his voting record. <u>A Republican not being forthright—gee, imagine that!</u>"
Criterion 2: "Spin and Misrepresentative Exaggeration"	Candidate's issue positions were out of sync with those of the electorate	Civil Negative	"The candidate had effective and convincing advertisements and more money to spend."
Use of a much more extreme, inflammatory word or phrase that makes an individual or action seem more radical, immoral, or corrupt		Uncivil Negative	"The candidate <u>manipulated the public</u> and <u>essentially bought the election.</u>"

Criteria of Incivility	Example Claim	Type	Example Statement
Criterion 3: "Emotionality/ Digital Stridency" Language suggests that an individual or group should be feared or is responsible for sadness. Also includes obscenity. Additionally, visual elements: thoughts that are purposefully exaggerated through uppercase letters, multiple exclamation points, and quotes.	Candidate's election is somewhat worrisome	Civil Negative	"The election of the candidate has me worried about the direction of the country"
		Uncivil Negative	"I fear for what will happen to this country if the candidate is elected. It will be a sad day for America. -and- "WE SHOULD ALL BE SCARED!!!!!!!"
Criterion 4: "Conspiracy Theory" Accusations of very sinister motives/actions/ background. Although unreasonable, presented as factual	No base claim; claim made without merit	Uncivil Negative	"The candidate is a Manchurian candidate, controlled by foreigners bent on destroying America.

We also supposed, a priori, that given that the vast majority of tweets were innocuous and self-promotional, the UCs might be primed to view tweets with only a hint of partisanship as uncivil. That is, relatively tame but negative tweets might seem more uncivil when appearing among a sea of positive and neutral tweets than they would if they appeared in isolation or among only negative tweets (as they likely appear on users' actual Twitter feeds).

This realization, in conjunction with the initial coding results, prompted us to do additional coding. We put aside tweets that received all 0s or just a single 1 and conducted a second round of coding on the tweets that received two or three 1s from the UCs. For the second round of coding, three research assistants went through extensive training before independently coding the sample subset of about 1,600 tweets (as in the first round, members' names were not attached to the tweets). This time, intercoder reliability was much higher, producing a Krippendorf's alpha of 0.70. The coders then met to extensively discuss differences before agreeing upon a master set. The recoded subset of tweets was then recombined with the rest of the 112th and 113th sample datasets to form the training set. In the end, about 1.5 percent of the sample tweets were deemed uncivil.

Tea Partiers on the National Stage

The 2012 and 2016 Presidential Elections

Donald Trump's surprising competitiveness for and subsequent clinching of the 2016 Republican nomination for president brought lots of popular attention to a political science theory known as the *The Party Decides* (TPD) thesis, based on a book of the same name by Cohen, Karol, Noel, and Zaller (2008). In short, the TPD authors argue that party insiders coordinate their support for a candidate for their party's presidential nomination who they believe to be generally acceptable on policy grounds to the multiple factions within the party establishment, and electable (i.e., she or he has potential as a vote getter in the general election). This coordination game takes place during a period known as the "Invisible Primary," before primary and caucus voting begins, when candidates are vetted (Cohen et al. 2008). Once a candidate becomes a focal point (selected), insider support (e.g., endorsements and financial support) can propel her or him to the nomination. That is, the public follows the signals of elites. The fact that Trump won the nomination without the support of Republican insiders raised the question as to whether intra-party squabbling between "establishment" and Tea Party factions prevented the party from converging on any candidate and resulted in a vacuum that allowed Trump to surge to the top of polls and ultimately win (Noel 2016).

Other types of elite signals may have an impact on vote choice, too. As Trump soared to the head of polls in the summer of 2015, many political observers expressed befuddlement as to how Republican voters came to view Trump's rhetoric as acceptable for the nominee of their party (never mind a president) (see McCarthy 2015; Schlesinger 2016). Others suggested that Republicans had built up support for a candidate like Trump among their base after years of similar, if less severe, rhetoric. As one scholar put it, in the run-up to the Trump era, the Republican Party "seized vitriol and disdain and personal distrust and even hatred as a means of accomplishing political victory or making political distinctions," (Hudak 2015). This had the effect of encouraging Republican voters to support a candidate like Trump, who offered outrageous, brash, "anti-politically correct" commentary (Hudak 2015). According to this account, the line that Trump was the "candidate that Twitter built" is only half true: Trump was the candidate that uncivil Republicans built on Twitter.[1]

In this chapter, we focus on the influence Tea Party representation has had on the biggest national stage—presidential elections. Specifically, we consider the endorsement behavior of members of Congress during the two presidential elections that have occurred since the Tea Party movement came to be (2012 and 2016) and ask whether our Tea Party Association measures predict endorsements for some presidential aspirants over others—namely, outsider, "establishment" candidates. Given the surprising finish to the 2016 elections, we also consider whether Tea Party representation influenced vote choice in the fight for the 2016 Republican nomination and general elections. We additionally reflect on whether that less direct type of elite signaling—legislators' incivility on social media, which we have shown to be more prevalent among legislators who attached themselves to the Tea Party in the 113th Congress—had an impact on vote choice in the 2016 primary and general elections. In short, we investigate whether Trump was the candidate built by uncivil elites on Twitter in the years before his rise.

Endorsing Romney and "Non-Romneys" in 2012

One of the most significant media narratives of the 2012 Republican primaries was Tea Party supporters' ostensible preference for "anybody but Romney," leading to a series of fleeting "boomlets" for several other candidates—including former Texas governor Rick Perry, former speaker of the house Newt Gingrich (R-GA), and businessman and lobbyist Herman Cain—along with sustained support for former senator Rick Santorum (R-PA) (Sides and Vavreck 2013, 32, 41–63). However, as Sides and Vavreck (2013, 59–60, 86–87) demonstrate, the story is more complicated, as the vast majority of self-identified Tea Party "members" tended to have a favorable view of Romney. Moreover, Romney worked hard to portray himself as a "champion of the Tea Party" (Skocpol 2012) and, in the end, was strongly backed by Tea Party sympathizers in the general election (Bradberry and Jacobson 2013).

Mitt Romney may have received favorable support from Tea Party sympathizers during the race for the 2012 Republican nomination for president. But given the salience of stories describing the "establishment" Romney as in conflict or at least not completely simpatico with the Tea Party (e.g., Ball 2012; Friedersdorf 2012; Gonyea 2011; Vogel 2011), it would not be surprising if this storyline influenced how closely members of the House associated with the Tea Party attached themselves to Romney. Some members associated with the Tea Party may have also rejected the "establishment" Romney out of principle, preferring more outsider candidates—Michele Bachmann, the founder of the Tea Party Caucus, threw her hat in the ring after all. Whatever the motivation, we consider the impact of association with the Tea Party on endorsements of Romney and endorsements of candidates other than Romney during the Invisible Primary (so endorsements made before the January 3 Iowa Caucuses).

Table 9.1 displays the results of several models predicting endorsements made during the 2012 Invisible Primary. In each, we control for the "usual suspects" (ideology, gender, year took office, party leadership position, and committee leadership position). Column 1 regresses endorsements of a "non-Romney" candidate onto our Tea Party Association measures. That is, we are looking to see if those associated with the Tea Party were more likely to back "anybody but Romney," including Perry, Gingrich, Cain, Santorum, Bachmann, Representative Ron Paul (R-TX), former Minnesota governor Tim Pawlenty, and former ambassador and Utah governor John Huntsman.[2] Neither Tea Party Support nor Tea Party Association is significant. This remains the case when, as shown in column 2, we divide Tea Party Association into the dichotomous "Moderate Attachment" and "High Attachment" categories.

Tea Party Association measures might not predict endorsements of candidates other than Romney during the Invisible Primary, but perhaps they predict not supporting Romney during this period—that is, endorsing someone else or not making an endorsement at all. Column 3 regresses endorsement of Romney during the Invisible Primary onto the Tea Party Association measures and the control variables. Again, we see that both Association measures are insignificant. And this remains the case when, as shown in column 4, we use the dichotomous "Moderate" and "High Attachment" variables.

There is little evidence that members associated with the Tea Party displayed different endorsement behavior than Coffee members during the Invisible Primary. But perhaps this is not surprising: as Sides and Vavreck (2013, 37–40) discuss, many Republicans struggled to identify a candidate they thought would satisfy both the establishment and Tea Party wings, and thus many adopted a "wait and see" approach. The period before the 2012 Iowa Caucuses stands out, Sides and Vavreck (2013, 38–39) show, for the small percentage of Republican elites who issued endorsements relative to similar contemporary election cycles. Thus, it makes sense to look at endorsements after the primaries and caucuses begin. We thus consider endorsements of Romney and candidates other than Romney made before April 10 (the date when Romney's last remaining significant challenger, Rick Santorum, dropped out of the race, making Romney the presumptive nominee) (Sides and Vavreck 2013, 86).

Table 9.1 **Predicting Romney and Non-Romney Endorsements during the 2012 Invisible Primary**

Variable	MC Endorsed Non-Romney		MC Endorsed Romney	
	(1)	(2)	(3)	(4)
Tea Party Support	−0.03	−0.03	−0.06	−0.07
	(0.057)	(0.057)	(0.068)	(0.069)
Tea Party Attachment	0.18	—	−0.09	—
	(0.120)	—	(0.121)	—
High Tea Party Attachment	—	0.37	—	−0.23
	—	(0.237)	—	(0.249)
Moderate Tea Party Attachment	—	−0.43	—	0.26
	—	(0.362)	—	(0.278)
DW-Nominate	0.86	1.02	−0.91	−0.98
	(0.642)	(0.660)	(0.628)	(0.631)
Gender	−0.14	−0.18	**0.68**	**0.71**
	(0.348)	(0.351)	**(0.284)**	**(0.286)**
Year Took Office	−0.00	−0.00	−0.01	−0.01
	(0.014)	(0.014)	(0.013)	(0.013)
Party Leadership	0.16	0.27	0.07	−0.02
	(0.521)	(0.545)	(0.518)	(0.519)
Committee Leadership	−0.42	−0.40	0.13	0.08
	(0.426)	(0.431)	(0.329)	(0.334)
Constant	5.24	0.54	11.24	15.11
	(28.315)	(28.458)	(25.456)	(25.726)
Observations (N)	242	242	242	242
Adj. R^2	0.05	0.06	0.05	0.06

Note: Coefficients are probit regression. Standard errors are in in parentheses. Boldface indicates significance at $p < .05$ (one-tailed test).

Table 9.2 displays the results of models predicting endorsements for Romney and other "non-Romney" candidates before Romney became the presumptive nominee. As shown in column 1, the Tea Party Association variables are again insignificant. However, when we incorporate the dichotomous Tea Party Attachment variables, as shown in column 2, we see that those with high attachment to the Tea Party were less likely to endorse Romney before the nomination battle was all but wrapped up. To better interpret the size of this effect, we calculate the predicted probabilities of endorsing Romney by those

Table 9.2 **Predicting Romney and Non-Romney Endorsements before Romney Becomes Presumptive Nominee in 2012**

Variable	MC Endorsed Romney		MC Endorsed Non-Romney	
	(1)	*(2)*	*(3)*	*(4)*
Tea Party Support	−0.07	−0.07	−0.07	−0.07
	(0.061)	(0.063)	(0.070)	(0.071)
Tea Party Attachment	−0.17	—	0.11	—
	(0.113)	—	(0.124)	—
High Tea Party Attachment	—	**−0.40**	—	0.22
	—	**(0.232)**	—	(0.246)
Moderate Tea Party Attachment	—	0.33	—	**−0.99**
	—	(0.262)	—	**(0.517)**
DW-Nominate	−0.73	−0.81	0.94	1.23
	(0.585)	(0.590)	(0.670)	(0.708)
Gender	**0.67**	**0.71**	−0.22	−0.27
	(0.283)	**(0.285)**	(0.388)	(0.394)
Year Took Office	−0.01	−0.01	−0.00	0.00
	(0.012)	(0.012)	(0.015)	(0.015)
Party Leadership	**1.22**	**1.08**	—	—
	(0.504)	**(0.506)**	—	—
Committee Leadership	0.02	−0.04	−0.07	−0.04
	(0.313)	(0.317)	(0.388)	(0.397)
Constant	13.24	18.81	2.77	−1.88
	(23.943)	(24.238)	(29.189)	(29.383)
Observations (N)	242	242	242	242
Adj. R^2	0.07	0.09	0.03	0.07

Note: Coefficients are probit regression. Standard errors are in parentheses. Boldface indicates significance at $p < .05$ (one-tailed test). Party leadership is dropped from the "non-Romney" models due to lack of variation.

with and without High Tea Party Attachment in the 112th Congress.[3] As shown in Figure 9.1, whereas the predicted probability of endorsing Romney among those who did not foster high attachment to the Tea Party was 36 percent, it was 24 percent among those who did make significant efforts to link themselves to the movement. Although the difference in probabilities does not quite reach statistical significance, we think it highlights at least mild resistance to endorsing Romney among the members most strongly attached to the Tea Party in the 112th.

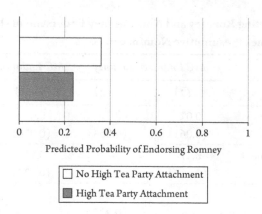

Figure 9.1 Predicted Probability of Member of Congress Endorsing Romney in 2012 (after Invisible Primary) by High Tea Party Attachment.
Bars represent predicted probabilities of endorsing Romney based on probit regression and calculated using the observed value approach (Hanmer and Kalkan 2013).

Table 9.2 also displays models predicting endorsements of a "non-Romney" candidate after the Invisible Primary but before Romney became the presumptive nominee.[4] Note that before April 10, Romney had collected endorsements from legislators who had previously backed other candidates during the Invisible Primary—thus, to have a standing endorsement of a "non-Romney" at this point in the campaign was indicative of true resistance to Romney's candidacy. The results in column 3 show that neither Tea Party Association measure significantly predicts backing a non-Romney at this point. However, something interesting happens when we break Tea Party Attachment down into the dichotomous Moderate and High Attachment variables, as displayed in column 4: those with moderate attachment to the Tea Party were less likely to endorse a non-Romney. As indicated in Figure 9.2, the probability of endorsing a non-Romney candidate falls from almost 17 percent among those without moderate attachment to less than 4.5 percent—although, again, the differences in probabilities are not quite statistically distinct.

This tells us, in conjunction with the fact that those with high attachment were less likely to endorse Romney, that there is some evidence those who made only some attempts to link themselves to the Tea Party in the 112th Congress were less concerned than those who made significant attempts to do so with preserving "anti-establishment" bona fides. When push came to shove, those with moderate attachment did not take the step of endorsing someone other than the ostensible front runner. This finding also highlights something we have seen repeatedly: during the 112th, Tea Party Attachment was not a reliable predictor of behavior presumed to characterize Tea Partiers.

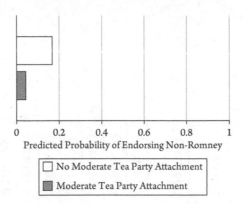

Predicted Probability of Endorsing Non-Romney

□ No Moderate Tea Party Attachment
■ Moderate Tea Party Attachment

Figure 9.2 Predicted Probability of Member of Congress Endorsing a Non-Romney Candidate in 2012 (after Invisible Primary) by High Tea Party Attachment.
Bars represent predicted probabilities of endorsing a non-Romney candidate based on probit regression and calculated using the observed value approach (Hanmer and Kalkan 2013).

Tea Party Constituency Support for Romney in 2012

There may not have been clear signaling from Tea Party members as to whether to back Romney during the primaries, but the general election is a whole new ball game.[5] After all, it was the 2008 election of Romney's general election opponent (Barack Obama) that launched the Tea Party movement in the first place (Parker and Barreto 2014). Tea Party sympathizers appeared to vote for Romney (or against Obama) at greater rates than other Republicans. Were constituents of members associated with the Tea Party more likely to vote for Romney?

To answer this question, we leverage data from the 2012 Cooperative Congressional Election Studies (CCES), which asked respondents about their vote choice in the general election. As there was no consequential third-party candidate in 2012, and approximately 96.5 percent reported voting for Obama or Romney, we construct a dichotomous "Romney Vote" variable, where a 1 represents a vote for Romney and 0 represents a vote for someone other than Romney (a vote for Obama, essentially).[6] Table 9.3 presents the results of four multilevel logit models, predicting support for Romney by our 112th Tea Party Association measures, with CCES respondents clustered into (112th) congressional districts. In the first models, we restrict the sample to those who reported casting a ballot in the general election and white voters. In model 1, we use the single, ordinal Tea Party Attachment measure. In the second model, we use the two dichotomous measures: Moderate Tea Party Attachment and High Tea Party Attachment. The third and fourth models are identical to the first two, except we include all voters (not just white voters).

Table 9.3 **Predicting Romney Votes in the 2012 General Election**

Variable	White Voters Only		All Voters	
	Model 1	Model 2	Model 3	Model 4
Tea Party Support	0.03 (0.06)	0.03 (0.05)	0.04 (0.05)	0.03 (0.05)
Tea Party Attachment	0.09 (0.06)	—	**0.11 (0.06)**	—
High Tea Party Attachment	—	0.14 (0.13)	—	0.19 (0.12)
Moderate Tea Party Attachment	—	**0.38 (0.19)**	—	0.29 (0.18)
Racial Resentment	**0.20 (0.04)**	**0.20 (0.04)**	**0.24 (0.04)**	**0.24 (0.04)**
Anti-Immigration Views	**0.19 (0.03)**	**0.19 (0.03)**	**0.20 (0.03)**	**0.20 (0.04)**
Age	**0.01 (0.00)**	**0.01 (0.00)**	**0.01 (0.00)**	**0.01 (0.00)**
Gender (Female = 1)	0.07 (0.09)	0.07 (0.09)	0.11 (0.09)	0.11 (0.09)
Race (White = 1)	—	—	**0.26 (0.13)**	**0.26 (0.13)**
Education (6 cat)	**0.19 (0.03)**	**0.19 (0.03)**	**0.19 (0.03)**	**0.19 (0.03)**
Party ID (7 cat)	**0.76 (0.03)**	**0.76 (0.03)**	**0.76 (0.03)**	**0.76 (0.03)**
Ideology (5 cat)	**0.56 (0.07)**	**0.56 (0.07)**	**0.60 (0.07)**	**0.60 (0.07)**
Born Again Christian	**0.38 (0.10)**	**0.38 (0.10)**	**0.37 (0.09)**	**0.37 (0.09)**
Knows MC's Party	**0.87 (0.11)**	**0.87 (0.10)**	**0.87 (0.10)**	**0.87 (0.10)**

Negative National Economic Perceptions	**0.71 (0.05)**	**0.72 (0.05)**	**0.69 (0.04)**	**0.69 (0.04)**
Decrease in Household Income	0.05 (0.04)	0.05 (0.04)	0.07 (0.04)	0.06 (0.04)
Constant	**−10.61 (0.52)**	**−10.64 (0.52)**	**−11.17 (0.49)**	**−11.19 (0.49)**
District-Level Variance	**0.39 (0.07)**	**0.40 (0.08)**	**0.40 (0.07)**	**0.39 (0.07)**
Observations (N)	17,569	17,569	20,471	20,471
Districts (N)	317	317	324	324
LR χ^2	358.73; $p < .000$	356.70; $p < .000$	289.25; $p < .000$	289.99; $p < 0.000$

Note: Robust standard errors are in parentheses. Boldface indicates significance at $p < .05$ (one-tailed test). Coefficients are the results of multilevel logit regression models. All data, except Tea Party Association variables, are from the 2012 Cooperative Congressional Election Study.

For all the models, we utilize the sampling weights provided by the CCES. In addition, we incorporate a number of control variables, including a Racial Resentment scale, a measure of anti-immigrant positions, age, gender, education, race, whether respondents identify as a born-again Christian, party identification (on a 7-point scale), political ideology (on a 5-point scale), perceptions of the state of the national economy over the previous year, and reports of how household income has changed over the past four years. We also control for whether or not respondents could identify their House member's political party (which serves as a measure of political sophistication and a check on the likelihood of legislators' political associations influencing respondents' political behavior). More details on these variables can be found in Appendix I.

As can be seen in the first model, neither Tea Party Support nor Tea Party Attachment predicts voting for Romney among white voters. Yet in model 2, we can see that moderate Tea Party Attachment significantly predicts voting for Romney. This is consistent with the primary results in Table 9.2, in which legislators with moderate attachment to the movement were less likely to endorse one of Romney's "anti-establishment" competitors. In 2012, at least, members who made some effort to link themselves to the movement helped to bolster support for (or at least not undermine) the establishment Romney among white voters. As Figure 9.3 indicates, the probability of voting for Romney increased from about 52 percent to 55 percent when a voter's legislator had moderate Tea Party Attachment. Given that more than nine in ten voted in line with their partisanship in the 2012 general election and that Romney won 59 percent of the white vote, a three-percentage-point difference is substantial.[7]

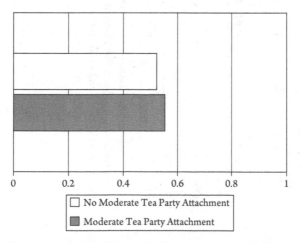

Figure 9.3 Predicted Probability of Voting for Romney in General Election among White Voters by Moderate Tea Party Attachment.
Bars represent predicted probabilities of voting for Romney based on multilevel logit regression and calculated using the observed value approach (Hanmer and Kalkan 2013).

Models 3 and 4 in Table 9.3, which include all voters represented by a Republican member (but control for race), show slightly different results. The single Tea Party Attachment variable in model 3 is positive and significant, but both of the dichotomous Attachment variables in model 4 fall just outside of significance. A move from no attachment to the highest value increases the probability of voting for Romney from about 49 percent to about 51 percent. This difference, two points, is consequential: receiving less than 50 percent of the vote in districts controlled by Republicans would likely have made for a landslide win for Obama.

Given Romney's entreaties to the Tea Party movement, his strong showing among Tea Party supporters, and Republicans' stated goal of making Obama a "one-term president," it is not surprising that constituents of members attached to the Tea Party would support Romney at higher rates than constituents of other Republicans. That is, although the conventional wisdom has been that Romney had difficulties with Tea Party voters, strong dislike for Obama among Tea Partiers (along with the lack of a salient third-party candidate) meant that those who elected members attached to the movement were less likely to defect from the Republican ticket. The preponderance of evidence, then, suggests that members attached to the Tea Party helped Romney more than they hurt him—or that negative partisanship was at least stronger in districts represented by legislators who attached themselves to the Tea Party.

When it comes to other factors we include in the above models, the models are consistent, and the results are not all that surprising—pessimism about the national economy, for example, is associated with voting for Romney, a reflection that partisanship tends to color economic evaluations (e.g., Gerber and Huber 2010). But there are a pair of results worth highlighting. Even controlling for partisanship and ideology, anti-immigrant attitudes predict support for Romney, a sign of the connection between hostility toward immigrants and the Republican vote—and something Romney seemed to recognize.[8] The same goes for racial resentment. Four years later, these attitudes would have a sizable impact on vote choice in the Republican nomination battle and the general election.

Endorsing Cruz and other "Non-Trumps" in 2016

In the preceding chapter, we mentioned Ted Cruz's (R-TX) influence among Tea Party members in the 113th Congress and reported that these members helped propel his candidacy for the 2016 Republican nomination for president. Here we provide one test of this claim by looking at how good a job our measures of Tea Party Association do at predicting Cruz endorsements during the 2016 primary contests. That is, did Cruz's ostensible allies in the 113th Congress back him when he threw his hat in the ring for president?

For this analysis, we exclude members who did not serve in the 114th Congress or who left Congress before the end of the 2016 primary season.[9] Despite Cruz's reputation as "speaker in all but name" and reputed close relationship with a number of Black and Green Tea Republicans, he did not initially draw all of their support. A group of High Attachment members from the 113th—Amash (R-MI), Reid Ribble (R-WI), Raul Labrador (R-ID), Matt Salmon (R-AZ), Trent Franks (R-AZ), and Joe Barton (R-TX)—initially backed other candidates.[10] However, each of them would come over to Cruz— most before Marco Rubio (R-FL) suspended his campaign on March 15. Prior to his surprisingly strong victory in Wisconsin on April 5, Cruz had consolidated Black and Green Tea support.[11]

Indeed, even when controlling for the variables that we incorporated in our other models (including ideology), Tea Party Attachment is a significant predictor of endorsing Cruz, while Tea Party Support is insignificant (see Table 9.4).[12] Figure 9.4 displays the predicted probabilities of endorsing Cruz by Tea Party Attachment.[13] Whereas the probability of endorsing Cruz was just below 8.5 percent for members with no attachment to the Tea Party in the 113th, it increases 20 percent among those with moderate attachment, and more than 37 percent for members with a high level of attachment. The difference between those with no attachment and high attachment is statistically significant, indicating that it is High Attachment scores that are driving this effect.[14]

Thus, Cruz did finally garner support from members who attached themselves to the Tea Party but initially backed candidates like Rubio, Wisconsin governor Scott Walker, former Texas governor Rick Perry, and former Arkansas governor Mike Huckabee. By the time Rubio dropped out, most of Cruz's purported House allies had lined up behind him—and, notably, not Donald Trump. As displayed in Figure 9.5, of the twenty-six endorsements Cruz received from members who served in both the 113th and 114th Congresses, seventeen were from Black or Green Tea Republicans. Also shown in Figure 9.5 is the breakdown of endorsements received by libertarian senator Rand Paul (R-KY): like Cruz, he received more endorsements from Black and Green Tea members than Coffee members, despite the latter making up a much larger proportion of the 113th Republican Conference. However, Paul received far fewer endorsements than Cruz overall.

The flip side of Tea Party support for Cruz was the absence of Tea Party support for the mainstream, establishment choices. As shown in Figure 9.5, Ohio governor John Kasich and former Florida governor Jeb Bush did not collect a single endorsement from a Black or Green Tea member. Of the twenty-eight members of the House who served in the 113th and 114th Congresses who endorsed

Table 9.4 **Predicting Cruz Endorsements in 2016**

Variable	MC Endorsed Cruz	
	(1)	*(2)*
Tea Party Support (113th)	0.02	0.02
	(0.058)	(0.060)
Tea Party Attachment (113th)	**0.59**	—
	(0.212)	—
Moderate Tea Party Attachment (113th)	—	**0.54**
	—	**(0.297)**
High Tea Party Attachment (113th)	—	**1.22**
	—	**(0.473)**
DW-Nominate (113th)	**2.72**	**2.70**
	(0.923)	**(0.919)**
Gender	–0.06	–0.06
	(0.506)	(0.506)
Year Took Office	–0.02	–0.02
	(0.017)	(0.017)
Committee Leadership (113th)	–0.49	–0.49
	(0.532)	(0.532)
Constant	36.61	36.36
	(34.985)	(34.878)
Observations (N)	196	196
R^2	0.24	0.24

Note: Coefficients are probit regression. Standard errors are in parentheses. Boldface indicates significance at $p < .05$ (one-tailed test).

Bush or Kasich, twenty-five were Coffee members. The exceptions were three Whites Tea members who initially threw their support behind Bush.[15]

Marco Rubio, who, despite losing the Republican nomination, collected the most endorsements, had a far more mixed collection. He received the same number of Black Tea endorsements as Cruz and drew only one less Green Tea endorsement. However, a far larger share of his endorsements came from Coffee members: nearly 60 percent were from members with no Tea Party association, whereas less than one in three of Cruz's endorsements were from Coffee members. The breakdown of Rubio's endorsements by Tea type reflects, and is also indicative of, his reputation as a Republican with both Tea Party and "establishment" credentials (e.g., Balz 2015; French 2016).

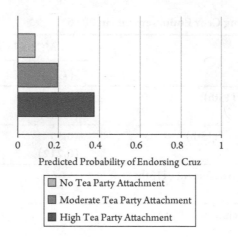

Figure 9.4 Predicted Probability of a Member of Congress Endorsing Cruz in 2016 by Tea Party Attachment, 113th Congress.

Bars represent predicted probabilities of endorsing Cruz based on probit regression and calculated using the observed value approach (Hanmer and Kalkan 2013).

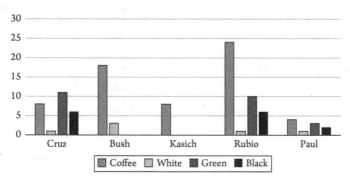

Figure 9.5 2016 Primary Endorsements by Tea Types, 113th Congress.

Bars represent the number of endorsements received from members of each Tea type.

Support for Trump on Twitter

Generally, the TPD thesis does a good job of predicting major party nominees in the post-1968 reform era—excepting 2016.[16] Donald Trump received very few endorsements from party insiders during his 2016 run. Before Trump won the February 24 Nevada Caucuses, he had attracted no endorsements from state governors, US senators, or members of the House (Bycoffe 2015; Gass 2016). In the end, Trump would receive very few endorsements from Republican elites. From House members, Trump would receive only eleven endorsements, nine of which were made by Coffee Republicans in the 113th Congress, five of whom initially endorsed other candidates (there were three Jeb Bush backers). The two non-Coffee members were Green Tea Scott DesJarlais (R-TN) and White Tea Kevin Cramer (R-ND). Trump would clinch the nomination with little institutional support—Tea Party or otherwise.[17]

However, beyond formal endorsements, there are other ways members could express public approbation of Trump's candidacy and his political positions—namely via Twitter.[18] Trump's stature as a political influencer grew with his promotion of the "birther" conspiracy theory in 2011 (e.g., Tesler 2016a). However, even as Trump's stature grew among some Republican voters—fueled by his "birther" talk—he received little attention from Republican legislators, judging by their mentions of Trump on Twitter. In the 112th Congress, Republicans as a whole directly referenced Trump only four times (there was also a tweet to Ivanka Trump). However, three of these four references were made by Black and Green Tea members and featured themes Trump would highlight in his subsequent presidential run.[19]

In the 113th Congress, the number of direct references to Trump grew to twenty-one, fourteen of which were made by Black or Green Tea members, and another by a White Tea member. While this is not a huge number, it does suggest a growing appreciation for Trump's political influence, as does the fact that most of the tweets were ingratiating; for example, White Tea Cathy McMorris Rodgers (R-WA) tweeted in June 2013, "Enjoyed meeting "the donald" @realDonaldTrump to discuss America's bright future," and Black Tea Steve King (R-IA) tweeted in October 2014, "@realDonaldTrump. Thanks for outstanding press conference and 3 stage events in Iowa last evening. You strengthened our agenda and resources."[20] Other tweets promoted some of Trump's criticisms of Obama, as well as some of his more controversial views; for example, on May 2014 Green Tea Doug LaMalfa (R-CA) tweeted, "RT @realDonaldTrump: The global warming we should be worried about is the global warming caused by NUCLEAR WEAPONS in the hands of crazy or impotent leaders."

However, given the volume of tweets Republicans posted during the 113th Congress, the limited references suggest ambivalence toward Trump. Even in the heat of the election in the fall of 2016, references on Twitter to Trump or his slogan "Make America Great Again" were limited, and the majority of posts either were neutral in tone or could be considered critical of Trump—especially after the release of the "Access Hollywood" tapes (Gervais 2018). There were only a handful of tweets promoting and defending Trump—but even these were not overly effusive; among these was one by Jim Bridenstine (R-OK): "Given the stakes of this election, if Paul Ryan isn't for Trump, then I'm not for Paul Ryan." This tweet is likely more indicative of negative partisanship and tension between Tea Partiers and House leadership than of support from Trump.

Even when we look at campaign accounts rather than official accounts, only a fraction of tweets referenced Trump. The vast majority were posted by a group of ten members (Gervais 2018). Eight of these were Coffee members in the 113th Congress. Among members associated with the Tea Party, only the campaign accounts of Black Tea Mark Meadows (R-NC) and Green Tea Todd Rokita (R-IN) made more than two references to Trump.

Tea Party Constituency Support in the 2016 Primaries

On March 4, 2016, Ben Carson dropped out of the race for the Republican nomination for president, leaving four contenders: Trump, Cruz, Rubio, and Kasich. As we have shown, Black and Green Tea members largely backed Cruz and Rubio during the 2016 Republican nomination battle; however, a plurality of Rubio's support came from Coffee members. Kasich and Trump, who did not collect many endorsements, drew predominantly from Coffee members (Kasich exclusively so).

If endorsements have an impact on the voting decisions of primary voters, then we should see that the Tea Party attachment of members has a positive effect on support for Cruz, a variable effect on support for Rubio, and a null or negative effect on support for Trump and Kasich. In fact, that is exactly what we find when we analyze data from the 2016 CCES, which asked respondents if and how they voted in a primary or caucus.

Table 9.5 presents the results of a series of multilevel models predicting support for Kasich, Rubio, and Cruz, with CCES respondents clustered into (113th) congressional districts. We restrict the sample to those who reported voting in a primary or caucus and those who were continuously represented by the same member from the 112th through the 114th Congress.[21] In addition, we utilize the sampling weights provided by the CCES.

Included in the models are Tea Party Attachment and Tea Party Support measures from the 112th and 113th Congresses. For the sake of parsimony, we show only the results of the models with separate Moderate Attachment and High Attachment dichotomous variables; however, models with the single Tea Party Attachment variables are included in Table A9.1 in Appendix II. In addition, we include controls for the same demographic factors we control for in the 2012 general election model.[22]

Racial resentment and anti-immigration attitudes are two factors that have been found to predict Trump support (Schaffner et al. 2017). We used several new measures of these attitudes (measures that were not in the 2012 CCES). For racial resentment, we constructed separate measures of Cognitive and Apathetic Racism—the former being a measure of awareness or acknowledgment of the existence of racism in the United States (see Neville et al. 2000), and the latter a measure of how bad people feel about the existence of racism (Schaffner et al. 2017). We also constructed a measure of anti-immigrant attitudes from four items included in the CCES, with 4 indicating strong hostility toward immigrants.

The first column of Table 9.5 displays the results for Kasich support. The model indicates that legislators' attachment to the Tea Party in the 113th

Table 9.5 **Tea Party Representation and Vote Choice in the Race for the 2016 Republican Nomination**

Variable	Vote in 2016 Primary/Caucus				
	Voted Kasich	Voted Rubio	Voted Cruz	Voted Trump	
Tea Party Support (113th)	−0.02 0.04)	−0.01 (0.03)	−0.01 (0.03)	**0.04 (0.02)**	
Tea Party Support (112th)	0.05 (0.06)	**−0.08 (0.05)**	**−0.09 (0.04)**	**0.05 (0.03)**	
High Tea Party Attachment (113th)	−0.37 (0.49)	0.45 (0.30)	**0.41 (0.25)**	**−0.59 (0.17)**	
Moderate Tea Party Attachment (113th)	**−0.44 (0.21)**	0.25 (0.20)	−0.07 (0.16)	0.18 (0.12)	
High Tea Party Attachment (112th)	−0.17 (0.22)	0.17 (0.17)	0.23 (0.15)	−0.02 (0.13)	
Moderate Tea Party Attachment (112th)	0.06 (0.23)	0.23 (0.25)	**0.44 (0.17)**	**−0.28 (0.12)**	
Cognitive Racism	**−0.06 (0.04)**	**0.08 (0.03)**	**0.13 (0.02)**	**0.08 (0.02)**	
Apathetic Racism	0.02 (0.05)	**−0.07 (0.04)**	−0.01 (0.03)	**0.11 (0.03)**	
Anti-Immigration Views	**−0.18 (0.07)**	**−0.20 (0.05)**	**0.13 (0.05)**	**0.37 (0.03)**	
Age	−0.00(0.01)	0.01 (0.00)	−0.01 (0.00)	**0.01 (0.00)**	
Gender (Female = 1)	−0.11(0.11)	**0.28 (0.13)**	**−0.36 (0.09)**	−0.10 (0.07)	
Race (White = 1)	**0.46 (0.22)**	−0.29 (0.21)	**0.28 (0.15)**	0.19 (0.15)	
Education (6 cat)	**0.13 (0.04)**	**0.25 (0.05)**	**0.09 (0.03)**	**−0.12 (0.03)**	
Party ID (7 cat)	**0.39 (0.04)**	**0.58 (0.05)**	**0.23 (0.03)**	**0.49 (0.03)**	
Ideology (5 cat)	−0.02 (0.08)	−0.15 (0.07)	**0.69 (0.05)**	**−0.22 (0.05)**	
Born Again Christian	**−0.35 (0.15)**	0.11 (0.12)	**0.52 (0.09)**	**−0.31 (0.09)**	

(continued)

Table 9.5 Continued

Variable	Vote in 2016 Primary/Caucus				
	Voted Kasich	Voted Rubio	Voted Cruz	Voted Trump	
Knows MC's Party	**0.40 (0.16)**	**0.50 (0.17)**	**0.65 (0.13)**	**−0.50 (0.09)**	
Negative National Economic Perceptions	**−0.20 (0.08)**	**−0.18 (0.07)**	0.00(0.06)	**0.43 (0.05)**	
Decrease in Household Income	−0.07 (0.07)	0.04(0.07)	0.02(0.05)	**0.09 (0.04)**	
Constant	**−3.98 (0.50)**	**−6.85 (0.47)**	**−7.36 (0.38)**	**−5.99 (0.36)**	
District-Level Variance	0.61 (0.11)	0.36 (0.10)	0.32 (0.06)	0.16 (0.03)	
Observations (N)	9,816	9,816	9,816	9,816	
Districts (N)	130	130	130	130	
LR χ^2	166.98; p <.000	48.88; p <.000	135.45; p <.000	74.11; p <.000	

Note: Robust standard errors are in parentheses. Boldface indicates significance at $p < .05$ (one-tailed test). Coefficients are the results of multilevel logit regression models. All data, except Tea Party Association variables, are from the 2016 Cooperative Congressional Election Study. Samples in all models are restricted to voters who participated in a Republican primary or caucus and who were represented by the same House member from the 112th through the 114th Congress.

Congress had a negative effect on voting for Kasich (this is also the case with the model that uses the single Attachment measures, included in Appendix II). Specifically, moderate attachment reduces Kasich support. Other notable factors include the negative effect that cognitive racism and anti-immigration views have on Kasich support, as do negative sociotropic and "pocketbook" economic evaluations. Kasich voters, in short, were less likely to come from districts with members who made some efforts to attach themselves to the Tea Party in the 113th Congress, were less ideological, were less likely to hold antagonistic views toward immigrants and deny that racism is a problem in the United States, and were more sanguine about national and personal economies than other voters. A picture is painted of the Kasich voter as fiscally conservative, more optimistic, and less motivated by out-group resentment than the Republican primary electorate at large.

Marco Rubio's voter base was different, as can be seen in the second column of Table 9.5. Notably, support from the Tea Party in the 112th Congress had a negative effect on voting for Rubio in a primary or caucus. This was also the case for Cruz—but support for Trump was boosted by voters from districts that received Tea Party support during the 2010 campaign season. We flesh out what we think this means later, but highlight it here to demonstrate that Rubio's (and Cruz's) relationship to the Tea Party is complicated, and consideration of Tea Party association as existing along a single dimension misses the bigger picture.

Neither Moderate nor High Tea Party Attachment is a significant predictor of voting for Rubio. This partly reflects the diversity of Rubio's endorsements—he collected as many from Black and Green Tea Republicans as Cruz did, but he also collected more endorsements from Coffee members than any other candidate, and these made up a significant proportion of all of his endorsements. Yet there is some evidence of attachment to the Tea Party boosting Rubio support—when we use the single Attachment measure (as we do in Table A9.1, Appendix II), we see that voters represented by members who attached themselves to the Tea Party had a positive effect on voting for Rubio. What this tells us is that Rubio's support was rather balanced—attachment to the Tea Party aided him, but whether the legislator had a moderate or high level of attachment did not seem to matter.

It is also worth pointing out that conservative ideology has a negative effect on Rubio support, just as Apathetic Racism and Anti-Immigration views do, but cognitive racism has a positive effect—in short, doubt that racism is a big problem in the United States predicts Rubio support, but his supporters were more empathetic toward people of other races and open to immigrants. Looking at these models, we can understand why Rubio was often cast as someone who could unite the various factions of the Republican Party but who was at the same time labeled a candidate without a base (Silver 2016). It is not obvious what the average Rubio voter looked like—which could be a good thing, if not for the fact that other candidates in the race were collecting significant support from loyal factions. Rubio's role might be interpreted as that of a spoiler, which is ironic given that he attracted the most endorsements. But this support was not sufficient. Like voters for Kasich, his voters were not uniformly resentful of African Americans and immigrants and were optimistic about the national economy—but there is some evidence that Tea Party representation (attachment) boosted support for Rubio, unlike Kasich.

Support from constituents of House members who attached themselves to the Tea Party was something Rubio would share with Ted Cruz. And for the senator from Texas, the connection to voters in Black and Green Tea districts was much more clean-cut: the support he received from Black and Green Tea members—especially those with high Attachment scores—translated into support, with a high level of attachment having a positive effect on the Cruz vote. Moderate attachment to the Tea Party in the 112th also boosted support for Cruz—among members with high Tea Party Salience scores or who tweeted about the Tea Party often but were not members of the Tea Party Caucus.

Cruz's campaign also appeared to tap into some ethnic resentment: both Cognitive Racism and Anti-Immigration views predicted Cruz support, but Apathetic Racism was not significant. There are several unique results in the Cruz models, too—most notably, he was the only candidate for which Ideology was positive and significant, indicating that he did the best with strong conservatives. In addition, both the Gender and Age variables are negative and significant, suggesting that a higher proportion of younger and male voters made up his coalition—and the Born Again Christian variable was positive and significant.

However, it was Donald Trump who appeared to have the most unique coalition of voters, as shown in Table 9.5. First, take a look at variables related to attitude and demographic factors in the model. If the true mark of an ethnocentric worldview is the harboring of attitudes that register high on the Cognitive Racism, Apathetic Racism, and Anti-immigration scales, then Trump alone collected the ethnocentric vote, as all three scales were positive and significant for Trump, a "feat" no other candidate accomplished.[23]

In addition, Trump was the only candidate for which Education and Knows MC's Party were negative and significant—indicative of a less politically sophisticated base, compared with the other candidates—and for which the Age variable was positive and significant. Finally, negative perceptions of the economy—both sociotropic and personal—predicts support for Trump, whereas for the other candidates, these variables are either insignificant or the signs are flipped. Like Rubio, Trump attracted fewer strong conservatives and, like Kasich, fewer born-again Christians.

There are unique results for Trump when it comes to the Tea Party variables as well. High Tea Party Attachment in the 113th Congress, which had a positive effect on the Cruz vote, had a negative effect on the Trump vote, as did Moderate Tea Party Attachment in the 112th (the single Tea Party Attachment variable is not significant in the model included in Appendix II). So, as with Kasich, being represented by a member of Congress who attached her- or himself to the Tea Party correlated with not supporting Trump. But, unlike Kasich, Trump did have some connection to the Tea Party: Tea Party Support in the 112th and 113th was positive and significant. That is, being represented by a member backed by the Tea Party movement is a strong predictor of voting for Trump.

This is an interesting finding—especially in light of the fact that 112th Tea Party Support had a negative effect on support for Rubio and Cruz. Why would support given to candidates from the organized Tea Party during the 2010 election season have such predictive power during the 2016 nomination race? After all, many Tea Party movement elites who were active during the 2010 campaign would be divided over Trump and Cruz (see Costa 2016; Zezima 2016). For example, Sarah Palin made a high-profile endorsement of Trump, but Glenn Beck, anointing Cruz the next "George Washington," remained a fervent "Never Trumper" even after Trump's election (Beinart 2017). Tea Party organizations like FreedomWorks expressed coolness toward Trump's candidacy (e.g., Lovelace 2015), while the president of the Tea Party Patriots would later take some credit for Trump's victory, arguing that "the values and principles that gave rise to the tea party movement in 2009 are finally gaining the top seat of power in the White House" (Martin 2016).

Here we offer one explanation for this finding. As we have argued, the rationale for Tea Party support was often more strategic than ideological. Members who drew support from the Tea Party movement came from competitive districts—for example, they had the highest support for Obama in both 2008 and 2012. Recall also from Chapter 3 that White Tea members were less ideological and that the districts they served had above-average unemployment. While the motivations of many organizations might have been libertarian, these were districts and voters that organizations and activists associated with the Tea Party movement believed it could win over with populist, anti-establishment messaging, focused on bogeymen like Obama and immigrants—think "take our country back." When Sarah Palin, in conjunction with other Tea Party strands, worked to boost the prospects of congressional candidates before and during the 112th Congress, it was hard to miss the populist tone of her messaging (Broder 2010). Consider this excerpt from a speech she gave in early 2011:

> The government created the problem, now government presents itself as a solution, trying to convince us the [sic] we can "Win the Future" by letting that little intellectual elite in a far distant capitol win it for us . . . Today big business, big labor, big government, they have seats at the table. The little guy doesn't but we're the ones left holding the tab. We are paying the bill. This is not the way it's supposed to be. This is not the way it must be. (Newton-Small 2011)

Critics of Palin and the organized Tea Party have panned the idea that "populist" is the right adjective to describe them, pointing to free-market capitalist policies they advocated for (see Milbank 2010d; Postel 2010; Rich 2010)—criticism that would also be leveled at Trump. Regardless, the language they have used can have lasting effects in promoting populist attitudes. And the organized Tea Party was quite active during the 2010 election season, offering this type of rhetoric. In contrast to the election season of 2010, which featured Tea Party organizations sponsoring bus tours, protests, and rallies to promote a message about an out-of-control federal government staffed with out-of-touch elites (Skocpol and Williamson 2012, 104–109), the 2012 election season saw less activity of this sort (we found that far fewer endorsements and campaign expenditures and less digital activism occurred during the season). This is likely for two reasons: first, the organized Tea Party at least partially accomplished its mission by helping Republicans handily retake the House of Representatives; second, congressional races were overshadowed by the presidential election.

Given that the 2010 activism (grassroots and "astro turf") was significant, there is reason to believe its effects could carry over to the 2016 election. The emotions that particular ads, rallies, and speeches evoke are evanescent. But proximity to protests and mass activism can help form political attitudes that are less fleeting (Wallace et al. 2014). The populist, anti-Obama, anti-establishment, and anti-Washington rhetoric of the 2010 Tea Party movement may have helped affirm and crystallize negative affective attitudes towards out-groups and adversaries held by those exposed—even well after the rallies, ads, and activism died down. There is agreement across the political spectrum that the Tea Party movement during this time did not embody a mere "mood"; rather, it infused Republican Party politics with an enduring populist brashness that lasted long after the Tea Party brand became less prominent.[24] As the scholar Walter Russell Mead (2011) penned in a 2011 *Foreign Affairs* article on Tea Party foreign policy:

The Tea Party movement is best understood as a contemporary revolt of Jacksonian common sense against elites perceived as both misguided and corrupt. And although the movement itself may splinter and even disappear, the populist energy that powers it will not go away.

We think these words are prophetic, and the same point is made by Skocpol and Williamson (2012) in their analysis of Tea Party organizations. Sarah Palin, Tea Party organizations, and Tea Party activists may no longer have as salient a role in backing candidates and policies in congressional districts that they did in 2010. But cultural resentment and populist attitudes, elements that would help propel the Tea Party into the center of American politics, would remain. And as Williamson (2016) argues, with common themes in anti-immigrant views, racial resentment, and ethno-nationalism, "the Trump presidency is of a piece with the Tea Party movement that preceded it."

Thus, the reactions provoked by Tea Party support prior to the 112th Congress were not momentary spikes in affect, but deep-rooted, simmering attitudes that were still festering in the fall of 2015. And for voters who were not tethered to strong (traditional) conservative ideological positions, who perceived government as unfairly rewarding people of color, and whose allegiance to the parties and people in Washington was limited, Trump was the only horse to back. In districts where representatives were targeted for Tea Party Support in 2010, it seems likely that the populist message was heard and accepted. However, allegiance to the Tea Party wing in Congress was tenuous. Voters in these districts, rather than turning to the senators in Washington ostensibly backed by the institutional Tea Party in 2016, gravitated to a person with a very anti-elite, populist message, one who had never served a day in government. Cruz, despite his attempts to seem unconventional and anti-Washington, was seen as too orthodox and too Washington.[25]

In short, the Tea Party electorate broke in two. Educated, ideological voters, familiar with their member of Congress and attuned to whomever they endorsed, split between Cruz and Rubio. But populist voters, whose districts once attracted Tea Party support and would have also been labeled "Tea Party" voters, threw their support behind Trump, who also honed a populist message (and won the endorsement of Palin). On the other hand, legislators' attachment to the Tea Party had a negative effect on support for the ostensibly more "establishment" John Kasich.

Voters who were represented by members who attached themselves to the Tea Party also held such anti-establishment sentiments. As we showed in Chapter 7, such members did make use of angry and sad rhetoric to incite latent resentment toward out-groups and the federal government. However, voters in districts represented by Black and Green Tea Republicans threw their support behind two different anti-establishment candidates, Cruz and Rubio.

To see the extent to which association with the Tea Party influenced vote choice during the primaries, we calculated the predicted probabilities of voting for Trump and Cruz or Rubio when a voter's representative did and did not have a High Tea Party Attachment score in the 113th Congress, as well as high and low Tea Party Support scores in the 112th.[26] The probabilities are shown in Figure 9.6. Whereas the predicted probability of supporting Trump moves from about 26 percent to 28 percent when 112th Tea Party Support goes from low to high (keeping all other variables at their observed values; see Hanmer and Kalkan 2013), it drops from about 27 percent to less than 20 percent when 113th Tea Party Attachment goes from not high to high.

It was the opposite for the Cruz or Rubio vote. When 112th Tea Party Support scores move from low to high (setting all other variables at their observed values), the probability of voting for either senator drops from about 37 percent to 29 percent. On the other hand, moving from not High Tea Party attachment in the 113th to a high level of attachment increases the probability of voting for Cruz or Rubio from 33 percent to about 45 percent.

There is a point we should make about the size of these effects, which applies to many of the findings we report throughout this chapter. Some of the effects—like the impact of support from the Tea Party in the 112th Congress on voting for Trump—may seem minute. For example, the effect of moving from the lowest value on the Anti-immigration scale to the highest value increases the probability of voting for Trump from 43 percent to 59 percent. However, our argument is not that legislators' Tea Party associations are the biggest factor in voting for Trump, but are, rather, important contributory factors. And given the closeness of many primary and caucus races, and the way various state parties dole out delegates to candidates, two or five or seven

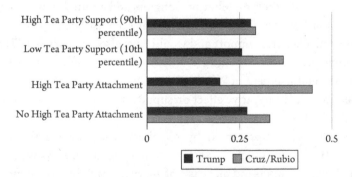

Figure 9.6 2016 Primary Vote Choice Probabilities by Representative's Tea Party Association.
Bars represent predicted probabilities of voting for Trump or Cruz/Rubio based on multilevel logit regression and calculated using the observed value approach (Hanmer and Kalkan 2013).

percentage points can make a big difference and ultimately decide who wins the nomination.

In the end, what we see here is how much a factionalized Republican Party enabled Trump's victory. One conclusion is that the upstart Tea Party wing in the House, hoping to resist another "establishment" candidate and to see one of its own claim the nomination. But the legislators remained divided over Cruz and Rubio. Had an institutionalized Tea Party not existed, it is hard to see how the candidacies of Cruz and even Rubio would have endured as long as they did—high Tea Party Attachment scores boosted the probability of voting for either significantly. A race without the two Tea Party–backed senators might have meant that Kasich, or another more traditional candidate, would have consolidated more endorsements and votes, early in the campaign. Perhaps if Rubio had not run or had dropped out earlier, Kasich would have had the "establishment lane" to himself. And the lack of agreement among House Tea Partiers mattered, too: without Rubio, Cruz would have consolidated more Tea Party support from voters in districts represented by Black and Green Tea Republicans.

These thoughts are counterfactual. Yet we think it likely that the divisions in the Republican Party in the period leading up to the primary race not only invited many to throw their hats in the ring (a record seventeen candidates initially)[27] but, even after the field had narrowed down to four candidates, the major bases of power—the so-called establishment and the Tea Party—remained divided, with three candidates competing over the voters roughly falling into these two camps. The sizable group of members who associated with the Tea Party movement in the 113th Congress spurned endorsing more conventional candidates, like Kasich, and instead divided their loyalties between Cruz and Rubio. That left Trump, who produced the most unique coalition, to clinch the nomination for himself.

Contrary to the predictions of the TPD thesis, the party did not coordinate on any candidate during the Invisible Primary. In fact, we believe that in the Tea Party era, the ability of insiders to coordinate on a single candidate has been severely curtailed (and we are not alone in this belief).[28] In 2016, House Tea Partiers appear to have played a big role in generating an impasse that left an opening for Trump to rabble-rouse his way to the top of the polls in the summer of 2015. Intra-party disputes would also forestall a united, extensive, and capable challenge to his candidacy during the nomination fight. By the time Kasich was the lone "establishment" choice, Trump had cemented a hold on many Republican votes.

That is not the only way we think the Tea Party in the House helped Trump during the primaries. While Trump's rhetoric on Twitter seems to many to be highly inappropriate, it is agreeable to many others—which raises the question as to how it became acceptable for a political elite to use such language. As we demonstrated in the preceding chapter, before Trump's rise, Black and Green Tea Party members had a penchant for uncivil rhetoric on Twitter. And although uncivil rhetoric was not absent from the posts of Coffee members, we have argued that the Tea Party movement was a critical element in establishing incivility as appropriate for political elites.

We consider whether Republican legislators' use of incivility in the years before 2016 influenced the likelihood of their constituents' voting for Kasich, Rubio, Cruz, and, of course, Trump.[29] In a set of multilevel models displayed in Table 9.6 (with voters again clustered into districts), we regress voting for each of the four candidates onto legislators' 112th and 113th incivility rates. We also include a measure of social media use on a scale of 0 to 6, where 0 means that the voter (within the past twenty-four hours) did not use social media at all, 1 means that the voter used social media but not for any political activities, and 2–6 indicate the number of political activities the voter engaged in on social media.[30] As we expect the influence of members' incivility has the greatest impact on voters who are politically engaged on social media (they are the most likely to see their members' tweets), we interact legislator incivility use and voter social media use. Finally, we control for the same demographic and attitudinal variables in the previous set of models, along with other types of media use (television, radio, and newspapers). Sampling weights are applied in each model.

Legislators' incivility use in the 112th Congress is not significant in any of the models, nor is the interaction between 112th incivility use and social media use (because this variable has little impact on the models, we leave it out of the models presented in the table). Perhaps this is not all that surprising—it is something of a stretch to assume that voters who engaged on social media during the 2016 campaign were also politically engaged on social media in 2011 and 2012. It is only more recently that social media use and the following of members of Congress on social media have swelled—in fact, the number of registered voters following a political elite doubled between 2010 and 2014, and the rate tripled among voters between the ages of thirty and fifty (Anderson 2015).

On the other hand, incivility use during the 113th Congress positively predicts voting for Rubio. This is not surprising, given that attachment to the Tea Party predicts incivility use in the 113th (as shown in the preceding chapter) and voting for Rubio (as shown in Table A9.1). But this is not the most interesting finding, in our opinion. While social media use had a negative effect on voting for Kasich and Rubio and no effect on voting for Cruz, it had a positive effect on voting for Trump—that is, the more politically engaged a person was on social media, the more likely the person was to vote for Trump. What is most notable is that the interaction between legislator incivility use in the 113th Congress and voters' reported social media use is negative and significant for Kasich, Rubio, and Cruz

Table 9.6 Incivility, Social Media Engagement, and Vote Choice in 2016 Republican Primaries

Variable	Vote in 2016 Primary/Caucus				
	Voted Kasich	Voted Rubio	Voted Cruz	Voted Trump
MC 112th Incivility Rate	-0.67 (1.58)	1.53 (1.48)	-2.00 (1.70)	-0.37 (0.70)
MC 113th Incivility Rate	0.19 (0.78)	2.86 (1.26)	0.40 (1.09)	-0.67 (0.09)
Social Media Use (0–6)	-0.10 (0.03)	-0.09 (0.03)	-0.04 (0.02)	0.05 (0.02)
Social Media*MC 113th Incivility Rate	-0.96 (0.37)	-0.83 (0.31)	-1.09 (0.26)	1.32 (0.31)
Uses TV (1 = yes)	-0.14 (0.14)	0.29 (0.15)	-0.39 (0.11)	0.37 (0.09)
Uses Radio (1 = yes)	-0.20 (0.13)	-0.18 (0.11)	0.63 (0.09)	-0.28 (0.09)
Uses Newspaper (1 = yes)	0.56 (0.14)	0.10 (0.13)	-0.15 (0.10)	-0.00 (0.09)
Cognitive Racism	-0.06 (0.04)	0.09 (0.03)	0.13 (0.03)	0.08 (0.02)
Apathetic Racism	0.01 (0.06)	-0.11 (0.036)	-0.01 (0.03)	0.14 (0.03)
Anti-Immigration Views	-0.18 (0.07)	-0.21 (0.05)	0.12 (0.05)	0.39 (0.03)
Age	-0.01 (0.01)	-0.00 (0.00)	-0.00 (0.003)	0.01 (0.00)
Gender (Female = 1)	-0.13 (0.11)	0.30 (0.13)	-0.26 (0.10)	-0.12 (0.07)
Race (White = 1)	0.35 (0.22)	-0.18 (0.21)	0.23 (0.16)	0.25 (0.15)
Education (6 cat)	0.13 (0.05)	0.25 (0.05)	0.07 (0.04)	-0.10 (0.03)
Party ID (7 cat)	0.40 (0.04)	0.58 (0.05)	0.22 (0.03)	0.47 (0.03)

(continued)

Table 9.6 **Continued**

Variable	Vote in 2016 Primary/Caucus			
	Voted Kasich	*Voted Rubio*	*Voted Cruz*	*Voted Trump*
Ideology (5 cat)	−0.01 (0.09)	−0.11 (0.07)	**0.70 (0.06)**	**−0.20 (0.06)**
Born Again Christian	**−0.30 (0.15)**	0.07 (0.13)	**0.50 (0.10)**	**−0.33 (0.09)**
Knows MC's Party	**0.44 (0.15)**	**0.68 (0.19)**	**0.70 (0.12)**	**−0.58 (0.09)**
Negative National Economic Perceptions	**−0.22 (0.09)**	**−0.17 (0.08)**	0.03 (0.06)	**0.45 (0.05)**
Decrease in Household Income	−0.04 (0.08)	0.08 (0.07)	−0.01 (0.06)	0.04 (0.05)
Constant	**−3.76 (0.51)**	**−6.72 (0.47)**	**−7.31 (0.40)**	**−6.55 (0.39)**
District-level variance	0.68 (0.13)	0.43 (0.11)	0.37 (0.07)	0.19 (0.04)
N Observations (N)	9,001	9,001	9,001	9,001
N Districts (N)	119	119	119	119
LR χ^2	180.34; $p < .00$	57.91; $p < .00$	134.23; $p < .00$	80.85; $p < .00$

Note: Robust standard errors are in parentheses. Boldface indicates significance at $p < .05$ (one-tailed test). Coefficients are the results of multilevel logit regression models. All data, except MC incivility use rates, are from the 2016 Cooperative Congressional Election Study. The sample in both models is restricted to voters who participated in a Republican primary or caucus and who were represented by the same House member throughout the 112th through the 114th Congress.

and positive for Trump. That is, the combination of voters being politically engaged on social media and their representatives frequently using incivility on Twitter in the years before 2016 boosted support for Trump at the expense of his competition.

To determine how big a boost this was for Trump, we calculate the predicted probability of voting for Trump versus Kasich, Rubio, or Cruz when the interaction between social media use and incivility use moves from a middle-of-the-road value to a high value.[31] The probability of voting for Trump and not one of his four main competitors is about 50 percent when the value is low and all other variables are set to their observed values—but when legislator incivility use and voter social media use are both high, the probability jumps to about 58 percent. The probability of voting for Trump versus *any* other candidate moves from 25 to 30 percent when the interaction between incivility rates and social media use goes from a low to high value. Did uncivil legislators cause Trump to win? No, not by themselves—absent feelings of racial resentment and anti-immigration attitudes, negative perceptions of the national economy, and so on, Trump would not likely have won even with members of Congress tweeting out uncivil posts. However, as with the Tea Party Association measures, we argue that it was an important contributory factor, and without the boost it provided to the Trump vote, his path to the nomination would likely have been more difficult or completely obstructed had the outcome in a few close primary races gone a different way. Moreover, as we have highlighted in the Chapters 7 and 8, there appears to be a connection between uncivil, emotional tweets and resentment among the electorate. This resentment invited legislators to say and do things they might normally not—they provided the red meat—and exposure to their rhetoric may perhaps have amplified feelings of resentment. In short, these factors are interconnected and related and also contributed to Trump's surprising clinching of the Republican nomination in July 2016.

Tea Party Constituency Support for Trump in the 2016 General Election

In the fight for the 2016 Republican nomination, Donald Trump did well with voters from districts that had attracted Tea Party support during the height of Tea Party activism. However, voters represented by members who strongly attached themselves to the Tea Party in the 113th Congress were less likely to support Trump than primary/caucus voters from other districts represented by Republicans. However, the general election was a whole new ball game, and

Trump was no longer competing against Kasich, Rubio, and Cruz, but Hillary Clinton, the Democratic nominee. Given strong dislike for Clinton among Republicans—and the power of negative partisanship—this was perhaps good news for Trump, in that he did not have to worry as much about the Republican base failing to support him. Nonetheless, a "Never Trump" movement among Republicans was active during the fall of 2016. Given how they affected the Trump vote during the primaries, we wondered how legislators' association with the Tea Party affected voter choice in the general election. Did some factors encourage voters to become "Never Trumpers" and cast either a protest vote (for a third-party candidate like Libertarian Party candidate Gary Johnson or independent candidate Evan McMullin) or even hold their nose and vote for Clinton?[32] Or did having a legislator associated with the Tea Party in some way reinforce support for Trump and reduce the likelihood of casting a protest or Clinton vote?

To assess whether Tea Party representation aided, hindered, or had no impact on voting for Trump, we construct a Trump Vote scale, where 1 represented a vote for Clinton, 2 indicated a vote for someone other than Clinton or Trump, and 3 signified a vote for Trump. This variable captures the range of vote choices possible in the general election, with voting for Clinton representing the strongest resistance to Trump and protest, third-party votes serving as a neutral category.

We designed two multilevel ordered probit regression models—one with the single Tea Party Attachment variable and one with the two dichotomous variables—with the Trump Vote scale serving as the dependent variable in both. As before, respondents are clustered into 113th congressional districts, and the samples are restricted to voters who were represented by the same members from the 112th Congress through the 114th. As we expect that any connection between the Tea Party Association variables and support for Trump will be limited to white voters, we exclude voters from minority groups from these analyses.

Among white voters, racial resentment and anti-immigration views, along with a negative outlook on the national economy, all boosted support for Trump (along with a number of demographic factors, including education). Yet even after these factors are controlled for, the results of both models, displayed in Table 9.7, demonstrate that Tea Party representation affected support for Trump during the general election. First, both models show that 113th Tea Party Support had a negative effect on support for Trump. This result is somewhat surprising, given that support from the Tea Party in the 112th boosted Trump during the nomination contests. We have a pair of explanations. First, as we have argued, support from the organized Tea Party is not based strictly on the ideology of candidates, but is doled out strategically. As we demonstrated in Chapters 3 and 5, it is most likely to go to members who do not have particularly conservative records and represent competitive districts, with White

Tea districts giving more support to Obama than Coffee districts. But voters were not more likely to support Clinton because their representatives received support from the Tea Party. Rather, the districts that received Tea Party support had voters more inclined to vote Democratic than other Republican districts to begin with.

Second, support from the Tea Party was much more limited in the 113th Congress than in the 112th (fewer endorsements, less money, and less activism). In fact, with the exception of predicting the number of sponsored bills that became law in Chapter 6, it has had little significance in any of the analyses we have run. While the 112th Congress featured forty-six White Tea members, the 113th featured only sixteen. Thus, in contrast to its 112th counterpart, which featured what was the zenith of Tea Party activity during the 2010 election season, 113th Tea Party Support may not be all that meaningful a variable.

In contrast, Tea Party Attachment may be a more meaningful variable in the 113th Congress, as the motivation and means (the Tea Party Caucus) to connect to the movement had declined for legislators—and so those who did attach themselves to the movement were likely true believers. And thus it is especially interesting that, as shown in model 1 of Table 9.7, attachment to the Tea Party in the 113th had a positive effect on Trump support in the general election, given the negative effects it had on Trump support during the primaries and how limited Republicans' support for Trump was, even on Twitter. Among white voters represented by Republican legislators, the effect on the probability of supporting Trump in the general election is modest: holding all other variables at their observed values, the predicted probability increases by more than two percentage points. Yet in an election where Trump won four critical states by less than this amount (Florida, Michigan, Pennsylvania, and Wisconsin), an effect this size was enough to affect the outcome of the election.

So in an election characterized by negative partisanship, and in which more than 90 percent of partisans on both sides voted for their party's candidate (Dalton 2017), why would a legislator's Tea Party affiliation boost support for Trump at all, especially after attachment to the Tea Party had a negative effect on Trump support in the primaries? Part of the explanation might be that those represented by members attached to the Tea Party have a penchant for anti-establishment outsiders, and with Cruz and Rubio no longer running against Trump, they were especially likely to back him now, going against an establishment insider Democrat named Clinton.

Yet it could also be that familiarity with Black and Green Tea Republicans and their rhetoric made acceptance of Trump and his rhetoric much more likely. Model 2 in Table 9.7, which breaks down Tea Party Association into Moderate and High Association, hints at this. Here we see that it is Moderate Tea Party Attachment in the 113th driving this effect. As you might recall, it was this

Table 9.7 **Tea Party Representation and the Trump Vote in the 2016 General Election**

Variable	Trump Vote Scale (0–2)	
	Model 1	Model 2
Tea Party Support (113th)	**–0.02 (0.01)**	**–0.02 (0.01)**
Tea Party Support (112th)	–0.00 (0.01)	0.00 (0.01)
Tea Party Attachment (113th)	**0.07 (0.04)**	—
Tea Party Attachment (112th)	–0.03 (0.03)	—
High Tea Party Attachment (113th)	—	0.07 (0.07)
Moderate Tea Party Attachment (113th)	—	**0.12 (0.06)**
High Tea Party Attachment (112th)	—	–0.06 (0.06)
Moderate Tea Party Attachment (112th)	—	–0.08(0.064)
Cognitive Racism	**0.16 (0.02)**	**0.16 (0.02)**
Apathetic Racism	**0.07 (0.02)**	**0.07 (0.02)**
Anti-Immigration Views	**0.24 (0.02)**	**0.24 (0.02)**
Age	0.00 (0.00)	0.00 (0.00)
Gender (Female = 1)	–0.07 (0.05)	–0.07 (0.05)
Education (6 cat)	**–0.05 (0.02)**	**–0.05 (0.02)**
Party ID (7 cat)	**0.41 (0.02)**	**0.41 (0.02)**
Ideology (5 cat)	**0.16 (0.03)**	**0.16 (0.03)**
Born Again Christian	**0.24 (0.06)**	**0.24 (0.06)**
Knows MC's Party	0.03 (0.04)	0.03 (0.04)
Negative National Economic Perceptions	**0.45 (0.03)**	**0.45 (0.03)**
Decrease in Household Income	**0.05 (0.03)**	**0.05 (0.03)**
Cut 1		
Constant	**4.81 (0.19)**	**4.81 (0.19)**
Cut 2		
Constant	**5.31 (0.18)**	**5.31 (0.18)**
District-Level Variance	**0.02 (0.007)**	**0.02 (0.007)**
Observations (N)	11,237	11,237

Table 9.7 **Continued**

Variable	Trump Vote Scale (0–2)	
	Model 1	*Model 2*
Districts (N)	130	130
LR χ^2	14.92; $p < .001$	14.03; $p < .001$

Note: Robust standard errors are in parentheses. Boldface indicates significance at $p < .05$ (one-tailed test). Coefficients are the results of multilevel ordered probit regression models. All data, except Tea Party Association variables, are from the 2016 Cooperative Congressional Election Study. The sample in both models is restricted to white voters who were represented by the same House member throughout the 112th through the 114th Congress.

variable that had a positive relationship with legislator incivility use in all of the Chapter 8 analyses (see Table 8.2). Trump's rhetoric and behavior might have made a number of Republicans uneasy, so much so that they declined to support him.[33] But voters inured to political incivility might readily accept a candidate for president whose campaign was significantly based on insulting and demeaning others on Twitter particularly if, as we saw with the primary analyses, the voter was politically engaged on social media.

This is precisely what we see. Table 9.8 breaks down the CCES sample into two groups: white general election voters who were not politically engaged on social media (or did not use social media at all) and white general election voters who engaged in at least one political activity on social media (and, again, we restrict the sample to voters represented by the same member of Congress through all three congresses). We again control for other types of media use. In the model containing just individuals who did not use social media (for political activities or in general), their members' incivility use in the 113th Congress had no effect on Trump support.[34] However, among individuals who were politically engaged on social media, a legislator's incivility use in the 113th had a positive effect on Trump support.[35] The predicted probability of voting for Trump among white voters politically engaged on social media increases from about 49 percent to about 50 percent (when all other variables are held at their observed values)—and while this is a one-percentage-point difference, given the controls in the model, the context of the race (high partisan allegiance), and the outcome of the election (Clinton won the popular vote by two percentage points and lost four states by just over a percentage point or less), this is a meaningful difference.

Of course, imprecision might lead to an underestimation of the effects as well. Reporting political activity on social media in 2016 does not mean exposure to the tweets of one's legislator in 2013 and 2014—it is reasonable to assume that if

Table 9.8 Incivility, Social Media Engagement, and Voting Trump in the General Election

Variable	Trump Vote Scale (0–2)	
	No Political Engagement on Social Media	Political Engagement on Social Media
MC 113th Incivility Rate	−0.30 (0.37)	**0.61 (0.35)**
MC 112th Incivility Rate	0.21 (0.78)	0.94 (0.68)
Uses TV (1 = yes)	**−0.16 (0.07)**	−0.01 (0.09)
Uses Radio (1 = yes)	0.08 (0.07)	**0.20 (0.08)**
Uses Newspaper (1 = yes)	0.06 (0.07)	−0.03 (0.07)
Cognitive Racism	**0.14 (0.02)**	**0.17 (0.02)**
Apathetic Racism	**0.06 (0.02)**	**0.08 (0.02)**
Anti-Immigration Views	**0.19 (0.02)**	**0.29 (0.03)**
Age	**0.01 (0.00)**	0.00 (0.00)
Gender (Female = 1)	**−0.21 (0.06)**	0.02 (0.07)
Education (6 cat)	−0.03 (0.02)	**−0.07 (0.03)**
Party ID (7 cat)	**0.44 (0.02)**	**0.39 (0.02)**
Ideology (5 cat)	**0.09 (0.04)**	**0.09 (0.05)**
Born Again Christian	**0.22 (0.07)**	**0.28 (0.08)**
Knows MC's Party	−0.06 (0.07)	0.05 (0.11)
Negative National Economic Perceptions	**0.46 (0.04)**	**0.43 (0.05)**
Decrease in Household Income	0.05 (0.04)	0.04 (0.03)
Cut 1		
Constant	**4.82 (0.22)**	**4.79 (0.26)**
Cut 2		
Constant	**5.29 (0.21)**	**5.33 (0.26)**
District-Level Variance	0.03 (0.01)	0.03 (0.01)
Observations (N)	5,346	5,818
Districts (N)	176	119
LR χ^2	4.73; $p < .05$	10.89; $p < .001$

Note: Robust standard errors are in parentheses. Boldface indicates significance at $p < .05$ (one-tailed test). Coefficients are the results of multilevel ordered probit regression models. All data, except MC incivility use rates, are from the 2016 Cooperative Congressional Election Study. The sample in the first model is restricted to white voters who were not politically engaged on social media and who were represented by the same House member throughout the 112th through the 114th Congress. The sample in the second model is restricted to white voters who were politically engaged on social media and who were represented by the same House member throughout the 112th through the 114th Congress. Sample weights were used in both models.

we could identify which voters were following their members on Twitter during these years, the effect size might be larger. In addition, as we have argued, traditional media coverage of members' tweets means that some non–social media users are exposed to uncivil tweets—in fact, offensive tweets are probably the most likely to receive coverage.[36] This type of exposure may also help normalize uncivil elite discourse among voters.

It is reasonable to think there is some self-selection happening here, in which voters who are less dedicated to or concerned about norms of incivility are more apt to become politically engaged on social media.[37] In turn, astute legislators, hoping to connect with constituents by fostering a digital homestyle, offer up the type of red meat they sense their followers want. But just as with other types of media, the reasons some people choose to use (or not use) social media are varied and not always straightforward (Correa et al. 2010; Hughes et al. 2012).[38] In addition, political communication scholarship demonstrates that social media use can affect offline political participation (Gil de Zuniga et al. 2012, 2014). In short, while tastes and personality characteristics may in part determine who joins social networking sites, people's political behavior can be influenced through engagement on social media.

As such, we think it likely that social media helps to normalize uncivil political discourse, in particular when it comes to the rhetoric of political elites. Legislators may offer up red meat rhetoric because they think it is what people want to hear, but that does not mean the messages do not have an impact on the attitudes of those exposed. For users whose members of Congress leveraged incivility frequently in their Twitter posts, Donald Trump's Twitter rhetoric might have seemed new and different—he takes incivility to a level that few other political elites have—but not inappropriate to the extent that they cannot back him.

The public is exposed to uncivil political discourse from other elites as well. We expect that incivility among members of Congress on social media during the 112th and 113th Congresses was neither as frequent or in most cases as severe as the incivility of other elites—namely those in partisan media. Yet we would again emphasize the legitimacy granted to a coarser type of discourse when legislators adopt it and use it via their official accounts. In addition to such rhetoric becoming more acceptable, there is the effect of the uncivil messages themselves. Scholars are still unwrapping the differential effects of pro-attitudinal and counter-attitudinal uncivil messages, the affective reactions they induce, and the role of personality in mediating these effects (Institute for Policy Research 2017; Gervais 2017a,b; Mutz 2015). But we think it likely that tweets such as those we highlighted in Chapters 7 and 8 help to activate and reinforce feelings of resentment, and this effect is compounded when an elected official is spreading the messages; claims that illegal immigrants are collecting food stamps or that Obama's so-called illegal and radical moves are allowing dangerous illegal immigrants to invade their towns are granted more gravitas and prominence when coming from a sitting member of Congress than a random poster.[39] And as Americans increasingly use social media to keep tabs on their elected officials, and social media platforms make it easier to do so, we expect the influence of congressional tweets to increase in the years to come (Anderson 2015; Fung 2017).

To be clear, uncivil and hyperbolic commentary is not limited to Republican officeholders or voters. Yet the Democratic Party has yet to embrace or promote a personality like Trump, who admittedly relishes talking (or tweeting) in a "politically incorrect" fashion. Moreover, it is hard to ignore the prominence of uncivil talk in Republican politics; for instance, other contenders for the 2016 Republican nomination attempted to emulate Trump. It became apparent that some level of incivility by the candidates was not only welcome, but requisite, for a segment of the Republican electorate. Consider this contemporaneous description of the 2016 Republican debates by political scientist Stephen Nuño (2016):

> The GOP debates have descended into afternoon talk show brawls with rowdy audiences egging their prospective candidates on to cast personal insults at their challengers. From Donald Trump boasting about the size of his genitals to Ted Cruz resorting to school yard antagonizations, "breathe Donald, breathe . . . ," I marveled at the state of the "Grand Old Party" and what it has become . . . If you watched the [March 3 debate in Detroit, Michigan], you learned nothing of substance except that the GOP popularity contest is inversely proportional to the display of civility by the candidates. John Kasich has shown restraint and measure throughout the campaign season and continues to find himself on the fringes of the election and of the discussion over how the GOP proposes to lead the country.

There is plenty of vitriol and incivility (and beyond) coming from individuals on the left (e.g., Beinart 2017)—including that from contenders for the 2016 Democratic nomination (Phillips 2017)—but we think it is a fair assessment that the Democratic debates were rather tame and civil in comparison.[40] Democratic voters may lust for red meat as well, but so far the Democratic Party has not fully adopted this tactic as a means of retaking power, and organized resistance to Trump on the left that (with the exception of extreme, fringe groups like the Antifa movement) has vowed to embrace tactics and rhetoric based on "respect" and devoid of "viciousness" (Levin et al. 2017). But stay tuned—if anger and incivility are intricately linked, then the pressure on Democratic candidates to tell the people what they want to hear is likely to be intense.

There is no factor that alone accounts for this appetite for incivility among the Republican base. Commentators, including the political psychologist Jonathan Haidt, have suggested that anti-politically correct sentiment during 2016 was a reaction to the perceived "liberal social justice overreach" when it comes to the policing of language, experienced as oppressive and a restriction on freedom and liberty.[41] We cannot reflect on the accuracy of this claim one way or the other. But as we have laid out, the willingness of the Tea Party–aligned Republicans and the circumstances Republicans found themselves in—out of power, just as a new tool for communication was growing in popularity—likely played a role in fomenting a craving for coarseness and crassness in political talk. Resentment of out-groups simmered beneath the surface and was fomented by the rhetoric of Republicans during the Tea Party era.

Perceived norms of discourse (and the lack thereof) play a role as well. The culture of social media is likely to shape the way legislators engage on social media platforms. Political leaders, rather than setting the tone of discourse on social media, acquiesce to it; their messages, at times, are delivered with the same blistering, acidic, and snarky tone that defines much of social media discourse. In addition, political elites are incentivized to offer uncivil rhetoric by an absence of norms constraining attacks on the other side, as well as underlying negative partisanship among their base (Iyengar and Westwood 2015). As such, genuine instances of bipartisanship (not just platitudes) and goodwill between legislators on both sides of the aisle might be perceived as normatively wrong among core supporters.

Accordingly, recent observers concerned with the coarsening of American discourse have often argued that while Trump has not helped the tone of discourse, he is not the cause but a manifestation of this trend.[42] Here we offer some support for this. A strong predictor of someone voting for Trump is having had a legislator who was uncivil on Twitter. Nearly all members were less uncivil on their official accounts—in terms of both frequency and intensity—than Trump has been on his personal account, and this was likely critical to acceptance of Trump. Occasional uncivil messages spread through congressional Twitter altered expectations for how elected officials conduct themselves, but there was not an instantaneous jump from relatively placid political talk to Trumpian bombast. That is not to say American discourse was devoid of incivility prior to social media and the Tea Party, but Americans were also not exposed to uncivil messages on a regular basis during their leisure time in the past.[43] Campaign ads attacking opponents appear only during campaign season and may not feature the candidates themselves (until they "approve this message" at the end). Thus, the ads lack a personal, off-the-cuff touch.[44] While legislators may be strategic (at times) with social media, tweets may seem genuine and impulsive, and exposure to your member of Congress attacking political adversaries in such tweets can be perceived as a sincere call to arms.

The Tea Party on the National Stage

In comparison with the Tea Party's status during the 2012 campaign season, the movement was supposed to have been washed up in 2016, a non-factor. Ironically, our findings indicate that the institutional Tea Party was more consequential in the latter election than the former. In 2012, Tea Party legislators likely did more to help the "establishment" (in the form of Mitt Romney) than they did to hurt it. However, during the 2016 battle for the Republican nomination, members of the House of Representatives who tied themselves to the Tea Party rejected mainstream, prominent candidates and threw their support behind two senators who espoused anti-establishment rhetoric (Cruz and Rubio). Rubio, on the other hand, battled for control of the "establishment lane" with John Kasich. With the Republican Party factionalized, an even *more* outsider candidate was able to put together a unique base by mobilizing populist resentment, a fire the Tea Party Movement had helped to stoke in 2010. This candidate, Donald Trump, did much of this mobilization via the social media platform Twitter. He thus took advantage of the normalization of uncivil, brash rhetoric from political elites that had taken place over the past half decade, led by Tea Party members. In Trump's general election face-off with Hillary Clinton, Trump received a boost in support from constituents of members attached to the Tea Party and from those who used incivility on Twitter.

While we believe any monocausal explanation for Trump's 2016 victories will be deficient, we think uncivil discourse had a part in Trump's success. Some readers may wish to point out that while we have been talking about incivility in discourse, we have not mentioned other phenomena that permeated social media during 2016—including so-called fake news and Twitter bots (or automated social media accounts run by software, not actual people) (Guilebeault and Woolley 2016). Both of these have been linked to a coordinated Russian effort to influence the outcome of the 2016 election, or at least encourage cynicism toward American political institutions (Phillip 2017; Timberg 2016). We cannot comment on the possibility of these factors influencing voting outcomes either way, but to the extent that Twitter bots and genuinely fake news stories contain conspiracy theories and demean candidates, these phenomena are related to the incivility we have been discussing, and we would expect reactions among those exposed to be similar. Moreover, just as uncivil discourse made Trump's candidacy more acceptable, rhetoric suggesting the worst about opponents makes it easier to accept conspiratorial fake news. We can understand how bizarre stories floating on the internet about Hillary Clinton gained traction—like the "pizzagate" conspiracy theory, which purported that Clinton was involved in a child sex abuse ring house in a Washington, DC, pizzeria—when we consider that House Republicans dedicated hundreds of tweets to framing Clinton in a negative light during the 113th Congress (Griffin 2016).

Election 2016 also saw the growing influence of alt-right, or white nationalist, sources on the web. The online news site Breitbart News, which, in the words of former chair Steve Bannon, became "the platform for the alt-right," enthusiastically embraced and promoted Trump's candidacy (Borchers 2017; Grynbaum and Herrman 2016). Bannon, who previously promoted Michele Bachmann and Sarah Palin, resigned his position as chair at Breitbart to join the Trump campaign and, for the first seven months of the Trump presidency, served as chief strategist in the Trump White House (Grynbaum and Herrman 2016; Shane 2016). Following his controversial stint in the White House, he returned to Breitbart and threatened to promote challenges to "establishment" Republicans ahead of the 2018 midterm elections who he deemed insufficiently loyal to Trump and committed to his populist-nationalist revolution within the Republican Party (Martin and Peters 2017; Peters 2018).[45] Trump's connection to Breitbart is plain to see. However, Breitbart, which Bannon began running in 2012, was embraced within Republican circles well before Trump's rise: members of Congress tweeted about or retweeted Breitbart stories 152 times during the 113th Congress, with most of the references coming from Black and Green Tea members.[46] Some of them, including Justin Amash, Jason Chaffetz (R-UT), and Louis Gohmert (R-TX), did so with significant frequency. These tweets often contained biting accusations that minority groups and others were receiving undeserved benefits provided by taxpayers. Consider two tweets posted by members who have attached themselves to the Tea Party. Marsha Blackburn shared a Breitbart story with her followers in November 2014, entitled "Exclusive—Report: Obama's Executive Amnesty Will Give Illegal Aliens Public Benefits," along with her own message: "The President's amnesty is lawless & will result in taxpayer funded welfare for illegal aliens. It must be stopped." Likewise, Steve King (R-IA) tweeted out in April 2013 that he and Breitbart had been vindicated after promoting a story that the Obama administration was sending money to Hispanic and female farmers who had made fraudulent discrimination claims.[47] It is not hard to imagine how these stories played out among white voters resentful of the perceived treatment the federal government and Obama administration extended to undocumented workers, Hispanics, and other groups. Others highlighted the threat of radical

Islam and its presence in the United States; for instance, in 2014, Green Tea Louie Gohmert tweeted out a link to a video of him discussing a Breitbart article on the House floor entitled, "Muslim Brotherhood Overruns National Cathedral in DC" (the article was written by Sebastian Gorka, a Bannon ally who served as a deputy assistant to President Trump during the same period Bannon was in the White House) (Rucker 2017; Smith 2017).

The spread and influence of genuinely fake news and alt-right sources via social media during the 2016 campaign was made possible because people were primed to accept them. The messages posted by House Republicans—particularly those who attached themselves to the Tea Party—in the years before 2016 reinforced resentment toward out-groups and disenchantment with government, normalized uncivil discourse among political elites, and aggravated negative feelings about the "other side"—all of which made the claims asserted by fake news, alt-right sources, and Trump not only tolerable but coveted among Republican voters in 2016.

Appendix I

CCES Questions Referenced

The following lists contain the questions/statements from the 2012 and 2016 Cooperative Congressional Election Study used in this chapter.

2012 CCES
- Racial Resentment
  - *Question(s)*:
    - CC422b: Racial Resentment B—"Generations of slavery and discrimination have created conditions that make it difficult for Blacks to work their way out of the lower class."
  - *Response Options*: 1 = strongly agree, 2 = somewhat agree, 3 = neither agree nor disagree, 4 = somewhat disagree, 5 = strongly disagree
- Anti-Immigration Views
  - *Question(s)*:
    - CC322_1: Immigration—"Grant legal status to all illegal immigrants who have held jobs and paid taxes for at least 3 years, and not been convicted of any felony crimes."
    - CC322_2: Immigration—"Increase the number of border patrols on the US–Mexican border."
    - CC322_3: Immigration—"Allow police to question anyone they think may be in the country illegally."

- CC322_5: Immigration—"Prohibit illegal immigrants from using emergency hospital care and public schools."
- CC322_6: Immigration—"Deny automatic citizenship to American-born children of illegal immigrants."
- *Response Options*: 1 = Yes, 2 = No (for each question)
- *Note*: For each question, all responses have been recoded so that the anti-immigrant view = 1 and the pro-immigrant view = 0; this variable is coded on a scale from 0 to 5, based on the sum of the responses to these questions.
- Age
  - Each respondent's age (in years)
- Gender
  - *Question(s)*:
    - gender: Gender—"Are you male or female?"
  - *Response Options*: 1 = Male, 2 = Female
  - *Note*: This variable is recoded such that female = 1, male = 0.
- Race
  - *Question(s)*:
    - race: Race—"What racial or ethnic group best describes you?"
  - *Response Options:* 1 = White, 2 = Black, 3 = Hispanic, 4 = Asian, 5 = Native American, 6 = Mixed, 7 = Other, 8 = Middle Eastern
  - *Note*: This variable is recoded such that white = 1, other = 0.
- Education
  - *Question(s)*:
    - educ: Education—"What is the highest level of education you have completed?"
  - *Response Options*: 1 = No high school, 2 = High school graduate, 3 = Some college, 4 = 2-year, 5 = 4-year, 6 = Post-grad
- Party ID
  - *Question(s)*:
    - pid7: 7 Point Party Identification (PID)—"Would you call yourself a strong Democrat or a not very strong Democrat? Would you call yourself a strong Republican or a not very strong Republican? Do you think of yourself as closer to the Democratic or Republican Party?"
  - *Response Options*: 1 = Strong Democrat, 2 = Not very strong Democrat, 3 = Lean Democrat, 4 = Independent, 5 = Lean Republican, 6 = Not very strong Republican, 7 = Strong Republican
- Ideology
  - *Question(s)*:
    - ideo5: Ideology—"Thinking about politics these days, how would describe your own political viewpoint?"

- *Response Options*: 1 = Very liberal, 2 = Liberal, 3 = Moderate, 4 = Conservative, 5 = Very Conservative
- Born Again Christian
  - *Question(s)*:
    - pew_bornagain: Born Again (Pew version)—"Would you describe yourself as a born-again or evangelical Christian, or not?"
  - *Response Options*: 1 = Yes, 2 = No
  - *Note*: This variable is recoded such that 1 = born again, other = 0.
- Knows MC's Party
  - *Question(s)*:
    - CC310d: Party Recall + Name Recognition—Rep—"Please indicate whether you've heard of this person and if so which party he or she if affiliated with . . ."
  - *Response Options*: 1 = Never heard of person, 2 = Republican, 3 = Democrats, 4 = other Party/Independent, 5 = Not sure
  - *Note*: Responses were matched with a correct list of each respondent's member of Congress. This variable is recoded such that 1 = respondent knows MC's party, 0 = respondent does not know MC's party.
- Negative National Economic Perceptions
  - *Question(s)*:
    - CC302: National Economy—"Would you say that OVER THE PAST YEAR the nation's economy has . . .?"
  - *Response Options*: 1 = Gotten much better, 2 = Gotten better, 3 = Stayed about the same, 4 = Gotten worse, 5 = Gotten much worse, 6 = Not sure
  - *Note*: "Not sure" or skipped responses were recorded as neutral ("stayed about the same").
- Decrease in Household Income
  - *Question(s)*:
    - CC304: Household Income Last 4 Years—"Over the past FOUR YEARS, has your household's annual income . . ."
  - *Response Options*: 1 = Increased a lot, 2 = Increased somewhat, 3 = Stayed about the same, 4 = Decreased somewhat, 5 = Decreased a lot
  - *Note*: Skipped responses were recorded as neutral ("stayed about the same").

2016 CCES

- Cognitive Racism
  - *Question(s)*:
    - CC16_422d: Racial Advantages—"White people in the U.S. have certain advantages because of the color of their skin."

- CC16_422f: Racial Problems Isolated—"Racial problems in the U.S. are rare, isolated situations."
- Response Options: 1 = Strongly agree, 2 = Somewhat agree, 3 = Neither agree nor disagree, 4 = Somewhat disagree, 5 = Strongly disagree
- *Note*: CC16_422f is recoded so that the "most racist" view = 5 and the "least racist" view = 1; the "cognitive racism" variable is a combination of CC16_422d + CC16_422f.
- *Note*: CC16_422f is recoded so that the "most racist" view = 5 and the "least racist" view = 1; the "cognitive racism" variable is a combination of CC16_422d + CC16_422f.
- Apathetic Racism
  - *Question(s)*:
    - CC16_422c: Angry Racism Exists—"I am angry that racism exists."
    - CC16_422e: Racial Fear—"I often find myself fearful of people of other races."
  - *Response Options*: 1 = Strongly agree, 2 = Somewhat agree, 3 = Neither agree nor disagree, 4 = Somewhat disagree, 5 = Strongly disagree
  - *Note*: CC16_422e was recoded so that the "most racist" view = 5 and the "least racist" view = 1; the "apathetic racism" variable is a combination of CC16_422c + CC16_422e.
- Anti-Immigration Views
  - *Question(s)*:
    - CC16_331_1: Immigration—"Grant legal status to all illegal immigrants who have held jobs and paid taxes for at least 3 years, and not been convicted of any felony crimes."
    - CC16_331_2: Immigration—"Increase the number of border patrols on the U.S.–Mexican border."
    - CC16_331_3: Immigration—"Grant legal status to people who were brought to the US illegally as children, but who have graduated from a U.S. high school."
    - CC16_331_5: Immigration—"Admit no refugees from Syria."
    - CC16_331_6: Immigration—"Increase the number of visas for overseas workers to work in the U.S."
  - *Response Options*: [Respondents are directed to select all that apply to the question of "What do you think the U.S. government should do about immigration?"]
  - *Note*: For each question, all responses have been recoded so that the anti-immigrant view = 1 and the pro-immigrant view = 0; the "anti-immigration views" variable is then coded on a scale from 0 to 5, based on the sum of the responses to these questions.

- Age
  - Each respondent's age (in years)
- Gender
  - *Question(s)*:
    - gender: Gender—"Are you male or female?"
  - *Response Options*: 1 = male, 2 = female
  - *Note*: This variable is recoded such that female = 1, other = 0.
- Race
  - *Question(s)*:
    - race: Race—"What racial or ethnic group best describes you?"
  - *Response Options*: 1 = White, 2 = Black, 3 = Hispanic, 4 = Asian, 5 = Native American, 8 = Middle Eastern, 6 = Mixed, 7 = Other
  - *Note*: This variable is recoded such that white = 1, other = 0.
- Education
  - *Question(s)*:
    - educ: Education—"What is the highest level of education you have completed?"
  - *Response Options*: 1 = No high school, 2 = High school graduate, 3 = Some college, 4 = 2-year, 5 = 4-year, 6 = Post-grad
- Party ID
  - *Question(s)*:
    - pid7: 7 point Party ID
  - *Response Options*: 1 = Strong Democrat, 2 = Not very strong Democrat, 3 = Lean Democrat, 4 = Independent, 5 = Lean Republican, 6 = Not very strong Republican, 7 = Strong Republican, 8 = Not sure
- Ideology
  - *Question(s)*:
    - ideo5: Ideology—"In general, how would you describe your own political viewpoint?"
  - *Response Options*: 1 = Very liberal, 2 = Liberal, 3 = Moderate, 4 = Conservative, 5 = Very conservative
- Born Again Christian
  - *Question(s)*:
    - pew_bornagain: Born Again (Pew version)—"Would you describe yourself as a born-again or evangelical Christian, or not?"
  - *Response Options*: 1 = Yes, 2 = No
  - *Note*: This variable has been recoded such that born again = 1, other = 0.
- Knows MC's Party
  - Question(s):
    - CC16_322d: Party Recall + Name Recognition—Rep—"Please indicate whether you've heard of this person and if so which party he or she is affiliated with . . ."

- *Response Options:* 1 = Never heard of person, 2 = Republican, 3 = Democrat, 4 = Other party/Independent, 5 = Not sure
- *Note*: Responses were matched with a correct list of each respondent's member of Congress. This variable is recoded such that 1 = respondent knows MC's party, 0 = respondent does not know MC's party.
- Negative National Economic Perceptions
  - *Question(s)*:
    - CC16_302: National Economy—"OVER THE PAST YEAR the nation's economy has . . .?"
  - *Response Options*: 1 = Gotten much better, 2 = Gotten better, 3 = Stayed about the same, 4 = Gotten worse, 5 = Gotten much worse, 6 = Not sure
  - *Note*: "Not sure" or skipped responses were recorded as neutral ("stayed about the same").
- Decrease in Household Income
  - *Question(s)*:
    - CC16_303: Past year—household income—"Over the past FOUR YEARS, has your household's annual income . . .?"
  - *Response Options*: 1 = Increased a lot, 2 = Increased somewhat, 3 = Stayed about the same, 4 = Decreased somewhat, 5 = Decreased a lot
  - *Note*: Skipped responses were recorded as neutral ("stayed about the same").
- Social Media Use
  - *Question(s)*:
    - CC16_300_5: Social Media—"In the past 24 hours have you . . . (check all that apply)"
    - CC16_300d_1: Posted a story, photo, video or link about politics—"Did you do any of the following on social media (such as Facebook, YouTube or Twitter)?"
    - CC16_300d_2: Posted a comment about politics—"Did you do any of the following on social media (such as Facebook, YouTube or Twitter)?"
    - CC16_300d_3: Read a story or watched a video about politics—"Did you do any of the following on social media (such as Facebook, YouTube or Twitter)?"
    - CC16_300d_4: Followed a political event—"Did you do any of the following on social media (such as Facebook, YouTube or Twitter)?"
    - CC16_300d_5: Forwarded a story, photo, video or link about politics to friends—"Did you do any of the following on social media (such as Facebook, YouTube or Twitter)?"
  - *Note*: This variable is scaled from 0 to 6 (how many of these political engagement activities each respondent did). E.g., 0 = no social media use, 1 = social media use but no political engagement ("no" on

5 questions, CC16_300d_1—CC16_300d_5), 6 = engaged in all five political engagement activities.

- Use TV
  - *Question(s)*:
    - CC16_300_2: TV—"In the past 24 hours have you . . . (check all that apply)"
  - *Note*: This variable is recoded such that 1 = use TV, 0 = do not use TV.
- Use Radio
  - *Question(s)*:
    - CC16_300_4: Radio—"In the past 24 hours have you . . . (check all that apply)"
  - *Note*: This variable is recoded such that 1 = use radio, 0 = do not use radio.
- Use Newspaper
  - *Question(s)*:
    - CC16_300_3: Newspaper—"In the past 24 hours have you . . . (check all that apply)"
  - *Note*: This variable is recoded such that 1 = use newspaper, 0 = do not use newspaper.

Appendix II

Multivariate Results

Table A9.1 **Tea Party Representation and Vote Choice in the Race for the 2016 Republican Nomination, Alternative Model**

Variable	Vote in 2016 Primary/Caucus			
	Kasich	*Rubio*	*Cruz*	*Trump*
Tea Party Support (113th)	0.00 (0.04)	−0.01 (0.03)	0.01 (0.03)	0.01 (0.03)
Tea Party Support (112th)	0.06 (0.06)	−0.08 (0.05)	**−.07 (0.04)**	0.04(0.03)
Tea Party Attachment (113th)	**−0.30 (0.19)**	**0.24 (0.13)**	0.09 (0.11)	−0.08 (0.09)
Tea Party Attachment (112th)	−0.08 (0.11)	0.10 (0.08)	**0.13 (0.07)**	−0.01 (0.06)
Cognitive Racism	**−0.06 (0.04)**	**0.08 (0.03)**	**0.12 (0.02)**	**0.09 (0.02)**
Apathetic Racism	0.02 (0.05)	**−0.07 (0.04)**	−0.01 (0.03)	**0.11 (0.03)**
Anti-Immigration Views	**−0.18 (0.07)**	**−0.20 (0.05)**	**0.14 (0.05)**	**0.37 (0.03)**
Age	−0.00 (0.01)	0.01 (0.00)	**−0.01 (0.00)**	**0.01 (0.00)**
Gender (Female = 1)	−0.11 (0.11)	**0.28 (0.13)**	**−0.36 (0.09)**	−0.10 (0.07)
Race (White = 1)	**0.46 (0.22)**	−0.29 (0.21)	**0.28 (0.15)**	0.19 (0.146)
Education (6 cat)	**0.13 (0.04)**	**0.26 (0.05)**	**0.09 (0.03)**	**−0.12 (0.03)**
Party ID (7 cat)	**0.39 (0.04)**	**0.58 (0.05)**	**0.23 (0.03)**	**0.49 (0.03)**
Ideology (5 cat)	−0.02 (0.08)	**−0.15 (0.07)**	**0.69 (0.05)**	**−0.22 (0.05)**
Born Again Christian	**−0.35 (0.15)**	0.11 (0.12)	**0.52 (0.09)**	**−0.31 (0.09)**

(*continued*)

Table A9.1 **Continued**

Variable	Vote in 2016 Primary/Caucus			
	Kasich	*Rubio*	*Cruz*	*Trump*
Knows MC's Party	**0.40 (0.16)**	**0.50 (0.17)**	**0.65 (0.13)**	**−0.50 (0.09)**
Negative National Economic Perceptions	**−0.20 (0.08)**	**−0.18 (0.07)**	0.00 (0.06)	**0.43 (0.05)**
Decrease in Household Income	−0.07 (0.07)	0.04 (0.07)	0.02 (0.05)	**0.09 (0.04)**
Constant	**−3.97 (0.50)**	**−6.83 (0.47)**	**−7.33 (0.38)**	**−6.02 (0.36)**
District-Level Variance	0.61 (0.11)	0.37 (0.10)	0.34 (0.06)	0.18 (0.03)
Observations (*N*)	9,816	9,816	9,816	9,816
Districts (*N*)	130	130	130	130
LR χ^2	170.21; *p* < .000	49.59; *p* < .000	145.16; *p* < .000	90.93; *p* < .000

Note: Robust standard errors are in parentheses. Boldface indicates significance at *p* < .05 (one-tailed test). Coefficients are the results of multilevel logit regression models. All data, except Tea Party Association variables, are from the 2016 Cooperative Congressional Election Study. The sample in all models is restricted to voters who participated in a Republican primary or caucus and who were represented by the same House member throughout the 112th through the 114th Congress.

Table A9.2 **Incivility, Social Media Engagement, and Vote Choice in 2016 Republican Primaries, Alternative Model**

Variable	Voted Trump
MC 112th Incivility Rate	0.10 (1.038)
MC 113th Incivility Rate	−0.85 (1.293)
Social Media Use (0–6)	**0.07 (0.022)**
Social Media*MC 113th Incivility Rate	**1.49 (0.371)**
Uses TV (1 = Yes)	**0.38 (0.105)**
Uses Radio (1 = Yes)	**−0.35 (0.093)**
Uses Newspaper (1 = Yes)	−0.07 (0.094)
Cognitive Racism	0.01 (0.023)
Apathetic Racism	**0.11 (0.031)**
Anti-Immigration Views	**0.31 (0.041)**
Age	**0.01 (0.003)**
Gender (Female = 1)	−0.02 (0.087)
Race (White = 1)	0.09 (0.169)
Education (6 cat)	**−0.16 (0.032)**
Party ID (7 cat)	**0.14 (0.039)**
Ideology (5 cat)	**−0.43 (0.067)**
Born Again Christian	**−0.32 (0.096)**
Knows MC's Party	**−0.89 (0.101)**
Negative National Economic Perceptions	**0.36 (0.053)**
Decrease in Household Income	0.01 (0.050)
Constant	**−1.41 (0.471)**
District-Level Variance	**0.26 (0.048)**
Observations (N)	4,558
Districts (N)	119
LR χ^2	105.68; $p < .000$

Note: Robust standard errors are in parentheses. Boldface indicates significance at $p < .05$ (one-tailed test). Coefficients are the results of multilevel logit regression models. All data, except MC incivility use rates, are from the 2016 Cooperative Congressional Election Study. The sample in both models is restricted to voters who participated in a Republican primary or caucus and who were represented by the same House member throughout the 112th through the 114th Congress.

10

Tea Party-ness, Trump, and the Future of the Republican Party

In January 2009, the Republican Party found itself out of power at the national level. Building on their majorities in the House and Senate and reclaiming the White House in the November 2008 elections, Democrats controlled both houses of Congress and the presidency for the first time in fourteen years. As dire as the situation might have seemed for Republicans at the time, conditions were in place that would make Democratic dominance of Washington short-lived. In recent years, majorities in Congress have been insecure, and party control can quickly flip (Lee 2016). The party out of power can rapidly bounce back in the next federal election, incentivizing partisan conflict and activities meant to degrade the opposition (Lee 2016). On top of this, Republicans had the option of tapping into a resource that might make sweeping victories in 2010 and beyond a possibility. A deep-seated resentment was felt by many white voters who would become active in the Tea Party, fueled by the idea that undeserving "others" had "cut in line" (Hochschild 2016). Obama's victory enhanced the sense that their social status and an American way of life and culture they knew and were attached to were coming to an end (Parker and Barreto 2014).

For parties and elected officials, this type of simmering resentment is a resource. It is a close relative of anger, which political psychologists know is a powerful mobilizer (Marcus et al. 2006; Valentino 2011). As such, resentment among white voters, if properly focused, could blaze a path back to power in Congress (and perhaps make Barack Obama a one-term president). In their efforts to foster this anger, congressional Republicans would have a lot of help. A complex web of conservative media outlets, well-financed conservative organizations, and grassroots activists would waste little time in the opening months of the Obama administration organizing opposition with the mantra "Take our country back" (Skocpol and Williamson 2012, 8–10). These elements coalesced into the amorphous Tea Party movement, which had taken the center stage of American politics by the summer of 2009.

The roles of the conservative media establishment, resentment among the reactionary grassroots, and conservative advocacy organizations in ginning up the Tea Party movement have all been the subject of rigorous analysis by scholars (Berry and Sobieraj 2013; Parker and Barreto 2013; Skocpol and Williamson 2012). But there is a fourth element that has received little scholarly attention until now—the role of political elites in intensifying white identity and resentment via emotional appeals during the Tea Party era (Kreiss et al. 2017). It has been our purpose in this book to come to a better understanding of the Tea Party wing in Congress, an understudied but crucial element of the Tea Party movement whose influence and relevance may prove to be the longest lasting.

As we have argued, the dearth of research on the Tea Party in Congress stems in part from the difficulty of discerning who is and is not a Tea Party Republican. But we have also endeavored to correct the record on the Tea Party in the House. Here we summarize a few claims about the Tea Party that are not borne out in our analyses.

1. *Tea Party association was limited to a small minority of Republicans.*

We have argued that strategies for measuring "Tea Party-ness" among House members that rely solely on caucus memberships or organizational endorsements lead to significant underestimations of the role of the movement in congressional politics. In addition, focusing on one and not the other ignores the dimensionality of the Tea Party association: part of the story is who is *supported by* the Tea Party, and the other is who wishes to *attach* her- or himself to the Tea Party.

We have thus reimagined Tea Party association as falling along two distinct dimensions: support from the Tea Party movement and efforts to attach to the movement. Using scores on these scales, we divided members of Congress during the 112th and 113th Congresses into four groups: Black Tea, Green Tea, White Tea, and Coffee members. During the 112th Congress, only four in ten Republicans were Coffee members—they had low levels of support and attachment. In the 113th, the demise of the Tea Party Caucus and a reduced presence of Tea Party organizations during the 2012 elections meant more Coffee members—approximately 64 percent of the Republican Conference were Coffee. However, those with moderate to high levels of association with the Tea Party still made up more than a third of House Republicans. Moreover, those who fell in the Coffee camp were not necessarily devoid of any type of Tea Party association, but were below average on both dimensions. These numbers indicate that the Tea Party in the House was far from a small, niche group of legislators. Instead, a substantial portion of the Republican Conference in both congresses was associated with the Tea Party.

2. *Republicans associated with the Tea Party were more fiscally conservative than other Republicans.*

According to a common story, the Tea Party was formed in reaction to Washington's perceived free-spending ways, including its Troubled Asset Relief Program (TARP) bailout of 2008, the American Recovery and Reinvestment Act of 2009 ("the stimulus package"), and the Affordable Care Act ("Obamacare"). The House members elected during the Tea Party wave of 2010 were sent to Washington to restore fiscal discipline and focus on fiscal issues, backed by fiscally focused Tea Party organizations and activists (e.g., Adler 2010). These members succeeded in directing Washington's attention toward issues like the federal deficit and took an uncompromising approach to cutting federal spending—resulting in high-profile showdowns like the debt ceiling crisis of 2011, the "fiscal cliff" crisis of late 2012 and early 2013, and the government shutdown of the fall of 2013 (e.g., Dionne 2016).

However, this story appears to be not quite right. We find little evidence not only of a relationship between attachment to the Tea Party and fiscal conservatism, but of a relationship between support from the Tea Party and fiscal conservatism. Instead, we find that Republican House members are quite fiscally conservative regardless of their Tea Party association. And while we do find that House members associated with the Tea Party are more likely to adopt anti-deliberative, uncompromising rhetoric than members with low or no connection to the movement, it is members who attach themselves to the Tea Party who do this, not those who were backed by Tea Party organizations and activists.

Legislators who made efforts to attach themselves to the Tea Party were more conservative on social and racial issues. That is, it is social and racial conservatism that sets Tea Party and Coffee Republicans apart and drives more conservative voting records. These findings dovetail with research on Tea Party activists which finds that rather than being purely against spending and government programs, activists' views are far more nuanced (Skocpol and Williamson 2012; also see Cramer 2016). They are motivated not by restoring fiscal discipline or small government, but by preventing perceived undeserving "others" from receiving support from the government. Accordingly, members who made efforts to attach themselves to the Tea Party movement were distinct from other Republicans when it came to voting on issues that predominantly affect racial and ethnic minorities.

3. *Tea Party Republicans were very junior backbenchers who were less legislatively active and less legislatively effective than other Republicans.*

As one *Newsweek* article announced the day after the 2010 midterms elections, "The Tea Party–backed victors . . . will be relatively powerless freshmen" (Adler 2010). This perception of Tea Party House members—that they were very

junior backbenchers during the 112th and 113th Congresses who could obstruct but had limited legislative success—has been a popular one (e.g., Clancy
2014; Douthat 2015; Tomasky 2014; Umana 2014).

Yet the story is much more complicated than this. For one, members of
the House leadership, including John Boehner (R-OH), Eric Cantor (R-VA),
Kevin McCarthy (R-CA), and Paul Ryan (R-WI), were all associated with the
Tea Party in the 112th Congress. Ryan and Cantor, especially, were viewed as
leaders of the Tea Party in government at one point, only to become the focus
of the Tea Party's ire later. Moreover, while on average Black, Green, and White
Tea Republicans had served less time in Congress than Coffee Republicans,
the relationship between Tea Party association and legislative ineffective-
ness is nonexistent. In fact, we find some evidence that support from the Tea
Party is positively related to ushering sponsored bills into law during the 113th
Congress, and those who attached themselves to the Tea Party sponsored more
bills and had higher levels of legislative effectiveness in the 112th. Tea Party–
aligned members appear to have been more skilled at legislating than many have
presumed and to have enjoyed some institutional cachet.

Although Tea Party Support scores had some predictive power when it came
to legislative success, this was the exception to the rule. A common theme
throughout the analyses we present is that Tea Party Support was not a significant predictor, particularly when it came to behavior commonly associated with
Tea Party members. This is likely because support was doled out from different
elements of the Tea Party movement for different reasons. The various entities
might not have agreed on who to back, but what they had in common was taking
a strategic rather than purely ideological approach to picking candidates to
support. The Tea Party movement lent support to candidates who they believed
they could influence and who they believed could, or at least were motivated
to, shepherd their policies into law. By the same token, the candidates who
succeeded in getting into office with some support from the movement were
not always the most conservative, but were in many cases vulnerable—and their
precarious position was likely to have led to less distinctive conduct in terms of
legislative and extra-legislative behavior. When money, time, and energy are finite, it would be silly for Tea Party organizations and activists to waste resources
on candidates in no danger of losing, who already support their agenda, or who
cannot be trusted to get the job done.

On the other hand, Tea Party Attachment—especially in the 113th Congress,
after the ranks of Black and Green Tea Republicans had been culled of Tea Party
Caucus "imposters"—is a consistent significant predictor overall. This makes
sense. If a member is going to make the effort to associate with the movement,
then it would be odd if the member's legislative and extra-legislative behavior
did not reflect the reputation of being a Tea Party member and expectations of

the movement's supporters. The label "Tea Party Republican" is pretty useless if the movement's supporters are disappointed with you. Moreover, and less cynically, principles probably play a role, too; at least some Black and Green Tea members (especially in the 113th Congress, when associating with the Tea Party was more difficult and the dividends were less obvious) were true believers.

A Strategic Blunder?

In January 2017, with the swearing in of Donald J. Trump as the country's forty-fifth president, Republicans completed a comeback of epic proportions. Eight years after finding themselves locked out of power in Washington, Republicans now had majorities in both houses of Congress, along with a Republican president. Even more, the elections of 2016 augmented Republican dominance of state governments, putting the party in a position of power not seen in roughly a century (Bosman and Davey 2016). Yet for many of the Republicans who were plotting a path back to power in 2009, this may have proved to be a hollow victory. Their goal of retaking power was met, but it had come at the cost of losing control of the direction of the party, its unity, and, in some cases, their own positions of influence within it.

The changes the Republican Party has undergone stem from the rise of the Tea Party. We have highlighted at various points in this book that the institutionalization of the Tea Party in the House was enabled by decisions made by influential House members. It was the choice of Eric Cantor, Paul Ryan, and Kevin McCarthy, aspiring to leadership positions in a Republican-controlled Congress, to encourage and recruit Tea Party-esque members in the lead-up to the 2010 midterm elections (the Young Guns strategy). It was a choice to aggravate populist, simmering anger toward Obama and Washington as both the inchoate Tea Party movement and a new method for communicating with the public emerged—something John Boehner led the way in before and after the 112th Congress. And it was a choice not to more directly and forcefully confront a rising populist, ethno-nationalist tide that would overtake the party.

The fanfare that the Tea Party movement once attracted has subsided. Tea Party events are far rarer than they were in 2010 and certainly do not draw the media attention they once did. Alas, those looking for men dressed in tricornered hats must again seek out historical reenactments. Yet the institutionalized Tea Party is not done—in fact, it may be more influential than ever. It has largely neutralized the old "establishment" in the House: the same House leaders who hoped to benefit from inviting Tea Party–aligned members into Congress now find themselves under assault or out of a job. The Freedom Caucus is as much a force in Congress as it has ever been, and the legislative efforts on big-ticket items—from debt ceiling increases to the complete repeal of Obamacare—have slim chances of surviving without the blessing of its members (e.g., DeBonis and Paletta 2017).

The Tea Party has also injected a dose of more potent social and racial conservatism into the House, which aggravates bitter feelings toward "undeserving" out-groups. Myriad commentaries have compared current Republican rhetoric regarding immigration to that of President Reagan and both presidents Bush (e.g., DeFrancesco Soto 2015; Lee 2017; Sakuma 2016). This change is reflected in our analyses of Tea Party Twitter rhetoric. Evincing this growing "mainstreaming" of ardent anti-immigration positions and rhetoric, controversial (and once isolated) Tea Party members like Steve King have found their stock rising after the unexpected ending to the 2016 elections (Graham 2017).

Tea Party positions, attitudes, and rhetoric on immigrants helped to pave the way to Trump. And with Trump's Electoral College victory, the institutional Tea Party gained a foothold in the executive branch. Trump himself, we have argued, is an outgrowth of the Tea Party. The communicative strategies he employs have their antecedents in the Twitter behavior of many Black and Green Tea Republicans. And House leaders who have found themselves under attack by their Tea Party colleagues have surely noticed the rhetorical bombs being flung their way from down Pennsylvania Avenue.

There has been plenty of debate over whether Trump is a "true" Republican (e.g., Danforth 2017; Letter to the Editor 2017). Regardless, he holds substantial sway over the party now. Mr. Trump was not party insiders' first choice to win the nomination—in many cases, he was probably the last choice (Noel 2016). In what has been described as a "hostile takeover," Trump's substantial following on Twitter and Facebook minimized the help he would need from the party and party leaders in reaching the public and demonstrated that the party could not mediate the messaging (e.g., Von Drehle 2017). As president, his relationship with congressional leaders has not been entirely productive, and he has shown that he is willing to spurn and embarrass Paul Ryan and Mitch McConnell (R-KY) (DeBonis et al. 2017).

Trump has also brought House Tea Party veterans into his administration. The former Green Tea Tom Price (R-GA) briefly served as secretary of Health and Human Services, overseeing the effort to deconstruct Obamacare.[1] Another former Green Tea member and former Freedom Caucus chair, Mick Mulvaney (R-SC), currently serves as director of the Office and Management and Budget—a position that gives him influence over a number policy issues important to Tea Party Republicans, including Obamacare repeal, debt ceiling increases, and slashing social safety net programs (Bernstein 2017). Former White Tea Mike Pompeo (R-KS) serves as director of the CIA, while Green Tea Jim Bridenstine (R-OK) was recently nominated to become the administrator of NASA. If confirmed by the Senate, Bridenstine would be the first politician to run the space agency (Guarino 2017b). Former Michigan representative Pete Hoekstra (R-MI), a founding member of the Tea Party Caucus in the 111th Congress, was confirmed as the US ambassador to the Netherlands. Hoekstra, who has attracted controversy for comments he made in 2015 that have been characterized as anti-Muslim (Rosenberg and Nadhir 2018), joined another founding member of the Tea Party Caucus in the Trump administration: Mike Pence (R-IN), the current vice president of the United States.

Rather than waning, the relevance and influence of the institutionalized Tea Party are at an apex. And a rhetorical strategy for gaining and protecting power has proved effective, eclipsing suggestions that the GOP needed to adopt a more inclusive rhetorical approach that appealed to minority groups in the aftermath of Obama's 2012 re-election. Uncivil, anti-deliberative discourse, emotional claims about the unfairness and ineptness of government policies and institutions, suggestions that the old society and order familiar to many white Americans are being supplanted by a new set of rules governing speech and restricting liberty—this type of rhetoric works. If anything, then, the incentives to adopt this approach should appear greater to political elites, and the frequency and extremity of this style of rhetoric should have increased after 2016.

From Incivility to Violence?

Signs of increasingly extreme rhetoric were much in evidence on the campaign trail in 2016. Trump violated discursive norms of presidential candidates by advocating violence against journalists and protesters at his campaign rallies. As president, he has continued to promote violence against journalists and news media perceived to be against him and has suggested that law enforcement officers should treat "bad guys" roughly (Berman 2017; Sullivan and Haberman 2017; Victor 2017). The response of Trump and his aides to criticism of this type of rhetoric is that the president was merely joking around. But there may be real consequences of using language of this kind.[2] Among these is the normalization of violence.

Racist fringe groups have become emboldened and see fit to make their presence known in public demonstrations, and they have interpreted Trump's relatively muted response to their activities as an endorsement (Porter 2017; Wang 2017). In turn, the response among some on the left to Trump and an energized white nationalist movement has been the promotion of violent imagery and tactics. The comedian Kathy Griffin attracted intense criticism for sharing via Twitter a photo of her holding a fake, bloody severed head of Donald Trump (Hill 2017). The radical left group Antifa, which has existed for decades but is enjoying renewed interest, has advocated violent resistance to not just white nationalist groups but Trump supporters more broadly (Beinart 2017).

Unfortunately, the belief that violence against political opponents is appropriate or necessary has been acted upon on more than one occasion during the still young Trump presidency. Not even two months after Trump's inauguration, fringe activists on the left violently shut down multiple events on college campuses that were set to feature controversial conservative speakers (Beinart 2017). Violence between "fascist" and "anti-fascist" groups in Portland, Oregon, during the spring of 2017 was punctuated by the murder of two men and the injuring of a third who rushed to the defense of two girls (one African American and one Muslim) being berated by a Trump supporter on a light-rail train (Beinart 2017). In May 2017, the Republican candidate for Montana's vacant House seat, Greg Gianforte, assaulted a reporter for the *Guardian* after being asked a question about legislation to replace the Affordable Care Act. Gianforte would go on to win the special election and was seated in Congress, after pleading guilty to misdemeanor assault (Borchers 2017). In June 2017, a self-declared Bernie Sanders supporter and Trump opponent opened fire on Republican members of Congress practicing for the annual congressional baseball game in Alexandria, Virginia, seriously wounding Majority Whip Steve Scalise (R-LA) (Shear et al. 2017). Just as voices on the left implicated figures on the right (including Sarah Palin) in the 2011 Gabby Giffords (D-AZ) shooting, voices on the right blamed liberal efforts to incite anger toward Republicans for the Alexandria shooting (Weigel 2017). Scalise survived the attack but has since had to relearn how to walk (Tillett 2017). In August 2017, nineteen activists counterprotesting at a white supremacist rally in Charlottesville, Virginia, were struck by a car driven by one of the white nationalists. One of the counterprotesters, Heather Heyer, passed away from the injuries she sustained (Silverman and Laris 2017). In addition, an African American protester was beaten by six white supremacists elsewhere during the rally.

This litany of political violence is not exhaustive. We thus find ourselves in a time where there are bitter feelings of anger and resentment on both the left and right, as well as energized fringe groups who view violence as a legitimate tactic. It will be tempting for some political elites to try to take advantage of this energy and make subtle—and not so subtle—allusions to violence. But while this may be politically expedient, such tactics threaten to further unravel social bonds and escalate tension between the Left and Right to the point where political violence is not restricted to a few isolated events but a regular occurrence (Allen 2017).

So far, embrace of rhetoric encouraging or condoning violence has been limited among members of Congress. But for both Democrats and Republicans, the temptation to appease a segment of active, mobilized members of the base will be strong at times, and challenges in targeting such messages to these audiences (in 280 characters or fewer) are nonexistent.[3] It may be that norms against violence are too strongly ingrained in American society to be pushed aside the way norms of civility have been. We expect that many self-identified Democratic and Republican voters do not condone any level of political violence, and, to their credit, members of Congress have condemned recent violence in a strong and bipartisan fashion.

Yet the avoidance of widespread violent rhetoric does not mean an era of civil discourse online is around the corner. It is worth reiterating that the incivility of House members' tweets—at least from their official accounts—was relatively rare from 2011 to 2015. But Trump's ascendance represents a victory for those who dismiss the importance of civil discourse. Unless it becomes apparent that Trump's choice of words is a liability (this is a popular talking point, but we suspect many pundits also recognize the power of Trump's incivility among a sizable segment of the electorate), then incivility among the political elite is apt to increase. For the time being, "Trump-esque culture warriors" wielding blunt, incendiary rhetoric will increasingly be found on Republican tickets (Blake 2017a). Accepting Trump and his approach to politics would not just be a stylistic adjustment for the Republican Party; as George Will (2017) put it, to embrace Trump means to "embrace a political style that entails a political substance . . . suited to it."

This brings us to an important question: Can a unifying message be communicated without civility? Can a divided country find a middle ground in which to cooperate on shared policy goals even while embracing uncivil discourse? We suspect the answer to this is no. Neuroscience has given political scientists insights into how much information processing occurs at the preconscious level (Lodge and Taber 2013; Marcus et al. 2000). Information that is presented to us in an antagonistic way is dismissed from active consideration with little input from our conscious minds—or "us." To the extent that incivility engenders aversive affective reactions at the preconscious level, the chances of bipartisan cooperation are slim when discourse increasingly incorporates language that communicates a lack of respect for one's in-group. The likelihood that the country can be brought together when one or both sides insults the other, or imputes malicious motives to the other, is likely slimmer. Perhaps the normalization of incivility in political talk, and its increasing frequency, will force Americans to develop thicker skins and to no longer be offended by breaches of discursive norms (for a discussion of this idea see Herbst 2010). But such a day may be a long way off or may never come. In the meantime, we suspect that a more constructive course will be to embrace civility. But when incivility seems to bring rewards (even when they turn out to be hollow), why would politicians follow such a course? In the second to last section of this chapter, we evaluate another option for Republicans moving forward, one that might deliver electoral success without hollow rewards.

Another Way? The Outlook for Republicanism in the Age of Trump and Twitter

In the aftermath of Democratic victories in 2008, congressional Republicans made the explicit choice to aggravate (rather than temper) resentment for political gain. They arguably have lost control of the fire they fanned. As John Wagner (2017) writes in the *Washington Post*:

> President Trump pardoned a tough-on-immigration Arizona sheriff accused of racial profiling. He threatened a government shutdown if Congress won't deliver border wall funding. He banned transgender people from serving in the military. And he is expected to end a program that shields from deportation young undocumented immigrants who consider the United States home.

Is this the future of the Republican Party? Maybe. But the party can also make the choice to embrace different strategies (and find success in doing so).

There are signs of a course correction among at least one high-profile Republican in the House. In early 2016, newly minted speaker Paul Ryan instructed a group of House interns on the importance of civility in political discourse, arguing that Americans cannot be insulted into agreeing with each other (Feheery 2016). This speech came at a time when the frontrunner for his party's presidential nomination was drawing attention for his barrage of insults aimed at opponents on Twitter. Ryan's remarks were a not so subtle denunciation of Trump's tactics. However, they also included a more tacit acknowledgment that the rhetoric he himself had employed in the past had not always met the standard of decorous debate he was now promoting—namely, the demonization of opponents, of which there is plenty in the Young Guns manifesto.

Ryan's reluctance to embrace Trumpism may prove to be short-lived (Blake 2017b). However, there have been other recent instances of high-profile Republicans promoting markedly different paths than Trump's. Among them are Governor John Kasich and Senator Jeff Flake (R-AZ), who have advocated compromise and more civil, tasteful discourse, while criticizing Trump's rhetoric and behavior (Coppins 2017; Rubin 2017). Kasich, however, will leave office in January 2019 due to term limits. And Flake, facing a primary threat from a challenger aligned with Trump (and who previously challenged John McCain (R-AZ) and has been compared to previous Tea Party Senate challengers), announced he would not seek re-election in 2018 (Catanese 2017; Stolberg 2017). In an October 2017 speech on the Senate floor announcing his decision to retire from the Senate, Flake sharply denounced Trump (without mentioning Trump by name). In addition, Flake suggested that he and his Republican colleagues were complicit in enabling Trump's behavior by acting as if it were "normal" and that, rather than resisting resentful impulses from the public, they had embraced a politics of resentment. He expressed:

> Regret because of [the] indecency of our discourse. Regret because of the coarseness of our leadership. Regret for the compromise of our moral authority, and by our, I mean all of our complicity in this alarming and dangerous state of affairs . . . Reckless, outrageous and undignified behavior has become excused and countenanced as telling it like it is when it is actually just reckless, outrageous and undignified . . . With respect and humility, I must say that we have fooled ourselves for long enough that a pivot to governing is right around the corner, a return to civility and stability right behind it . . . It is . . . clear to me for the moment that we have given in or given up on [our] core principles in favor of a more viscerally satisfying anger and resentment. To be clear, the anger and resentment that the people feel at the royal mess that we've created are justified. But anger and resentment are not a governing philosophy.[4]

McCain, too, has criticized Trump, as has Senator Bob Corker (R-TN), but Corker has also announced his retirement from the chamber, and it is expected that McCain, having been diagnosed with brain cancer, will not serve in the Senate for much longer (Hulse 2017). If the only vocal critics of Trump are those set to leave government, is there realistically another path for Republican officeholders, or have the Tea Party and Trump consumed the party at this point? Here we highlight two other examples of Republicans rejecting the Tea Party strategy and, often conspicuously, Trump and his tactics.

Charlie Baker: The Latest Republican Governor in Liberal Massachusetts

Shortly after he became governor, Charlie Baker was the subject of an *Atlantic* article entitled "The Bluest Republican: Why Staunchly Democratic Massachusetts

Loves Its New GOP Governor" (Ball 2015). Ball (2015) highlights both Baker's moderate policy positions—particularly on social issues—and his engaging demeanor. The article points out the "easy, natural likability" of Baker (in explicit contrast to former Massachusetts governor and Republican presidential nominee Mitt Romney) and notes that "[i]n Kansas, he would almost certainly be considered a Democrat."

Baker's path to the Republican nomination was quite a bit more complicated than what he faced in 2010 when he won the nomination but lost to then-governor Deval Patrick. At the 2014 Massachusetts Republican convention, Baker received more than 82 percent of the delegate vote. His closest opponent, business executive Mark Fisher, received just less than 15 percent of the delegate vote. The rules of the Massachusetts Republican Party require candidates to receive 15 percent of the delegate vote in order for their names to be placed on a primary ballot. Since Fisher had failed to receive the required 15 percent, it appeared that Baker had won the nomination without the need for a primary. However, more than 2 percent of the ballots were returned blank. Fisher argued—correctly—that as these ballots were not included in the total, he would have received more than 15 percent of the delegates' votes and should be included on the primary ballot. Controversy over the proper handling of the blank ballots finally ended up being resolved in court. Following various claims and counterclaims about Fisher's request for a large financial settlement to drop the suit, he was added to the ballot.

Ironically, Fisher was a Tea Party activist. In his one debate with Baker, the candidates clashed on a number of issues, including abortion rights and gun control (Metzger and Deehen 2014). To highlight the distinction between his own political views and those of his Tea Party opponent Fisher, Baker described himself as a "fiscal conservative, social moderate" (Miller 2014). When both candidates were asked to identify a current political figure they considered a role model, Baker struggled, finally naming former Florida governor Jeb Bush. Fisher quickly named Wisconsin governor (and fellow Tea Party associate) Scott Walker. In the primary election, Baker soundly defeated Fisher by a vote margin of 3 to 1.

Baker faced a much more difficult race with Democrat Martha Coakley. Though he focused on economic issues—arguing that he could make the Massachusetts state government more efficient and more effective—he also highlighted his relatively liberal positions on a host of issues related to social policy and racial/ethnic policy. As Ball (2015) writes:

> [Baker] aggressively promoted his liberal stances on hot-button issues. The campaign produced a video featuring Baker and his gay brother; his very first ad, released before the Republican primary, touted his support

for gay marriage and abortion rights. During the summer border crisis, Baker endorsed housing migrant children in Massachusetts, to howls from the right wing.

Analysts have also commented on the change in Baker's public persona from the lost 2010 race to the successful 2014 campaign. In 2010, Baker's campaign slogan was the hard-edged "Had enough?" In 2014, his campaign slogan—"Let's be great, Massachusetts"—was warmer, more encouraging, and more civil, and this was after an additional four years of Democratic control of the state government. Quinn's (2014) analysis of Baker's victory highlights the dramatic stylistic change between Baker's 2010 candidate self and his 2014 candidate self:

> One of Baker's biggest problems in 2010 was that he came across frequently as angry. Baker fed off the national rage that birthed the Tea Party movement and that ultimately damaged his standing with Massachusetts voters.
>
> The Tea Party thing that worked in some parts of the state for the likes of State Rep. Shaunna O'Connell ultimately damaged Baker. His campaign slogan then "Had Enough?" was aimed more at placating bombastic talk radio listeners than it was [aimed at] swing voters in Framingham.
>
> He had to recast himself and be who he is: a likable dorky dad that happens to be really, really smart and somewhat funny.

By 2014, the style matched the politics. In 2010, Baker's campaign anger may have been consistent with what he saw as a movement of fiscal conservatives. But as we saw in the 112th and 113th Congresses, key actors in the Tea Party movement—particularly those Republican House members focused on attaching themselves to the movement—had reoriented the substantive focus of the movement to issues that had nothing to do with fiscal policy. And Baker's own moderate positions on these issues and his personal style—collaborative, civil, funny—made the Tea Party a particularly poor fit.

Staking out a position as a pragmatic fiscal conservative with moderate views in other realms of policy, Baker won a tight general election race. In a state essentially dominated by Democrats, victory required a large number of Democratic votes, but Baker was also quite popular with Republicans. He did, after all, receive 85 percent of the delegate vote at the Republican state convention—a fact he often mentions (Ball 2015).

Baker and President Trump are worlds apart in their personal style, and Baker is a frequent critic of Trump. Recently, he has consistently criticized Trump on a wide array of policy issues. He has broken with the president on climate change and environmental policy, criticizing Trump's withdrawal from the Paris climate agreement.[5] Baker was appalled by Trump's plan to cut funding for scientific research, specifically at the National Institutes of Health (Schoenberg 2017), and he has taken the president to task for his response to the Charlottesville tragedy and his failure to quickly condemn white supremacists. Not surprisingly, Baker did not support Trump during the 2016 election.

Larry Hogan: Successfully Republican in a Very Blue State

In a recent edition of the *Washington Post*'s Sunday Magazine, the lead article featured the current governor of Maryland, Republican Larry Hogan. In the article, entitled "The Un-Trump Republican: Gov. Larry Hogan's Radically Normal Model for the GOP," Mosk (2017) outlines the distinctions between Governor Hogan and President Trump, arguing that Hogan offers an alternative pathway for future electoral success. In short, if Hogan's strategy will work in decidedly blue Maryland, it will work anywhere.

That Maryland is a blue state is uncontroversial. Lists of the most liberal and most Democratic states almost always include Maryland. A 2017 Gallup Report (Newport 2017) ranks Maryland as the ninth most liberal state. According to a 2016 Gallup Report (Jones 2016), Maryland has the seventh most Democratic electorate. By any standard measure, Maryland is a strongly Democratic state. Still, in 2014 it elected a Republican governor, Larry Hogan, over a popular lieutenant governor (Anthony Brown), who would go on to become a member of the House of Representatives. When he won, he became only the second Republican governor of Maryland since Spiro Agnew in the late 1960s.

Early in the election season, a Hogan victory in the Republican primary was not even a sure thing. The owner of a very successful real estate business, Hogan had politics in his blood. His father served as a member of the House of Representatives from Maryland's Fifth Congressional District and subsequently as the Prince George's County executive. Though he himself had served as Maryland's state secretary of appointments during Robert Ehrlich's administration (the last Republican governor), his competitors included a sitting state delegate and a county administrator from one of the largest traditionally Republican counties in the state. But his idiosyncratic style (and a significant fundraising advantage) helped Hogan to secure the nomination with a plurality of the vote in a four-candidate race.

Outspent by Democratic opponent Anthony Brown, Hogan was still able to pull off one of the most surprising upsets of the 2014 election season. In fairness to Brown, winning a gubernatorial election as a lieutenant governor is extremely difficult, at least in Maryland, and it is worth noting that the last Democrat to attempt that move, Kathleen Kennedy Townshend, also lost (to Robert Ehrlich, who endorsed Governor Hogan). In an election that saw a surprisingly low turnout among Democrats and Republicans, Hogan carried the day in a particularly inhospitable political environment for Republicans.

How did he do that? During the campaign, he focused on core economic issues: taxes and economic growth. As Mosk (2017) writes, "When Hogan entered the race, he decided lower taxes and more jobs would be his message." He decried the business environment in Maryland, and he promised to scale back taxes and government regulation to improve the opportunities available to commercial interests in Maryland. He assiduously avoided hard-line, traditional Republican stances on key social issues such as abortion and gun control. On the issue of abortion, for example, while Hogan admitted his own pro-life perspective, he also accepted the current legal status of abortion rights. These positions—and his positive personality and effective political style—carried him to victory in November 2014.

It is Hogan's positive personality and political style that figure most prominently in the recent *Washington Post* feature on the governor. Mosk's comparison of Trump and Hogan focuses on stylistic differences. In one particularly telling passage, Mosk (2017) points out that

> Hogan has two powerful, though seemingly contradictory, things going for him. On the one hand, he was elected by the same category of voters who, from Pennsylvania to Ohio to Wisconsin, would later vault Trump to the White House: a potent wave of disaffected blue-collar and suburban whites. On the other hand, he has worked to create a personal brand that is affable, bipartisan, pragmatic—pretty much the opposite of Trump.

Quoting a prominent state Democrat, Comptroller Peter Franchot, Mosk (2017) writes:

> "Nobody is a bigger critic of Trump than I am. I consider him to be a reckless and vulgar individual," Franchot told me. "And I find Governor Hogan to be about as far removed from him in how he interacts with people, the respect he has for people, the public interest that he expresses from his perspective—I think he is as far removed from Donald Trump as anybody could possibly be."

Ironically these stylistic differences manifest in men who have a lot in common. Even Mosk (2017) admits that the similarities between Trump and Hogan are inescapable: Both are conservative, straight-talking businessmen with backgrounds in real estate. Both entered politics as outsiders who gave voice to a frustrated working class but forged common cause with corporate executives. Yet their personas couldn't be more different.

Again, the article focuses on the personal differences between the president and the governor, suggesting that demeanor alone provides entrée to constituencies that would be otherwise unavailable.

For us, efforts to separate style and substance are frequently (inescapably?) problematic. Incivility breeds incivility, and incivility provides fertile ground for the racial/ethnic conservatism and social conservatism that are crucial components of the reactionary Republicanism that produced a Trump victory in 2016. We see the same difference in demeanor between Trump and Hogan that Mosk describes; where we differ is in our assessment of the distinctiveness of their political views. For us, differences in style are often married to differences in substance.

As we noted, Hogan has staked out a more moderate position on abortion than Trump. Likewise, Hogan and Trump have taken different tracks on immigration policy. Hogan is certainly no liberal on immigration issues—he has supported cooperation with federal Immigration and Customs Enforcement officers, and he opposed what has been referred to as the "Sanctuary State" bill considered in the Maryland legislature. But he has also attacked Trump's immigration policy, particularly those aspects of it relating to legal immigration. He described one Trump proposal as "a solution in search of a problem" (Lang 2017). Governor Hogan has also taken a significantly more moderate position on environmental policy—particularly as it relates to cleaning up and preserving the Chesapeake Bay—than President Trump. On LGBTQ issues, Governor Hogan's positions fall well to the left of Trump's. Hogan has indicated that his own position on gay marriage has "evolved" (Lavers 2014), and he allowed pro-LGBTQ legislation to become law without a veto. The gap between Trump and Hogan on these fundamental issues is clearest in their respective responses to the controversy surrounding Confederate statuary. While Trump's response has been, at best, equivocal in the aftermath of the Charlottesville tragedy, Hogan authorized the removal of the statue of Justice Roger B. Taney from the State House grounds. Crucially, this policy difference centers on racial/ethnic policies and social policies in which Trump (and Tea Partiers before him) staked out conservative positions.

What we see goes well beyond a difference in style: we see a difference in policy. While Hogan's winning coalition included a large swath of voters—many blue-collar whites who would vote for Trump two years later—his victory depended heavily on the support of what have been referred to as "Hogan Democrats" (McDonald 2015). Hogan attracted these voters with promises of tax relief and an improved economy. The same voters would not have approved of a more conservative line on social policy issues or racial/ethnic policy issues—regardless of Hogan's affable political style. This is a key reason why Hogan was able to win in Maryland and Trump was not.

Like Mosk (2017), we see Governor Hogan's approach as a model for the future success of the Republican Party. It is not a model based on style alone; rather, it is fundamentally about style *and* policy. Incivility precludes the type of cooperative and pragmatic politics that Hogan espouses. By the same token, civility without substance is not enough. Hogan's story—and the kernel of his example for the future of the Republican Party—is the marriage of style and substance.

Concluding Thoughts

When we started this project—before Obama's re-election campaign had even begun—we certainly never expected to be where we are now. Our early fascination with the Tea Party's manifestation in the House and the surprising realization that legislators supported by Tea Party organizations were often not the same legislators trumpeting in town meetings and on Twitter accounts the benefits of the movement. We were likewise surprised by the social and racial/ethnic conservatism of the policy positions of a significant number of Tea Party legislators. That the digital homestyles of these members trafficked frequently in incivility was not, however, unexpected. In this way, they pioneered a style that would become synonymous with President Trump. We certainly didn't predict Trump's victory, but given our research maybe we should have seen it coming. At the least, we now have a better understanding of why it came.

We can never underestimate the connection between style and substance. Are we surprised that incivility is married to reactionary policy positions? No. Are we surprised that the style and substance of a House member influence the level of support for a presidential candidate with a similar message from the same party? Yes, we are. But we find it difficult to avoid this conclusion.

Throughout, we have focused on Republicans. The nature of the Tea Party in the House set that boundary. In closing, we can't help but think about what tomorrow will bring for the party, for its politicians, and for its supporters. President Trump offers one way forward, a path paved by Tea Party legislators. As our descriptions of Governor Baker and Governor Hogan suggest, other roads are available. In a recent survey of nearly 250,000 registered voters, Charlie Baker and Larry Hogan ranked as the two most popular governors in

America (Easley 2018). Resentment has staying power, but it needn't have a stranglehold on our future. And what of Democrats and the prospect for a "Tea Party on the left"? A mirror image of the Tea Party arising to take hold of the Democratic Party seems unlikely to us for several reasons. First, Democratic voters have been less committed to abstract ideological principles—and more committed to programmatic victories—than Republicans. Thus, Democratic lawmakers have been open to compromise in order to satisfy the programmatic demands of the various social groups that make up the Democratic coalition (Grossman and Hopkins 2015). Other elements that were a part of and enabled the Tea Party movement are absent on the left—including a collection of well-funded advocacy organizations and an ideological media establishment with a devoted following (Williamson 2017). Thus, a Tea Party movement on the left, uncompromising in its push for "bigger government," is unlikely to take hold of the Democratic Party in the way that the Tea Party took hold of the Republican Party.

Moreover, it is unlikely Democrats will try to stoke racial resentment or focus much on race at all in their 2018 messaging. A more diverse base means that it is more difficult to identify a single strand of simmering racial resentment within the Democratic electorate and identify a messaging strategy that broadly aggravates these feelings. The crux of the debate over "identity politics" as an electoral strategy for Democrats is whether it is too divisive—that is, whether it leaves some members of the coalition (namely, whites) feeling like they are being ignored or even belittled (Gopnik 2016; Lilla 2016; Williams 2017). The truth of this and the extent to which Democrats have relied on an identity politics strategy are less important to the topic at hand than the fact that the party is unlikely to attempt to foster any sort of racial resentment ahead of the 2018 midterm elections. This is because the surprise ending of 2016 will likely convince party leaders to adopt a message that ostensibly appeals to all members of their coalition, including white voters they believe they have lost, and because midterm electorates are far less diverse than presidential electorates (see Smith 2017).

Finally, while the activist Left may have energy, it is also disjointed. The Tea Party is amorphous and decentralized, consisting of a variety of activist groups, organizations, and elected officials, but it is still a single coalition movement united under a single banner. The energized, activist Left that has emerged during the Trump presidency is even more diffuse, with activists organizing under a plethora of banners. To name a few, there is the Indivisible network, started by a group of former Democratic congressional staffers, which joined several existing grassroots networks organizations, including Moveon.org, Black Lives Matter, and Our Revolution (an outgrowth of Bernie Sanders's (I-VT) presidential campaign). In addition, 2017 saw coordinated anti-Trump protest marches, including the Women's Marches on January 22—reported to be the largest protest day in American history (Bloomfield 2017)—and the Marches for Science in April (Mooney 2017). And, of course, there is also Antifa. Each of these groups, along with others, are sometimes placed under the banner of "the Resistance" (and to make things really confusing, there is a separate grassroots organization that calls itself the "The Resistance").[6] We suspect that there is some coordination between these efforts (e.g., Indivisible and Black Lives Matter chapters organizing protests against Confederate statues). But "the Resistance" largely refers to a collection of decentralized and amorphous movements, not a single movement like the Tea Party. It also remains to be seen whether any candidates will run under the label "Resistance Democrat" (or any other group label) in the 2018 midterms or whether this or any other cue will mean much to most voters.

The fact that a "Tea Party on the left" is unlikely to emerge does not mean that the various activist groups cannot influence the direction of the Democratic Party during the 2018 midterm elections. Nor does it mean that populism, anger, incivility, and conspiracy theories will not be embraced by those on the left (Martin 2017; Nyhan 2017). While the founders of the Indivisible movement, for example, have pledged to follow the Tea Party playbook, they claim that they will, in contrast, embrace a politics of respect (Levin et al. 2017); the rhetoric on their Twitter accounts, however, indicates otherwise.[7] In the aftermath of Trump's victory, much discussion has been devoted to how Democratic leaders can tap into the energy of angry anti-Trump activists without falling victim to these forces and losing control of the party, as happened to Republican leaders with the Tea Party (e.g., Kabaservice 2017; Kane 2017). This discussion is not just trivial punditry. Passion is integral to democracy, and emotion in politics is unavoidable (Marcus 2002). In a well-functioning democracy, the sentiments of citizens should be translated into policy, and not ignored or dismissed. But unchecked passion can be merciless and destructive, and when the leaders of political parties, engaged in a constant campaign, make it their goal to aggravate rather than assuage such passion, they are derelict in their duties.

As James Madison argued in *Federalist* No. 49, "The passions ought to be controlled and regulated by the government." Institutions play a critical role in moderating passion, and by convention, as well as changes in Madison's constitutional design, much of this duty has fallen to the political parties.[8] However, external influences can cause parties to abandon this role or prevent them from executing it (e.g., Grossman and Hopkins 2015; La Raja and Schaffner 2015; Masket 2009). And in a highly charged and polarized era, the seductiveness of extreme rhetoric will be intense for legislators, as it has the dual function of mobilizing electoral support and warding off criticism from those who favor tough talk about the other side. Surrendering to these pressures may be politically expedient and, in an era where competition for control of Congress is intense, bring about short-term electoral victory for parties (Lee 2016). Yet a political environment in which both parties engage in an arms race of incivility and anger is not one conducive to policymaking, stability, or strengthening frayed social bonds.[9] It also normalizes demagoguery, and at a time when the parties no longer have a monopoly on access to the eyes and ears of the public, party leaders can quickly lose control of their own parties. It takes but two adversarial firebrands who command attention and have little regard for democratic norms for rhetoric to escalate to the point of encouraging political violence. But this is not inevitable. The parties can recognize and respond to resentment within their base without being consumed by it. The path they choose is the choice of their leaders, but the consequences are for all of us to bear.

NOTES

Chapter 1: Reactionary Republicanism

1. Gallup, http://www.gallup.com/poll/147635/tea-party-movement.aspx (accessed August 2, 2017).
2. See Gervais and Morris (2012).
3. Cramer (2016b) has also tied rural resentment to Trump's 2016 victory. For a summary of this, see Wallis (2016).

Chapter 2: Tea Party to Trump

1. Also see Maxwell and Parent (2013).
2. In *The Teavangelicals: The Inside Story of How the Evangelicals and the Tea Party Are Taking Back America*, David Brody (2012) provides a compelling treatment of this important aspect of the Tea Party movement.
3. Dionne (2016, 259) refers to the same phenomenon as "racial, cultural, and economic conservatism."
4. Also see Williamson et al. (2011).

Chapter 3: The Tea Party in the House of Representatives

1. The presumption that the Tea Party in the House is limited to Republicans is widely accepted.
2. The original link cited in Carson and Pettigrew (2013) is no longer active, but see the following source, which contains the same type of information: "How the Tea Party Fared," *New York Times*, November 4, 2010, http://www.nytimes.com/interactive/2010/11/04/us/politics/tea-party-results.html.
3. At least not during the 112th Congress. Gosar's current congressional website lists the Tea Party Caucus among the dozens of caucuses of which he is a member. Just what 2016 membership in the Tea Party Caucus means is unclear.
4. This is a somewhat more inclusive list than that used by some other researchers (see Gallagher and Rock 2012; Ragusa and Gaspar 2016) because we did not require membership in the Tea Party Caucus in both the 111th and 112th Congresses to count in either. Given our broader measurement strategy, this is unlikely to pose significant inferential difficulties.
5. We were able to locate a formerly public list of Liberty Caucus members from its chair's website: https://web.archive.org/web/20130220000241/http://houselibertycaucus-amash.house.gov/membership. We also reviewed which members were being followed by the caucus's official Facebook page (https://www.facebook.com/houselibertycaucus) and reports on attendance at Caucus events in various news stories. Of course, interest from a Facebook page is not the same as being the member of a group, and attending a meeting

should not be interpreted as formal membership. Thus, in the end, only members who were listed on the chair's website were coded as members of the Liberty Caucus. While this method is not ideal, there is substantial overlap between the various sources, which gives us confidence in its workability.

6. The search parameters for the 112th Congress were from 12:00 p.m. on January 5, 2011, until 12:00 p.m. on January 3, 2013. The parameters for the 113th Congress were from 12:00 p.m. on January 3, 2013, until 12:00 p.m. on January 3, 2015.

7. This measure was first utilized by Gervais and Taylor (2016).

8. See ABC News (2010) and Sheets (2013).

9. This would be consistent with other research examining the relationship between various potential indicators of the association between legislators and the Tea Party movement (see Bailey et al. 2012; Ragusa and Gaspar 2016).

10. According to Gallagher and Rock (2012, 94), "If there is a difference between Tea Party and non-Tea Party Republicans, voting data alone does not reveal a difference."

11. Shelley Moore Capito (R-WV) has since been elected to the US Senate.

12. We realize the problematic issues associated with using DW-Nominate scores to measure ideology, but this is still a common practice in the broader congressional literature. And more significant for our purposes, the use of these scores to measure ideology is ubiquitous in the literature on the Tea Party in Congress.

13. Because the average scores for the various types are based on data for only a small sample of legislators, it does not necessarily follow that, just because the Coffee Republicans had the lowest scores of the set of small sample types, they would necessarily have a score below the average for the Republicans in the chamber as a whole.

14. Students of southern politics identify the southern states as those that made up the Confederacy during the Civil War. Missouri was not a Confederate state.

15. This relationship is not uncomplicated, and though the relative size of the politically mobilized African American population plays a far more important role than it did (or even could have) in Key's (1949) time, the basic character of the relationship remains a prominent aspect of southern politics.

16. See Schwartz (2015).

17. Boehner's first tweet was in August 2007: https://discover.twitter.com/first-tweet#SpeakerBoehner. Twitter was launched in the first quarter of 2006, but it did not gain a significant user base until late 2006 to early 2007; See Carlson 2011. Boehner was a Twitter pioneer among members of Congress.

18. Of the nine members, Justin Amash (R-MI), Thomas Massie (R-KY), and Ted Yoho (R-FL) qualified as Black Tea Republicans in the 113th Congress, while Raul Labrador (R-ID), Jim Bridenstine (R-OK), Paul Broun (R-GA), Louie Gohmert (R-TX), and Tim Huelskamp (R-KS) qualified as Green Tea Republicans. Steve Pearce was the exception, although his scores on both Tea Party Association dimensions were above the median values for the Republican Conference. Pearce would later join the Freedom Caucus in the 114th Congress.

19. A couple of years after leaving Congress, Boehner publicly derided some of these members—reserving particular scorn for a co-founder of the Freedom Caucus, Jim Jordan (R-OH) (see Alberta 2017).

20. This meant a lot more in the 113th Congress, as far fewer endorsements were doled out from Tea Party organizations in 2012 than in 2010.

21. The Tea Party Express statement about Ryan can be seen here: http://www.teapartyexpress.org/5047/congressman-paul-ryan-strong-tea-party-choice-for-vice-president. As we count only endorsements for congressional seats, Tea Party Express's endorsement of Ryan for vice president did not factor into his Tea Party Support score for the 113th Congress.

22. This is according to an analysis conducted by a machine intelligence research company. See Kircher (2017) for details.

23. In their study of roll call voting, Ragusa and Gaspar (2016) examine the effect of Tea Party Caucus and Liberty Caucus memberships as well as the effects of endorsements by Tea Party organizations and the prevalence of Tea Party activists in members' constituencies. In our work, caucus membership is a signal from a member and endorsements are a signal from Tea Party organizations. From their perspective, ideologically pliable members are influenced by

their participation in caucus activities and by the support they receive from Tea Party organizations. In essence, they see the ideological dimension, which drives roll call behavior, as flowing from caucus memberships and endorsements. We see caucus membership as driven by ideology (and electoral considerations). Likewise, we see organizational support as driven by member ideology (and electoral considerations)—albeit from the perspective of the organizations.

Chapter 4: The Representational Foundations of Tea Party Association in the House

1. It is worth noting that because no representatives of color joined the Tea Party Caucus, we could not include a variable for the race/ethnicity of the member of Congress. Had we done this, it is at least conceivable that one or more of the racial/ethnic constituency context variables would have been significant.
2. We are not aware of any cases in which a member of Congress returned a lawful contribution from a registered organization clearly aligned with the Tea Party movement.
3. As our analysis in this chapter is limited to the 112th Congress, we focus solely on membership in the Tea Party Caucus in this context.
4. We realize that using the actual margin of victory—and the sample is such that all of the candidates were victors—is a suboptimal choice. Unfortunately, the available alternatives also suffer from significant shortcomings. Because election returns are tied to candidates, use of the 2008 results is problematic. A particularly large number of the candidates in this election are new, and so 2008 results would provide an inferior indicator of security. Likewise, any effort to create an instrument for the 2010 results would depend on variables we include in our most comprehensive models. Finally, we doubt that the causal ordering issue is significant in this case. If it is, then our results suggest that Tea Party Support has a substantial *negative* effect on electoral outcomes; if Tea Party Support is driving votes, then the greater the level of support, the poorer the electoral outcomes. This strikes us as unlikely.
5. All probability estimates are based on the observed value approach developed by Hanmer and Kalkan (2013).
6. This is the Racial Resentment B question. The specific wording is "Generations of slavery and discrimination have created conditions that make it difficult for Blacks to work their way out of the lower class." Disagreement is consistent with racial resentment.
7. We found little evidence that other attitudinal measures tapping various dimensions of constituency conservatism were significant determinants of either Tea Party support or Tea Party attachment. As the constituency-level estimates are based on average sample sizes well below 100, this is not especially surprising.

Chapter 5: Tea Party-ness and Roll Call Voting in the House

1. It is important to note that the data on which Bailey et al. (2012) base their DW-Nominate scores are drawn from less than a single session/year of the 112th Congress.
2. We are not suggesting, however, that fiscal conservatism plays no role in Tea Party support. See Arceneaux and Nicholson (2012) and Maxwell and Parent (2013).
3. Or their future constituents if they might have an interest in higher-level offices.
4. Legislators holding the following positions were coded 1 for the Party Leadership variable: speaker of the House, majority leader, majority whip, Republican conference chair, conference vice-chair, campaign committee chair, and conference secretary. All others were coded 0.
5. Legislators holding the following committee leadership positions were coded 1 for the Committee Leadership variable. All others were coded 0.
6. We calculate the estimates for the 113th Congress because no other calculations were available, not because we have any concerns about the calculations for the 112th Congress. The lack of calculated estimates for the 113th Congress is a result of the change in a significant number of district boundaries from the 112th Congress to the 113th Congress. As the boundaries changed, there was no simple translation from the 112th to the 113th Congress,

and we were simply the first to invest in calculating the new estimates (with GIS software). Details are available from the authors.

7. All multivariate model results can be found in the Appendix.

8. This subtle shift, like the much larger shift among Republicans, was in the conservative direction.

9. Note the consistency with results presented in Ragusa and Gaspar (2016).

10. For the latest scores, see http://www.nfib.com/advocacy/how-congress-voted/ (accessed January 4, 2017).

11. Recent data indicate that the percentage of African Americans living in poverty and the percentage of Hispanics living in poverty are more than twice the percentage of whites living in poverty (Kaiser Family Foundation 2016).

12. Walter Jones (R-NC) not only had the most liberal racial policy score of all members in the High Tea Party Attachment category, but was tied for the seventh most liberal score among Republicans in the 113th Congress. When Jones is excluded from the analysis, the significant relationship between High Tea Party Attachment and racial policy voting disappears.

13. Though they do not conceptualize Tea Party association in the way we do, it's important to note that other scholars have noted the distinction between the effects of Tea Party endorsements and Tea Party Caucus membership (see Bailey et al. 2012; Ragusa and Gaspar 2016).

Chapter 6: Tea Party-ness, Bill Sponsorship, and Legislative Effectiveness

1. This is calculated by dividing the number of bills the member sponsored that passed the House by the total number of bills sponsored.

2. Because many members had identical scores on the 113th Tea Party Support measure—especially on the low end, the groups are not divided into even thirds. Roughly half of Republicans fell into the Low Tea Party Support group in the 113th.

3. Holding all other variables at their means, those with High Tea Party Attachment had an expected value of 19.2 bills, while all others had an expected value of 16.1 sponsored bills.

4. These members were Chris Stewart (R-UT), Tom Cotton (R-AR), Keith Rothfus (R-PA), Jackie Walorski (R-IN), Richard Hudson (R-NC), Kevin Cramer (R-ND), Steve Stockman (R-TX), Steve King (R-IA), Ted Yoho (R-FL), Paul Gosar (R-AZ), Andy Barr (R-KY), and Jason Chaffetz (R-UT).

5. Note that Steve Stockman (R-TX) previously served in Congress from 1997 to 2013, before returning in 2015.

6. Renewed interest in and conflict over federal land use has been attributed to "tea party politics" (McKinnon and Sanchez 2012).

7. See E. Scott Adler and John Wilkerson for more information on the how bills are categorized by topic: *Congressional Bills Project: (2011–2015)*, NSF 00880066 and 00880061.

8. Volden and Wiseman define above-average scores as LES-to-Benchmark ratios above 1.50. Below-average scores are defined as LES-to-Benchmark ratios below 0.50.

Chapter 7: Tea Party-ness and Public Presentation

1. *New York Times* reporter Kate Zernike's (2010) book on the movement is entitled *Boiling Mad: Inside Tea Party America.*

2. We might more accurately describe this as an example of reciprocal causation, where the media's agenda influences what elites tweet about, and what elites tweet about influences the media's agenda. See Neuman et al. (2014).

3. For discussions and reviews of automated coding programs, including LIWC, see Grimmer and Stewart (2013) and Young and Soroka (2012).

4. Curious readers who tweet can assess their own tweets via LIWC by visiting www.analyzewords.com.

5. These numbers are based on the LIWC2015 dictionary.

6. Freshman member Markwayne Mullin (R-OK) was not included in the analysis of the 113th Congress, as his account issued few tweets during the analysis (eleven), totaling just 248

words, which was deemed too few to allow an accurate assessment of his proclivity for emotional language.

7. Several other factors appeared to drive the use of emotion, unrelated to Tea Party Association in the 112th: those newer to Congress used slightly fewer angry or anxious words in their posts, committee chairs were more likely to use sad words, and more conservative members used significantly more sad words than their more moderate colleagues. There is little evidence of differentiation between members otherwise.

8. Other factors have significant effects on the percentages of affective words used. Newer members were again less likely to use angry or anxious language in the 113th Congress, and conservatism had a positive relationship with the percentage of anxious and sad words used. Committee leaders used fewer anxious words, and the posting of more tweets was associated with a slightly higher percentages of anxious words.

9. These examples were taken from the tweets of Michelle Bachmann (R-MN), Jim Bridenstine (R-OK), John Fleming (R-LA), and Timothy Huelskamp (R-KS).

10. John Boehner infamously "rejected" the word in an interview on *60 Minutes* in 2011 while serving as speaker of the House. See Tannen (2011). This might be interpreted as evidence of the influence of the Tea Party rather than evidence that an anti-compromise spirit is not restricted to Tea Party members.

11. House Republicans of the 1990s may have shut down the government and impeached Bill Clinton, but they also came to a number of compromise agreements with Clinton.

12. This is in reference to former Indiana state treasurer Richard Mourdock, who was endorsed by Tea Party Express and FreedomWorks (Livingston 2011), as well as Sarah Palin (via Facebook); see https://www.facebook.com/note.php?note_id=10150713388963435.

13. For a list of Tea Party Express's endorsements, see http://www.teapartyexpress.org/previous-endorsements.

14. We searched for the term "bipartisan" in addition to "bipartisanship." However, the search for the former returned more than 1,500 references, mainly to "bipartisan" legislation. It became apparent that the term is used most frequently as a tool to grant legitimacy to legislation, and not necessarily as an endorsement of bipartisanship.

15. Searching for the stem "negotiat*" returns words such as "negotiation," negotiates," and "negotiating."

16. Coders were largely in agreement: in the 112th and 113th Congresses, they chose the same category in 89 percent of cases, producing a Krippendorf's alpha of 0.84 and 0.82 in the 113th. Differences between coders were ironed out during subsequent meetings, to produce two master lists.

17. Members who issued no tweets were excluded from this analysis.

18. However, the insignificance of Tea Party Attachment appears to be driven by one outlier— Dana Rohrabacher (R-CA), whose interactive behavior on Twitter (with both the public and other legislators) is notably different from that of other Republicans (and indeed most Democrats). Although, he scores a 0 on the Tea Party Attachment scale in the 113th, he might as well be coded as a 1; his Tea Party Salience score just misses the cutoff, and a number of nonofficial sources link him to the Liberty Caucus in the 113th Congress. Either giving him a 1 on Tea Party Attachment or leaving him out of the analysis results in Tea Party Attachment being significant in the model.

19. These members were Paul Gosar (R-AZ), Tom Price (R-GA), Justin Amash (R-MI), and Jeff Duncan (R-SC).

20. See Davidson (2014) and the House *Members' Congressional Handbook*: http://cha.house.gov/handbooks/members-congressional-handbook#Members-Handbook-Comms-Websites.

21. Royce's tweet read, "Cosponsored @RepMcGoverns #Magnitsky bill 2 stand w/ the Russian people, who (from recent protests) R tired of corruption & abuse of power."

22. Gerlach's tweet read, "Thank you 2 @RepJasonAltmire for working with us to secure MOH for Sgt. Leslie H. Sabo Jr."

23. Issa's tweet to Dingell read, "And a warm welcome to my colleague, and new follower, @john_dingell."

24. Issa's tweet to Hoyer read, "Happy birthday to.@whiphoyer. This is your birthday song. It doesn't last too long. Hey! (lyrics/music:.@speakerboehner)."

25. Members also seemed to believe wishing their colleagues across the aisle "happy birthday" qualified as bipartisanship. We found several examples of birthday tweets accompanied by the hashtag "#bipartisanship," as well as this one from Issa: "And in the spirit of bipartisanship, a very happy birthday to my #CA colleague @NancyPelosi."

Chapter 8: Civility and Tea Party Rhetoric

1. See Todd et al. (2010).
2. See the National Institute for Civil Discourse, University of Arizona, http://nicd.arizona. edu/revivecivility/about.
3. See Gervais and Morris (2015b).
4. For the complete list, see Lee and Quealy (2016).
5. For example, during the 2017 debate over Republican plans to repeal the Affordable Care Act, Senator Elizabeth Warren (D-MA) claimed, "Repeal and run is for cowards" (Warren 2017). Before entering the Senate, *Saturday Night Live* alum Al Franken (D-MN) authored political books with titles like *Lies and the Lying Liars Who Tell Them: A Fair and Balanced Look at the Right*. In a satirical book written after he entered the Senate, Franken devotes a chapter to describing how much he hated Ted Cruz (R-TX), calling Cruz, among others things, a sociopath (Ball 2017). And, of course, this is not close to an exhaustive list of uncivil commentary by current Democratic politicians. Also see Blankley (2009).
6. Berry and Sobieraj (2013, 6) argue that outrage is incivility expressed with greater intensity and that some visual examples of incivility used by Mutz and Reeves (2005), such as eye-rolling, are not outrageous because "they do not incorporate the elements of malfeasant inaccuracy and intent to diminish that characterize outrage." However, one could argue that eye-rolling is an intent to diminish, and one might be hard-pressed to identify an example of incivility that does not do so. The distinction between this type of incivility and some of the examples of outrage that Sobieraj and Berry cite—including obscene language and verbal sparring—is not entirely clear. Do eye-rolling and smirking not elicit emotion, one of the defining features of outrage? Mutz (2015) persuasively demonstrates that they do. While Berry and Sobieraj note that eye-rolling does not qualify as an "emotional display," as the category is reserved for egregious behaviors (28), a case could even be made for including eye-rolling in the category of "belittling." In short, the distinction between incivility and outrage incivility is not entirely clear, and so we treat them as the same concept.
7. *Direct threats* can also be included as a type of incivility (e.g., Massaro and Stryker 2012).
8. Incivility among elites may have the additional effect of discouraging more civil, temperate candidates from seeking public office in the first place. This creates a troubling cycle where the extent to which incivility crowds out civility—both among legislators and in their public statements—grows, leaving an increasingly uncivil legislative body and an increasingly uncivil public discourse.
9. The percentage of those selected was not a whole number because the total number of tweets for some members increased after the sample tweets were selected and coded but before the machine learning took place. Initially, the samples of some members who were frequent tweeters were truncated, as Twitter's application programming interface (API) limits the number of total tweets that can be retrieved per user account. We devised a means of collecting the missing tweets at a later date.
10. We cross-validated the results of the ME model with a supervised vector network (SVM). The models were in agreement on 99 percent of the cases. Collingwood and Wilkerson (2012) found that these two approaches, on average, were the most accurate.
11. The Pew Research Center (2017) found that "indignant disagreement," which we deem to be a broader and more inclusive category than incivility, is rare in members' Facebook posts, appearing in only 9 percent of postings. However, the Pew study also found significant variation among members.
12. Rohrabacher's replies to other Twitter users are frequently dismissive and combative, such as this one from December 2011: "@brhackett ours could have been good exchange, but U ignored substance even of first point. So sad. This is last communication with U." The same is

true of this tweet from November 2012, "@Truthbuster U seem to be only one not admitting Obama lie in this case, or at least keeping quiet in faced of clear evidence of deceit."

13. See Alvarez (2012b).

14. This rhetoric is also prevalent in Michele Bachmann's (R-MN) 2011 response to the State of the Union speech; her response was sponsored by Tea Party Express (which competed with the official Republican response by Paul Ryan). For a transcript of the speech, see http://www.cnn.com/2011/POLITICS/01/25/sotu.response.bachmann/.

15. Some may wonder whether terms like "failed policies" and "failed presidency" really amount to uncivil discourse. This, we think, likely reflects the kind of coarseness in our political discourse, which makes milder forms of incivility seem rather pedestrian. To make this point, we ask you to imagine accusing a colleague (or superior), "laughing off" her "failed policies," in a meeting (Republicans on numerous occasions asked Obama not to "laugh off" his "failed presidency").

16. Not two hours before McCarthy's June 14 tweet, the official Twitter account for the Heritage Foundation, the conservative think tank, tweeted, "Unemployment is not a laughing matter, Mr. President," along with a link to a Heritage Foundation piece. It is likely that McCarthy was referencing this same piece; a link to the official whip website was included in the tweet, but the page is no longer active. We found the same Heritage piece on a Tea Party blog: http://teapartyorg.ning.com/profiles/blogs/mr-president-unemployment-is?xg_source=activity. Heritage is cited as having been a prominent backer of the Tea Party movement during the Obama years—especially after hiring "Tea Party godfather" Senator Jim DeMint (R-SC) as CEO in 2012—focused on fostering anti-Obama sentiment (Shepard 2017). Skocpol and Williamson (2012, 114) found that the Heritage Foundation was among the most referenced advocacy groups on Tea Party blogs and websites during the summer of 2011. DeMint and Heritage reportedly also played a role in getting conservatives on board with Donald Trump in 2016 (Shepard 2017).

17. For commentary on Sanders and his embrace of the label "Democratic socialist," see Keith (2015).

18. For example, one tweet, originally posted by the Republican Study Committee Twitter handle and retweeted by Green Tea Republican Timothy Huelskamp (R-KS) read, "RT @RepublicanStudy: It must be crystal clear in '12 who backs govt mandates and venture socialism vs. liberty and free enterprise."

19. Steve Scalise (R-LA), Blaine Luetkemeyer (R-MO), and Christopher Smith (R-NJ) did not tweet in the 112th Congress. Rob Bishop (R-UT) did not tweet either. Rich Nugent (R-FL) did not tweet from his official account at all during the 113th Congress, but did tweet during the 112th.

20. Andy Harris (R-MD) and Ralph Hall (R-TX) were Tea Party Caucus members who served in both congresses, but they did not issue their first tweets until the 113th Congress.

21. In fairness to Speaker Boehner, Vice President Biden (a fellow Catholic), who, as we noted above, has not always been a paragon of civility, was also honored by Notre Dame (Capehart 2016).

22. See Bobic (2016). The full video can be seen here: http://www.theonion.com/video/after-obama-victory-shrieking-white-hot-sphere-of--30284.

23. We are satirizing one of Donald Trump's more infamous tweets during the 2016 campaign, which read, "I refuse to call Megyn Kelly a bimbo, because that would not be politically correct. Instead I will only call her a lightweight reporter!": https://twitter.com/realDonaldTrump/status/692312112115380224. Trump is referencing former Fox News Channel host Megyn Kelly, with whom he took issue following her questioning of him during an August 2015 debate between candidates for the Republican nomination for president (see Cassella et al. 2016).

24. At least one analysis, based on data from the full 2016 American National Election Study, concludes that symbolic racism was a much better predictor of Trump support than authoritarianism. See Wood (2017).

25. Ball (2016) offers an alternative take: that Trump is an amalgamation of the establishment and Tea Party wings of the GOP, combining the "win-at-all-costs" pragmatism of the establishment with the "passionate angers" of the Tea Party grassroots.

26. In fact, the official account has yet to issue a tweet with the trademark "Sad!" and, through May 2017, made only two references to the "failing New York Times" and one reference to the "failing career" of rapper Snoop Dogg.
27. This claim was not altogether wrong. For commentary on Trump's claim and some context, see Long and Luhby (2016).
28. Huelskamp tweeted in November 2014, referencing video footage of ACA architect Jonathan Gruber, "#WhiteHouse website praises #Gruber. This is what Liberals think about average Americans. #Stupid," and in February 2014, "Federal job-killing over regulations will cost average American family $60,000 in 2014 #TEA #TrimTheGovt."
29. Bridenstine tweeted in November 2014, "Amnesty is unfair to legal immigrants that have played by the rules, and it's unfair to the workforce as labor rates will decline.#NoAmnesty," and in May 2013, "Today @JimDeMint said the total cost of granting #amnesty to illegal immigrants is $6.3 trillion. #tcot." He also warned that "Obama's illegal amnesty order" led to "#IllegalImmigrants already lining up for #Amnesty workshops."
30. Rokita tweeted on September 2013, "Johnny M wants to use illegal immigrants to build wall. He says we can't afford #Obamacare. #DefundObamacare #Danville."
31. For example, in June 2013, King tweeted, "20 brazen self-professed illegal aliens have just invaded my DC office. Obama's lawless order gives them de facto immunity from U.S. law." In July 2014, King tweeted, "Intel says Obama #amnesty busload of UAC #illegals are headed to Iowa from border. Iowans, keep an eye out and let me know what you see."
32. Carter tweeted in November 2013, "Pls take a moment to read my latest OpEd about the #FortHood Shooting 'The Cost of Being Politically Correct' http://t.co/KnoFGUOlJn#FtHood."
33. Trump made this announcement via a campaign press release. For additional context and reactions to Trump's announcement, see Diamond (2015).
34. Gohmert tweeted in May 2012: "Big thanks to The @DailyCaller for this news story: #DHS Documents Advise Deference to Muslim Extremists—VIDEO: http://t.co/vyiKt5OeSZ." The URL links to a video of Gohmert commenting on an article from the *Daily Caller* on the House floor.
35. Jones tweeted in January 2013, "Yesterday I spoke out against an NEH-funded program to promote Muslim cultures at Craven Community College http://t.co/eiXheDdW."
36. Duncan tweeted in June 2013, "Taking a quick break to huddle up with @SenRandPaul this morning to talk about how to move the country back towards the Constitution #PJNET," and in July 2013 he retweeted, "RT @2000Vance: @RepJeffDuncan @mericanrefugeeJeff, stand your ground and do the right thing. Time to take our country!"
37. Committee for a Responsible Federal Budget, "Rigell Releases Sequester Replacement Plan," October 21, 2015, http://www.crfb.org/blogs/rigell-releases-sequester-replacement-plan.
38. Black Tea Republican Tim Griffin (R-AR) tweeted in July 2011, "America's economy can be great again, but we must address Washington's over regulation." Green Tea Republican Lynn Jenkins (R-KS) tweeted in May 2012, "We—as Republican women—are leading the charge to make America great again." Green Tea Connie Mack (R-FL) retweeted the following (via a campaign account) in June 2012, "RT @marklarflash: @ConnieMackIV—Wholeheartedly support your campaign to make America great again."
39. We made two addendums to the training set for the coding of Trump's tweets. First, we added several of Trump's tweets from his unofficial account that used the hashtag #crookedhillary, which refers to Trump's preferred epithet for Hillary Clinton. As "crooked" did not appear in the tweets of members in the 112th and 113th Congresses, and we deemed this nickname for Clinton to be uncivil, a selection of tweets with the hashtag were coded as uncivil and included in the training set. Second, we included a small coded sample of tweets from the official account (1 percent of the total) in the training set.
40. A pair of reviews by journalists: Barbaro (2015) and Tharoor (2017). In addition, cognitive linguist George Lakoff describes a "taxonomy of Trump tweets" in the following interview: http://www.wnyc.org/story/taxonomy-trump-tweets/.
41. For example, see commentary by Wayne (2017), Navarrette Jr. (2017), and Rountree (2016). Also see: National Institute for Civil Discourse, University of Arizona, http://nicd.arizona.edu/revivecivility/about.

42. The 1994 and 2010 elections shared a number of features that made the resultant congresses especially ripe for incivility. Jamieson (2011), analyzing instances of incivility in the House of Representative up to the 112th Congress (measured as instances when members refer to other members as "liars" or "hypocrites" or call into question their integrity on the House floor), finds that incivility reached a peak in 1995 with the Gingrich-led Republican takeover of the House in the 104th Congress. The 1995 levels were rivaled only by those in 1946, which followed the end of World War II and the death of Franklin Roosevelt—suggesting that spikes in incivility come after major political changes. Between the 105th and 111th Congresses, incivility on the floor of the House did not greatly exceed its historical average (Jamieson 2011). As such, Jamieson notes that a number of factors that led to heightened incivility in the 104th would be present in the 112th, including the facts that both were turnover congresses, a Republican majority was elected in a campaign centered on attacking Democratic healthcare legislation, and the Democratic president's poll numbers raised doubt about his re-election, thus "decreas[ing] the political cost and increas[ing] the political benefits of unparliamentary attacks," (Jamieson 2011). However, unlike the economy in 1995, that in 2011 was in poor condition, and the 112th Congress featured "freshman tea-party adherents" ready to break ranks with leadership (Jamieson 2011).

43. As one analysis of speeches made by congressional Republican leaders regarding the Affordable Care Act (ACA) in 2009 and 2010 found, Obama and Democrats were regularly vilified and accused of having ulterior motives (Darr 2013). There is also plenty of anecdotal evidence that, in the lead-up to the 112th Congress, leveling uncivil criticism against Obama was a strategy for retaking the House. For example, on the day the ACA passed the House of Representatives, as Tea Party activists protested outside the Capitol, Ryan and Boehner were among the legislators making uncivil comments inside. Boehner took to the floor and reportedly yelled at Democrats, referring to them as a "disgrace to Jeffersonian values" (Milbank 2010c).

44. According to the Pew (2017) study, congressional leaders were significantly more likely to express "indignant disagreement" with the other side in Facebook postings during the 114th Congress than were rank-and-file members. The rate was the highest among Republican leaders (24 percent). Democratic leaders were only slightly more likely to include indignant opposition in their postings than were rank-and-file Republicans (17 percent vs. 15 percent). These types of posts were rarer among rank-and-file Democrats (4 percent).

45. It also, according to one analysis, made him the most influential member on Twitter shortly afterward, as indicated by the number of times he was retweeted. Among the few other House Republicans deemed "influential" during this time (i.e., their tweets received larger audiences) were John Boehner (R-OH), Eric Cantor (R-VA), Michele Bachmann (R-MN), and Jason Chaffetz (R-UT), and John Culberson (R-TX). See http://techpresident.com/blog-entry/who-has-most-twitter-klout-congress-answer-will-surprise-you.

46. For an example of controversial comments by Chaffetz about "undeserving" others, see Bump (2017).

47. In a July 2016 tweet, Walsh seemingly threatened then–President Obama (McCaskill 2016) and subsequently received backlash in May 2017 for a comment labeled "outrageous" responding to a plea from late-night host Jimmy Kimmel to keep protections for people with preexisting conditions in place that included a personal story, (Zorn 2017).

48. For reporting on Huelskamp's think tank appointment, see Wong (2017). For reporting on the think tank, the Heartland Institute, see Gillis and Kaufman (2012).

Chapter 9: Tea Partiers on the National Stage

1. We adapt this line from presidential historian Gil Troy, who was quoted as saying that Trump "is in many ways the candidate that Twitter made—with all of life, let alone politics, reduced to a series of 140-character rhetorical drive-by shootings" (Jackson 2016).

2. Some might object that Huntsman, and perhaps even Pawlenty, did not possess the same "anti-establishment" profiles of the other "non-Romneys," and so endorsements of Huntsmen (and Pawlenty) should not be considered measures of anti-establishment leanings. Excluding

endorsements of Huntsman (and Pawlenty) does not affect the significance of variables in the models included in columns 1 and 2 of Table 9.1.

3. To calculate the predicted probabilities, we leverage the simulation method using the observed value approach developed by Hanmer and Kalkan (2013).

4. Party leadership was dropped from this model, as it is a perfect predictor (i.e., no member of the party leadership endorsed a candidate other than Romney).

5. While we were curious whether members' association with the Tea Party influenced constituents' vote choice during the 2012 nomination battle, the 2012 Cooperative Congressional Election Study unfortunately did not ask respondents about their vote choice in a primary or caucus. Other surveys conducted during the 2012 campaign did ask about voters' primary vote choice (e.g., the 2012 Cooperative Campaign Analysis Project) but did not include sizable district-level samples or did not include 112th district IDs.

6. We also constructed an ordinal variable, where 0 signifies that someone voted for Obama, 1 signifies a vote for a third-party candidate, and 2 signifies a vote for Romney, and ran ordered probit versions of the models we present later in the chapter. This had no impact on our conclusions.

7. For more details, see https://ropercenter.cornell.edu/polls/us-elections/how-groups-voted/how-groups-voted-2012/.

8. Romney proposed a "self-deportation" plan, which received support from conservatives and restrictionist immigration groups. See Preston (2012).

9. This includes twenty-eight Republican members who did not run for re-election in 2014, two members who lost re-election in 2014, and four members who left Congress before the end of the primary campaign; see https://ballotpedia.org/114th_United_States_Congress.

10. Amash (R-MI) and Labrador (R-ID) initially endorsed Rand Paul. Reid Ribble (R-WI) initially endorsed Scott Walker, then switched to Marco Rubio, before endorsing Cruz in early April 2016. Matt Salmon (R-AZ) initially endorsed Rubio, Trent Franks (R-AZ) initially endorsed Mike Huckabee, and Joe Barton (R-TX) initially endorsed Governor Rick Perry.

11. See Barabak and Finnegan (2016) for reporting of Cruz's primary win in Wisconsin in April 2016 and what it meant for the nomination race at the time.

12. We use probit regression to predict Cruz endorsements. The model controls for ideology in the 113th Congress (DW-Nominate scores), House member gender, year took office, and committee leadership in the 113th. Party leadership in the 113th is dropped from the model, as only four members of the 113th leadership served through the 2016 primary season, and none supported Cruz.

13. We again leverage the simulation method using the observed value approach (Hanmer and Kalkan 2013).

14. In support of this, when separate High Attachment and Moderate Attachment dummy variables are used, in lieu of the three-category variable, Moderate Attachment is significant only at $p < .1$, while High Attachment remains significant at $p = .01$.

15. The White Tea members who backed Bush were Chris Stewart (R-UT) Daniel Webster (R-FL), and Ann Wagner (R-MO). Wagner would endorse Cruz following Bush's exit from the race.

16. The post-reform era refers to the changes the parties made to their nominating processes that ostensibly weakened the influence of party insiders and strengthened the power of voters (via primaries) to determine the nominee. However, as Cohen et al. (2008) show, since 1976 elites have retained influence through the Invisible Primary.

17. Trump's endorsement record is most similar to New Jersey governor Chris Christie's during the 2016 campaign. Christie collected five endorsements from members serving in both the 113th and 114th Congresses, all of whom were Coffee members.

18. Though pre-election endorsements for Trump were rare among elected Republicans (including those associated with the Tea Party), this did not preclude ex post support for the outcome. As former representative and chair of the Tea Party Caucus Tim Huelskamp (R-KS) told us, "[I know] what motivated America to elect Donald Trump. If I played any such role in that race, I'm happy to take credit" (Huelskamp, personal communication).

19. These tweets included a retweet of Trump by Green Tea Joe Wilson (R-SC) in July 2011: "RT @realDonaldTrump: If only @Obama was as focused on balancing the budget as he is on weakening Israel's borders then America would be path to solvency." In addition, there was this December 2011 retweet by Black Tea Bill Huizenga (R-MI): "RT @realDonaldTrump: The new job figures don't include 315,000 people who have given up looking for jobs." Also, Green Tea member Marsha Blackburn (R-TN) tweeted to Trump in April 2012, ".@ realDonaldTrump I'd love to hear from you and your followers about the impact #EPA's toxic regulations are having on your businesses."

20. Presaging the controversy over Russia's attempts to influence the 2016 presidential elections and questions about Trump's connections to Russian power players, Steve King tweeted in February 2014, "Donald Trump just said, 'Lighten up on the Russians' on #Olympics. Enjoy the games and save criticism for substance, not minutia. I agree."

21. If a member did not serve in the 113th and/or 114th Congress, we would not expect the member's Twitter habits to have as strong an influence, or any influence, on constituents' political behavior in 2015 and 2016.

22. We also control for age, gender, education, race, identification as a born-again Christian, party identification (on a 7-point scale), political ideology (on a 5-point scale), perceptions of the state of the national economy over the previous year, and reports of how household income has changed over the past year. We also control for whether or not respondents could identify their House member's political party (which serves as a measure of political sophistication and a check on the likelihood of legislators' political associations influencing respondents' political behavior). More details on the variables can be found in Appendix I.

23. In fact, moving from left to right in Table 9.5, we can see a gradual increase in ethnic resentment among the candidates.

24. For instance, see Williamson (2016) for a perspective from a Brookings Institution scholar, and Hayes (2016) for perspectives from panelists participating in a lecture event sponsored by the Heritage Foundation.

25. As one Wisconsin voter put it, "Trump is the right person to put in here, because we need somebody who everyone thinks is nuts. Cruz is just saying what the establishment wants him to say. He's a puppet," (Barabak and Finnegan 2016).

26. The predicted probability of voting for Cruz or Rubio is based on a model included in Table A9.1 in Appendix II, where the dependent variable is coded as 1 for having voted for Cruz or Rubio and as 0 for having voted for another candidate in a primary or caucus. High Tea Party Attachment is positive and significant in the model.

27. See Linshi (2015).

28. As Hans Noel (2016), one of the authors of *The Party Decides*, argued in a *New York Times* op-ed, this might signal that the political environment had changed, with partisan news, influential factions like the Tea Party, and the influence of super PACs all loosening the party elite's grip on the nominating process. In addition, Noel suggests it might be that the party is falling apart: one only need look at the challenges the House Freedom Caucus and Ted Cruz have posed for House leadership in recent years. We think both of these explanations have some weight.

29. As before, the sample is restricted to those who reported voting in a primary or caucus and those who were continuously represented by the same member from the 112th through the 114th Congress.

30. These activities include posting a story, photo, video, or link about politics; posting a comment about politics; reading a story or watching a video about politics; following a political event; or forwarding a story, photo, video, or link about politics.

31. Specifically, we predict support for Trump when the value of the interaction is set at the 50th percentile and the 99th percentile. Predicted probabilities are based on a model included in Table A.9.2 in Appendix II, in which the dependent variable is coded as 0 for a vote for Kasich, Rubio, or Cruz and 1 for a vote for Trump.

32. See Frum (2016) for a discussion of the dilemma some Republicans faced in 2016.

33. For some high-profile examples of "Never Trumpers," see Draper (2016) and Ball (2015b).

34. Ironically, given Trump's history as a reality TV star and close connections to a number of individuals associated with Fox News, television use had a negative effect on Trump support. It is likely that this measure is too general to determine the impact of television viewing on Trump support.

35. Moreover, factors that were significant in the model consisting of voters not politically engaged on social media—such as age, gender, and television use—are not significant in the model consisting of social media users.

36. See, e.g., Lefler (2010) for local coverage of a controversial tweet by then-Rep Mike Pompeo (R-KS). Also see Elizalde (2017) and Steinhauer (2017) for national coverage of controversial tweets by Steve King.

37. Notably, the effect of incivility use in the 113th Congress is not restricted to white voters: it has a positive, significant effect on all voters.

38. In addition, different personality types may be attracted to different social networking sites (e.g., Facebook and Twitter). See Hughes et al. (2012).

39. For instance, Green Tea Republican Diane Black (R-TN) tweeted in June 2013, "I offered amdt to the #FarmBill to STOP sending food stamps to Mexican nationals & illegal immigrants. Learn more: http://t.co/FjJutYeqTN." The tweet linked to a Facebook post issued by Black that included the line, "STOP this outrageous abuse of taxpayer dollars!" It has never been the policy of the Supplemental Nutrition Assistance Program (which provides food stamps) to give assistance to undocumented noncitizens: https://www.fns.usda.gov/sites/default/files/Non-Citizen_Guidance_063011.pdf.

40. For a comparison of a Democratic debate with a Republican debate, see Cassidy (2015b).

41. See Edsall (2016) and Soave (2017).

42. For discussion of the role of Trump's rise has played in the coarsening of American discourse (and vice versa), see Bruni (2017) and Editorial Board (2017).

43. Taunts directed toward the other side can be found in congressional press releases (Grimmer and King 2011), but these are often released via social media, which is likely to be the place voters encounter them (Glassman et al. 2013).

44. Of course, many member of Congress Twitter posts are not actually posted by the legislator, or are very personal— i.e., written in the first-person. We encourage researchers to investigate whether this affects the impact of uncivil Twitter posts.

45. As of this writing, it seems that Steve Bannon has been defenestrated from conservative circles following the loss of Roy Moore, a controversial candidate he backed, in a December 2017 Senate special election in Alabama, and his subsequent public falling-out with Trump. He again resigned as chair of Breitbart in January 2018 (Peters 2018). See: https://www.nytimes.com/2018/01/09/us/politics/steve-bannon-breitbart-trump.html.

46. In total, forty-three members tweeted about Breitbart in some way. Of these members, only sixteen were Coffee members (the largest group), and only eight of these were also Coffee members in the 112th Congress.

47. King tweeted, "NY Times vindicates King & Breitbart! Vilsack/Holder/Obama culpable, corrupt $4.4bil in Pigford claims. http://t.co/X580LjTjw9 #Pigford." The "Pigford claims" refer to efforts by Hispanic and female farmers to get compensation for being systematically rejected for federal loans by biased officials. African American farmers had received compensation, to the tune of $50,000, during the Clinton administration. The Obama administration chose to compensate Hispanic and female claimants similarly. However, as King and Breitbart alleged, the claims were largely fraudulent. In short, with this tweet, King not only weds himself to Breitbart, but sends the message to followers that the Obama administration was sending billions in taxpayer money to women and minority group members under false pretenses of "discrimination."

Chapter 10: Tea Party-ness, Trump, and the Future of the Republican Party

1. Ironically, Price was pressured to resign following reports of wasteful spending on private air travel (Baker et al. 2017).

2. In addition, Corey Lewandowski, who served as Trump's campaign manager, was charged with battery in March 2016 after grabbing and pushing a Breitbart News reporter. Lewandowski

was also caught on camera grabbing a protester after a March 2016 Trump rally in Arizona (Haberman and Grynbaum 2016).

3. Notably, in November 2017, Twitter officially increased its character limit, doubling the maximum allowed characters from the original 140 to 280. Time will tell if this change has any meaningful effect on political discourses on the platform.

4. The full transcript of Flake's speech is available from the *New York Times*: "Full Transcript: Jeff Flake's Speech on the Senate Floor," *New York Times*, October 24, 2017, https://www.nytimes.com/2017/10/24/us/politics/jeff-flake-transcript-senate-speech.html?smid=tw-share.

5. See "Massachusetts Gov. Baker: Trump Climate Action Disappointing," *Associated Press*, June 1, 2017, http://www.apnewsarchive.com/2017/Gov._Baker%3A_Trump_climate_action_disappointing/id-84feeb60287747b588043de05a75a6c0.

6. See the website for the "Resistance Party": https://www.theresistanceparty.org/.

7. For instance, the Twitter account of one chapter of the Indivisible movement, located in Texas's Twenty-first Congressional District, regularly tweeted and retweeted belittling commentary about the district's Republican member of Congress (Lamar Smith) during , the state's two senators, the governor, and Trump throughout 2017.

8. For example, by convention, members of the Electoral College almost never vote contrary to the popular vote in their states, and the Seventeenth Amendment established the popular election of US senators in lieu of state legislatures.

9. See "Anger Runs High on Both Sides of the Trump Divide," *Rasmussen Reports*, June 20, 2017, http://www.rasmussenreports.com/public_content/politics/general_politics/june_2017/anger_runs_high_on_both_sides_of_the_trump_divide.

BIBLIOGRAPHY

ABC News. 2010. "The Conversation: Understanding 'Hashtag Politics.'" *ABCnews.com.* http://abcnews.go.com/WN/tcot-drives-tea-party-republican-message-social-media/ story?id=11682222 (accessed August 21, 2017).

Abrajano, Marisa, and Zoltan L. Hajnal. 2015. *White Backlash: Immigration, Race, and American Politics.* Oxford: Oxford University Press.

Acosta, Jim. 2012. "Is the Tea Party Ready to Deal on Fiscal Cliff?" *CNN.com.* http://politicalticker. blogs.cnn.com/2012/12/12/is-the-tea-party-ready-to-deal-on-fiscal-cliff/ (accessed January 9, 2017).

Adler, Ben. 2010. "How the Tea Party Plans to Put the Pressure on the GOP." *Newsweek,* November 4. http://www.newsweek.com/how-tea-party-plans-put-pressure-gop-69825 (accessed February 7, 2018).

Agarwal, Sheetal D., et al. 2014. "Grassroots Organizing in the Digital Age: Considering Values and Technology in Tea Party and Occupy Wall Street." *Information, Communication & Society* 17(3): 326–341.

Alberta, Tim. 2017. "John Boehner Unchained." *Politico Magazine.* http://politi.co/2zhDZXN (accessed December 15, 2017).

Allen, Danielle. 2017. "No, Don't Punch More Nazis." *Washington Post.* https://www. washingtonpost.com/opinions/no-dont-punch-more-nazis/2017/08/24/e1364e96-8445-11e7-902a-2a9f2d808496_story.html (accessed September 9, 2017).

Allen, Jonathan, and John Bresnahan. 2011. "Sources: Biden Likened Tea Partiers to 'Terrorists.'" *Politico,* August 2. http://www.politico.com/news/stories/0811/60421.html (accessed March 31, 2017).

Alvarez, Lizette. 2012a. "Allen West Faces Challenge in New Florida District." *New York Times.* http://www.nytimes.com/2012/07/20/us/politics/allen-west-faces-challenge-in-new-florida-district.html (accessed March 20, 2017).

Alvarez, Lizette. 2012b. "Republican Concedes House Race in Florida." *New York Times.* http:// www.nytimes.com/2012/11/21/us/politics/in-florida-republican-concedes-house-race. html?mcubz=1 (accessed February 7, 2018).

Anderson, Ashley A., Dominique Brossard, Dietram A. Scheufele, Michael A. Xenos, and Peter Ladwig. 2014. "The 'Nasty Effect': Online Incivility and Risk Perceptions of Emerging Technologies." *Journal of Computer-Mediated Communication* 19(3): 373–387.

Anderson, Monica. 2015. "More Americans Are Using Social Media to Connect with Politicians." Pew Research Center. http://www.pewresearch.org/fact-tank/2015/05/19/more-americans-are-using-social-media-to-connect-with-politicians/ (accessed May 22, 2015).

Ansolabehere, Stephen, and James M. Snyder Jr. 2011. "Weak Tea." *Boston Review*, March 1. http://bostonreview.net/stephen-ansolabehere-james-snyder-jr-tea-party (accessed August 6, 2014).

Arceneaux, Kevin, and Stephen P. Nicholson. 2012. "Who Wants to Have a Tea Party? The Who, What, and Why of the Tea Party Movement." *PS: Political Science and Politics* 45(4): 700–710.

Azari, Julia. 2016. "Was Hillary Clinton's 'Delete Your Account' Tweet 'Unpresidential'?" *Mischiefs of Factions*, January 10. http://www.vox.com/mischiefs-of-faction/2016/6/10/11906468/clinton-trump-delete-your-account (accessed March 29, 2017).

Bacon, Perry. 2010. "With New Book, Cantor Disavows Power Grab." *Washington Post*. http://www.washingtonpost.com/wp-dyn/content/article/2010/09/13/AR2010091306667.html (accessed February 5, 2018).

Bade, Rachael. 2016. "Freedom Caucus Knives out for Ryan after Huelskamp Loss." *Politico*, August 3. http://politi.co/2aRwpYN (accessed September 9, 2017).

Bade, Rachael, and Elena Schneider. 2016. "GOP Establishment Trounces Tea Party in Congressional Primaries." *Politico*. http://www.politico.com/story/2016/08/congress-primaries-establishment-trounces-tea-party-227609 (accessed January 23, 2017).

Bailey, Michael A., Jonathan Mummolo, and Hans Noel. 2012. "Tea Party Influence: A Story of Activists and Elites." *American Politics Research* 40(5): 769–804.

Baker, Peter, Glenn Thrush, and Maggie Haberman. 2017. "Health Secretary Tom Price Resigns After Drawing Ire for Chartered Flights." *New York Times*. https://www.nytimes.com/2017/09/29/us/politics/tom-price-trump-hhs.html (accessed February 10, 2018).

Ball, Molly. 2012. "The Tea Party's Mitt Romney Crisis." *Atlantic*. https://www.theatlantic.com/politics/archive/2012/04/the-tea-partys-mitt-romney-crisis/256008/ (accessed August 18, 2017).

Ball, Molly. 2015a. "The Bluest Republican: Why Staunchly Democratic Massachusetts Loves Its New GOP Governor." *Atlantic*. https://www.theatlantic.com/magazine/archive/2015/03/the-bluest-republican/384969/ (accessed September 8, 2017).

Ball, Molly. 2015b. "'The Republican Party Created Donald Trump,'" *Atlantic*, https://www.theatlantic.com/politics/archive/2015/08/erick-erickson-the-republican-party-created-donald-trump/400847/ (accessed September 8, 2017).

Ball, Molly. 2016. "Is the Tea Party Responsible for Donald Trump?" *Atlantic*. https://www.theatlantic.com/politics/archive/2016/05/did-the-tea-party-create-donald-trump/482004/ (accessed August 23, 2017).

Ball, Molly. 2017. "Al Franken Has Been Sitting on Jokes for a Decade. Now He's Ready to Tell Them." *New York Times*. https://www.nytimes.com/2017/05/29/books/review/al-franken-giant-of-the-senate.html (accessed September 9, 2017).

Balz, Dan. 2014. "Tea Party vs. Establishment as Primary Season Opens." *Washington Post*. https://www.washingtonpost.com/politics/tea-party-vs-establishment-as-primary-season-opens/2014/05/05/5ebadc1c-d461-11e3-8a78-8fe50322a72c_story.html (accessed August 24, 2017).

Balz, Dan. 2015. "Marco Rubio's Moment: Can He Meld Establishment Cash, Outsider Appeal?" *Washington Post*. https://www.washingtonpost.com/politics/marco-rubios-moment-can-he-meld-establishment-cash-outsider-appeal/2015/10/31/2274fe48-7fe8-11e5-b575-d8dcfedb4ea1_story.html (accessed June 9, 2017).

Banks, Antoine J. 2014. *Anger and Racial Politics: The Emotional Foundation of Racial Attitudes in America*. New York: Cambridge University Press.

Barabak, Mark Z., and Michael Finnegan. 2016. "Cruz Wins Wisconsin, Complicating Trump's Path to the Nomination." *Los Angeles Times*. http://www.latimes.com/nation/politics/la-na-gop-primary-wisconsin-20160405-story.html (February 10, 2018).

Barbaro, Michael. 2015. "Pithy, Mean and Powerful: How Donald Trump Mastered Twitter for 2016." *New York Times*. http://www.nytimes.com/2015/10/06/us/politics/donald-trump-twitter-use-campaign-2016.html (accessed October 5, 2015).

Barberá, Pablo. 2014. "Birds of the Same Feather Tweet Together: Bayesian Ideal Point Estimation Using Twitter Data." *Political Analysis* 23(1): 76–91.

Barreto, Matt, Betsy L. Cooper, Benjamin Gonzalez, Christopher S. Parker, and Christopher Towler. 2011. "The Tea Party in the Age of Obama: Mainstream Conservatism or Out-Group Anxiety?" *Political Power and Social Theory* 22(1): 105–137.

Barrett, Ted. 2015. "Republicans Rebuke Cruz over His Charge McConnell Lied." *CNN.* http://www.cnn.com/2015/07/26/politics/cruz-senate-mcconnell-lied/index.html (accessed July 27, 2015).

Barrouquere, Brett. 2017. "Gohmert Feared Arrest if Trump Had Lost." *Houston Chronicle,* March 4. http://www.chron.com/news/politics/texas/article/Gohmert-feared-arrest-if-Trump-had-lost-10977316.php (accessed September 9, 2017).

Bazelon, Emily. 2017. "How Do We Contend with Trump's Defiance of 'Norms'?" *New York Times.* https://www.nytimes.com/2017/07/11/magazine/how-do-we-contend-with-trumps-defiance-of-norms.html (accessed November 9, 2017).

Beckel, Michael. 2013. "'Tea Party' Nonprofits Rarely Endorsed Political Candidates." Center for Public Integrity. http://www.publicintegrity.org/2013/05/17/12672/tea-party-nonprofits-rarely-endorsed-political-candidates (accessed July 25, 2014).

Beinart, Peter. 2017a. "Glenn Beck's Regrets." *Atlantic.* https://www.theatlantic.com/magazine/archive/2017/01/glenn-becks-regrets/508763/ (accessed September 11, 2017).

Beinart, Peter. 2017b. "The Rise of the Violent Left." *Atlantic.* https://www.theatlantic.com/magazine/archive/2017/09/the-rise-of-the-violent-left/534192/ (accessed September 6, 2017).

Bennett, Brian. 2017. "'America First,' a Phrase with a Loaded Anti-Semitic and Isolationist History." *Los Angeles Times.* http://www.latimes.com/politics/la-na-pol-trump-america-first-20170120-story.html (February 10, 2018).

Berman, Mark. 2017. "Trump Tells Police Not to Worry about Injuring Suspects, Drawing Rebukes from Law Enforcement." *Washington Post.* https://www.washingtonpost.com/news/post-nation/wp/2017/07/28/trump-tells-police-not-to-worry-about-injuring-suspects-during-arrests/?utm_term=.7a7e12d68cd1 (accessed September 6, 2017).

Bernstein, Jared. 2017. "OMB Director Mulvaney Could Not Be More Wrong: We Need the Congressional Budget Office Now more than Ever." *Washington Post.* https://www.washingtonpost.com/posteverything/wp/2017/06/05/omb-director-mulvaney-could-not-be-more-wrong-we-need-the-congressional-budget-office-now-more-than-ever/ (accessed February 10, 2018).

Bernstein, J. M. 2010. "The Very Angry Tea Party." *New York Times.* http://opinionator.blogs.nytimes.com/2010/06/13/the-very-angry-tea-party/ (accessed January 2, 2017).

Berry, Jeffrey M., and Sarah Sobieraj. 2014. *The Outrage Industry Political Opinion Media and the New Incivility.* Oxford: Oxford University Press.

Bimber, Bruce. 2014. "Digital Media in the Obama Campaigns of 2008 and 2012: Adaptation to the Personalized Political Communication Environment." *Journal of Information Technology & Politics* 11(2): 130–150.

Binder, Sarah A. 2015. "Boehner's Departure Won't Bring about Change." *New York Times.* https://www.nytimes.com/roomfordebate/2015/09/30/the-house-after-john-boehners-departure/boehners-departure-wont-bring-about-change?mcubz=1 (accessed September 9, 2017).

Blackmon, Douglas A., and Jennifer Levitz. 2011. "Tea Party Sees No Triumph in Compromise." *Wall Street Journal,* August 2. http://www.wsj.com/articles/SB10001424053111903635604576474050402040650 (accessed January 7, 2017).

Blake, Aaron. 2011. "The Misappropriation of the Tea Party Label (and the Headaches It's Causing)." *Washington Post.* https://www.washingtonpost.com/blogs/the-fix/post/the-misappropriation-of-the-tea-party-label-and-the-headaches-its-causing/2011/03/17/ABws7Il_blog.html (accessed August 23, 2017).

Blake, Aaron. 2015. "Here Are the Republicans Who Voted against John Boehner for Speaker." *Washington Post.* https://www.washingtonpost.com/news/the-fix/wp/2015/01/06/here-are-the-republicans-who-voted-against-john-boehner-for-speaker/ (accessed September 9, 2017).

Blake, Aaron. 2017a. "'Trumpism without Trump' Lost in Virginia. But Don't Write Its Obituary Just Yet." *Washington Post*. https://www.washingtonpost.com/news/the-fix/wp/2017/11/08/trumpism-without-trump-lost-in-virginia-dont-write-its-obituary-just-yet/ (accessed February 8, 2018).

Blake, Aaron. 2017b. "Paul Ryan Erases Any Doubt: 'We're with Trump.'" *Washington Post*. https://www.washingtonpost.com/news/the-fix/wp/2017/11/08/paul-ryan-erases-any-doubt-were-with-trump/ (accessed November 9, 2017).

Blankley, Tony. 2009. "End the Coarsening of Civic Discourse." *Washington Times*. http://www.washingtontimes.com/news/2009/sep/22/end-the-coarsening-of-civic-discourse/ (accessed September 9, 2017).

Blodget, Henry. 2013. "There's Nothing 'Partisan' about Trashing the Selfish Extremists Who Just Shut Down Our Government." *Slate*. http://www.slate.com/blogs/business_insider/2013/10/01/government_shutdown_tea_party_republicans_are_to_blame.html (accessed July 17, 2015).

Bloomfield, Matt. 2017. "Women's March against Donald Trump is the Largest Day of Protests in US History, Say Political Scientists." *Independent*, January 23. https://www.independent.co.uk/news/world/americas/womens-march-anti-donald-trump-womens-rights-largest-protest-demonstration-us-history-political-a7541081.html (accessed February 10, 2018).

Blum, Rachel. 2017. "What Donald Trump's Rhetoric Borrows from the Tea Party." *Vox*, February 9. https://www.vox.com/mischiefs-of-faction/2017/2/9/14552930/trump-tea-party-rhetoric-immigrants-liberal-media (accessed February 10, 2018).

Bobic, Igor. 2016. "The Onion Totally Called The Rise Of Donald Trump 4 Years Ago." *Huffington Post*. https://www.huffingtonpost.com/entry/donald-trump-the-onion-prediction_us_572a3381e4b016f3789462cc (accessed February 10, 2018).

Bode, Leticia, Alexander Hanna, Junghwan Yang, and Dhavan V. Shah. 2015. "Candidate Networks, Citizen Clusters, and Political Expression Strategic Hashtag Use in the 2010 Midterms." *Annals of the American Academy of Political and Social Science* 659(1): 149–165.

Bolton, Alexander. 2006. "Bloggers Prefer Shadegg or Boehner." *The Hill*, January 25. http://thehill.com/homenews/news/10382-bloggers-prefer-shadegg-or-boehner (accessed May 19, 2017).

Bond, Jon R. 2013. "Life Ain't Easy for a President Named Barack: Party, Ideology, and Tea Party Freshman Support for the Nation's First Black President." *Forum* 11: 243–258.

Borchers, Callum. 2017. "Body-Slamming Congressman Greg Gianforte Might as Well Get His Awkward Interview over with." *Washington Post*. https://www.washingtonpost.com/news/the-fix/wp/2017/08/30/body-slamming-congressman-greg-gianforte-might-as-well-get-his-awkward-interview-over-with/ (accessed September 6, 2017).

Bosman, Julie, and Monica Davey. 2016. "Republicans Expand Control in a Deeply Divided Nation." *New York Times*. https://www.nytimes.com/2016/11/12/us/republicans-expand-control-in-a-deeply-divided-nation.html (accessed September 7, 2017).

Bouie, Jamelle. 2013. "Michele Bachmann Is Gone, but Her Paranoid Politics Has Become the Norm for GOP." *Washington Post*. https://www.washingtonpost.com/blogs/plum-line/wp/2013/05/29/michele-bachmann-is-gone-but-her-paranoid-politics-will-live-on/?utm_term=.862d537cf8d4 (accessed March 8, 2017).

Boyer, Peter J. 2010. "House Rule: Will John Boehner Control the Tea Party Congress?" *New Yorker*. https://www.newyorker.com/magazine/2010/12/13/house-rule-peter-j-boyer (accessed February 7, 2018).

Bradberry, Leigh A., and Gary C. Jacobson. 2013. "Does the Tea Party Still Matter? Tea Party Influence in the 2012 Elections." Paper prepared for the Annual Meeting of the American Political Science Association, Chicago, August 29–September 1, 2013.

Brader, Ted. 2006. *Campaigning for Hearts and Minds: How Emotional Appeals in Political Ads Work*. Chicago: University of Chicago Press.

Bresnahan, John, and Jake Sherman. 2011. "Bachmann's Thin Legislative Résumé." *Politico*, June 28. http://politi.co/kxlYqc (accessed January 24, 2017).

Broder, David S. 2006. "Republicans in Search of Answers." *Washington Post.* http://www.washingtonpost.com/wp-dyn/content/article/2006/05/05/AR2006050501662.html (accessed May 19, 2017).

Broder, David S. 2010. "Sarah Palin Displays Her Pitch-Perfect Populism." *Washington Post.* http://www.washingtonpost.com/wp-dyn/content/article/2010/02/10/AR2010021002451.html (accessed September 11, 2017).

Brody, David. 2012. *The Teavangelicals: The Inside Story of How the Evangelicals and the Tea Party Are Taking Back America.* New York: Zondervan.

Brooks, David. 2016. "The Governing Cancer of Our Time." *New York Times.* http://www.nytimes.com/2016/02/26/opinion/the-governing-cancer-of-our-time.html (accessed December 31, 2016).

Brooks, Deborah Jordan, and John G. Geer. 2007. "Beyond Negativity: The Effects of Incivility on the Electorate." *American Journal of Political Science* 51(1): 1–16.

Brown, Heath A. 2015. *The Tea Party Divided: The Hidden Diversity of a Maturing Movement.* New York: Praeger.

Bruni, Frank. 2017. "I'm O.K.—You're Pure Evil." *New York Times,* https://www.nytimes.com/2017/06/17/opinion/sunday/im-ok-youre-pure-evil.html (accessed September 9, 2017).

Bullock, Charles S. III, and M. V. Hood III. 2012. "The Tea Party, Sarah Palin, and the 2010 Congressional Elections: The Aftermath of the Election of Barack Obama." *Social Science Quarterly* 93(5): 1424–1435.

Bump, Philip. 2014. "Coming Soon: A Campaign Run Entirely by Super PACs." *Washington Post.* http://www.washingtonpost.com/blogs/the-fix/wp/2014/07/28/coming-soon-a-campaign-run-entirely-by-super-pacs/July28 (accessed August 6, 2014).

Bump, Philip. 2015. "The Exceptional Campaign Timing of Ted Cruz's Ferocious Floor Speech." *Washington Post.* http://www.washingtonpost.com/blogs/the-fix/wp/2015/07/24/the-exceptional-campaign-timing-of-ted-cruzs-ferocious-floor-speech/?postshare=4821437750154029 (accessed July 24, 2015).

Bump, Philip. 2016. "Rep. Steve King Wonders What 'Sub-Groups' besides Whites Made Contributions to Civilization." *Washington Post.* https://www.washingtonpost.com/news/the-fix/wp/2016/07/18/rep-steve-king-wonders-what-sub-groups-besides-whites-made-contributions-to-civilization/ (accessed September 14, 2016).

Bump, Philip. 2017. "Jason Chaffetz's iPhone Comment Revives the 'poverty Is a Choice' Argument." *Washington Post.* https://www.washingtonpost.com/news/politics/wp/2017/03/07/jason-chaffetzs-iphone-comment-revives-the-poverty-is-a-choice-argument/ (accessed February 10, 2018).

Burghart, Devin, and Leonard Zeskind. 2010. *Tea Party Nationalism: A Critical Examination of the Tea Party Movement and the Size, Scope, and Focus of Its National Factions.* Report for the Institute for Research & Education on Human Rights.

Burghart, Devin, and Leonard Zeskind. 2015. *The Tea Party Movement in 2015.* Special report for the Institute for Research & Education on Human Rights.

Bycoffe, Aaron. 2015. "The 2016 Endorsement Primary." *FiveThirtyEight,* June 7. http://projects.fivethirtyeight.com/2016-endorsement-primary/ (accessed June 8, 2017).

Cadei, Emily. 2015. "Tea Party Conservatives Take Aim at GOP Leaders." *Newsweek,* October 8. http://www.newsweek.com/house-freedom-caucus-conservatives-take-aim-kevin-mccarthy-house-speaker-380857 (accessed November 23, 2015).

Calamur, Krishnadev. 2017. "A Short History of 'America First.'" *Atlantic.* https://www.theatlantic.com/politics/archive/2017/01/trump-america-first/514037/ (accessed: February 10, 2018).

Campbell, Angus, Phillip Converse, Warren Miller, and Donald Stokes. 1960. *The American Voter.* New York: Wiley.

Campbell, David E., and Robert D. Putnam. 2011. "Crashing the Tea Party." *New York Times.* http://www.nytimes.com/2011/08/17/opinion/crashing-the-tea-party.html (accessed February 7, 2018).

Capehart, Jonathan. 2014. "Herman Cain Is Absolutely Right . . . about the Tea Party." *Washington Post.* http://www.washingtonpost.com/blogs/post-partisan/wp/2014/08/07/herman-cain-is-absolutely-right-about-the-tea-party/?hpid=z2 (accessed August 7, 2014).

Capehart, Jonathan. 2016. "How Notre Dame Honors Joe Biden, John Boehner and Political Civility." *Washington Post.* https://www.washingtonpost.com/blogs/post-partisan/wp/2016/05/14/how-notre-dame-honors-joe-biden-john-boehner-and-political-civility/?utm_term=.2bac7a816be5 (accessed May 12, 2017).

Carlson, Nicholas. 2011. "The Real History of Twitter." *Business Insider.* http://www.businessinsider.com/how-twitter-was-founded-2011-4 (accessed February 9, 2018).

Carney, Timothy P. 2013. "Tea Party Needs to Recognize That It's Playing with Live Ammo." *Washington Examiner,* October 19. http://www.washingtonexaminer.com/tea-party-needs-to-recognize-that-its-playing-with-live-ammo/article/2537427 (accessed January 24, 2017).

Carson, Jamie L., and Stephen Pettigrew. 2013. "Strategic Politicians, Partisan Roll Calls, and the Tea Party: Evaluating the 2010 Midterm Elections." *Electoral Studies* 32(1): 26–36.

Cassella, Megan, Susan Heavey, and Dustin Volz. 2016. "Trump Steps up Attacks with 'Bimbo' Tweet before Fox News Debate." *Reuters.* https://www.reuters.com/article/us-usa-election-trump/trump-jabs-fox-anchor-after-exiting-republican-debate-in-iowa-idUSKCN0V51PU (accessed February 9, 2018).

Casselman, Ben. 2016. "Why Are White People So Pessimistic about the Economy?" *FiveThirtyEight,* June 10. https://fivethirtyeight.com/features/for-blacks-and-hispanics-the-economic-glass-is-still-half-full/ (accessed June 1, 2017).

Cassidy, John. 2015a. "After Being Reëlected as Speaker, Boehner Will Need More Cigarettes." *New Yorker,* January 6. http://www.newyorker.com/news/john-cassidy/boehner-reelected-speaker-cigarettes (accessed May 15, 2017).

Cassidy, John. 2015b. "Democratic Debate Offers Up No Winners, but a Clear Choice." *New Yorker.* December 20. https://www.newyorker.com/news/john-cassidy/democratic-debate-offers-up-no-winners-but-a-clear-choice (accessed February 10, 2018).

Cassone, Chris, and Robert Stacy McCain. 2012. *Take Our Country Back: One Song and One Man's Story of the Tea Party.* Plano, TX: Dunham Books.

Catanese, David. 2017. "Kelli Ward: The Trump Torch-Bearer Rattling Arizona's Senate Race." *US News & World Report.* https://www.usnews.com/news/the-run/articles/2017-08-30/kelli-ward-the-trump-torch-bearer-rattling-arizonas-senate-race (accessed October 25, 2017).

Chait, Jonathan. 2016. "Donald Trump Hasn't Killed the Tea Party. He Is the Tea Party." *Daily Intelligencer,* May 19. http://nymag.com/daily/intelligencer/2016/05/donald-trump-is-the-tea-party.html (accessed June 28, 2016).

Cho, Wendy K. Tam, James G. Gimpel, and Daron R. Shaw. 2012. "The Tea Party Movement and the Geography of Collective Action." *Quarterly Journal of Political Science* 7(2): 105–133.

Cillizza, Chris. 2013a. "The Fix's Complete Guide to Understanding House Republicans." *Washington Post.* http://www.washingtonpost.com/blogs/the-fix/wp/2013/07/09/the-fixs-complete-guide-to-understanding-house-republicans/ (accessed July 25, 2014).

Cillizza, Chris. 2013b. "The Failure of the Farm Bill—and Why House Republicans Can't Be Led." *Washington Post.* http://www.washingtonpost.com/blogs/the-fix/wp/2013/06/20/the-failure-of-the-farm-bill-and-why-house-republicans-cant-be-led/ (accessed July 17, 2015).

Clancy, Dean. 2014. "The Tea Party's Weakness, Exposed." *US News & World Report.* http://www.usnews.com/opinion/blogs/opinion-blog/2014/06/17/eric-cantors-demise-exposes-the-tea-partys-weakness (accessed January 29, 2017).

Clement, Scott, and John C. Green. 2011. "The Tea Party, Religion, and Social Issues." *Pew Forum on Religion and Public Life.* http://pewresearch.org/pubs/1903/tea-party-movement-religion-social-issues-conservative-christian (accessed on February 7, 2018).

Cline, Seth. 2012. "Tea Party House Members Even Wealthier than Other GOP Lawmakers." OpenSecrets (blog). https://www.opensecrets.org/news/2012/01/tea-party-house-members-wealthy-gop/ (accessed August 21, 2017).

Coblenz, Mike. 2014. "How Angry Is the Tea Party?" *Daily Kos*. http://www.dailykos.com/story/2014/6/29/1310378/-How-Angry-is-the-Tea-Party (accessed January 2, 2017).

Coe, Kevin, Kate Kenski, and Stephen A. Rains. 2014. "Online and Uncivil? Patterns and Determinants of Incivility in Newspaper Website Comments." *Journal of Communication* 64(4): 658–679.

Cohen, Marty, David Karol, Hans Noel, and John Zaller. 2008. *The Party Decides: Presidential Nominations before and after Reform*. Chicago: University of Chicago Press.

Cohn, Alicia. 2011. "Sen. McCain Won't Apologize for 'Tea Party Hobbits' Comment." *The Hill*, August 9. http://thehill.com/blogs/blog-briefing-room/news/176055--mccain-not-sorry-for-tea-party-hobbits-comment (accessed September 9, 2017).

Cohn, Nate. 2014. "Why Did Cantor Lose? Not Easy to Explain." *New York Times*. https://www.nytimes.com/2014/06/11/upshot/why-did-cantor-lose-not-easy-to-explain.html (accessed January 23, 2017).

Colleoni, Elanor, Alessandro Rozza, and Adam Arvidsson. 2014. "Echo Chamber or Public Sphere? Predicting Political Orientation and Measuring Political Homophily in Twitter Using Big Data." *Journal of Communication* 64(2): 317–332.

Collingwood, Loren, and John Wilkerson. 2012. "Tradeoffs in Accuracy and Efficiency in Supervised Learning Methods." *Journal of Information Technology & Politics* 9(3): 298–318.

Converse, Philip E. 1964. "The Nature of Belief Systems in Mass Publics." In *Ideology and Discontent*, edited by David E. Apter, 206–261. Ann Arbor: University of Michigan Press.

Conway, Bethany A., Kate Kenski, and Di Wang. 2015. "The Rise of Twitter in the Political Campaign: Searching for Intermedia Agenda-Setting Effects in the Presidential Primary." *Journal of Computer-Mediated Communication* 20(4): 363–380.

Cooper, Helene, and Jeff Zeleny. 2011. "In Tucson, Obama Urges Americans to New Era of Civility." *New York Times*. http://www.nytimes.com/2011/01/13/us/13obama.html (accessed August 12, 2016).

Coppins, McKay. 2017. "Jeff Flake's Gamble." *Atlantic*. https://www.theatlantic.com/magazine/archive/2017/09/jeff-flakes-gamble/534201/ (accessed October 16, 2017).

Correa, Teresa, Amber Willard Hinsley, and Homero Gil de Zúñiga. 2010. "Who Interacts on the Web? The Intersection of Users' Personality and Social Media Use." *Computers in Human Behavior* 26(2): 247–253.

Costa, Robert. 2014. "Sen. Ted Cruz of Texas Is a Rising Republican Power in House, as Well as a Whip." *Washington Post*. https://www.washingtonpost.com/politics/sen-ted-cruz-of-texas-is-a-rising-republican-power-in-house-as-well-as-a-whip/2014/07/31/10e5a87a-18ed-11e4-85b6-c1451e622637_story.html?utm_term=.5199e06a342e (accessed February 7, 2018).

Costa, Robert. 2015. "What John Boehner Told Me the Night before He Said He Was Quitting." *Washington Post*. https://www.washingtonpost.com/politics/john-boehner-in-twilight/2015/09/25/124fc54a-6399-11e5-8e9e-dce8a2a2a679_story.html?utm_term=.312466baa281 (accessed May 15, 2017).

Costa, Robert. 2016. "Palin's Endorsement the Latest Prize as Trump, Cruz Battle for Conservatives." *Washington Post*. https://www.washingtonpost.com/politics/palins-endorsement-the-latest-prize-as-trump-cruz-battle-for-conservatives/2016/01/19/c243b326-bede-11e5-83d4-42e3bceea902_story.html (accessed September 11, 2017).

Costa, Robert. 2017. "Freedom Caucus Leaders Vent to Paul Ryan after Talks with Steve Bannon." *Washington Post*. https://www.washingtonpost.com/news/powerpost/wp/2017/09/06/freedom-caucus-leaders-vent-to-ryan-following-talks-with-bannon/ (accessed September 9, 2017).

Cottle, Michelle. 2016a. "Keeping the President's Hands Off Utah's Land." *Atlantic*. http://www.theatlantic.com/politics/archive/2016/09/utah-public-lands-rob-bishop/499316/ (accessed January 25, 2017).

Cottle, Michelle. 2016b. "Freedom Caucus Members Want to Punish Paul Ryan." *Atlantic*. https://www.theatlantic.com/politics/archive/2016/10/no-rest-for-paul-ryan/505931/ (accessed September 9, 2017).

Cramer, Katherine J. 2016a. *The Politics of Resentment: Rural Consciousness in Wisconsin and the Rise of Scott Walker*. Chicago: University of Chicago Press.

Cramer, Katherine J. 2016b. "Here's What Trump Is Telling Resentful Americans (and Sanders Is Not)." *Washington Post*. https://www.washingtonpost.com/news/monkey-cage/wp/2016/03/15/heres-what-trump-is-telling-resentful-americans-and-sanders-is-not/ (accessed April 25, 2017).

Daley, William M. 2015. "The GOP's Dysfunction All Started with Sarah Palin." *Washington Post*. https://www.washingtonpost.com/opinions/the-gops-dysfunction-all-started-with-sarah-palin/2015/10/25/bdd34892-7442-11e5-8248-98e0f5a2e830_story.html?utm_term=.5a703bc2699f (accessed January 2, 2017).

Dalton, Russell J. 2017. "The Blinders of Partisanship and the 2016 US Election." OUPblog: Oxford University Press, January 9. https://blog.oup.com/2017/01/partisanship-voting-presidential-election/ (accessed February 10, 2018).

Danforth, John. 2017. "The Real Reason Trump Is Not a Republican." *Washington Post*. https://www.washingtonpost.com/opinions/trump-is-exactly-what-republicans-are-not/2017/08/24/9909a320-8832-11e7-a50f-e0d4e6ec070a_story.html?utm_term=.9cce06b3d562 (accessed September 8, 2017).

Darr, Christopher. 2013. "A 'Dialogue of the Deaf': Obama, His Congressional Critics, and Incivility in American Political Discourse." In *Venomous Speech: Problems with American Political Discourse on the Right and Left*, edited by Clarke Rountree, 19–40. New York: Praeger.

Davidson, C. Simon. 2014. "When Is a Tweet an Ethics Violation? A Question of Ethics." *Roll Call*, July 22. http://www.rollcall.com/news/home/when-is-a-tweet-an-ethics-violation-a-question-of-ethics (accessed September 8, 2017).

Davis, Susan. 2016. "House GOP's 2010 Tea Party Class Heads for the Exits." NPR.org. http://www.npr.org/2016/04/03/472852016/house-gops-2010-tea-party-class-heads-for-the-exits (accessed August 23, 2017).

DeBonis, Mike, and Damian Paletta. 2017. "Freedom Caucus Leader Warns: Don't Attach Harvey Aid to Debt-Ceiling Increase." *Washington Post*. https://www.washingtonpost.com/powerpost/freedom-caucus-leader-warns-dont-attach-harvey-aid-to-debt-ceiling-increase/2017/08/31/6b53ebc6-8e58-11e7-91d5-ab4e4bb76a3a_story.html (accessed September 6, 2017).

DeBonis, Mike, Kelsey Snell, Philip Rucker, and Elise Viebeck. 2017. "Trump Sides with Democrats on Fiscal Issues, Throwing Republican Plans into Chaos." *Washington Post*. https://www.washingtonpost.com/powerpost/house-prepares-for-harvey-relief-vote/2017/09/06/62919058-92fc-11e7-89fa-bb822a46da5b_story.html (accessed September 8, 2017).

Deckman, Melissa. 2016. *Tea Party Women: Mama Grizzlies, Grassroots Leaders, and the Changing Face of the American Right*. New York: New York University Press.

DeFrancesco Soto, Victoria. 2015. "Remember When The GOP Actually Courted Latinos?" *Talking Points Memo*. http://talkingpointsmemo.com/cafe/bush-administration-courting-latinos (accessed September 7, 2017).

DeSilver, Drew. 2014. "In Late Spurt of Activity, Congress Avoids 'Least Productive' Title." *Pew Research Center*. http://www.pewresearch.org/fact-tank/2014/12/29/in-late-spurt-of-activity-congress-avoids-least-productive-title/ (accessed April 15, 2018).

Devroy, Ann, and Charles R. Babcock. 1994. "Gingrich Speech Gives Lobbyists a Strategy for Midterm Elections." *Washington Post*, October 14. Archived at: http://tech.mit.edu/V114/N48/gingrich.48w.html (accessed February 9, 2018).

Diamond, Jeremy. 2015. "Donald Trump: Ban All Muslim Travel to U.S." *CNN.com*. https://www.cnn.com/2015/12/07/politics/donald-trump-muslim-ban-immigration/index.html (accessed February 10, 2018).

Dickey, Jack. 2015. "Why Kevin McCarthy Likes Jason Chaffetz." *Time*, October 5. http://time.com/4061668/kevin-mccarthy-jason-chaffetz/ (accessed May 21, 2017).

Dionne, E. J. 2016. *Why the Right Went Wrong: Conservatism—From Goldwater to the Tea Party and Beyond.* New York: Simon & Schuster.

Dionne, E. J., Thomas E. Mann, and Norman J. Ornstein. 2017. "How the GOP Prompted the Decay of Political Norms." *Atlantic.* https://www.theatlantic.com/politics/archive/2017/09/gop-decay-of-political-norms/540165/ (accessed February 7, 2018).

Douthat, Ross. 2015. "Wanted: A Tea Party Speaker." *New York Times.* https://www.nytimes.com/2015/10/11/opinion/sunday/wanted-a-tea-party-speaker.html (accessed February 7, 2018).

Draper, Robert. 2011. "How Kevin McCarthy Wrangles the Tea Party." *New York Times Magazine.* http://www.nytimes.com/2011/07/17/magazine/how-kevin-mccarthy-wrangles-the-tea-party.html (accessed May 22, 2017).

Draper, Robert. 2016. "How Donald Trump Set Off a Civil War within the Right-Wing Media." *New York Times Magazine.* https://www.nytimes.com/2016/10/02/magazine/how-donald-trump-set-off-a-civil-war-within-the-right-wing-media.html (accessed February 7, 2018).

Duggan, Maeve, and Joanna Brenner. 2013. "The Demographics of Social Media Users—2012." *Pew Research Center: Internet, Science & Tech.* http://www.pewinternet.org/2013/02/14/the-demographics-of-social-media-users-2012/ (accessed August 21, 2017).

Duran, Nicole. 2017. "Tea Party Merges with 'Trumpism,' for Now." *Washington Examiner,* February 12. http://www.washingtonexaminer.com/tea-party-merges-with-trumpism-for-now/article/2614512 (accessed August 23, 2017).

Easley, Cameron. 2018. "America's Most and Least Popular Governors—January 2018." *Morning Consult.* https://morningconsult.com/2018/02/01/governor-rankings-jan-2018 (accessed February 8, 2018).

Eddlem, Thomas R. 2014. "The War on the Tea Party." *New American,* February 5. http://www.thenewamerican.com/usnews/item/17529-the-war-on-the-tea-party (accessed November 23, 2015).

Editorial Board. 2017. "Trump Didn't Birth American Intolerance. He's The Manifestation of Our Long-Disturbed National Dialogue." *Los Angeles Times,* June 3. http://www.latimes.com/opinion/editorials/la-ed-political-discourse-trump-tolerance-racism-20170603-story.html (accessed February 8, 2018).

Edsall, Thomas. 2016. "The Anti-P.C. Vote." *New York Times.* https://www.nytimes.com/2016/06/01/opinion/campaign-stops/trump-clinton-edsall-psychology-anti-pc-vote.html (accessed March 31, 2017).

Egan, Timothy. 2012. "The Fraud of the Tea Party." *New York Times.* http://opinionator.blogs.nytimes.com/2012/01/15/the-fraud-of-the-tea-party/ (accessed July 17, 2015).

Eligon, John, and Michael Schwirtz. 2012. "Todd Akin Provokes Ire with 'Legitimate Rape' Comment." *New York Times.* http://www.nytimes.com/2012/08/20/us/politics/todd-akin-provokes-ire-with-legitimate-rape-comment.html (accessed March 30, 2017).

Elizalde, Elizabeth. 2017. "Rep. Steve King Mocks Latina with 'Offensive' Tweet Questioning Whether She Speaks English." *New York Daily News,* April 25. http://www.nydailynews.com/news/national/rep-king-mocks-latina-tweet-questioning-english-skills-article-1.3101291 (accessed August 20, 2017).

Elkins, Emily. 2017. "The Five Types of Trump Voters." *Democracy Fund Voter Study Group.* https://www.voterstudygroup.org/reports/2016-elections/the-five-types-trump-voters (accessed June 23, 2017).

Engels, Jeremy. 2015. *The Politics of Resentment: A Genealogy.* University Park: Pennsylvania State University Press.

Economist. 2011. "Scheme, Stonewall and Fulminate." July 21. http://www.economist.com/node/18988614 (accessed February 7, 2018).

Entin, Harry. 2014. "The Eric Cantor Upset: What Happened?" *FiveThirtyEight.* https://fivethirtyeight.com/features/the-eric-cantor-upset-what-happened/ (accessed February 7, 2018).

Farenthold, David A., Rosalind S. Helderman, and Ed O'Keefe. 2013. "What the 'Fiscal Cliff' Means for the Tea Party Movement." *Washington Post.* https://www.washingtonpost. com/news/post-politics/wp/2013/01/01/what-the-fiscal-cliff-means-for-the-tea-party-movement/ (accessed January 9, 2017).

Feehery, J. 2016. Paul Ryan Is Right. Will Anyone Listen? *USA Today,* March 23.

Fenno, Richard F. 1978. *Home Style: House Members in Their Districts.* London: Longman.

Ferrechio, Susan. 2014. "Libertarian Wing of GOP Gains Strength in Congress." | *Washington Examiner,* January 24. http://www.washingtonexaminer.com/libertarian-wing-of-gop-gains-strength-in-congress/article/2542802 (accessed March 23, 2015).

Foley, Elizabeth Price. 2012. *The Tea Party: Three Principles.* New York: Cambridge University Press.

Formisano, Ronald P. 2012. *The Tea Party: A Brief History.* Baltimore: Johns Hopkins University Press.

Fox News. 2011. "Bachmann Wins Iowa Straw Poll, Cements Her Top-Tier Status in GOP Race." http://www.foxnews.com/politics/2011/08/13/finally-here-ames-straw-poll-first-test-2012.html (accessed: February 10, 2018).

Freedlander, David. 2013. "Anger over Fiscal-Cliff Deal Fires Up Tea Party." *Daily Beast.* http:// www.thedailybeast.com/articles/2013/01/03/anger-over-fiscal-cliff-deal-fires-up-tea-party.html (accessed January 7, 2017).

French, David. 2013. "On Intra-Conservative Incivility." *National Review Online,* October 17. http://www.nationalreview.com/corner/361545/intra-conservative-incivility-david-french (accessed March 29, 2017).

French, David. 2016. "Marco Rubio and the Difference between Being 'Establishment' and Someone Establishment Voters Can Support." *National Review,* February 2. http://www. nationalreview.com/corner/430704/marco-rubio-and-different-definitions-establishment (accessed June 9, 2017).

Fridkin, Kim L., and Patrick J. Kenney. 2008. "The Dimensions of Negative Messages." *American Politics Research* 36(5): 694–723.

Friedersdorf, Conor. 2011. "Why the Tea Party Should Stop Fearing Compromise." *Atlantic.* http://www.theatlantic.com/politics/archive/2011/07/why-the-tea-party-should-stop-fearing-compromise/241925/ (accessed January 2, 2017).

Friedersdorf, Conor. 2012. "Could Election 2012 Be Going Any Worse for the Tea Party?" *Atlantic.* https://www.theatlantic.com/politics/archive/2012/01/could-election-2012-be-going-any-worse-for-the-tea-party/251104/ (accessed June 6, 2017).

Frum, David. 2010. "Post-Tea-Party Nation." *New York Times Magazine.*http://www.nytimes. com/2010/11/14/magazine/14FOB-idealab-t.html (accessed December 4, 2015).

Frum, David. 2016. "A Guide for Undecided Republicans." *The Atlantic.* https://www.theatlantic. com/politics/archive/2016/10/deciding-how-to-vote/504977/.

Fung, Brian. 2017. "You Can Now Call Your Elected Officials through Facebook." *Washington Post.* https://www.washingtonpost.com/news/the-switch/wp/2017/03/27/you-can-now-call-your-congressman-through-facebook/ (accessed August 11, 2017).

Gainous, Jason, and Kevin M. Wagner. 2013. *Tweeting to Power: The Social Media Revolution in American Politics.* New York: Oxford University Press.

Gallagher, Ian, and Brian Rock. 2012. "Reading the Tea Leaves: Tallying the Votes of the Tea Party in the 112th Congress." *Journal of Legal Metrics* 1(1): 87–112.

Gans, Curtis. 2013. "Why Only Republicans Can Save Us from the Tea Party." *Washington Monthly.* http://washingtonmonthly.com/2013/10/18/why-only-republicans-can-save-us-from-the-tea-party/ (accessed January 10, 2017).

Gass, Nick. 2016. "Trump Lands His First Congressional Endorsements." *Politico,* February 24. http://politi.co/1QcRaXm (accessed June 8, 2017).

Gerber, Alan S., and Gregory A. Huber. 2010. "Partisanship, Political Control, and Economic Assessments." *American Journal of Political Science* 54(1): 153–173.

Gerson, Michael. 2010. "Tea Party Complications." *Washington Post.* http://www.washingtonpost. com/wp-dyn/content/article/2010/11/29/AR2010112905134.html.

Gervais, Bryan T. 2014. "Following the News? Reception of Uncivil Partisan Media and the Use of Incivility in Political Expression." *Political Communication* 31(4): 564–583.

Gervais, Bryan T. 2015. "Incivility Online: Affective and Behavioral Reactions to Uncivil Political Posts in a Web-Based Experiment." *Journal of Information Technology & Politics* 12(2): 167–185.

Gervais, Bryan T. 2017a. "More than Mimicry? The Role of Anger in Uncivil Reactions to Elite Political Incivility." *International Journal of Public Opinion Research* 29(3): 384–405.

Gervais, Bryan T. 2017b. "Does Elite Incivility Provoke Partisan Citizenship? A Test of Affective Intelligence Theory." Working paper, Department of Political Science and Geography, University of Texas at San Antonio.

Gervais, Bryan T. 2018. "What to Tweet when the Top is Toxic? Gauging References to the 2016 Presidential Candidates in House Members' Social Media Posts." In *The Roads to Congress 2016*, edited by Sean Foreman and Marcia Godwin, 43–56. London: Palgrave Macmillan.

Gervais, Bryan T., and Irwin L. Morris. 2012. "Reading the Tea Leaves: Understanding Tea Party Caucus Membership in the US House of Representatives." *PS: Political Science & Politics* 45(2): 245–250.

Gervais, Bryan T., and Irwin L. Morris. 2014. "Black Tea, Green Tea, Herbal Tea, and Coffee: Understanding the Variation in Attachment to the Tea Party among Members of Congress." Paper prepared for the Annual Meeting of the American Political Science Association, August 28–31, Washington, DC.

Gervais, Bryan T., and Irwin L. Morris. 2015a. "Tea(s) and Coffee: Understanding the Variation in Attachment to the Tea Party among Members of Congress." Paper prepared for the Annual Meeting of the Western Political Science Association, April 2–4, Las Vegas.

Gervais, Bryan T., and Irwin L. Morris. 2015b. "Predicting Tea Party Association in the United States Senate." Paper prepared for the American Political Science Association Annual Meeting, September 3–6, San Francisco.

Gervais, Bryan T., and Jeffrey A. Taylor. 2016. "Sub-Partisan Cues and Ideological Distinctions: The Effect of the Tea Party Label on Voter Perceptions of Congressional Candidates." *Social Science Quarterly.* 97(5): 1130–1143.

Gervais, Bryan T., and Walter Wilson. 2017. "New Media for the New Electorate? U.S. Representatives' Use of Spanish in Tweets." *Politics, Groups, and Identities.* Advance online publication. doi: http://dx.doi.org/10.1080/21565503.2017.1358186.

Gest, Justin. 2016. *The New Minority: White Working Class Politics in an Age of Immigration and Inequality.* New York: Oxford University Press.

Gil de Zúñiga, Homero, Nakwon Jung, and Sebastián Valenzuela. 2012. "Social Media Use for News and Individuals' Social Capital, Civic Engagement and Political Participation." *Journal of Computer-Mediated Communication* 17(3): 319–336.

Gil de Zúñiga, Homero, Logan Molyneux, and Pei Zheng. 2014. "Social Media, Political Expression, and Political Participation: Panel Analysis of Lagged and Concurrent Relationships." *Journal of Communication* 64(4): 612–634.

Gillis, Justin, and Leslie Kaufman. 2012. "In Heartland Institute Leak, a Plan to Discredit Climate Teaching." *New York Times.* https://www.nytimes.com/2012/02/16/science/earth/in-heartland-institute-leak-a-plan-to-discredit-climate-teaching.html (accessed February 10, 2018).

Glassman, Matthew Eric, Jacob R. Straus, and Colleen J. Shogan. 2009. *Social Networking and Constituent Communication: Member Use of Twitter During a Two-Week Period in the 111th Congress.* Washington DC: Congressional Research Service.

Glassman, Matthew Eric, Jacob R. Straus, and Colleen J. Shogan. 2013. *Social Networking and Constituent Communication: Member Use of Twitter during a Two-Month Period in the 112th Congress.* Washington DC: Congressional Research Service.

Golbeck, Jennifer, Justin M. Grimes, and Anthony Rogers. 2010. "Twitter Use by the U.S. Congress." *Journal of the American Society for Information Science and Technology* 61(8): 1612–1621.

Gold, Hadas. 2017. "Jason Chaffetz Signs with Fox News." *Politico.* https://www.politico.com/story/2017/06/28/jason-chaffetz-fox-news-240045 (accessed February 10, 2018).

Gold, Matea. 2014. "Tea Party PACs Reap Money for Midterms, but Spend Little on Candidates." *Washington Post*. http://www.washingtonpost.com/politics/tea-party-pacs-reap-money-for-midterms-but-spend-little-on-candidates/2014/04/26/0e52919a-cbd6-11e3-a75e-463587891b57_story.html (accessed July 25, 2014).

Goldberg, Jonah. 2017. "Republican Health-Care Bill Fails as Trump Supporters Blame Paul Ryan." *National Review Online*, March 29. http://www.nationalreview.com/article/446207/republican-health-care-bill-fails-trump-supporters-blame-paul-ryan (accessed May 19, 2017).

Goldfarb, Zachary. 2013. "Tea Party Lawmakers See the Culmination of Years of Effort in Shutdown." https://www.washingtonpost.com/politics/with-shutdown-tea-party-lawmakers-see-the-culmination-of-years-of-effort-to-downsize-government/2013/10/02/3207126a-2ab3-11e3-8ade-a1f23cda135e_story.html?utm_term=.aa3b3d06098f (accessed August 24, 2017).

Gonyea, Don. 2011. "Tea Party Looks to Recapture Election Magic in 2012." NPR.org. http://www.npr.org/2011/11/08/142123503/tea-party-looks-to-impact-presidential-election (accessed June 6, 2017).

Gonyea, Don. 2016. "How Sarah Palin Paved The Way For Donald Trump." NPR.org. https://www.npr.org/2016/01/23/464068087/how-sarah-palin-paved-the-way-for-donald-trump (accessed February 8, 2018).

Gopnik, Adam. 2016. "The Democrats and the Seesaw of Identity Politics." *New Yorker*, December 2. https://www.newyorker.com/news/daily-comment/the-democrats-and-the-seesaw-of-identity-politics (accessed September 11, 2017).

Graham, David A. 2017. "Steve King's Improbable Ascendance." *Atlantic*. https://www.theatlantic.com/politics/archive/2017/03/steve-king-nearer-the-throne/519336/ (accessed March 25, 2017).

Greenblatt, Alan. 2012. "The Public Respects Civility, But Rewards Rudeness." *NPR*. https://www.npr.org/2012/01/26/145910143/the-public-respects-civility-but-rewards-rudeness (accessed February 10, 2018).

Griffin, Andrew. 2016. "What Is Pizzagate? The Hillary Clinton Conspiracy Theory That Led to a Man Opening Fire in a Restaurant." *Independent*, December 5. http://www.independent.co.uk/life-style/gadgets-and-tech/news/pizzagate-what-is-it-explained-hillary-clinton-paedophile-conspiracy-gunman-fake-news-a7456681.html (accessed September 9, 2017).

Grimmer, Justin, and Gary King. 2011. "General Purpose Computer-Assisted Clustering and Conceptualization." *Proceedings of the National Academy of Sciences* 108(7): 2643–2650.

Grimmer, Justin, and Brandon M Stewart. 2013. "Text as Data: The Promise and Pitfalls of Automatic Content Analysis Methods for Political Texts." *Political Analysis* 21(3): 267–297.

Grossman, Matt, and David A. Hopkins. 2015. "Ideological Republicans and Group Interest Democrats: The Asymmetry of American Party Politics." *Perspectives on Politics* 13(1): 119–139.

Groenendyk, Eric W., and Antoine J. Banks. 2014. "Emotional Rescue: How Affect Helps Partisans Overcome Collective Action Problems." *Political Psychology* 35(3): 359–378.

Grynbaum, Michael M., and John Herrman. 2016. "Breitbart, Reveling in Trump's Election, Gains a Voice in His White House." *New York Times*, November 13.

Grynbaum, Michael M., and Sydney Ember. 2016. "If Trump Tweets It, Is It News? A Quandary for the News Media." *New York Times*. https://www.nytimes.com/2016/11/29/business/media/if-trump-tweets-it-is-it-news-a-quandary-for-the-news-media.html (accessed March 7, 2017).

Guarino, Ben. 2017a. "How All-Caps Came to Signify Shouting, as in Trump's 'SEE YOU IN COURT . . .'" *Washington Post*. https://www.washingtonpost.com/news/morning-mix/wp/2017/02/10/how-all-caps-came-to-signify-shouting-as-in-trumps-see-you-in-court/ (accessed March 28, 2017).

Guarino, Ben. 2017b. "Trump Nominates Oklahoma Politician and Climate Skeptic to Run NASA." *Washington Post*. https://www.washingtonpost.com/news/speaking-of-science/

wp/2017/09/05/trump-nominates-oklahoma-politician-and-climate-skeptic-to-run-nasa/ (accessed September 7, 2017).

Guilebeault, Douglas, and Samuel Woolley. 2016. "How Twitter Bots Are Shaping the 2016 Presidential Election." *Atlantic.* https://www.theatlantic.com/technology/archive/2016/11/election-bots/506072/ (accessed September 9, 2017).

Gulati, Girish J., and Christine B. Williams. 2015. "Congressional Campaigns' Motivations for Social Media Adoption." In *Controlling the Message: New Media in American Political Campaigns*, edited by Victoria A. Farrar-Myers and Justin S. Vaughn, 32–52. New York: New York University Press.

Gutmann, Amy, and Dennis Thompson. 2012. *The Spirit of Compromise: Why Governing Demands It and Campaigning Undermines It.* Princeton: Oxford: Princeton University Press.

Haberman, Maggie, and Michael M. Grynbaum. 2016. "Corey Lewandowski, Donald Trump's Campaign Manager, Is Charged with Battery." *New York Times.* https://www.nytimes.com/2016/03/30/us/politics/trump-campaign-manager-corey-lewandowski.html (accessed February 10, 2018).

Hanmer, Michael J., and Kerem Ozan Kalkan. 2013. "Behind the Curve: Clarifying the Best Approach to Calculating Predicted Probabilities and Marginal Effects from Limited Dependent Variable Models." *American Journal of Political Science* 57(1): 263–277.

Harcourt, Bernard E. 2012. *The Politics of Incivility.* Rochester, NY: Social Science Research Network. SSRN Scholarly Paper. http://papers.ssrn.com/abstract=2020679 (accessed May 29, 2014).

Hayes, Stephen. 2016. "A New Era in Conservative Politics: The Tea Party's Lasting Influence." *The Heritage Foundation.* https://www.heritage.org/political-process/report/new-era-conservative-politics-the-tea-partys-lasting-influence (accessed February 10, 2018).

Healy, Patrick, and Jonathan Martin. 2016. "In Second Debate, Donald Trump and Hillary Clinton Spar in Bitter, Personal Terms." *New York Times.* https://www.nytimes.com/2016/10/10/us/politics/presidential-debate.html?_r=1 (accessed March 29, 2017).

Hemmer, Nicole. 2017. "What Donald Trump's Two Twitter Accounts Reveal about His Presidency." *US News & World Report.* https://www.usnews.com/opinion/thomas-jefferson-street/articles/2017-05-30/what-donald-trumps-two-twitter-accounts-reveal-about-his-presidency (accessed June 2, 2017).

Hemphill, Libby, Jahna Otterbacher, and Matthew Shapiro. 2013a. "What's Congress Doing on Twitter?" In *Proceedings of the 2013 Conference on Computer Supported Cooperative Work*, CSCW '13, New York: ACM, 877–886. http://doi.acm.org/10.1145/2441776.2441876.

Hemphill, Libby, Aron Culotta, and Matthew Heston. 2013b. *Framing in Social Media: How the US Congress Uses Twitter Hashtags to Frame Political Issues.* Rochester, NY: Social Science Research Network. SSRN Scholarly Paper. http://papers.ssrn.com/abstract=2317335 (accessed July 23, 2015).

Henry, P. J. and David O. Sears. 2002. "The Symbolic Racism 2000 Scale." *Political Psychology* 23(2): 253–283.

Herbst, Susan. 2010. *Rude Democracy: Civility and Incivility in American Politics.* Philadelphia: Temple University Press.

Hesse, Monica. 2017. "Misery Is Being Paul Ryan." *Washington Post.* https://www.washingtonpost.com/lifestyle/style/misery-is-being-paul-ryan/2017/05/18/560d6e52-3b53-11e7-8854-21f359183e8c_story.html?utm_term=.0fd22a624b12 (accessed May 19, 2017).

Hetherington, Marc J. 2001. "Resurgent Mass Partisanship: The Role of Elite Polarization." *American Political Science Review* 95(3): 619–631.

Hetherington, Marc J., and Jonathan Weiler. 2009. *Authoritarianism and Polarization in American Politics.* New York: Cambridge University Press.

Hill, Dan. 2015. "The Surprising Emotion Driving Ted Cruz." *Reuters Blogs.* http://blogs.reuters.com/great-debate/2015/12/29/the-surprising-emotion-driving-ted-cruz/ (accessed January 2, 2017).

Hill, Libby. 2017. "Kathy Griffin Shocks in Gory Photo Shoot with Donald Trump's (Fake) Head." *Los Angeles Times*, May 30. http://www.latimes.com/entertainment/

la-et-entertainment-news-updates-may-kathy-griffin-shocks-in-gory-photo-1496183372-htmlstory.html (accessed September 9, 2017).

Ho, Catherine. 2016. "U.S. Chamber of Commerce President Tom Donohue Announces Revamp of Group's Lobbying Arm." *Washington Post*. https://www.washingtonpost.com/news/powerpost/wp/2016/11/15/u-s-chamber-of-commerce-president-tom-donohue-announces-revamp-of-groups-lobbying-arm/ (accessed August 23, 2017).

Hochschild, Arlie Russell. 2016. *Strangers in Their Own Land: Anger and Mourning on the American Right*. New York: New Press.

Hoggett, Paul, Hen Wilkinson, and Pheobe Beedell. 2013. "Fairness and the Politics of Resentment." *Journal of Social Policy* 42(3): 567–585.

Hohmann, James. 2013. "The House's New Ron Paul." *Politico*. http://www.politico.com/story/2013/04/the-houses-new-ron-paul-justin-amash-89485.html (accessed November 20, 2015).

Hood, M. V. III, Quentin Kidd, and Irwin L. Morris. 2015a. "Race and the Tea Party in the Old Dominion: Split-Ticket Voting in the 2013 Virginia Elections." *PS: Political Science and Politics*. 48(1): 107–114.

Hood, M. V. III, Quentin Kidd, and Irwin L. Morris. 2015b. "Tea Leaves and Southern Politics: Explaining Tea Party Support among Southern Republicans." *Social Science Quarterly* 96(4): 923–940.

Hook, Janet, and Patrick O'Connor. 2014. "GOP Sees Primaries Taming the Tea Party." *Wall Street Journal*, May 21. http://online.wsj.com/news/articles/SB10001424052702304422704579574292535157208 (accessed July 25, 2014).

Hook, Janet, and Patrick O'Connor. 2015. "Grass-Roots Anger Transforms Republican Party in Congress and Presidential Campaign." *Wall Street Journal*, October 9. http://www.wsj.com/articles/grass-roots-anger-transforms-republican-party-in-congress-and-presidential-campaign-1444430748 (accessed January 2, 2017).

Howard, Marcus E. 2015. "Rep. Jason Chaffetz to Challenge Kevin McCarthy in Race for House Speaker." *Los Angeles Times*, October 4. http://www.latimes.com/nation/politics/la-na-chaffetz-speaker-announce-20151004-story.html (accessed May 21, 2017).

Hudak, John. 2015. "The Republicans Brought the Trump Circus on Themselves." *Newsweek*, July 29. http://www.newsweek.com/republicans-brought-trump-circus-themselves-357965 (accessed August 11, 2017).

Huelskamp, Timothy. 2017. Personal communication (email). October 17.

Hughes, David John, Moss Rowe, Mark Batey, and Andrew Lee. 2012. "A Tale of Two Sites: Twitter vs. Facebook and the Personality Predictors of Social Media Usage." *Computers in Human Behavior* 28(2): 561–569.

Hulse, Carl. 2009. "Boehner Reaches into Bag of Tricks to Disrupt Democrats." *New York Times*. https://www.nytimes.com/2009/07/05/us/politics/05hill-web.html (accessed on February 7, 2018).

Hulse, Carl. 2017. "Another Republican Call to Arms, but Who Will Answer?" *New York Times*. https://www.nytimes.com/2017/10/24/us/politics/republican-party-flake-mccain-corker-bush-trump.html (accessed October 25, 2017).

Institute for Policy Research. 2017. Working Paper, Northwestern University.

Iyengar, Shanto, Gaurav Sood, and Yphtach Lelkes. 2012. "Affect, Not Ideology a Social Identity Perspective on Polarization." *Public Opinion Quarterly* 76(3): 405–431.

Iyengar, Shanto, and Sean J. Westwood. 2015. "Fear and Loathing across Party Lines: New Evidence on Group Polarization." *American Journal of Political Science* 59(3): 690–707.

Jackson, David. 2016. "Trump's Rhetoric Is Harsher than Previous Nominees." *USA Today*. https://www.usatoday.com/story/news/politics/elections/2016/06/23/donald-trump-hillary-clinton-rhetoric/86293780/ (accessed August 11, 2017).

Jacobson Gary. 2000. "Party Polarization in National Politics: The Electoral Connection." In *Polarized Politics: Congress and the President in a Partisan Era*, edited by J. R. Bond and R. Fleisher, 9–30. Washington, DC: CQ Press.

Jalonick, Mary Claire. 2016. "Ted Cruz Does Have Friends in Washington. Check the House" *Associated Press*. http://www.pbs.org/newshour/rundown/ted-cruz-does-have-friends-in-washington-check-the-house/ (accessed May 26, 2017).

Jamieson, Kathleen Hall. 2011. "Civility in Congress (1935–2011) as Reflected in the Taking Down Process." *Report Series: The Annenberg Public Policy Center of the University of Pennsylvania*. http://www.annenbergpublicpolicycenter.org/Downloads/Civility/Civility_9-27-2011_Final.pdf.

Jamieson, Kathleen Hall, and Joseph N. Cappella. 2009. *Echo Chamber: Rush Limbaugh and the Conservative Media Establishment*. New York: Oxford University Press.

Johnson, Jenna, and Matea Gold. 2017. "Trump Calls the Media 'the Enemy of the American People.'" *Washington Post*. https://www.washingtonpost.com/news/post-politics/wp/2017/02/17/trump-calls-the-media-the-enemy-of-the-american-people/ (accessed February 10, 2018).

Jones, Jeffrey M. 2016. "Red States Outnumber Blue for First Time in Gallup Tracking." *Gallup Report*. http://www.gallup.com/poll/188969/red-states-outnumber-blue-first-time-gallup-tracking.aspx (accessed September 8, 2017).

Jones, Robert P. 2016. *The End of White Christian America*. New York: Simon & Schuster.

Jones, Richard P., Daniel Cox, Betsy Cooper, and Rachel Lienesch. 2015. "Anxiety, Nostalgia, and Mistrust: Findings from the 2015 American Values Survey." Public Religion Research Institute. http://www.prri.org/research/survey-anxiety-nostalgia-and-mistrust-findings-from-the-2015-american-values-survey/.

Jossey, Paul H. 2016. "How We Killed the Tea Party." *Politico Magazine*. http://www.politico.com/magazine/story/2016/08/tea-party-pacs-ideas-death-214164 (accessed August 24, 2017).

Jurka, Timothy P, Loren Collingwood, Amber E Boydstun, Emiliano Grossman, and Wouter van Atteveldt. 2013. "RTextTools: A Supervised Learning Package for Text Classification." *R Journal* 5(1): 6–12.

Kabaservice, Geoffrey. 2017. "Are Democrats Becoming Extremists?" *Politico Magazine*, March 15. http://politi.co/2njDUwn (accessed September 8, 2017).

Kagan, Robert. "Trump Is the GOP's Frankenstein Monster. Now He's Strong Enough to Destroy the Party." *Washington Post*. https://www.washingtonpost.com/opinions/trump-is-the-gops-frankenstein-monster-now-hes-strong-enough-to-destroy-the-party/2016/02/25/3e443f28-dbc1-11e5-925f-1d10062cc82d_story.html?utm_term=.1705824cadba (accessed March 21, 2017).

Kaiser Family Foundation, Henry J. 2016. "Poverty Rate by Race/Ethnicity." http://kff.org/other/state-indicator/poverty-rate-by-raceethnicity/?currentTimeframe=0 (accessed January 12, 2017).

Kalkan, Kerem Ozan. 2016. "What Differentiates Trump Supporters from Other Republicans? Ethnocentrism." *Washington Post*. https://www.washingtonpost.com/news/monkey-cage/wp/2016/02/28/what-differentiates-trump-supporters-from-other-republicans-ethnocentrism/ (accessed May 31, 2017).

Kalman, Yoram M., and Darren Gergle. 2014. "Letter Repetitions in Computer-Mediated Communication: A Unique Link between Spoken and Online Language." *Computers in Human Behavior* 34: 187–193.

Kane, Paul. 2010. "'Tea Party' Protesters Accused of Spitting on Lawmaker, Using Slurs." *Washington Post*. http://www.washingtonpost.com/wp-dyn/content/article/2010/03/20/AR2010032002556.html (accessed March 24, 2017).

Kane, Paul. 2017. "A New, Liberal Tea Party Is Forming. Can It Last without Turning against Democrats?" *Washington Post*. https://www.washingtonpost.com/powerpost/a-new-liberal-tea-party-is-forming-can-it-last-without-turning-on-democrats/2017/02/11/94421200-efdf-11e6-9973-c5efb7ccfb0d_story.html (accessed September 8, 2017).

Kane, Paul, and Ed O'Keefe. 2014. "House GOP Leaders Spike Border Bill Rather than See It Defeated." *Washington Post*. https://www.washingtonpost.com/politics/house-gop-leaders-spike-border-bill-rather-than-see-it-defeated/2014/07/31/1b720ff2-18e0-11e4-9e3b-7f2f110c6265_story.html (accessed February 5, 2018).

Kang, Taewoo, Erika Franklin Fowler, Michael M. Franz, and Travis N. Ridout. 2018. "Issue Consistency? Comparing Television Advertising, Tweets, and E-Mail in the 2014 Senate Campaigns." *Political Communication* 35(1): 32–49.

Karpowitz, Christopher F., J. Quin Monson, Kelly D. Patterson, and Jeremy C. Pope. 2011. "Tea Time in America? The Impact of the Tea Party Movement on the 2010 Midterm Elections." *Political Science & Politics*. 44(2): 303–309.

Keith, Tamara. 2015. "4 Speeches to Hear before Bernie Sanders' Socialism Address." NPR. http://www.npr.org/2015/11/18/456401100/listen-4-speeches-bernie-sanders-should-hear-before-his-socialism-address (accessed February 9, 2018).

Kernell, Samuell. 2006. *Going Public: New Strategies of Presidential Leadership*. 4th edition. Washington, DC: CQ Press.

Key, V.O. 1949. *Southern Politics in State and Nation*. New York: Vintage Books.

Kinder, Donald R., and Cindy D. Kam. 2009. *Us Against Them: Ethnocentric Foundations of American Opinion*. Chicago: University of Chicago Press.

Kinder, Donald R, and David O. Sears. 1981. "Prejudice and Politics: Symbolic Racism versus Racial Threats to the Good Life." *Journal of Personality and Social Psychology*. 40(3): 414–431.

Kircher, Madison Malone. 2017. "Paul Ryan Is the Most Hated Man on Twitter, Scientifically." *New York Magazine*. http://nymag.com/selectall/2017/05/paul-ryan-has-worst-ratio-on-twitter.html (accessed February 9, 2018).

Klein, Ezra. 2013. "'People Don't Fully Appreciate How Committed the Tea Party Is to Not Compromising.'" *Washington Post*. https://www.washingtonpost.com/news/wonk/wp/2013/10/04/people-dont-fully-appreciate-how-committed-the-tea-party-is-to-not-compromising/ (accessed January 2, 2017).

Kreiss, Daniel, Joshua O. Barker, and Shannon Zenner. 2017. "Trump Gave Them Hope: Studying the Strangers in Their Own Land." *Political Communication* 34(3): 470–478.

Lang, Robert. 2017. "Hogan on Trump Immigration Plan: 'Solution in Search of a Problem.'" *WBAL Newsradio 1090*. http://www.wbal.com/article/256156/21/hogan-on-trump-immigration-plan-solution-in-search-of-a-problem (accessed September 8, 2017).

La Raja, Raymond J., and Brian F. Schaffner. 2015. *Campaign Finance and Political Polarization: When Purists Prevail*. Ann Arbor: University of Michigan Press.

Lassen, David S., and Aaron R. Brown. 2010. "Twitter: The Electoral Connection?" *Social Science Computer Review*, 29(4), 419–436. doi:10.1177/0894439310382749.

Lavers, Michael K. 2014. "Larry Hogan: Position on Same-Sex Marriage Has 'Evolved.'" *Washington Blade*. http://www.washingtonblade.com/2014/08/08/larry-hogan-position-sex-marriage-evolved/ (accessed September 8, 2017).

Lawless, Jennifer L. 2012. "Twitter and Facebook: New Ways to Send the Same Old Message?" In *iPolitics*, edited by Richard L. Fox and Jennifer Ramos, 206–232. New York: Cambridge University Press.

Layman, Geoffrey C., Thomas M. Carsey, and Juliana Menasce Horowitz. 2006. "Party Polarization in American Politics: Characteristics, Causes, and Consequences." *Annual Review of Political Science* 9(1): 83–110.

Lee, Frances E. 2016. *Insecure Majorities: Congress and the Perpetual Campaign*. Chicago: University Of Chicago Press.

Lee, Jasmine C., and Kevin Quealy. 2016. "The 319 People, Places and Things Donald Trump Has Insulted on Twitter: A Complete List." *New York Times*. https://www.nytimes.com/interactive/2016/01/28/upshot/donald-trump-twitter-insults.html (accessed March 16, 2017).

Lee, Timothy B. 2017. "This Video of Ronald Reagan Shows How Much the Republican Party Has Changed on Immigration." *Vox*, January 29. https://www.vox.com/2017/1/29/14429368/reagan-bush-immigration-attitude (accessed September 7, 2017).

Lefky, Tyler, Paul R. Brewer, and Michael Habegger. 2015. "Tweets on Television News: The Nature and Effects of Campaign Coverage of Twitter." *Electronic News* 9(4): 257–269.

Lefler, Dion. 2010. "Pompeo Apologizes for Tweet to 'Tremendously Offensive' Blog Post about Opponent Goyle." *Wichita Eagle*, August 12. http://www.kansas.com/news/article1041917.html (accessed March 16, 2017).

Letter to the Editor. 2017. "Mr. Danforth Is Wrong on Mr. Trump." *Washington Post* https://www.washingtonpost.com/opinions/mr-danforth-is-wrong-on-mr-trump/2017/08/27/cecaac50-89ba-11e7-96a7-d178cf3524eb_story.html?utm_term=.a05bfecf8a4c (accessed September 8, 2017).

Levin, Ezra, Leah Greenberg, and Angel Padilla. 2017. "To Stop Trump, Democrats Can Learn from the Tea Party." *New York Times*. https://www.nytimes.com/2017/01/02/opinion/to-stop-trump-democrats-can-learn-from-the-tea-party.html (accessed August 11, 2017).

Lilla, Mark. 2016. "The End of Identity Liberalism." *New York Times*. https://www.nytimes.com/2016/11/20/opinion/sunday/the-end-of-identity-liberalism.html (accessed February 8, 2018).

Linkins, Jason. 2013. "Michele Bachmann's Legislative Accomplishments in One Chart." *Huffington Post*. http://www.huffingtonpost.com/2013/05/29/michele-bachmann-legislative-accomplishments_n_3354476.html (accessed January 24, 2017).

Linshi, Jack. 2015. "More People Are Running for Presidential Nomination Than Ever." *Time*, July 8. http://time.com/3948922/jim-gilmore-virginia-2016/ (accessed February 10, 2018).

Livingston, Abby. 2011. "FreedomWorks Backs Richard Mourdock Over Dick Lugar." *Roll Call*. https://www.rollcall.com/news/freedomworks_backs_richard_mourdock_over_dick_lugar-209741-1.html (accessed February 9, 2018).

Livingston, Abby. 2016. "U.S. Rep. Louie Gohmert Calls Hillary Clinton 'Mentally Impaired.'" *Texas Tribune*. https://www.texastribune.org/2016/09/09/louie-gohmert-calls-hillary-clinton-mentally-impai/ (accessed September 9, 2017).

Lizza, Ryan. 2013. "The House of Pain." *New Yorker*. http://www.newyorker.com/magazine/2013/03/04/the-house-of-pain (accessed May 21, 2017).

Lizza, Ryan. 2015. "Paul Ryan Faces the 'Young Guns' Jinx." *New Yorker*, December 10. http://www.newyorker.com/news/daily-comment/paul-ryan-faces-the-young-guns-jinx (accessed May 19, 2017).

Lodge, Milton, and Charles S. Taber. 2013. *The Rationalizing Voter*. Cambridge: Cambridge University Press.

Long, Heather. 2016. "Is America's Middle Class Too Pessimistic?" *CNNMoney*. http://money.cnn.com/2016/07/21/news/economy/us-economy-middle-class/index.html (accessed February 10, 2018).

Long, Heather, and Tami Luhby. 2016. "Yes, This Is the Slowest U.S. Recovery since WWII." *CNNMoney*. http://money.cnn.com/2016/10/05/news/economy/us-recovery-slowest-since-wwii/index.html (February 10, 2018).

López, Haney. 2014. *Dog Whistle Politics: How Coded Racial Appeals Have Reinvented Racism and Wrecked the Middle Class*. New York: Oxford University Press.

Lovelace, Ryan. 2015. "FreedomWorks CEO Cautions Activists about Supporting Donald Trump." *Washington Examiner*, July 22. http://www.washingtonexaminer.com/freedomworks-ceo-cautions-activists-about-supporting-donald-trump/article/2568766 (accessed September 11, 2017).

MacKuen, Michael B., George E. Marcus, Jennifer Wolak, and Luke Keele. 2006. "The Measure and Mismeasure of Emotion." In *Feeling Politics: Emotion in Political Information Processing*, edited by David P. Redlawsk, 31–45. New York: Palgrave Macmillan.

MacKuen, Michael, Jennifer Wolak, Luke Keele, and George E, Marcus. 2010. "Civic Engagements: Resolute Partisanship or Reflective Deliberation." *American Journal of Political Science* 54(2): 440–458.

Malone, Noreen. 2011. "How Much, Exactly, Did the Tea Party 'Compromise'?" *New York Magazine*. http://nymag.com/daily/intelligencer/2011/08/how_much_exactly_did_the_tea_p.html (accessed January 6, 2017).

Mann, Thomas E., and Norman J. Ornstein. 2012. *It's Even Worse than It Looks: How the American Constitutional System Collided with the New Politics of Extremism*. New York: Basic Books.

Marcotte, Amanda. 2016. "War on Federal Parks: Radicalized Republicans Try to Prevent Turning Bears Ears in Utah into a National Monument." *Salon*. http://www.salon.com/2016/07/12/war_on_federal_parks_radicalized_republicans_try_prevent_turning_bears_ears_in_utah_into_a_national_monument/ (accessed January 25, 2017).

Marcus, George E. 2002. *The Sentimental Citizen: Emotion in Democratic Politics*. University Park: Pennsylvania State University Press.

Marcus, George E., Michael MacKuen, Jennifer Wolak, and Luke Keele. 2006. "The Measure and Mismeasure of Emotion." In *Feeling Politics: Emotion In Political Information Processing*, edited by David P. Redlawsk, 31–45. New York: Palgrave Macmillan.

Marcus, George E., W. Russell Neuman, and Michael MacKuen. 2000. *Affective Intelligence and Political Judgment*. Chicago: University of Chicago Press.

Margolin, Emma. 2016. "'Make America Great Again'—Who Said It First?" *NBC News*, September 9. http://www.nbcnews.com/politics/2016-election/make-america-great-again-who-said-it-first-n645716 (accessed June 1, 2017).

Martin, Jenny Beth. 2016. "The Tea Party Movement Is Alive and Well—And We Saw Trump Coming." *Politico Magazine*, November 19. http://politi.co/2fFNzsC (accessed September 11, 2017).

Martin, Jonathan. 2017. "Angry Democrats Study the Tea Party's Playbook." *New York Times*. https://www.nytimes.com/2017/01/23/us/politics/justice-democrats-liberal-progressive.html (accessed September 8, 2017).

Martin, Jonathan, and Jeremy W. Peters. 2017. "As G.O.P. Bends toward Trump, Critics Either Give In or Give Up." *New York Times*. https://www.nytimes.com/2017/10/25/us/politics/trump-republican-party-critics.html (accessed October 30, 2017).

Mascaro, Lisa, Michael A. Memoli, and Mark Z. Barabak. 2014. "Eric Cantor Defeat by Tea Party Shakes Republican Politics to Its Core." *Los Angeles Times*, June 10. http://www.latimes.com/nation/la-na-primaries-20140611-story.html (accessed January 23, 2017).

Masket, Seth. 2009. *No Middle Ground: How Informal Party Organizations Control Nominations and Polarize Legislatures*. Ann Arbor: University of Michigan Press.

Massaro, Toni M., and Robin Stryker. 2012. "Freedom of Speech, Liberal Democracy, and Emerging Evidence on Civility and Effective Democratic Engagement." *Arizona Law Review* 54(2): 375–441.

Matishak, Martin. 2015. "Meet the Freedom Caucus, the Group Inflaming Washington." *Fiscal Times*. https://www.thefiscaltimes.com/2015/10/20/Meet-Freedom-Caucus-Group-Inflaming-Washington (accessed November 23, 2015).

Maxwell, Angie. 2016. "A Tale of Two Tea Parties? Southern Distinctiveness and Tea Party Membership." *PS: Political Science & Politics* 49(2): 210–214.

Maxwell, Angie, and T. Wayne Parent. 2012. "The Obama Trigger: Presidential Approval and Tea Party Membership." *Social Science Quarterly* 93(5): 1385–1401.

Maxwell, Angie and T. Wayne Parent. 2013. "A 'Subterranean Agenda'? Racial Attitudes, Presidential Evaluations and Tea Party Membership." *Race and Social Problems* 5(3): 226–237.

Mayer, Jane. 2010. "Covert Operations: The Billionaire Brothers Who Are Waging a War against Obama." *New Yorker*, August 30.

Mayhew, David R. 1974. *Congress: The Electoral Connection*. New Haven, CT: Yale University Press.

McCarthy, Tom. 2015. "Is This Guy Serious? Could Republican Frontrunner Donald Trump Actually Win?" *Guardian*. https://www.theguardian.com/us-news/2015/jul/19/is-this-guy-serious-could-republican-frontrunner-donald-trump-actually-win (accessed September 11, 2017).

McCaskill, Nolan D. 2016. "Rep. Ellison Calls for DOJ to Investigate Joe Walsh Tweet." *Politico*. https://www.politico.com/story/2016/07/keith-ellison-joe-walsh-tweet-doj-225636 (accessed February 10, 2018).

McDaniel, Jason, and Sean McElwee. 2016. "Trump Supporters Have Cooler Feelings towards Many Groups, Compared to Supporters of Other Candidates." *New West.* https://thewpsa.wordpress.com/2016/05/16/trump-supporters-have-cooler-feelings-towards-many-groups-compared-to-supporters-of-other-candidates/ (accessed May 31, 2017).

McDonald, Jared. 2015. "Who Are the Democrats That Voted for Hogan?" Center for American Politics and Citizenship (CAPC), University of Maryland. https://gvpt.umd.edu/sites/gvpt.umd.edu/files/Who%20are%20the%20Hogan%20Democrats%20(2).pdf.

McKinnon, Shaun, and Yvonne Wingett Sanchez. 2012. "State Lawmakers Push to Take over Millions of Federal Acres." USAtoday.com http://www.usatoday.com/news/nation/story/2012-03-26/states-rights-federal-land/53786490/1 (accessed January 25, 2017).

McManus, Doyle. 2016. "A Race to Claim the Mantle of Anger." *Los Angeles Times.* http://www.latimes.com/opinion/op-ed/la-oe-0117-mcmanus-angry-reform-20160117-column.html (accessed February 4, 2018).

McNitt, Andrew D. 2014. "The Tea Party Movement and the 2012 House Election." *PS: Political Science & Politics* 47(4): 799–805.

Mead, Walter Russell. 2011. "The Tea Party and American Foreign Policy: What Populism Means for Globalism." *Foreign Affairs* 90(2): 28–44.

Mehta, Dhrumil. 2014. "The Age of Tea Party Members in Congress." *FiveThirtyEight,* May 5. http://fivethirtyeight.com/datalab/the-age-of-tea-party-members-in-congress/ (accessed July 22, 2014).

Mehta, Seema. 2016. "Trump's Grass-Roots Supporters Line up to Defend Him, Accuse Political Elite of Exploiting the Controversy." *Los Angeles Times,* October 8. http://www.latimes.com/politics/la-na-pol-trump-gop-voices-20161008-snap-story.html (accessed May 19, 2017).

Metzger, Andy, and Mike Deehan. 2014. "Republicans Baker, Fisher Meet in First Debate of Primary Race for Governor." *Metro West Daily News,* August 14. http://www.metrowestdailynews.com/article/20140813/NEWS/140818543 (accessed September 8, 2017).

Middlekauff, Robert. 2007. *The Glorious Cause: The American Revolution, 1763–1789.* 2nd ed. Oxford: Oxford University Press.

Milbank, Dana. 2010a. "What 'Republican Establishment' Is the Tea Party Rattling?" http://www.washingtonpost.com/wp-dyn/content/article/2010/09/17/AR2010091703198.html (accessed September 9, 2017).

Milbank, Dana. 2010b. "The Republican Party Could Use Some Adults." *Washington Post.* http://www.washingtonpost.com/wp-dyn/content/article/2010/10/29/AR2010102905833.html (accessed May 15, 2017).

Milbank, Dana. 2010c. "The Two Paul Ryans." *Washington Post.* http://www.washingtonpost.com/wp-dyn/content/article/2010/12/07/AR2010120706493.html (accessed May 21, 2017).

Milbank, Dana. 2010d. "A Tea Party of Populist Posers." http://www.washingtonpost.com/wp-dyn/content/article/2010/10/19/AR2010101906085.html (accessed September 11, 2017).

Miller, Joshua. 2014. "Few Similarities Between Baker and Fisher at Cordial Debate." *Boston Globe.* https://www.bostonglobe.com/metro/2014/08/25/few-similarities-between-charlie-baker-mark-fisher-cordial-debate/yuy6DKVVk2J6S4Cj9nOMwM/story.html (accessed September 8, 2017).

Montopoli, Brian. 2012. "Tea Party Supporters: Who They Are and What They Believe." Cbsnews.com., December 12. http://www.cbsnews.com/news/tea-party-supporters-who-they-are-and-what-they-believe/ (accessed January 2, 2017).

Mooney, Chris. 2017. "Historians Say the March for Science Is 'Pretty Unprecedented.'" *Washington Post.* https://www.washingtonpost.com/news/energy-environment/wp/2017/04/22/historians-say-the-march-for-science-is-pretty-unprecedented/?utm_term=.4f2f3ec3e524 (accessed September 8, 2017).

Morin, David T., and Mark A. Flynn. 2014. "We Are the Tea Party!: The Use of Facebook as an Online Political Forum for the Construction and Maintenance of in-Group Identification during the 'GOTV' Weekend." *Communication Quarterly* 62(1): 115–133.

Mosk, Matthew. 2017. "The Un-Trump Republican: Gov. Larry Hogan's Radically Normal Model for the GOP." *Washington Post*. https://www.washingtonpost.com/lifestyle/magazine/2017/07/27/e86813e8-6893-11e7-a1d7-9a32c91c6f40_story.html (accessed September 8, 2017).

Murray, Shailagh. 2006. "Aspiring House Leaders Cite Support." *Washington Post*. http://www.washingtonpost.com/wp-dyn/content/article/2006/01/12/AR2006011201853.html (accessed May 19, 2017).

Mutz, Diana C. 2006. *Hearing the Other Side: Deliberative versus Participatory Democracy*. Cambridge: Cambridge University Press.

Mutz, Diana C. 2015. *In-Your-Face Politics: The Consequences of Uncivil Media*. Princeton, NJ: Princeton University Press.

Mutz, Diana C., and Byron Reeves. 2005. "The New Videomalaise: Effects of Televised Incivility on Political Trust." *American Political Science Review* 99(1): 1–15.

Navarrette, Jr. Ruben. 2017. "The Golden Age of Incivility." *The Monitor*. http://www.themonitor.com/opinion/columnists/article_8114cf1a-4638-11e7-90bd-23be10b035cb.html (accessed February 10, 2018).

Neuman, W. Russell, Lauren Guggenheim, S. Mo Jang, and Soo Young Bae. 2014. "The Dynamics of Public Attention: Agenda-Setting Theory Meets Big Data." *Journal of Communication* 64(2): 193–214

Neville, Helen A. et al. 2000. "Construction and Initial Validation of the Color-Blind Racial Attitudes Scale (CoBRAS)." *Journal of Counseling Psychology* 47(1): 59–70.

Newhauser, Daniel. 2013. "What Happened to the Tea Party Caucus?" *Roll Call*, March 20. http://www.rollcall.com/news/what_happened_to_the_tea_party_caucus-223309-1.html (accessed March 23, 2015).

Newport, Frank. 2017. "Wyoming, North Dakota, and Mississippi Most Conservative." *Gallup News*, January 31. http://www.gallup.com/poll/203204/wyoming-north-dakota-mississippi-conservative.aspx (accessed September 8, 2017).

Newton-Small, Jay. 2011. "Palin's Populist Message." *Time*. http://swampland.time.com/2011/02/05/palin%E2%80%99s-populist-message/ (accessed September 11, 2017).

New York Times. 2010. "Where the Tea Party Candidates Are Running." Ohttp://www.nytimes.com/interactive/2010/10/15/us/politics/tea-party-graphic.html (accessed January 5, 2011).

New York Times Editorial Board. 2015. "Paul Ryan, a Speaker for the Freedom Caucus." *New York Times*. http://www.nytimes.com/2015/10/23/opinion/paul-ryan-a-speaker-for-the-freedom-caucus.html (accessed November 20, 2015).

Noel, Hans. 2016. "Why Can't the G.O.P. Stop Trump?" *New York Times*. https://www.nytimes.com/2016/03/01/opinion/campaign-stops/why-cant-the-gop-stop-trump.html (accessed August 15, 2017).

Norman, Jim. 2015. "In U.S., Support for Tea Party Drops to New Low." *Gallup.com*. http://news.gallup.com/poll/186338/support-tea-party-drops-new-low.aspx (accessed February 5, 2018).

Nuño, Stephen A. 2016. "Debate Takeaway: Incivility Rules, GOP Will Support Trump." *NBC News*, March 4. https://www.nbcnews.com/news/latino/debate-takeaway-incivility-rules-gop-will-support-trump-n531621 (accessed November 20, 2017).

Nyhan, Brendan. 2017a. "Why More Democrats Are Now Embracing Conspiracy Theories." *New York Times*. https://www.nytimes.com/2017/02/15/upshot/why-more-democrats-are-now-embracing-conspiracy-theories.html (accessed May 31, 2017).

Nyhan, Brendan. 2017b. "Norms Matter." *Politico Magazine*. https://www.politico.com/magazine/story/2017/09/05/why-norms-matter-politics-trump-215535 (accessed November 9, 2017).

Palmer, Anna, and Laura French. 2015. "House Rebels Crusade for Cruz." *Politico*. http://politi.co/1MEDd1g (accessed May 26, 2017).

Pareene, Alex. 2014. "House Conservatives Fed up with Conservative Caucus, Form Even More Conservative Caucus." http://www.salon.com/2014/01/17/house_conservatives_fed_up_with_conservative_caucus_form_even_more_conservative_caucus/ (accessed March 23, 2015).

Parker, Ashley, and Steve Eder. 2016. "Inside the Six Weeks Donald Trump Was a Nonstop 'Birther.'" *New York Times*. https://www.nytimes.com/2016/07/03/us/politics/donald-trump-birther-obama.html (accessed October 25, 2017).

Parker, Christopher. 2010. "2010 Multi-state Survey on Race and Politics." University of Washington Institute for the Study of Ethnicity, Race and Sexuality. http://depts.washington.edu/uwiser/racepolitics.html (accessed February 7, 2018).

Parker, Christopher S., and Matt A. Barreto. 2013. *Change They Can't Believe In: The Tea Party and Reactionary Politics in America*. 2nd ed. Princeton, NJ: Princeton University Press.

Pearlstein, Steven. 2017. "The GOP Cannot Fix Itself—Let Alone American Health Care." *Washington Post*. https://www.washingtonpost.com/news/wonk/wp/2017/07/20/pearlstein-on-gop-health-care-debacle/ (accessed August 23, 2017).

Peters, Jeremy W. 2018. "Steve Bannon Steps Down From Breitbart Post." *New York Times*. https://www.nytimes.com/2018/01/09/us/politics/steve-bannon-breitbart-trump.html (accessed February 10, 2018).

Pew Research Center. 2011. "More Now Disagree with Tea Party—Even in Tea Party Districts." Pew Research Center for the People and the Press. http://www.people-press.org/2011/11/29/more-now-disagree-with-tea-party-even-in-tea-party-districts/ (accessed August 21, 2017).

Pew Research Center. 2017. "Partisan Conflict and Congressional Outreach." Pew Research Center for the People and the Press. http://www.people-press.org/2017/02/23/who-is-going-negative-leadership-and-very-liberal-or-conservative-members-most-critical-of-other-side/ (accessed May 31, 2017).

Phillip, Abby. 2017. "The Curious Case of 'Nicole Mincey,' the Trump Fan Who May Actually Be a Bot." *Washington Post*. https://www.washingtonpost.com/politics/the-curious-case-of-nicole-mincey-the-trump-fan-who-may-actually-be-a-russian-bot/2017/08/07/7aa67410-7b96-11e7-9026-4a0a64977c92_story.html?utm_term=.7aa9761a311e (accessed August 17, 2017).

Phillips, Amber. 2016. "The Tea Party Just Officially Swiped John Boehner's House Seat." *Washington Post*. https://www.washingtonpost.com/news/the-fix/wp/2016/03/16/one-last-indignity-the-tea-party-swipes-john-boehners-seat/?utm_term=.94c776db9ddd (accessed May 15, 2017).

Phillips, Amber. 2017. "The Sorry State of Political Discourse Right Now, in Five Bernie Sanders Tweets." https://www.washingtonpost.com/news/the-fix/wp/2017/03/06/the-sorry-state-of-political-discourse-right-now-in-five-bernie-sanders-tweets/?utm_term=.5f728bc11f65 (accessed August 11, 2017).

Poole, Keith T. and Howard L. Rosenthal. 1997. *Congress: A Political Economic History of Roll Call Voting*. New York: Oxford University Press.

Porter, Tom. 2017. "White Nationalists from All Corners of the Internet Are Uniting for the 'Largest Racist Protest in Decades.'" *Newsweek*, August 8. http://www.newsweek.com/white-nationalists-kkk-demo-virginia-647748 (accessed September 6, 2017).

Postel, Charles. 2010. "Sarah Palin a Populist?" *Politico*, March 3. http://www.politico.com/news/stories/0310/33781.html (accessed September 11, 2017).

Postel. Charles. 2012. "The Tea Party in Historical Perspective: A Conservative Response to a Crisis of Political Economy." In *Steep: The Precipitous Rise of the Tea Party*, edited by Lawrence Rosenthal and Christine Trost, 25–46. Berkeley: University of California Press.

Preston, Julia. 2012. "Romney's Plan for 'Self-Deportation' Has Conservative Support." *New York Times*, January 24.

Prokop, Andrew. 2012. "Losing Obama's Favorite Republican." *New Yorker*, May 8. http://www.newyorker.com/news/news-desk/losing-obamas-favorite-republican (accessed May 15, 2017).

Quinn, Garrett. 2014. "How Charlie Baker Won and Quite Possibly Revived the Massachusetts Republican Party." *Mass Live*. http://www.masslive.com/news/boston/index.ssf/2014/11/how_charlie_baker_won.html (accessed September 8, 2017).

Ragusa, Jordan M., and Anthony Gaspar. 2016. "Where's the Tea Party? An Examination of the Tea Party's Voting Behavior in the House of Representatives." *Political Research Quarterly* 69(2): 361–372.

Raju, Manu. 2015. "Ted Cruz Accuses Mitch McConnell of Telling a 'Flat-out Lie.'" *Politico*. http://www.politico.com/story/2015/07/ted-cruz-says-mitch-mcconnell-lies-export-import-bank-120583.html (accessed July 24, 2015).

Rampell, Catherine. 2016. "Surprise—Trump, Cruz and Rubio Aren't All That Different." *Washington Post*. https://www.washingtonpost.com/opinions/surprise--trump-cruz-and-rubio-arent-all-that-different/2016/02/25/966954fe-dbfd-11e5-891a-4ed04f4213e8_story.html?utm_term=.d05c94b4f594 (accessed February 4, 2018).

Rauch, Jonathan. 2016. "How American Politics Went Insane." *Atlantic*. http://www.theatlantic.com/magazine/archive/2016/07/how-american-politics-went-insane/485570/ (accessed January 10, 2017).

Reinlin, Lauren. 2011. "Crowd Presses Congressman." *Northwest Florida Daily News*, March 23.

Rich, Frank. 2010. "Palin's Cunning Sleight of Hand." *New York Times*. https://www.nytimes.com/2010/02/14/opinion/14rich.html (accessed September 11, 2017).

Rosenberg, Eli, and Amar Nadhir. 2018. "After Drubbing by Media, Trump's Ambassador to the Netherlands Apologizes for Anti-Muslim Remarks." *Washington Post*. https://www.washingtonpost.com/news/worldviews/wp/2018/01/12/after-drubbing-by-the-press-trumps-netherlands-ambassador-apologizes-for-anti-muslim-remarks/ (accessed February 8, 2018).

Ross, Janell. 2016. "The Fix: From Mexican Rapists to Bad Hombres, The Trump Campaign in Two Moments." *Washington Post*. https://www.washingtonpost.com/news/the-fix/wp/2016/10/20/from-mexican-rapists-to-bad-hombres-the-trump-campaign-in-two-moments/?utm_term=.e49854201870 (accessed February 3, 2018).

Rothwell, Jonathan T. and Pablo Diego-Rosell, 2016. "Explaining Nationalist Political Views: The Case of Donald Trump." Working paper, Gallup. Available at SSRN: https://ssrn.com/abstract=2822059 or http://dx.doi.org/10.2139/ssrn.2822059.

Roundtree, Clark. 2016. "How American Politics Became so Uncivil." *AL.com*. http://www.al.com/opinion/index.ssf/2016/03/how_american_politics_became_s.html (accessed February 10, 2018).

Rubin, Jennifer. 2015. "My Gracious: What Has Happened to Our Politics?" *Washington Post*. https://www.washingtonpost.com/blogs/right-turn/wp/2015/09/27/my-gracious-what-has-happened-to-our-politics/?utm_term=.5f174fae5e9b (accessed May 15, 2017).

Rubin, Jennifer. 2017. "Paul Ryan and House GOP Are in Denial as Inferno Engulfs White House." *Washington Post*. https://www.washingtonpost.com/blogs/right-turn/wp/2017/05/18/paul-ryan-and-house-gop-are-in-denial-as-inferno-engulfs-white-house/?utm_term=.af88a9c4335f (accessed May 19, 2017).

Rucker, Philip. 2017. "Sebastian Gorka, a Fiery Nationalist and Bannon Ally, Abruptly Exits White House." *Washington Post*. https://www.washingtonpost.com/politics/sebastian-gorka-a-fiery-nationalist-and-bannon-ally-abruptly-exits-white-house/2017/08/25/426d3d6a-89f9-11e7-a94f-3139abce39f5_story.html (accessed October 30, 2017).

Sakuma. 2016. "How the GOP's Rhetoric on Immigration Created a Demagogue." *MSNBC*. http://www.msnbc.com/msnbc/how-the-gops-rhetoric-immigration-created-demagogue (accessed September 7, 2017).

Santos, Fernanda. 2012. "Results of Primary Elections in Arizona Give Democrats Hope." *New York Times*. http://www.nytimes.com/2012/08/30/us/politics/results-of-primary-elections-in-arizona-give-democrats-hope.html (accessed December 28, 2016).

Sapiro, Virginia. 1999. "Considering Political Civility Historically: A Case Study of the United States." Presented at the Annual Meeting of the International Society for Political Psychology, Amsterdam.

Sargent, Greg. 2016a. "Why Is Rubio Talking about Trump's Spray Tan and Small Hands? These Charts Explain It." *Washington Post.* https://www.washingtonpost.com/blogs/plum-line/wp/2016/02/29/why-is-rubio-talking-about-trumps-spray-tan-and-small-hands-these-charts-explain-it/?utm_term=.9fc9c1711949 (accessed March 31, 2017).

Sargent, Greg. 2016b. "Donald Trump Is a Racist Conspiracy Theorist. Don't Let Him Lie His Way out of It." *Washington Post.* https://www.washingtonpost.com/blogs/plum-line/wp/2016/09/16/donald-trump-is-a-racist-conspiracy-theorist-dont-let-him-lie-his-way-out-of-it/?utm_term=.c7e7d9a71388 (accessed October 25, 2017).

Saunders, Kyle L., and Alan I. Abramowitz. 2004. "Ideological Realignment and Active Partisans in the American Electorate." *American Politics Research* 32(3): 285–309.

Schaffner, Brian, Matthew MacWilliams, and Tatishe Nteta. 2017. "Explaining White Polarization in the 2016 Vote for President: The Sobering Role of Racism and Sexism." http://people.umass.edu/schaffne/schaffner_et_al_trump.pdf).

Schlesinger, Robert. 2016. "Donald Trump Is the Presumptive GOP Nominee: What Now?" *US News & World Report.* https://www.usnews.com/opinion/articles/2016-05-03/donald-trump-is-the-presumptive-gop-nominee-what-now (accessed September 11, 2017).

Schoenberg, Shira. 2017. "Donald Trump's Proposed Cuts to NIH." *Mass Live.* http://www.masslive.com/politics/index.ssf/2017/03/gov_charlie_baker_alarmed_by_p.html (accessed September 8, 2017).

Schouten, Fredreka. 2013. "Tea Party Groups Take Aim at Farm Bill, Republicans." *USA Today.* https://www.usatoday.com/story/news/politics/2013/10/23/tea--farm-bill-showdown/3172141/ (accessed September 9, 2017).

Schreckinger, Ben. 2015. "Ted Cruz's Most Provocative Quotes." *Politico,* http://www.politico.com/story/2015/03/ted-cruz-provocative-quotes-116304 (accessed February 10, 2018).

Schwartz, Ian. 2015. "Boehner: 'I Was In The Tea Party Before There Was A Tea Party.'" *Real Clear Politics.* https://www.realclearpolitics.com/video/2015/01/28/boehner_i_was_in_the_tea_party_before_there_was_a_tea_party.html (accessed February 9, 2018).

Schwartz, Ian. 2016. "Trump: I'm Not Against Free Trade, I Want Fair Trade; I Just Want Better Deals." *Real Clear Politics.* http://www.realclearpolitics.com/video/2016/06/30/trump_im_not_against_free_trade_i_want_fair_trade_i_just_want_better_deals.html (accessed February 9, 2018).

Shane, Scott. 2016. "Combative, Populist Steve Bannon Found His Man in Donald Trump." *New York Times.* https://www.nytimes.com/2016/11/27/us/politics/steve-bannon-white-house.html (accessed August 17, 2017).

Shapiro, Matthew A., and Libby Hemphill. 2016. "Politicians and the Policy Agenda: Does Use of Twitter by the U.S. Congress Direct *New York Times* Content?" *Policy & Internet.* doi: 10.1002/poi3.120.

Shear, Michael D. 2012. "Ryan Brings the Tea Party to the Ticket." *New York Times.* https://thecaucus.blogs.nytimes.com/2012/08/12/ryan-brings-the-tea-party-to-the-ticket/ (accessed August 17, 2017).

Shear, Michael D., and Matt Apuzzo. 2017. "F.B.I. Director James Comey Is Fired by Trump." *New York Times.* https://www.nytimes.com/2017/05/09/us/politics/james-comey-fired-fbi.html (accessed February 10, 2018).

Shear, Michael D., Adam Goldman, and Emily Cochrane. 2017. "Steve Scalise Among 4 Shot at Baseball Field; Suspect Is Dead." *New York Times.* https://www.nytimes.com/2017/06/14/us/steve-scalise-congress-shot-alexandria-virginia.html (accessed September 6, 2017).

Sheets, Connor Adams. 2013. "What Does TCOT Mean? About The #TCOT Hashtag Top Conservatives Use on Twitter." *International Business Times.* http://www.ibtimes.com/what-does-tcot-mean-about-tcot-hashtag-top-conservatives-use-twitter-1109812 (February 9, 2018).

Shephard, Alex. 2017. "The D.C. Think Tank Behind Donald Trump." *New Republic*, February 22. https://newrepublic.com/article/140271/dc-think-tank-behind-donald-trump (accessed May 17, 2017).

Shesgreen, Deirdre. 2015. "Speaker John Boehner Bids Farewell 'with No Regrets or Burdens.'" *USA Today.* https://www.usatoday.com/story/news/politics/2015/10/29/house-speaker-john-boehner-bids-farewell-no-regrets-burdens/74794780/ (accessed May 15, 2017).

Sides, John, and Lynn Vavreck. 2013. *The Gamble: Choice and Chance in the 2012 Presidential Election*. Princeton, NJ: Princeton University Press.

Silver, Nate. 2016. "Marco Rubio Never Had a Base." *FiveThirtyEight*, March 9. https://fivethirtyeight.com/features/marco-rubio-never-had-a-base/ (accessed August 3, 2017).

Silverman, Ellie, and Michael Laris. 2017. "Charlottesville Victim: 'She Was There Standing up for What Was Right.'" *Washington Post.* https://www.washingtonpost.com/local/public-safety/charlottesville-victim-she-was-there-standing-up-for-what-was-right/2017/08/13/00d6b034-8035-11e7-b359-15a3617c767b_story.html (accessed September 6, 2017).

Skocpol, Theda. 2012. "Mitt Romney, the Stealth Tea Party Candidate." *Washington Post.* https://www.washingtonpost.com/opinions/mitt-romney-the-stealth-tea-party-candidate/2012/01/31/gIQAy0BZnQ_story.html (accessed August 2, 2017).

Skocpol, Theda. 2014. "Tea Party Forces Still Control the Republican Agenda." *Talking Points Memo*, July 3. http://talkingpointsmemo.com/cafe/tea-party-forces-still-control-the-republican-agenda (accessed January 24, 2017).

Skocpol, Theda, and Vanessa Williamson. 2012. *The Tea Party and the Remaking of Republican Conservatism*. New York: Oxford University Press.

Smith, David. 2017. "Q&A: What Are Trump and the White House's Links to the Far Right?" *Guardian.* http://www.theguardian.com/us-news/2017/aug/14/donald-trump-steve-bannon-breitbart-news-alt-right-charlottesville (accessed September 9, 2017).

Smith, Jamil. 2017. "Why the Democrats' 'Better Deal' Is Political Suicide." *Vanity Fair.* https://www.vanityfair.com/news/2017/08/why-the-democrats-better-deal-is-political-suicide (accessed September 9. 2017).

Soave, Robby. 2017. "Frustration with Political Correctness Was a Huge Predictor of Whether You Voted for Trump." *Reason.* http://reason.com/blog/2017/05/10/frustration-with-political-correctness-w (accessed September 9, 2017).

Sobieraj, Sarah, and Jeffrey Berry. 2011. "From Incivility to Outrage: Political Discourse in Blogs, Talk Radio, and Cable News." *Political Communication* 28(1): 19–41.

Spivak, Joshua. 2012. "The Tea Party's New Model: Experienced Candidates Magnifying Movement's Influence." *Time.* http://swampland.time.com/2012/08/24/the-tea-partys-new-model-experienced-candidates-magnifying-movements-influence/ (accessed January 24, 2017).

Stasavage, David. 2007. "Polarization and Publicity: Rethinking the Benefits of Deliberative Democracy." *Journal of Politics* 69(1): 59–72.

Steinhauer, Jennifer. 2016. "Paul Ryan Faces Tea Party Forces That He Helped Unleash." *New York Times.* https://www.nytimes.com/2016/03/03/us/politics/paul-ryan-faces-tea-party-forces-that-he-helped-unleash.html?mcubz=1&_r=0 (accessed May 19, 2017).

Steinhauer, Jennifer. 2017. "Steve King, Hurling Insults at Immigrants, Is Rebuked by His Own Party." *New York Times.* https://www.nytimes.com/2017/03/13/us/politics/steve-king-babies-civilization.html (accessed August 20, 2017).

Stolberg, Sheryl Gay. 2017. "Jeff Flake, a Fierce Trump Critic, Will Not Seek Re-Election for Senate." *New York Times.* https://www.nytimes.com/2017/10/24/us/politics/jeff-flake-arizona.html (accessed October 25, 2017).

Sullentrop, Chris. 2006. "Majority Leader Boehner: Who's Happy?" *New York Times.* https://opinionator.blogs.nytimes.com/2006/02/03/majority-leader-boehner-whos-happy/?_r=0 (accessed May 19, 2017).

Sullivan, Eileen, and Maggie Haberman. 2017. "Trump Shares, Then Deletes, Twitter Post of Train Hitting Cartoon Person Covered by CNN Logo." *New York Times.* https://www.nytimes.com/

2017/08/15/us/politics/trump-shares-then-deletes-twitter-post-of-cnn-cartoon-being-hit-by-train.html (accessed September 6, 2017).

Tannen, Deborah. 2011. "Why Is 'Compromise' a Dirty Word?" *Politico*. https://www.politico.com/news/stories/0611/57044.html (accessed February 9, 2018).

Taub, Amanda. 2016. "The Rise of American Authoritarianism." *Vox*, March 1. https://www.vox.com/2016/3/1/11127424/trump-authoritarianism (May 31, 2017).

Tausczik, Yla R., and James W. Pennebaker. 2010. "The Psychological Meaning of Words: LIWC and Computerized Text Analysis Methods." *Journal of Language and Social Psychology* 29(1): 24–54.

Tesler, Michael. 2013. "The Return of Old-Fashioned Racism to White Americans' Partisan Preferences in the Early Obama Era." *Journal of Politics* 75(1): 110–123.

Tesler, Michael. 2016a. "Birtherism Was Why so Many Republicans Liked Trump in the First Place." *Washington Post*. https://www.washingtonpost.com/news/monkey-cage/wp/2016/09/19/birtherism-was-why-so-many-republicans-liked-trump-in-the-first-place/ (accessed June 13, 2017).

Tesler, Michael. 2016b. *Post-Racial or Most-Racial: Race and Politics in the Obama Era*. Chicago: University of Chicago Press.

Tharoor, Ishaan. 2017. "Trump's Twitter Feed Is a Gateway to Authoritarianism." *Washington Post*. https://www.washingtonpost.com/news/worldviews/wp/2017/03/06/trumps-twitter-feed-is-a-gateway-to-authoritarianism/ (accessed: March 7, 2017).

Theocharis, Yannis, et al. 2016. "A Bad Workman Blames His Tweets: The Consequences of Citizens' Uncivil Twitter Use When Interacting with Party Candidates." *Journal of Communication* 66(6): 1007–1031.

Thorson, Kjerstin, Emily Vraga, and Brian Ekdale. 2010. "Credibility in Context: How Uncivil Online Commentary Affects News Credibility." *Mass Communication and Society* 13(3): 289–313.

Tillett, Emily. 2017. "Steve Scalise Must 'Relearn' How to Walk after Alexandria Shooting, Paul Ryan Says." *CBS News*, August 22. https://www.cbsnews.com/news/steve-scalise-learning-to-walk-again-after-alexandria-shooting-paul-ryan/ (accessed September 6, 2017).

Timberg, Craig. 2016. "Russian Propaganda Effort Helped Spread 'Fake News' during Election, Experts Say." *Washington Post*. https://www.washingtonpost.com/business/economy/russian-propaganda-effort-helped-spread-fake-news-during-election-experts-say/2016/11/24/793903b6-8a40-4ca9-b712716af66098fe_story.html?utm_term=.b5c6ec023aba3 (accessed February 7, 2018).

Tobias, Jimmy. 2016a. "Beyond the Bundys: The Far Right and the Future of Conservation." *Pacific Standard*, January 28. https://psmag.com/beyond-the-bundys-the-far-right-and-the-future-of-conservation-aefcb6374c6f#.s0rbvqv1s (January 25, 2017).

Tobias, Jimmy. 2016b. "Land Grab Duplicity." *Pacific Standard*, May 10. https://psmag.com/land-grab-duplicity-d22e9328ce1#.srfom4yjz (accessed January 25, 2017).

Todd, Chuck, Mark Murray, Domenico Montanaro, and Ali Weinberg. 2010. "First Thoughts: Why Dems Are on the Verge of Losing the House." *NBC News*, http://firstread.nbcnews.com/_news/2010/10/27/5359501-first-thoughts-why-dems-are-on-the-verge-of-losing-the-house (accessed January 24, 2017).

Tomasky, Michael. 2014. "Where Does the Tea Party Find These People?" *Daily Beast*. http://www.thedailybeast.com/articles/2014/02/25/where-does-the-tea-party-find-these-people.html (accessed January 24, 2017).

Tope, Daniel, Justin T. Pickett, and Ted Chiricos. 2015. "Anti-Minority Attitudes and Tea Party Movement Membership." *Social Science Quarterly* 51: 322–337.

Tromble, Rebekah. 2016. "Thanks for (Actually) Responding! How Citizen Demand Shapes Politicians' Interactive Practices on Twitter." *New Media & Society*. http://journals.sagepub.com/doi/abs/10.1177/1461444816669158.

Tumasjan, Andranik, Timm O. Sprenger, Philipp G. Sandner, and Isabell M. Welpe. 2010. "Election Forecasts with Twitter: How 140 Characters Reflect the Political Landscape." *Social Science Computer Review*. http://journals.sagepub.com/doi/abs/10.1177/0894439310386557.

Tumulty, Karen, and Philip Rucker. 2015. "Trump Roils First Debate among GOP Contenders." *Washington Post*. https://www.washingtonpost.com/politics/donald-trump-dominates-raucous-republican-debate/2015/08/06/b8a5f0e6-3c79-11e5-8e98-115a3cf7d7ae_story.html?utm_term=.8e2082ab84c5 (accessed March 29, 2017).

Umana, Brian. 2014. "I'm a Democrat and I Helped the Tea Party Unseat Eric Cantor." *Washington Post*. https://www.washingtonpost.com/posteverything/wp/2014/06/13/im-a-democrat-and-i-helped-the-tea-party-unseat-eric-cantor/ (accessed January 23, 2017).

Uslaner, Eric M. 1993. *The Decline of Comity in Congress*. Ann Arbor: University of Michigan Press.

Valentino, Nicholas A., Ted Brader, Eric W. Groenendyk, Krysha Gregorowicz, and Vincent L. Hutchings. 2011. "Election Night's Alright for Fighting: The Role of Emotions in Political Participation." *Journal of Politics* 73(1): 156–170.

Van Dongen, Rachel. 2016. "Republicans Take to Social Media to Bash Obama's Gun Control Announcement." *Washington Post*. https://www.washingtonpost.com/news/powerpost/wp/2016/01/05/republicans-take-to-social-media-to-bash-obamas-gun-control-announcement/ (accessed May 23, 2017).

Victor, Daniel. 2017. "Trump, Calling Journalists 'Sick People,' Puts Media on Edge." *New York Times*. https://www.nytimes.com/2017/08/23/business/media/trump-rally-media-attack.html (accessed September 6, 2017).

Vogel, Kenneth P. 2011. "Tea Party Dilemma: What to Do about Mitt Romney." *Politico*, June 24. http://www.politico.com/news/stories/0611/57674.html (accessed June 6, 2017).

Volden, Craig, and Alan E. Wiseman. 2014. *Legislative Effectiveness in the United States Congress: The Lawmakers*. New York: Cambridge University Press.

Von Drehle, David. 2017. "Steve Jobs Gave Us President Trump." *Washington Post*. https://www.washingtonpost.com/opinions/steve-jobs-gave-us-president-trump/2017/09/05/f4f487e4-9260-11e7-aace-04b862b2b3f3_story.html (accessed September 8, 2017).

Wagner, John. 2017. "In Action after Action, Trump Appeals Primarily to His Dwindling Base." *Washington Post*. https://www.washingtonpost.com/politics/in-action-after-action-trump-appeals-primarily-to-his-dwindling-base/2017/09/03/a3ab9bf4-8f57-11e7-91d5-ab4e4bb76a3a_story.html?utm_term=.6d601cf6f3fe (accessed September 3, 2017).

Waldman, Paul. 2014. "The Tea Party May Be Losing Races, but It's Actually Winning." *Washington Post*. https://www.washingtonpost.com/blogs/plum-line/wp/2014/08/06/the-tea-party-may-be-losing-races-but-its-actually-winning/?tid=a_inl&utm_term=.42f08efbbb1d (accessed January 25, 2017).

Wallace, Sophia J., Chris Zepeda-Millán, and Michael Jones-Correa. 2014. "Spatial and Temporal Proximity: Examining the Effects of Protests on Political Attitudes." *American Journal of Political Science* 58(2): 433–448.

Walsh, Deirdre, Tal Kopan, and Manu Raju. 2015. "Kevin McCarthy Faces House Conservatives." *CNN*, October 6. http://www.cnn.com/2015/10/06/politics/house-speaker-mccarthy-chaffetz-freedom-caucus/index.html (accessed November 23, 2015).

Wang, Amy. 2017. "One Group Loved Trump's Remarks about Charlottesville: White Supremacists." *Washington Post*. https://www.washingtonpost.com/news/post-nation/wp/2017/08/13/one-group-loved-trumps-remarks-about-charlottesville-white-supremacists/?utm_term=.1c00403c9673 (accessed September 6, 2017).

Ward, Ian. 2015. "Tea Party Imitators? The Campaign against the Carbon Tax, the Media and a New Uncivil Politics." *Australian Journal of Political Science* 50(2): 1–16.

Warren, Elizabeth. 2017. "The GOP's Strategy for Obamacare? Repeal and Run." BostonGlobe.com. https://www.bostonglobe.com/opinion/2017/01/15/gop-strategy-for-aca-repeal-and-run/aCcjrJWQDjx4r4aRxkMCaL/story.html (accessed September 9, 2017).

Wasson, Erik. 2012. "Club for Growth Issues Tea Party Purity Scorecard on Freshmen." *The Hill*, May 15. http://thehill.com/policy/finance/227567-club-for-growth-issues-tea-party-purity-scorecard-on-freshmen (accessed August 6, 2014).

Wayne, Teddy. 2017. "The Culture of Nastiness." *New York Times*. https://www.nytimes.com/2017/02/18/fashion/donald-trump-hillary-clinton-nasty-woman-social-media.html (accessed March 7, 2017).

Weaver, David A., and Joshua M. Scacco. 2013. "Revisiting the Protest Paradigm: The Tea Party as Filtered through Prime-Time Cable News." *International Journal of Press/Politics* 18(1): 61–84.

Weber, Christopher. 2013. "Emotions, Campaigns, and Political Participation." *Political Research Quarterly* 66(2): 414–428.

Wehner, Peter. 2015. "Why Ben Carson's Nazi Analogies Matter." *New York Times*. https://www.nytimes.com/2015/10/20/opinion/why-ben-carsons-nazi-analogies-matter.html (accessed March 31, 2017).

Weigel, David. 2013. "The Tea Party Caucus Is Dead and That's OK." *Slate*. http://www.slate.com/blogs/weigel/2013/03/20/the_tea_party_caucus_is_dead_and_that_s_okay.html (accessed July 25, 2014).

Weigel, David. 2017. "Conservative Voices Blame Alexandria Shooting on Democrats and the Left." *Washington Post*. https://www.washingtonpost.com/news/powerpost/wp/2017/06/14/conservative-voices-blame-alexandria-shooting-on-democrats-and-the-left/ (accessed September 9, 2017).

Weiner, Rachel. 2013. "McCain Calls Paul, Cruz, Amash 'Wacko Birds.'" *Washington Post*. https://www.washingtonpost.com/news/post-politics/wp/2013/03/08/mccain-calls-paul-cruz-amash-wacko-birds/ (accessed September 9, 2017).

Weiner, Rachel. 2014. "For Rep. Dave Brat, a Tricky Balance." *Washington Post*. https://www.washingtonpost.com/local/virginia-politics/for-rep-dave-brat-a-tricky-balance/2014/11/26/c960cb22-7046-11e4-893f86bd390a3340_story.html?utm_term=.2acee6a8d9bb (accessed January 23, 2017).

Weisman, Jonathan, and Jennifer Steinhauer. 2014. "Local Tea Party Activists See Own Groups among Washington Adversaries." *New York Times*. http://www.nytimes.com/2014/05/13/us/politics/tea-party-activists-see-own-groups-among-washington-adversaries.html (accessed July 25, 2014).

Welch, David. 2012. "Where Have You Gone, Bill Buckley?" *New York Times*. http://www.nytimes.com/2012/12/04/opinion/where-have-you-gone-bill-buckley.html (accessed January 2, 2017).

White, Ben. 2016. "Strong Economic News Undercuts Trump's Doom-and-Gloom Message." *Politico*. https://www.politico.com/story/2016/10/us-economy-2016-third-quarter-trump-230441 (accessed February 10, 2018).

Will, George. 2017. "A Trumpian Shadow Hangs over the Virginia Election." *Washington Post*. https://www.washingtonpost.com/opinions/a-trumpian-shadow-hangs-over-the-virginia-election/2017/10/25/84919a74-b8e8-11e7-be94-fabb0f1e9ffb_story.html (accessed November 9, 2017).

Williams, Vanessa. 2017. "An Identity Crisis for Identity Politics." *Washington Post*. https://www.washingtonpost.com/news/post-nation/wp/2017/07/27/an-identity-crisis-for-identity-politics/ (accessed September 11, 2017).

Williamson, Vanessa. 2016. "What the Tea Party Tells Us about the Trump Presidency." *Brookings*. https://www.brookings.edu/blog/fixgov/2016/11/09/tea-party-and-trump-presidency/ (accessed August 17, 2017).

Williamson, Vanessa. 2017. "Could This Be the Left's Tea Party?" *CNN*. http://www.cnn.com/2017/02/12/opinions/tea-party-of-the-left-williamson-opinion/index.html (accessed February 9, 2018).

Williamson, Vanessa, Theda Skocpol, and John Coggin. 2011. "The Tea Party and the Remaking of Republican Conservatism." *Perspectives on Politics* 9(1): 25–43.

Wong, Scott. 2017. "Tea Party Favorite to Lead Conservative Think Tank." *The Hill*, June 29. http://thehill.com/homenews/house/339987-huelskamp-to-lead-conservative-think-tank (accessed February 10, 2018).

Wood, Thomas. 2017. "Racism Motivated Trump Voters More than Authoritarianism." *Washington Post.* https://www.washingtonpost.com/news/monkey-cage/wp/2017/04/17/racism-motivated-trump-voters-more-than-authoritarianism-or-income-inequality/ (accessed February 9, 2018).

Young, Lori, and Stuart Soroka. 2012. "Affective News: The Automated Coding of Sentiment in Political Texts." *Political Communication* 29(2): 205–231.

Zaller, John. 1992. *The Nature and Origins of Mass Opinion.* New York: Cambridge University Press.

Zezima, Katie. 2016. "Glenn Beck Endorses Ted Cruz." *Washington Post.* https://www.washingtonpost.com/news/post-politics/wp/2016/01/23/glenn-beck-endorses-ted-cruz/ (accessed September 11, 2017).

Zorn, Eric. 2017. "Joe Walsh's Tweets about Jimmy Kimmel's Baby Shed Light on Health Care Debate." *Chicago Tribune.* http://www.chicagotribune.com/news/opinion/zorn/ct-kimmel-walsh-health-care-zorn-perspec-0505-md-20170503-column.html (accessed February 10, 2018).

INDEX